THE BURNS MANTLE BEST PLAYS
OF 1949–1950

THE BURNS MANTLE
BEST PLAYS OF 1949–1950

AND THE

YEAR BOOK OF THE DRAMA

IN AMERICA

EDITED BY

JOHN CHAPMAN

DODD, MEAD AND COMPANY
NEW YORK   -   -   -   1966

INTRODUCTION

INTRODUCTION

THIS volume, thirty-third in the continuing series begun by the late Burns Mantle, is something of a milepost statistically—and perhaps it marks a turning point in the artistic record of the American theatre. It completes the record of the first fifty years of the Twentieth Century in theatrical affairs. The first volume, chronologically speaking, records all productions and the Best Plays from the season of 1899-1900 to 1909. The second covers 1909 to 1919. These books were prepared by Burns Mantle and Garrison P. Sherwood. The first of the year-by-year histories embraces the season of 1919-1920.

For many years, possessors of the Best Plays series have been asking for an over-all index volume, so that they may quickly locate the record of a play or a playwright. This much-wanted index is being published simultaneously with this volume, and it embraces, most appropriately, a half century of the New York stage.

This half century has seen great changes in the art of the theatre —changes that frequently but not always have been for the better. It has seen the appalling decline of the road—and the compensating growth of various types of regional dramatic groups. It has seen the American theatre grow to a position of world influence, with the best of our works being acclaimed, studied and imitated in the dramatic capitals of Europe. The half century has demonstrated the resilience, the inherent and indestructible life, of the stage in the face of threats to its existence by motion pictures, radio and now television. In fifty years the theatre has become a profession as well as an art—a profession which can and indeed must be studied in schools and colleges. The level of education in all branches of the drama is constantly rising. It may be that dramatists and actors, being geniuses, are born and not made—but without careful schooling these geniuses might not make the grade.

There have been golden years and locust years, booms and depressions. Skyrocketing costs have all but eliminated the individual manager who relied upon his own artistic judgment and his own money. Producers today are not individuals, but corporations selling stock to backers. It would take a phenomenally well-heeled manager to risk out of his own pocket the $100,000 or $300,000 a first-class production requires today. High costs and high losses have resulted in fewer and fewer productions. Unemployment among actors is a serious problem, and if it were not for television it would be frightening; but television has literally kept alive the acting pool which the New York stage needs.

This last season marked a low point in production—but perhaps it was the turning point, the last milepost on the down-grade, as well. All branches of the theatre, including dramatists, were grappling with the problems of cost. The arena-type theatre, or theatre-in-the-round, emerged as a resourceful solution of the high price of production and the high price of tickets. The American National Theatre and Academy, with a long-range program of national scope, increased in strength and influence. In New York, indications were that the building code, whose restrictions have been so severe as to discourage theatre construction, would be drastically revised and make the building of new playhouses economically attractive. The Fabulous Invalid was, as usual, alive and vigorously kicking and nowhere near the grave. It seemed to be saying to itself, "Oh, well, the first fifty years are the hardest."

There have been minor typographical changes in this volume which will, one hopes, make for greater readability. For the second season, the record includes the theatrical histories of Boston and Philadelphia, as well as those of Chicago, San Francisco and the Los Angeles area. One small innovation is the inclusion of stage managers among those responsible for each production. This is because many persons now important to the drama as managers and directors—and even as actors and dramatists—have begun in the professional theatre by being assistant stage managers and then stage managers.

I am grateful to the lady who goes to the theatre with me—my wife—for her careful maintenance of the statistical record and for her watchfulness over the innumerable events which have occurred Off Broadway.

JOHN CHAPMAN

Westport, Connecticut, June, 1950

CONTENTS

CONTENTS

THE BURNS MANTLE BEST PLAYS
OF 1949–1950

THE BURNS MANTLE BEST PLAYS
OF 1949–1950

THE SEASON IN NEW YORK

ONCE again, Economics has won over Art in New York's professional theatre. Skyrocketing production costs limited the 1949-1950 season to sixty-two offerings—an all-time low. Skyrocketing maintenance costs made financial failures out of plays and musicals which were, to all appearances, hits—plays and musicals which ran 100 or 200 performances and still wound up in the red.

There was not so much talk this time about the critics ruining the theatre. The reviewers were, indeed, far kinder than the public, which ruthlessly rejected many offerings which had received favorable notices. In moments of discouragement or annoyance, it often seemed to me that the public wanted to see only one show, "South Pacific," and it went grudgingly to something else because tickets for this astonishing box-office freak were not available. In better and clearer-minded moments, however, I was not so cynical; on at least two occasions—the submission of "The Cocktail Party" and "The Consul" to a popular vote—the New York theatregoer demonstrated that he is adult, intelligent and curious. Since there can be no theatre with artistic aspirations unless it can find an audience which *is* adult, intelligent and curious, this evidence was profoundly encouraging.

During the season there were two events which had an important bearing on the future of the New York stage, even though neither of them bore directly upon the art of the drama. The first was an action brought by the Attorney General of the United States against the Shuberts and their various corporations, accusing them of being a monopoly in restraint of trade. The Shuberts seemed unworried and were prepared to contest the action. They claimed that they by no means had a monopoly on New York theatres, there being many houses independently owned and others owned by the Astors' City Investing Company, and that a play could tour the U. S. without making its route through their United Booking Office. This action was brought just fifty years after Lee, J. J. and the late Sam S. Shubert came to Broadway from Syracuse as theatre operators and began a trust-busting action of their own which was successful—the breaking of the monopoly enjoyed by the Klaw & Erlanger "Combine."

The second important event was the submission to New York City of changes in the building code, fire laws and licensing regulations which would permit the construction of playhouses with office or store space above or below them. It seemed likely that these changes would be made, and that they would result in the construction of badly needed new playhouses. Part of the plan was to obtain from the State permission to build and license bars in theatres. At present, the only places of entertainment, aside from night clubs and hotel rooms, which are permitted to sell liquor are the Metropolitan Opera House and Carnegie Hall.

The public began its season of showgoing on July 15, 1949, by making a success out of a musical which had received few enthusiastic notices—"Miss Liberty," by Irving Berlin and Robert E. Sherwood. With such names as those of the authors and of their co-producer and director, Moss Hart, to count upon, the public bought "Miss Liberty" sight unseen. Before the opening there was an advance sale of more than $400,000—enough to keep the musical going two or three months. Without such an advance, "Miss Liberty" might have been a quick failure; but with it, the show had a breathing spell. In this breathing spell the public decided that it liked "Miss Liberty," and the musical had a run of 308 performances.

On July 7, S. Hurok, the busy and venturesome impresario, presented a Spanish revue, "Cabalgata," which had been running in Spain, Latin America and the West Coast of the U. S. for seven years. It proved only moderately interesting to New Yorkers. Mr. Hurok's great triumph of the season was bringing to the Metropolitan Opera House the brilliant and lavish Sadler's Wells Ballet Company. This troupe, generously subsidized by the British Government, was a revelation in splendor and quality; its principal ballerinas, Margot Fonteyn and Moira Shearer, became toasts of the town. Mr. Hurok estimated that he could have played the Opera House to its vast capacity for nine months—but he had to get out in a month because opera was to be done there.

The Metropolitan Opera is not theatre according to the limitations of this volume, but it was of more than ordinary interest to the Broadway theatre because of a change in management. Edward Johnson retired as general manager on June 1, 1950, after fifteen years at the post. Johnson began his career as a popular tenor in

Broadway musical comedies, and for many years was a leading tenor at the Met. He was to be replaced by Rudolph Bing, Vienna-born Englishman famed for his operation of the Glyndebourne and Edinburgh Festivals. Bing spent the entire season with Johnson at the Met, watching and observing. Then, when it came time for him to make his own plans for the 1950-1951 opera season, he astonished the old guard by going to Broadway and Hollywood for people he wanted. He asked Rouben Mamoulian, Margaret Webster and other theatre directors to restage operas for him, and asked men like Jo Mielziner and Donald Oenslager to design new settings; he even offered Danny Kaye the role of the jailer in his principal revival of the new season, "Die Fledermaus."

Indeed, the barrier between grand opera and Broadway was crumbling. Gian-Carlo Menotti's "The Consul," frankly an opera, became as much of a box-office hit as "Gentlemen Prefer Blondes." Marc Blitzstein had less good fortune with his opera version of "The Little Foxes," titled "Regina." Although the supporters of this work were staunch and vocal, "Regina" could not weather its notices and public indifference. Many people of high standing in the musical world maintained that "Regina" was many years ahead of its time, and that it may become a great success in 1960.

Ken Murray's vaudeville, "Blackouts," had run for more than seven years in Hollywood, but the best it could make was fifty-one performances at the Ziegfeld Theatre, beginning September 6. In Hollywood "Blackouts" had been performed in an intimate house and there was considerable informality about it, with visiting movie stars taking part from the audience. In New York it was no more than a vaudeville show, and for many years New Yorkers have refused to patronize vaudeville unless a movie goes with it.

Roger Stevens, a midwesterner of wealth, liked a performance of "Twelfth Night" at the Ann Arbor, Mich., Spring drama festival, and decided to sponsor it in New York. He presented it on October 3, with Frances Reid as Viola, Arnold Moss as Malvolio and Carl Benton Reid as Sir Toby Belch. The public's enthusiasm did not match Mr. Stevens', and "Twelfth Night" had a short run.

The first British import of the season, "Yes, M'Lord," arrived October 4 and was only moderately popular. But it did offer playgoers a pleasant reunion with A. E. Matthews, the one-time Bulldog Drummond, who celebrated his eightieth birthday during the run of the play. Also on October 4, S. M. Chartock hopefully launched a Gilbert & Sullivan revival series, with some new settings by Ralph Alswang. But there were only twenty-four performances of four operettas and they were not too enthusiastically patronized. New

York seems to want only the D'Oyly Carte Company on Broadway. In off-Broadway neighborhoods, however, two Gilbert & Sullivan companies kept busy all season long.

With high hopes, Maurice Evans offered in October two one-act plays by Terence Rattigan. "The Browning Version" was a study of an embittered schoolmaster, and "Harlequinade" was an unabashed farce about the acting profession. Although Mr. Evans was praised for his impersonation of the teacher, he could not make a go of his twin bill. One-act plays are not in favor these days.

George Abbott is a producer whose search for talent ranges wider than do the investigations of some of his Broadway-confined colleagues. At Catholic University, Washington, D. C., he found and liked a revue the sketches and lyrics of which had been written by two of the faculty, Jean and Walter Kerr. He also liked the music by Tin Pan Alley's Jay Gorney. So he brought "Touch and Go" to the Broadhurst for a lively 176 performances beginning October 16. He also presented two new comediennes, Nancy Andrews and Kyle MacDonnell; Miss MacDonnell had been known to television audiences as a highly telegenic singer.

Lillian Hellman, who usually writes plays out of her own head, was so impressed by a French play, "Montserrat," by Emmanuel Roblès, that she decided to make an adaptation of it. The whole season, in fact, abounded in adaptations. "Montserrat," dealing with an uprising led by the patriot Simon Bolivar against the Spanish in Venezuela, was an extraordinarily grim melodrama with Emlyn Williams in the role of a sadistic inquisitor. It was a failure.

The end of October brought two musicals, "Lost in the Stars" and the aforementioned "Regina." "Lost in the Stars" was an adaptation by Maxwell Anderson of Alan Paton's long novel of South Africa, "Cry, the Beloved Country." It had music by Kurt Weill, whose death in 1950 was a great loss to the musical stage. "Lost in the Stars" was carefully and beautifully staged by Rouben Mamoulian and impressively sung by Todd Duncan, Inez Matthews and other Negroes, and it was an artistic and box office success. In 1950 Weill and Anderson had been writing another musical, "Twain on the River," based on Mark Twain's "Life on the Mississippi," "Tom Sawyer" and "Huckleberry Finn." At the time of his death Weill had completed five songs for the new work, and during the Summer Anderson and the Playwrights' Company were looking for another musician to finish the score.

A more than ordinary event was the appearance on November 2 of Alfred Lunt and Lynn Fontanne in a comedy by S. N. Behrman, "I Know My Love." It marked the twenty-fifth year in which these favorite players had been acting together. It was a tailor-made play, of course, in which they ran the gamut of age, from being young lovers to being very, very old but still lovers. The comedy was a foreordained success, and ran until it came time for the stars to take their customary Summer holiday.

November also brought Doris Frankel's "Love Me Long," a trite and obvious comedy about the housing shortage. It did not last long. The next new production was a revival of Strindberg's "The Father," with Raymond Massey and Mady Christians as the antagonists. An off-Broadway revival of the same play ran longer than Mr. Massey's sixty-nine performances.

The appearance of Katharine Cornell always is an event, for her productions are staged with style and splendor. Her new play, "That Lady," was an unhappy choice—a rather dull and tearful fragment of history involving King Philip II of Spain and the one-eyed Princess of Eboli. Miss Cornell wore a black patch over an eye with charm and chic, but "That Lady" proved heavy going even for Cornell devotees. There were seventy-eight performances.

The next of the November offerings, "Texas, Li'l Darlin'," gave the reviewers their comeuppance by surviving discouraging reports and running into the 1950-1951 season. It was a musical about a grassroots Texas politician, with Kenny (Senator Claghorn) Delmar as the politician. The success of "Texas" was a comfort to and a triumph for Anthony Brady Farrell, the stubborn Albany millionaire whose earlier musical productions had been enormously expensive failures. Mr. Farrell also became co-producer with the Theatre Guild of another musical, "Arms and the Girl."

December was ushered in by "The Closing Door," a melodrama about a maniac by and with Alexander Knox. The theatre doors closed on "The Closing Door" in a little under three weeks. Next came "Clutterbuck," by Benn W. Levy. This English specialist in light comedy is best known in this country for "Springtime for Henry," a standard item for Summer stock. "Clutterbuck" was a frothy amusement which managed to go through the season and on into the new theatrical year.

"Metropole" set a new record for the season by opening on December 6 and closing on December 7—two performances. It was not as bad a play as this record indicates; it merely failed to accomplish what it tried to do. It was a comedy about a magazine editor who resembled Harold Ross, the famed individualist who edits *The New Yorker*. (But Wolcott Gibbs, critic for *The New Yorker*, said he thought the play was about an editor of *Time*.) "Metropole" could have made a struggle for existence, for it did have a colorful performance by Lee Tracy, but Max Gordon is a producer who will not waste time bucking newspaper notices. As soon as he read the reviews he closed the play.

The biggest musical comedy event since the openings of "South Pacific" and "Kiss Me, Kate" was the première of "Gentlemen Prefer Blondes," at the Ziegfeld. Carol Channing, playing the role of Anita Loos' Lorelei Lee, got the most enthusiastic notices of any musicomedienne of this generation, and the musical was an immense success. It did and does, however, find some patrons who abhor it. I believe those who do not find it amusing are those who take it literally—as a period piece about the prohibition, Paris and flapper days of the 1920s. Actually, it is a satire on those days, and therefore highly amusing to those old enough to remember the times.

The outstanding humorist of the season was, once again, Bernard Shaw. On December 21 his "Caesar and Cleopatra" was presented, with Sir Cedric Hardwicke as Caesar and Lilli Palmer as Cleopatra. The work was as brilliant, witty and modern as it was when it first was presented in 1899, and it enjoyed a satisfying run. The night after "Caesar" was presented, Garson Kanin offered a comedy, "The Rat Race," about two young people trying to get along in an unfriendly and sleazy neighborhood in New York. "The Rat Race" was one of Mr. Kanin's rare failures.

A surprising long-run contender was "The Velvet Glove"—surprising because it was quite frankly a Catholic play. Plays about any one religion often are limited in their appeal, but this one found a wide public. Written by Rosemary Casey and awarded a prize by the Christophers, "The Velvet Glove" dealt with educational controversies and mild intrigues in a convent. Grace George made her return to the stage in the leading role and was ably accompanied by another veteran, Walter Hampden. During the run of the play Miss George's husband, William A. Brady, died; and in the tradition of the theatre the show went on, with Miss George declining to close the play. At the end of the season Miss George was given the Drama League medal for the best performance of the season—the first prize she had ever won in a long and distinguished career.

A drama about a Negro politician and the color line, "How Long Till Summer," was offered in an elaborate setting, but it managed to last only seven performances, beginning December 27.

The New York City Theatre Company began a lively and encouraging season on December 28 with a production of Goldsmith's farce, "She Stoops to Conquer." This season at the City Center was the result of generous and unflagging work, entirely voluntary, by Maurice Evans, who had accepted the post of artistic director. For the first production Mr. Evans persuaded such players as Ezra Stone, Burl Ives, Carmen Mathews and Brian Aherne to work for two weeks (plus rehearsal time) for $50 a week.

The first hit of 1950 came on January 5, when Carson McCullers' "The Member of the Wedding" was presented at the Empire. It was generally acclaimed as a fine, sensitive character study, and the performances of Ethel Waters, Julie Harris and seven-year-old Brandon de Wilde were unstintingly praised. "The Member of the Wedding" won the Drama Critics Circle Award as the best play of the theatrical year.

For two years Burgess Meredith had been enthusiastic about an Irish fantasy by Donagh MacDonagh, "Happy as Larry." He thought it would make an interesting and unusual musical. By performing innumerable auditions he finally managed to obtain sufficient backing and "Happy as Larry" was produced on January 6— and it closed on January 7 after three performances. Here again is a case where the statistical record is unfair to a play. This musical novelty was not all it should have been, perhaps, but it was by no means an offense to the drama. In a happier economy, it could have had a modest run.

The second of Mr. Evans' revivals at the City Center was "The Corn Is Green," with Eva Le Gallienne in Ethel Barrymore's role. And, speaking of Miss Barrymore, that lady came from Hollywood late in January to be a particular star in the American National Theatre and Academy's ANTA Album, its third annual $100-a-seat benefit at the Ziegfeld Theatre. Miss Barrymore played "The Twelve Pound Look."

Another revue, "Alive and Kicking," was a January failure. It strove to be intimate and bright, but the public did not find it so. It was followed by an interesting failure, "The Enchanted." This fantasy was by the same combination which produced the successful "Madwoman of Chaillot"—the late Jean Giraudoux and Columbia University's Professor Maurice Valency. "The Enchanted" did not manage to find critical or popular favor, but in it were some trenchant observations on the follies of the human race.

Mel Dinelli, a screenwriter, essayed a play in "The Man." It was, to me, ingenious and interesting. A melodrama about a crazy handyman and a widowed houseowner, it had only two important characters—played by Dorothy Gish and Don Hanmer. It also had a trick ending which could not be anticipated. My own weakness for unabashed melodrama is not often shared by others, and "The Man" was lucky to get ninety-two performances.

One of the few managers alive who will back his judgment with his own money, instead of going into the angel markets, is Dwight Deere Wiman. Mr. Wiman supplied much of the large financing for a revue, "Dance Me a Song," which sought to recapture the informality and charm of his "Little Shows." For the revue he found an interesting new monologist, Wally Cox. But he could not find enough customers to go beyond thirty-five performances, ending in mid-February.

The outstanding play of the season arrived January 21. It was T. S. Eliot's "The Cocktail Party," a comedy in blank verse with philosophical and religious undertones. "The Cocktail Party" had been produced for a brief engagement at the Edinburgh Festival, and, detouring London, had been brought to New York by Henry Sherek and Gilbert Miller. It is certain that nobody connected with it anticipated any more than an intellectual and artistic success. The actors, all but one of whom were British, figured on a few weeks in New York at most.

The reviews of "The Cocktail Party" were interestingly divided. Some critics professed puzzlement; John Chapman, Richard Watts Jr. and Robert Garland labeled it a "masterpiece." Poet Eliot's play swiftly became the No. 1 dramatic hit of the year. London tired of waiting for the original company to return and set up its own production—which also became a hit. It is interesting that the London production cost only $7,000 and paid off in ten days. The success of "The Cocktail Party" is, to me, the highlight of the season, for it proves that one should never underestimate the interest and intelligence of the buying public. It also proves that controversy is fun. The play has violent partisans—those who loathe it as much as others admire it; and such partisanship is the greatest single factor in keeping the theatre alive and kicking.

Another drama with a historical background, "Design for a Stained Glass Window," was based by William Berney and Howard Richardson on the story of an English saint, Margaret Clitherow, who fought the Protestant Reformation in Elizabethan times. Berney and Richardson were the authors of the novel and successful "Dark of the Moon," but they had only a week's run of their new play late in January.

Whether they are producers or authors, or both, Richard Rodgers and Oscar Hammerstein are quite unfamiliar with failure. On January 24 they presented Samuel Taylor's play, "The Happy Time," based on stories by Robert Fontaine. It was a pleasant family fable with a French Canadian background, and was an immediate hit.

On January 25 Maurice Evans made his most brilliant production of the City Center season by offering, for two weeks, Shaw's "The

Devil's Disciple," with himself as the Disciple and Dennis King as Gentlemanly Johnny Burgoyne, the cynical general who impersonated Shaw in the Revolutionary War. This comedy was so obviously a "draw" that it could not be abandoned in a fortnight. A new production, necessitated by union rules, was made for a commercial run, and the play reopened at the Royale on February 21 and achieved a total of 127 performances. During the ensuing Summer Evans was to tour the comedy in Summer theatres, including the Opera House at Central City, Colorado.

On January 26 the Theatre Guild offered a scenically sumptuous "As You Like It," with Katharine Hepburn as Rosalind. Miss Hepburn's return from the movies was an event, and it was well publicized with many photographs of Miss Hepburn's legs in tights. The legs and a box office name boosted Shakespeare's idyll to a new long-run record of 145 performances.

What turned out to be the late Brock Pemberton's last production was, unhappily, a disappointment. On the last day of January Pemberton offered "Mr. Barry's Etchings," a comedy about a genial counterfeiter played by Lee Tracy.

A good many people have been tempted over the years to dramatize Henry James's eerie tale, "The Turn of the Screw." One who toyed with it, trying to make it either a screenplay or a drama, was Mel Dinelli, author of this season's "The Man." Dinelli gave it up as too tricky. Another who tried it and spent a couple of years on it was William Archibald, who has been an actor and a dancer as well as a writer. Mr. Archibald succeeded, and called his play "The Innocents." It was one of the successes of the season, starting in February, but had to close after 141 performances because its leading adult player, Beatrice Straight, was soon to become a mother. Miss Straight's husband, Peter Cookson, was the producer of "The Innocents." At the season's end he was hoping to resume the play's run in September. Jo Mielziner won Variety's poll of the critics as the best designer of the season for his setting for the play.

Another Guild offering, in February, was "Arms and the Girl," a musical based on Lawrence Langner's and Armina Marshall's successful comedy about "bundling," "The Pursuit of Happiness." The musical was something less than a pursuit of happiness, for dissensions and illnesses among, and withdrawals from, the cast shortened the run to 134 performances.

February brought another revival to the City Center for two weeks—"The Heiress." New in the title role was Margaret Phillips, and she won such favorable notices that her recognition as an able young actress was greatly enhanced. Subsequently Miss Phillips was engaged to replace Irene Worth in "The Cocktail Party" when Miss Worth left the company in June.

One of the season's curios was "All You Need Is One Good Break," a folk comedy by Hollywood's Arnold Manoff. It had involved and elaborate scenery and its principal character, played by the durable John Berry, talked almost incessantly. The play was withdrawn after four performances in February—and then was reopened by a still hopeful management nine nights later. It struggled along for thirty-two more performances.

A new playwright with more than ordinarily promising ability was William Inge, as was demonstrated when the Guild presented his play, "Come Back, Little Sheba," on February 15. This study of two drab lives ran out the season and won several acting awards for its principals, Shirley Booth and Sidney Blackmer. Another dramatist who showed promise when he wrote "Home of the Brave," Arthur Laurents, suffered a setback with "The Bird Cage," a night club melodrama which had its première on Washington's Birthday. It, too, had elaborate scenery, and it was directed by the top-flight Harold Clurman, who had done nobly with "The Member of the Wedding," but it did not last long.

A third in a series of elaborate productions, "Now I Lay Me Down to Sleep," made its bid early in March and failed. This adaptation of a Ludwig Bemelmans novel had excellent performances by Florence Eldridge and Fredric March, but the Bemelmans whimseys were somewhat lost in a place as big as a stage. One of the most tasteless productions of the season was Jack Kirkland's seven-performance revival of "Tobacco Road," this time with a Negro cast. What once was a potent folk comedy about poor whites now seemed to be an indignity and an embarrassment to its colored players.

The wonder boy of the season was, perhaps, Gian-Carlo Menotti, who first came to Broadway attention with his short operas, "The Medium" and "The Telephone." On the Ides of March his first full-length opera, which he also had staged, was offered and got a uniformly enthusiastic press. Titled "The Consul," it was given the Critics Circle Award as the best musical of the season, in spite of the fact that it was an opera, and it also got the Pulitzer Prize in music.

Vinton Freedley, another of those rare beings, a self-financing producer, essayed an elaborate and handsome musical, "Great to Be Alive," on March 23. But it failed to find favor and ended with fifty-two costly performances.

The final March production was "The Wisteria Trees," Joshua Logan's adaptation of "The Cherry Orchard." Helen Hayes played the Chekhov heroine as the chatelaine of a run-down plantation in

Louisiana, which prompted one joker to dub the play "Southern Fried Chekhov." It was Miss Hayes' first appearance since the death of her daughter, Mary MacArthur, and it was another personal triumph for the star. Opinions on the play differed. Some, including this reviewer, believed that Logan had done no ill to the Russian's fragile play—had, indeed, given it warmth. Others protested that the adaptation was a desecration of a work of art and a violation of a dramatic masterpiece. Once again, controversy did no harm— and, whoever was right, it was certain that "The Wisteria Trees" would have a far longer run than any previous production of "The Cherry Orchard."

A quick failure which was generally hooted at in April was "Cry of the Peacock," adapted from a French sex comedy by Jean Anouilh. With a wittier adaptation and a more properly chosen cast the comedy might have shown some quality; but as it was it showed just enough quality for two performances, thus sharing the season's short-run record with "Metropole." Another April foolishness was "With a Silk Thread," a kind of "switch" on Shaw's "Candida." A more successful entrant of the month was Katherine Dunham's always-tropical dance revue, which extended a short scheduled engagement to thirty-seven performances.

The most talked-of production of the Spring was the revival of Barrie's "Peter Pan," with Hollywood's Jean Arthur in the Maude Adams role and Boris Karloff as Captain Hook—and with background music and a few songs by Leonard Bernstein. From all angles it was a risky venture, for modern audiences are not noted for their devotion to gentle whimsey and any actress who attempts to step into Miss Adams' tights is courting odious comparisons. The risk paid off, for "Peter Pan" was a triumph as a production and a personal triumph for Miss Arthur and Mr. Karloff. It did an immense children's trade at its three weekly matinees, of course—and was almost as great a draw for night-prowling adults.

Great expectations were held for "A Phoenix too Frequent," a one-act comedy in verse by London's shining new favorite, the young Christopher Fry. Something happened to the play in transit across the Atlantic and it was greeted with enthusiastic disfavor. The management also made the mistake of preceding the playlet—which was, one hoped, saucy and witty—with a heavy, morbid one-acter about race problems, "Freight." The transition from documentary realism to the fancifulness of a versed-up Greek legend was impossible for an audience to make. The two plays had five performances each.

In May, Paul and Grace Hartman set up for a Summer's stand with an unpretentious and pleasant revue, "Tickets, Please!" It was on the order of their successful "Angel in the Wings." The final month of the season brought another visiting road company to the City Center—the much-traveled but still bright musical, "Brigadoon." But a failure which was generally and genuinely regretted was the musical version of Goldoni's *commedia dell' arte*, "The Liar," which for a long time had been the pet project of Alfred Drake. Drake, busy in "Kiss Me, Kate," could not take the title role himself, but he did direct the production and showed talent in this new field for him. However, "The Liar" did not quite succeed in being a *commedia dell' arte con musica*, and its performances numbered twelve.

The City Center had another road show, "A Streetcar Named Desire," as a May offering. The final production of the season, on May 31, was a novelty. It was a revival of George Kelly's "The Show-Off" in an arena-type auditorium. This simple method of production, familiar in Texas and elsewhere, had not been essayed before in New York, although several managements have had such projects in the planning stage for some time. "The Show-Off" was presented in the ballroom of the Hotel Edison, which had been converted into a four-sided arena with a square stage in the center. There was no scenery—just a rug, a table, a sofa and some chairs. The actors walked on and off along ramps leading to corner exits. Lee Tracy and Jane Seymour had the principal roles, and first-nighters found the production genuinely enjoyable.

Variety, which keeps tabs on things fiscal and physical, if not spiritual, in the theatre, summarized the season thus: "Despite the decline in production, the volume of business on Broadway has been only a shade below that for 1948-1949. On Broadway the gross for this season reached $28,614,500, compared to the 1948-1949 total of $28,840,700.

"Highest-grossing show was, of course, 'South Pacific,' which regularly topped $50,600 a week and had a season's total of $2,584,000."

Money invested in Broadway production was, according to *Variety*, $3,853,000—only about half the amount spent the previous year. As of May 31, money lost on failures amounted to $2,533,800 —as aginst $4,595,000 the year before. The most expensive failure was "Dance Me a Song," with $200,000 gone.

During the season death took its accustomed toll, and the losses were, as always, unaccustomed and grievous. The passing of Arthur Hopkins removed from the worldly stage the most influential man of his time in the American theatre. The loss of such as Brock Pemberton, Sir Harry Lauder, Philip Barry, Walter Huston, Frank

Morgan, George C. D. Odell, Bill Robinson and Kurt Weill was a heavy blow.

But, as always, there were others among the living—others at the height of their powers and others clambering boldly and bravely up. And so ends another annual report on the life of that fabulous, fabulous invalid, the theatre.

THE SEASON IN NEW YORK

THE SEASON IN BOSTON

By Elliot Norton

Drama Critic of the *Boston Post*

THE Boston theatre season of 1949-50 was neither as extensive nor as distinguished as it might have been. Between June 1, 1949, and May 31, 1950, only thirty-nine plays and musicals opened in the "regular" downtown playhouses. In the previous year there had been fifty-two.

In the previous year there had been thirty-four tryouts, shows being tested and sometimes repaired for Broadway. This time there were only twenty.

The smaller number of plays required fewer theatres. Although the landlords held on to all seven of our playhouses, two—the Majestic and the Copley—presented not a single "legitimate" show. Their operators, the Messrs. Shubert, have not withdrawn them from the field; there simply were not enough attractions for them.

This dwindling or shrinkage is, obviously, unfortunate. But if we had fewer shows than we might have been able to support this season, we could rejoice because we also saw fewer atrocities.

The previous year we had seen fourteen more tryouts. But many of the extras were shoestring productions which should never have been presented.

In 1949-50, it is true, there were two plays which opened and closed here abruptly, and never did get to Broadway. Yet neither Graham Greene's "The Heart of the Matter," an adaptation of his own novel which was presented by Richard Rodgers and Oscar Hammerstein, II, nor "An Old Beat-Up Woman," which Margo Jones brought here from her Theatre '50 in Dallas, was meretricious. Both plays were imperfect, and had to be withdrawn for rewriting, but both were the work of intelligent showmen and women who just had not done their work successfully this time.

Neither play in any way resembled such disasters of the previous season as "Grandma's Diary," for instance, which swelled the total statistics but did nothing else for anyone or for the drama itself.

"Happy as Larry," which was pretty much a shambles on the stage here and apparently not a great deal better on Broadway despite changes made in Boston, was no "turkey" either. There was

16

latent in it a charming idea and there were involved in it some good actors like Burgess Meredith, but their work was not properly bolstered.

The only show of our season which really seemed to make a clucking noise was a little darlin' called "Texas, Li'l Darlin'." This, however, went on to run for many months in New York, proving that if you have as much money as Anthony B. Farrell you can fool some of the people some of the time.

This emphasis on the better quality of the year's tryouts may seem a little strained, as though the recorder were trying to gloss over the bitter truth about the small total number of plays, but it is actually significant. Whether we like it or not, ours is largely a tryout town. There are some advantages in getting the shows before Broadway—when they are good, or even only promising. But a long procession of idiotic dramas can drive playgoers away from the theatre for years, or perhaps forever. Consider the fate of Atlantic City, which once got many tryouts and now has almost no theatre at all, because embittered playgoers finally revolted. Springfield, Mass., has a few shows a year now, but no more tryouts. Too many poor ones could do it to Boston, too.

Our season began lamely. On June 1, 1949, "Born Yesterday" was showing at the Colonial Theatre, the only play in town, a failure. On two previous occasions, Boston had accepted this Garson Kanin play and perhaps the seven weeks of those two engagements were enough. This third run was intended as an experiment and a gesture. Producer Max Gordon had decided that the trouble with the theatre's business is the theatre's prices. For this visit, "Born Yesterday" was offered at $1.80, including tax, for the highest-priced seats. At matinees the best seat in the house cost $1.20. But the public was not impressed.

The idea that there exists a large public just pining away to sit in the balconies and waiting only for the day when they can reach such an altitude for sixty cents, was exploded. They could not get anybody to go into the balconies at that price during the engagement of "Born Yesterday." What was expected to be an all-Summer run began on May 9 and ended June 11.

All the theatres of the city were dark from that date until Monday, September 19, when Madeleine Carroll appeared at the Schubert Theatre in "Goodbye, My Fancy."

In the meantime, however, the Boston Summer Theatre offered a season of nine plays during ten weeks beginning July 4. Run by cartoonists Lee Falk ("Mandrake the Magician") and Al Capp

("Li'l Abner"), this show shop operates in the 900-seat New England Mutual Hall, with stars and a professional company.

Their attractions during the Summer of 1949 were these:

Week of July 4, "Pretty Penny," a new musical revue, in tryout, with book and lyrics by Harold Rome, sketches by Jerome Chodorov, choreography by Michael Kidd, under the direction of George S. Kaufman.

Week of July 11: Ann Harding in "Yes, My Darling Daughter."

Week of July 18: Kay Francis in "Let Us Be Gay."

Week of July 25: Sarah Churchill in "The Philadelphia Story."

Week of August 1: Susan Peters in "The Barretts of Wimpole Street."

Week of August 8: Elisabeth Bergner in "Amphitryon 38."

Week of August 14: Joan Blondell in "Happy Birthday."

Week of August 21: Edward Everett Horton in "Present Laughter."

Week of August 28: Paul Lukas in "Accent on Youth."

Week of September 5: Return of Sarah Churchill in "The Philadelphia Story."

Madeleine Carroll opened the regular Boston season of 1949-50 pleasantly, if not brilliantly, in Fay Kanin's "Goodbye, My Fancy," proving herself the prettiest Congresswoman either party ever elected. Nobody here seemed to think the play was any great shakes, but it managed to do reasonably well for three weeks.

The first of the tryouts arrived in town on September 26, and then we knew we were in business again. Boston without a tryout is like Broadway without a new musical comedy hit, a dull place.

This first visitor was called in our town "Double Bill" and consisted of two plays, one very short, a comedy called "Harlequinade," and the other longer, called "The Browning Version," both written by the English playwright Terence Rattigan and both starring Maurice Evans and Edna Best. In New York, subsequently, these two used the one title, "The Browning Version."

We liked them better than Broadway did, though not so well as London, where they had prospered earlier.

October began with an engagement at the Boston Opera House of "The Student Prince," which nearly always does well here, no matter what the actors and singers do to it. The cast this time included Everett Marshall as Dr. Engel and Detmar Poppen as Lutz, the tutor.

On Monday, October 10, things theatrical took on a new color. On that evening we saw Alfred Lunt and Lynn Fontanne at the Plymouth Theatre in S. N. Behrman's adaptation of a French play,

"Auprès de ma Blonde," which was entitled "I Know My Love" here and subsequently in New York. It had had other names during the past season in a long western tour.

This flashy vehicle for the Lunts dazzled and delighted everyone so much that the receipts for each of the three weeks at the Plymouth Theatre were greater than those of any previous week in the history of the theatre. The record is a long one, since the Plymouth was first opened in 1911.

While the Lunts were getting under way, Rex Harrison and Joyce Redman burst into the Shubert Theatre with "Anne of the Thousand Days," the Maxwell Anderson play about Anne Boleyn and her Henry. There had been some minor replacements in the company since New York, but the overall excellence of the playing was unimpaired, and whatever Chicago may have decided later, "Anne" was a stirring theatrical event here, and well attended.

"Regina" was the first experimental theatre piece of 1949-50. Cheryl Crawford opened this opera—it seems to me to be nothing other than opera—at the Colonial Theatre on October 11.

It seemed to some of us that "Regina" represented a heroic attempt to bring new power and glory into the theatre, but that some of the people involved had failed to do their jobs effectively. "The Little Foxes" was a powerful play. There had to be a reason for setting it to music; the music must add depth or intensity, or give it some new or heightened values. Except in occasional scenes, it failed to do this. That it may eventually seem all that its composer, Marc Blitzstein, and its producer, Cheryl Crawford, wanted it to be, is not unlikely. Different players in key roles might lift it into success.

"Texas, L'il Darlin'," a musical sponsored by the angel Anthony Brady Farrell, followed "Regina" into the Colonial Theatre. It bored me, for one.

Also here in October was Tallulah the Terrific, in "Private Lives," which she can now enact in her sleep. The evening I attended she was wide awake and hilarious.

Raymond Massey, serving it as both star and director, arrived on Thursday evening, November 3, in Strindberg's propulsive drama, "The Father." As the captain whose wife drives him into insanity in a terrible contest for power, he seemed unfortunately limp, lacking the vital drive necessary for the part. Mady Christians, dropping the comfortable sweetness of the "Mama" everybody remembers, demonstrated tremendous force as the woman.

As usual, "Blossom Time" returned in October, which seems to be the right season for the kind of theatrical blooms it produces. It remained in bloom for two weeks at the Opera House.

"The Closing Door," by and with Alexander Knox, proved a creaking thing at the Wilbur Theatre, beginning November 14. Mr. Knox rebuilt the door but never managed to make it open and close smoothly and failed to call in other carpenters, who might have managed the job better.

An odd November attraction was "A Night in Spain," a concatenation of Spanish songs and dances by a horde of happy singers, dancers and musicians. Plotless and wordless, except for the curious comments of an American master of ceremonies whose dinner jacket and vocabulary were both blue, this had been called "Cabalgata" in New York and elsewhere. Here it was called good, and did good business.

Monty Woolley returned in "The Man Who Came to Dinner," opening against "A Night in Spain." He lacked this time some of the corrosive acidity which he had worked into his malevolently comical performance in the original production. He also lacked the kind of supporting actors who made the first version hum and hop along.

On Thanksgiving night, November 24, Garson Kanin's new play, "The Rat Race," opened at the Colonial Theatre. This had been anticipated more eagerly than any show so far, and the word was around that here was the big new hit of the season. The entire engagement of nine days was sold out in advance. But the play proved a bloomer.

Ordinarily, September and October are the most active theatrical months in Boston, but December took all honors this time.

Four shows opened on Christmas Day alone, and another the following night. For Boston, that's action.

First of the December offerings was a new revue called "Alive and Kicking," which lived up to its title only in part on the night of Thursday, December 8, when it was presented to its initial audience at the Shubert Theatre. Best number in it was a chantey by Lenore Lonergan, "French With Tears," the only surviving relic of the "Pretty Penny" revue which had been tried out in the Boston Summer Theatre by the same chanteuse. Best performer in it was Jack Cole, whose agile dancing antics impressed everybody.

Miss Hepburn arrived in "As You Like It" on Monday, December 12, and charmed pretty nearly everyone except those of us who, while admiring her personality and her pretty legs, felt that neither the charms nor the legs were those of Rosalind; the voice, too, was the voice of Hepburn. Altogether, this production seemed to be just a very pretty presentation of Katharine Hepburn in the Forest of

Arden. The public, however, made no distinction between Rosalind and Hepburn, and business was as lovely as the lady's limbs.

Grace George and Walter Hampden followed, in the Christophers' prize play, "The Velvet Glove," which seemed pretty thin, though Miss George and all the players were apt.

Christmas Day's openings included two at matinees and two at night, the matinee offerings being Burgess Meredith in Donagh McDonagh's "Happy as Larry," and a revival of "The Merry Widow," with Susanna Foster and Wilbur Evans. In the evening Tennessee Williams' "Summer and Smoke" was shown to Boston for the first time, with Katharine Balfour in the principal part instead of Margaret Phillips, who was very much missed. "Brigadoon," which had been here before, also returned on Christmas night, and proved a proper gift for the city's playgoers, who loved it.

Dwight Deere Wiman opened his new revue, "Dance Me a Song," the night after Christmas. It seemed promising if nothing more, what with the drolleries of comical Wally Cox and some other players, but it did not really catch fire.

"The Happy Time" was the first show of the new year, and a good way to start any year. It needed little work and did wonderful business for three weeks, with producers Richard Rodgers and Oscar Hammerstein, II, beaming about the Plymouth Theatre during that happy time.

"Design for a Stained Glass Window," a play about the obscure English martyr Margaret Clitherow, came to town with Martha Scott as Margaret on Tuesday, January 17. Written by William Berney and Howard Richardson, whose previous work was "Dark of the Moon," it promised more than it produced, and although the authors wrote an entirely new scene in the Ritz Carlton (as is required of authors in tryout here) it was obviously beyond succor when it quit Boston.

"Arms and the Girl," the Theatre Guild's musical comedy, enlivened the season, with Georges Guetary and Nanette Fabray re-creating in song and dance the principal parts of what had once been "The Pursuit of Happiness." We liked it and them here. I see by the papers New Yorkers did not.

On Monday, January 23, the Maurice Valency version of Jean Giraudoux' comic fantasy, "The Madwoman of Chaillot," opened at the Plymouth Theatre, and after a week moved to the Shubert Theatre to make way for Mae West in "Diamond Lil."

Just as in New York, "The Madwoman" proved a controversial work. At the intermission the night I attended, I overheard a harassed husband insisting to his wife that he considered it was "crazy" and he was not going back into the theatre for act two; he would spend the intervening time somewhere else, probably in the public library, and would meet her there later. He left, too. In the same crowd, I heard another shout ecstatically, "This is the finest thing I've seen all year."

By way of observation: the actors were not playing "The Madwoman" as well in Boston as they had during the first week on Broadway. In the second act, some of them were acting for personal amusement and not for the benefit of the drama.

As regards Mae West and "Diamond Lil," what can anyone possibly say for the record except that she did enormous business for two weeks at the Plymouth Theatre; so much business that she was invited to return and did. Beginning Monday, May 15, she offered it for another fortnight, this time at the larger Shubert Theatre. During this second visit, no one was trampled at the box office; on the other hand everyone, with the possible exception of the audience, derived some profit from the engagement.

Going back to January: The final attraction of that month was William Inge's "Come Back, Little Sheba," which did only moderately well in two weeks at the Colonial Theatre. Its weaknesses were apparent at the opening, and although Sidney Blackmer's performance was tremendous, that of Shirley Booth was at times unbalanced; this was later corrected by Miss Booth, with what results the New York record will show.

We got "Yes, M'Lord" from London, via New York, on Tuesday, February 6, and this did better business at the box office than "Sheba."

"Now I Lay Me Down to Sleep," by Ludwig Bemelmans, brought Fredric March and Florence Eldridge to the Shubert Theatre, on February 13. On the same evening, at the Plymouth Theatre, the return engagement of "A Streetcar Named Desire" began.

The Bemelmans play got a new first act from adaptor Elaine Ryan during its second week, but despite its occasional charms, failed to catch on here.

"Streetcar" was admirably played by a cast that included Uta Hagen and Anthony Quinn in the roles taken originally by Jessica Tandy and Marlon Brando. Miss Hagen seemed infinitely more penetrating and moving than Miss Tandy had been when the play tried out here in December, 1947. Mr. Quinn lacks the dazzle of his predecessor, yet he managed to plow through it with great conviction.

Another return engagement of February brought back "Lend

an Ear," this time with a second team. The substitutes failed to play it with the shine the first actors had bestowed on its antics. Nevertheless it prospered.

Between "Streetcar" and "Lend an Ear" we saw two more tryouts in February, neither of them satisfactory. The first was Joshua Logan's adaptation of "The Cherry Orchard," its locale shifted from provincial Russia to Louisiana. This one had been pre-tested during two evenings in Princeton, Mr. Logan's old college town, where it and he were acclaimed. At the Colonial Theatre in Boston, opening on the night of February 14, 1950, it was received coolly.

Mr. Logan waited two days to see whether the blame lay with the actors, with the Boston audiences, or with his own script. He decided the play was at fault and went then to the Ritz Carlton where, with the aid of his wife, a secretary and a dictating machine, he rewrote most of it. He was still rewriting a week later in New Haven and the two weeks after that in Philadelphia, and Helen Hayes and the others were learning new lines and business until three days before Broadway.

"The Heart of the Matter" proved to be a too literal, too crowded and not sufficiently dramatic dramatization by Graham Greene of his own novel of the same name. Producers Rodgers and Hammerstein decided it could not be repaired on the stage, so ordered it taken off and rewritten. For the record: Mr. Hammerstein said after the closing that he was "more than ever convinced there is a fine play in it."

The national company of "Mister Roberts" came here in March. This troupe, which had played a year in Chicago, was headed by John Forsythe as Lt. Roberts, Jackie Cooper as Ensign Pulver, James Rennie as the Captain and Robert Burton as the Doc. Mr. Forsythe disturbed some of us a little by his eerie resemblance in voice and manner to Henry Fonda, but the company is good, and the business has been fine.

In the course of the Boston engagement, longest of the season for any play, it was decided by producer Leland Hayward that Mr. Forsythe's playing entitled him to stardom, so it was announced that beginning June 1 his name would be billed above that of the show, marking the first time in more than fifteen years that any player has become a star in this city.

At the end of the season, on May 31, "Mister Roberts" was still running successfully and it seemed likely to continue through the summer.

Except for "Roberts" and a week of Cornelia Otis Skinner's mono-dramas, March came in and also went out like a lamb, theatrically.

From New York, on April 10, came "Miss Liberty" for three weeks of good business. The Broadway troupers were almost all present in the beginning, but Mary McCarty abdicated during the engagement here in favor of Sandra Deel, who had been Mary Martin's understudy in "South Pacific."

The season's final tryout was also an April matter. "Tickets, Please," with Paul and Grace Hartman, opened here at the Plymouth Theatre with a lot of good material poorly organized. One night later, a rescue party consisting entirely of George Abbott reached it, and the following day Mr. Abbott began quietly and rapidly restoring order. Very few people went to see it here, but the necessary work was done for Broadway.

Katharine Cornell came here in "That Lady" for a single week in April, and business was not good. Pretty nearly everybody liked her and Henry Daniell, as Ana De Mendoza and Philip II, but pretty nearly nobody liked the play.

The Mae West return engagement was the only incoming attraction during the month of May. Mae dominated May.

In addition to the regular attractions of the Boston season, some mention must be made of the Brattle Theatre. This is located in Cambridge, which is of course, immediately adjacent to Boston yet politically and otherwise quite separate.

The Brattle Theatre Company is a repertory group, whose original members began acting together just after the end of the war while most of them were students at Harvard. They called themselves then the Harvard Theatre Workshop.

In the mean time, with some summer theatre work also to their credit, they had bought old Brattle Hall, converted it into a modest playhouse seating 350, enrolled in the Actors' Equity Association, and being now graduated from college, set up as a fully professional troupe.

On October 6, 1949, at their Brattle Theatre, very close to Harvard College and even closer to Radcliffe College, they began their career with Betty Field in "Twelfth Night."

Since then they have presented twelve plays, most of them with visiting stars, all of them classics or semi-classics, some of them with considerable success.

Their acting has varied from the excellent to the very dubious, but they have kept their aim high and have managed to survive, and since their playhouse is only ten minutes by subway from the center of Boston, they seem likely to become a part of the Boston theatrical scene.

Their full schedule for their first season is as follows:

Betty Field in "Twelfth Night," opened October 6, 1949; Luise Rainer in "The Sea Gull," opened October 19; Claire Luce in "The Millionairess" and the Don Juan in Hell scene (Act 3 of "Man and Superman," by Bernard Shaw) opened November 2; "The Guardsman," by Ferenc Molnar, opened November 16; Ian Keith in Pirandello's "Henry IV," opened November 30; "Misalliance," by Shaw, opened December 13; "Troilus and Cressida," opened January 19, 1950; "Shadow and Substance," with Julie Haydon, opened February 8; "King Lear," with William Devlin, from the Old Vic's junior company at Bristol, England, opened February 22; Blanche Yurka in Ibsen's "The Wild Duck," opened April 11; "Yes Is For a Very Young Man," by Gertrude Stein, opened April 26, and "The Country Wife," by Wycherly, starring Cyril Ritchard as Sparkish, opened May 11, and was still playing June 1.

Turning back to the Boston scene: in addition to the regular attractions, our playhouses presented during 1949-50 four Yiddish language attractions: Maurice Schwartz in "Yosele, The Nightingale," for one week beginning January 22, at the Colonial Theatre; Maurice Schwartz in "Riverside Drive," for one week beginning Monday, April 3, at the Plymouth Theatre; Molly Picon, for five performances in "Abi Gesunt," beginning Friday, April 21, at the Boston Opera House, and Herman Yablokoff in "The Cantor's Boy," at the Plymouth Theatre on May 5.

We had three full weeks of ballet by the two major companies and one imported troupe during the year. The Ballet Theatre spent a week at the Boston Opera House beginning December 5, 1949, with Nora Kaye, Igor Youssekevitch, Nana Gollner and others featured in a more or less standard repertory.

The Ballets de Paris, presented sensationally as a peep show, was immensely successful in our city of culture for a week beginning January 16, at the Opera House.

On Monday, May 1, the Ballet Russe de Monte Carlo, an old standby, stood by at the Opera House.

At Jordan Hall, on May 3-4, those who enjoy the Hindu dancing of Uday Shan-Kar saw some.

The Boston Dance Theatre was formed during this season of 1949-50 under the aegis of Jan Veen. To the Boston Conservatory of Music Auditorium he brought, during the season, such dancers as Wasantha Wana Singh, Myra Kinch, Pola Nirenska and Charles Weidman, and seemed likely to establish the Boston Dance Theatre as a part of the local theatrical scene.

The Tributary Theatre of Boston went through its tenth season (the first season consisted only of one play), and at the end of the year was making plans to begin another in the fall.

Productions of the Tributary Theatre at New England Mutual Hall during the season of 1949-50 included the following: "Cyrano de Bergerac," October 7-8; "The Rivals," November 4-5, and November 11-12; the uncut version of "Macbeth," which is about ten minutes longer than the customary versions, December 2-3, and December 9-10; "The Devil's Disciple," January 13-14, and January 20-21, 1950; "Doctor Faustus," February 18; "Romeo and Juliet," February 24-25; "Two Gentlemen of Verona," March 17; "Murder in the Cathedral," April 14-15, and "Winterset," May 12-13 and May 20-21.

In its second season, playing also at New England Mutual Hall, the Boston Catholic Theatre presented some new plays with a religious background and some with none. Included were these: "Naughty Marietta," November 23; "The Hound of Heaven," an original about the Catholic poet, Francis Thompson, November 24; "Lump in My Throat," new Catholic play by Robert Todd, January 4; "A Voice in Rama," new Catholic play by James Coppinger, March 8, and "Man of Sorrows," also a religious work, April 3.

Boston got about as much opera as usual in 1949-50. The San Carlo company, which has its own following, played and sang at the Boston Opera House for eight days, beginning January 22, with the following operas: "Carmen," "Aïda," "La Traviata," "Madame Butterfly," "Cavalleria Rusticana," "Il Trovatore," "Faust," and "The Barber of Seville."

The Metropolitan Opera Company brought most of its stars and choristers here on March 27 for eight days and gave the elated citizenry "Manon Lescaut," "Faust," "Rigoletto," "Die Walkuere," "Tosca," "Simon Boccanegra," "Der Rosenkavalier," "Aïda," and Lohengrin."

Boris Goldovskys' New England Opera Theatre, a local company singing in English, appeared at the Boston Opera House three times during the year. On Sunday, November 13, they sang "The Turk in Italy"; on January 15, 1950, Benjamin Britten's "Albert Herring," and on February 12, "Rigoletto."

It was just as the curtain went up on "The Turk in Italy" that one of Boston's most respected critics, Leslie A. Sloper of the *Christian Science Monitor*, was suddenly and fatally stricken as he sat waiting for the performance. His passing was one of the season's most unfortunate happenings. He is greatly missed.

THE SEASON IN PHILADELPHIA

By Arthur B. Waters
Drama Critic of the Philadelphia *Gazette-Democrat*

PHILADELPHIA'S 1949-50 legitimate theatrical season, which came to a sluggish conclusion on Saturday, June 24, with the departure, Broadway-bound, of Michael Todd's rowdy revue, "Peep Show," must undoubtedly be characterized as one of the most unrewarding and undistinguished sessions that the local playhouses have ever known.

The total number of attractions—forty-two—set a new "low," at least for modern times. The season was abnormally late in getting under way (the first show didn't arrive until September 26 and it wasn't until a month later that three of the city's four regular legitimate houses were lighted), and it was abnormally early in its closing, in as much as after March 6 there were exactly six bookings and never more than one show in town at any one time.

In respect to the early Spring fold-up, 1949-50 resembled 1948-49, which would indicate that early or middle March and not middle May marks the city's theatrical swan song.

It was not merely in quantity, however, that the past season was dismal along the local rialto. The quality of the few bookings was very decidedly under par.

There were, in all, twenty-two tryouts in the four local theatres. Of these "Gentlemen Prefer Blondes," "The Consul" and "The Member of the Wedding" went on to become oustanding New York hits, while "Touch and Go," "Arms and the Girl," "The Wisteria Trees" and possibly "The Rat Race" might be said to have achieved some degree of Gotham success. Among the painful memories are "Montserrat," "Love Me Long," "Signor Chicago," "Metropole," "How Long Till Summer," "Alive and Kicking," "All You Need is One Good Break," "Now I Lay Me Down to Sleep," "What a Day," "Cry of the Peacock," "House on the Cliff" and "The Liar." As this is written, it is impossible to make any statement on "Peep Show."

Established New York hits which reached these shores (and there was a phenomenally small number of them) included "Goodbye, My Fancy," "Night in Spain," "Summer and Smoke," "Yes, M'Lord,"

27

"Lend an Ear" and "The Silver Whistle." Revivals and return engagements (in several cases with new stars) included "The Man Who Came to Dinner," "Philadelphia Story," "A Streetcar Named Desire," "Brigadoon," "The Barretts of Wimpole Street," "Tobacco Road," "Private Lives" and those perennial Shubert favorites, "Student Prince," "Merry Widow," and "Blossom Time." What might be classed as special bookings were "Ballets de Paris," Blackstone, Maurice Schwartz and another Yiddish offering, "Abi Gezunt."

Gone are the days when Labor Day saw the majority of local playhouses shedding the camphor, opening the doors and lighting up. Philadelphia playgoers and commentators had to wait until September 26 when the clever, intimate revue, "Touch and Go," bowed in at the Forrest for a two weeks' engagement. The same house also had the second booking—"Goodbye, My Fancy" on October 10. On the 13th, the season's first tryout, "Montserrat," made a delayed start at the Locust and had a mixed reception. "Love Me Long" drew the critics to the same house on October 24 and had very few favorable words said in its behalf; down the street the Shubert finally had its season opening with the arrival of "The Student Prince."

There was more activity and a little more relish on November 7 when "The Man Who Came to Dinner," with Monty Woolley back in his original role, finally teed off the Walnut's 1949-50 season, and "Signor Chicago" made its appearance at the Locust. During this same week, "Night in Spain" opened a ten days' run at the Shubert. The first real excitement of the season was reserved for Wednesday, November 17, when "Gentlemen Prefer Blondes" made its debut at the Forrest. It was acclaimed on all sides and did two and a half weeks of very fine business here, prior to its enthusiastic New York première.

"Metropole" (Walnut, November 21) proved a big disappointment despite Lee Tracy's sterling performance, but local playgoers and critics alike enjoyed Sarah Churchill in the revival of Philip Barry's "The Philadelphia Story" at the Locust. "Blossom Time" was a third opening on this date.

In the matter of openings, the week of December 5 proved to be most active of the season. "Summer and Smoke," Blackstone, and the returning "Brigadoon," at the Locust, arrived on Monday, and "The Rat Race" came to the Forrest on Wednesday, the 7th. All three did well, with the delightful "Brigadoon" developing almost immediately into a sellout as on its original appearance.

Two shows came to the city in the traditionally unprofitable week-before-Christmas and one of them, "The Member of the Wedding," proved to be the season's outstanding drama entrant, artistically speaking; it played a week and a half at the Walnut and completely outshone "How Long Till Summer," which tried out at the Locust over the same period.

"A Streetcar Named Desire" began a three weeks' return engagement at the Locust the day after Christmas. "Alive and Kicking," a tepid revue, opened at the Shubert on Tuesday, the 26th and the Theatre Guild's musical, "Arms and the Girl" made something of a local stir on Thursday, the 29th.

There was considerable difference of opinion locally as to the merits of "The Enchanted," which began a two weeks' tryout at the Walnut on January 2—first of 1950's offerings.

"The Madwoman of Chaillot" commenced a highly profitable stay at the Shubert on January 9; Maurice Schwartz and a revival of "The Merry Widow" followed on the 16th; and three attractions arrived during the week of the 23d, including the much-heralded but disappointing "All You Need is One Good Break" at the Shubert, "Yes, M'Lord" at the Walnut and "Ballets de Paris" at the Shubert.

February 6 was the last week of the 1949-50 period to see three openings; they were "Lend an Ear," "The Barretts of Wimpole Street" and "The Bird Cage" (a tryout at the Locust on Tuesday, the 7th).

After that activity began to taper off. "Tobacco Road" with a Negro cast started a fortnight's run at the Locust on the 20th. "What a Day" (which later changed its name to "Great to Be Alive") made its local bow at the Forrest on the next night, and on Wednesday, Philadelphia had its second big night of theatrical excitement when Menotti's dynamic "The Consul" had its world première at the Shubert.

"Private Lives" and "The Silver Whistle" came to the Locust and Walnut respectively on March 6, and with Helen Hayes' very necessary aid, "The Wisteria Trees" caused some furore when it reached the stage of the Shubert on the 13th. That was about the end.

The Walnut's season concluded offically on March 18. The Shubert booked the Yiddish piece, "Abi Gezunt," for a single week April 10 but otherwise was without bookings after Miss Hayes' vehicle departed March 25. The Locust had two tryouts, "Cry of the Peacock" (March 27 for one week), and "House on the Cliff" (April 17, for two weeks) and everybody agreed that they were about as incredibly bad as it's possible for a new play to be.

The Forrest, dark after the departure of "What a Day" on March 18, finally re-lit on April 24 with the musical, "The Liar," which received some fairly good notices here but did very little business. Then on June 5, Michael Todd's much-publicized "Peep Show" gave the fading season its third big first-night thrill and incidentally won general local acclaim.

No matter how you look at it, 1949–50 has been a thoroughly disappointing season.

THE SEASON IN CHICAGO

By Claudia Cassidy

Drama Critic of the *Chicago Tribune*

TWICE confounded by Chicago's 1949-50 theatre season, first in reality and then in retrospect, I decided on a fresh point of view for the archives. I asked Sam Gerson, overlord of the half dozen Shubert houses here, how he deciphered it. He replied obliquely in managerial code, "I think next season is going to be pretty good." I hope he has something more in mind than the delayed adrenalin of "South Pacific," for the fabulous invalid of our town is a pretty dead duck.

The boom has boomeranged in a homing curve. Its charted flight would take off about 1936-37 with thirty-six shows, touch its peak in 1945-46 with forty-two, mosey back to thirty-six in 1948-49, and nose dive to twenty-five in 1949-50. Hmmm, you say, that's bad. Sorry, it's worse. In 1945-46 forty-two shows ran 329 weeks. In 1948-49 thirty-six shows ran 249 weeks. In 1949-50 twenty-five shows ran 168 weeks.

You can blame television, taxes, transportation, or taciturn gentlemen of the box office, but the primary culprit would still be a shortage of shows. Because there weren't enough to go around the Studebaker joined the Civic as a television house, the Selwyn snatched at "The Third Man" to follow "The Red Shoes," and the Civic Opera house contented itself with opera, concert and ballet. Not one of the six active theatres could manage a full year's bookings. Few made even a respectable showing. Nothing new was tried out. Nothing came here that an inquisitive playgoer could not previously have seen elsewhere.

It still surprises Chicago to be a consumer rather than a producer of things theatrical. Pickings are slim at best, and neither the product nor the mood of the market is improved by delay and deterioration in transit. Of our twelve musicals only four were new even to Chicago. "Kiss Me, Kate," a topflight duplication headed by Anne Jeffreys and Keith Andes, was only a season late and so annexed the season's record of thirty-three weeks at the Shubert. The others were "Lend an Ear," "Les Ballets de Paris" of the combustible "Carmen," and "Miss Liberty," with Ann Crowley singing

31

where Allyn McLerie once danced. "Inside U.S.A." and "Allegro" lingered from the previous season. There were revivals or return engagements of "Oklahoma!," "Brigadoon," "Finian's Rainbow," "Blossom Time," "The Merry Widow" and "The Student Prince," some of them desperate bookings frowsy beyond description.

Of the thirteen plays, "Mister Roberts" stayed on from the previous season to make it fifty-four Erlanger weeks in all. But Tallulah Bankhead, who had a juicy twenty-six weeks at the Harris with "Private Lives" in 1947, mistakenly tried it again and lasted three.

The eleven plays new to Chicago revealed some interesting facets of the theatre mind at work. For instance, Elia Kazan prefers not to stage Chicago duplications of plays he has directed. He turned "Death of a Salesman" over to Harold Clurman, who had handled "A Streetcar Named Desire" the previous season, and Chicago suffered no loss. Mr. Clurman understood Arthur Miller's play in terms of Thomas Mitchell as he had revealed Tennessee Williams' in terms of Uta Hagen. Both were indelible theatre. Mr. Mitchell, whose vulnerability disarmed and tore the heart, had Miller musing, "I hadn't known I wrote this play about an Irish family." The twenty-two Erlanger weeks took the season's play record, but the "Salesman" should have run all season.

On the same plane of theatrical integrity was "The Madwoman of Chaillot," perhaps even a little richer here because the performance had deepened and Martita Hunt's medals had acquired patina, not tarnish. Katharine Cornell has only one standard, the highest she can achieve at the moment, so the fascinations of "That Lady" outweighed its flaws. A. E. Matthews reminded us of high comedy as a craft, so even the featherweight "Yes, M'Lord" was welcome. "Anne of the Thousand Days" expired in two weeks when even Joyce Redman and Rex Harrison failed to offset Maxwell Anderson's pedestrian play.

"Detective Story," with Chester Morris's jaw making Dick Tracy's look downright dimpled, was too second-rate a job to survive. "Summer and Smoke" was resuscitated by the Theatre Guild in "the original Dallas version" with Todd Andrews and Katherine Balfour, and was no improvement on the revised version. Glenn Anders and Sam Levene were all that was left of "Light Up the Sky," and a trustful Moss Hart had relegated the restaging to Mr. Levene, who is still a good actor.

"Goodbye, My Fancy" cherished the unlikely notion that a triangle involving Ann Harding, Bramwell Fletcher and Philip Reed would set audiences agog. It didn't, but Jean Casto was right as the spavined secretary. At season's end the Guild was still short a play, so it put its stamp on a revival of "Two Blind Mice," with Melvyn Douglas, Laura Pierpont and Mabel Paige in their original roles, and Kim Hunter in the part once played by Jan Sterling. This made it a Guild season composed entirely of non-Guild plays—"Death of a Salesman," "Yes, M'Lord" and "The Madwoman of Chaillot," along with "Summer and Smoke" and Sam Spewack's joust with the Office of Medicinal Herbs.

Not listed in the official count were a number of elusive items—the ice shows, Cornelia Otis Skinner's monologues, Spike Jones' musical mayhem, some hybrid corn called "Borschtcapades," Maurice Schwartz's "Riverside Drive," Blackstone's magic show, even the Black Hills Passion Play, woefully in need of the distance that lends enchantment. The Ballet Russe de Monte Carlo picked up $124,000 in eighteen performances, and the Sadler's Wells Ballet opened to sellout $90,000 for ten. Toscanini's concert sold out at a $9 top long before the box office had a chance to open, and the returning Metropolitan Opera rang up its curtain to some sold-out houses that must have delighted Edward Johnson's heart, because the performances in demand were so often the very ones Rudolf Bing has decided not to retain. The defunct Chicago Opera continued to invest its shrinking cash in the visiting New York City Opera, which paid few dividends.

For the record, the 1949-50 listing, compiled as of June 3:

Erlanger: 49 weeks—"Mister Roberts," 15 weeks' holdover, 54 in all; "Death of a Salesman," 22; "The Madwoman of Chaillot," 6; "Oklahoma!," 6 weeks' return engagement to date.

Shubert: 43 weeks—"Inside U.S.A.," 8 weeks' holdover, 11 in all; "Kiss Me, Kate," 33; "Miss Liberty," 2.

Harris: 27 weeks—"Summer and Smoke," 6; "At War with the Army," 5; "Goodbye, My Fancy," 5; "That Lady," 4; "Private Lives," 3 weeks' return engagement; "Two Blind Mice," 4 to date.

Great Northern: 24 weeks—"Allegro," 1 week holdover, 7 in all; "Brigadoon," 3 weeks' return engagement; "Finian's Rainbow," 2 weeks' return engagement; "Anne of the Thousand Days," 2; "The Student Prince," 3 weeks' return engagement; "Blossom Time," 3 weeks' return engagement; "Lend an Ear," 10 weeks to date.

Blackstone: 19 weeks—"Detective Story," 13; "The Merry Widow," 2; "Les Ballets de Paris," 2; "Goodbye, My Fancy," 2 after moving from Harris.

Studebaker: 6 weeks—"Yes, M'Lord," 3; "Light Up the Sky," 3.

THE SEASON IN SAN FRANCISCO

By Fred Johnson

Drama Editor of the San Francisco *Call-Bulletin*

WITH eyes ever alert for the silver lining, the show-minded San Franciscan has had his optimism under its severest test all through the last theatrical season. With much-needed patience he has grown to expect and enjoy only the occasional highlights in stage entertainment, meanwhile taking the nondescript and mediocre in the best possible stride. He is certain only that he will get more of the latter when, worse still, he is not surveying one or more completely dark playhouses.

Our loyal optimist is loth to agree that the show season of 1949-50 probably has been the city's leanest since the Argonauts of 1850 sat on rough benches to witness the theatre's burgeoning on this far outpost. In this State Centennial year he may even refuse to look at the figures of a theatre's booking list.

But because he has seen "Kiss Me, Kate," "Brigadoon," "A Streetcar Named Desire," "Inside U.S.A." and "Finian's Rainbow," don't imagine he is completely happy while awaiting the touring dates of "Death of a Salesman," "South Pacific" and "Lost in the Stars," all scheduled for months later and not among the items belonging in this inventory.

Thus dubiously fed on anticipation, he may or may not have gained much subsistence from Spike Jones' "Musical Depreciation Revue," which somebody must have relished in its twenty-four performances at the season's beginning. Under the nondescript heading there also came such divertissements as the Spanish "Cabalgata," which ran almost as long—a good San Francisco showing—before finding favor in New York; the Shipstads and Johnson "Ice Follies" and a drab edition of George White's "Scandals," calling it a revue but also calling it quits permanently after three thin weeks.

One of the autumn's weirdest offerings—of Los Angeles origin, but omitting any showings there—was a comedy with music called "Glamor Is the Gimmick," with Fortunio Bonanova as its spectacular star. Lasting one week, it was later to be voted the year's worst play by the San Francisco Critics Council, nosing out even the incredible "Mr. Adam," from the same geographical source.

Always a boon to the San Francisco theatre is the annual Civic Light Opera Association's festival, which had opened with "The Great Waltz" before the completion of last year's report. Three New York musical successes—"Brigadoon," with forty performances; "Kiss Me, Kate," with forty-eight, and "High Button Shoes," forty, accounted for most of the town's Summer entertainment. "Finian's Rainbow," not officially on the Civic schedule, fared less well as a follow-up, with twenty-four.

Opening the 1950 light opera season in May was General Director Edwin Lester's new production of "The Chocolate Soldier," with a ballet and new music added and Salvatore Baccaloni playing the Massakroff role for accentuated comedy. Wilbur Evans and Marion Bell were in the lead parts. "Rose Marie," "South Pacific" and "Lost in the Stars," with its "vacationing" New York cast, were to follow.

"A Streetcar Named Desire," teaming Judith Evelyn and Anthony Quinn, won the year's long-run honors with sixty-four performances. Beatrice Lillie brightened the early Winter for three weeks in "Inside U.S.A.," and "Oklahoma!" on a third visit returned for the same period.

There were such variations in theatrical fare as Cornelia Otis Skinner's one-woman playlets, more successful than on a preceding engagement, and the Ballet Theatre, welcomed here for the first time in a legitimate house. Monty Woolley made his first San Francisco appearance in "The Man Who Came to Dinner"—Alexander Woollcott had been his predecessor some years before. Woolley was well received for three weeks, ending March 11, when the Curran Theatre went dark, to remain so until Lloyd Nolan came in more than a month later as star of "The Silver Whistle," presented by Lewis and Young with several members of the New York cast in support. A play-hungry town responded happily, as it did for Olsen and Johnson's new French-style revue, "Tsk! Tsk! Tsk! Paree," for which they pledged a new title before taking it into New York's Winter Garden. Olsen was absent from the cast, due to a fractured leg sustained in a Southern California motor accident.

Meanwhile the next-door Geary Theatre was being intermittently occupied as the season closed, notably by "The Philadelphia Story," starring Sarah Churchill. Backed by Theatre Guild subscriptions, its run was profitable. Margaret Webster's Shakespearean Players were less fortunate in their one-week's occupancy of the same stage in "Julius Caesar" and "The Taming of the Shrew." The theatre then was given over to a screen showing of "The Bicycle Thief," not to be otherwise lighted until Thomas Mitchell's June appearance in "Death of a Salesman."

With hopes of reviving the days when Homer Curran and Fred Belasco regularly produced for both San Francisco and Los Angeles theatres, Gene Mann, of the latter city's Greek Theatre, planned to bring musical productions to San Francisco from that outdoor amphitheatre and perhaps from El Capitan in Hollywood. "Gentlemen Prefer Blondes," in the first category, was definitely booked for this city's Curran.

Long-deferred hopes of a local and professional theatre were realized in January of this year when Robert T. Eley, a Californian from the New York repertory group of the Cherry Lane Theatre, established the San Francisco Repertory Company in a small theatre that had been a church and then a music hall. In its first two months there was interference by theatrical union pickets, prior to labor settlement on a minimum basis. Opening with "Present Laughter," the able group then presented "An Inspector Calls," "Two Blind Mice," "The Adding Machine," "The Respectful Prostitute" and "Trio," with its California authors, Dorothy and Howard Baker, taking bows.

Playing to small audiences, the zealous adventurers still were hopeful of gaining a foothold with their presentation of plays which had been given no attention by the city's commercial theatres. The repertory company's career, it seemed, could go along with that of the Municipal Theatre, which has been successful for several years under authority of the Board of Education's adult department. The civic setup, under David W. Hunter's managing directorship, had its best year with the presentation of "Strange Bedfellows," "The Proud Age," "The Druid Circle," "Amphitryon 38," "The Glass Menagerie," "A Tale of Two Cities" and "Arms and the Man."

A highlight of the Stanford (University) Players' season was their July première of "Now I Lay Me Down to Sleep," an adaptation of the Ludwig Bemelmans novel by Elaine Ryan, a San Franciscan. The staging was by Hume Cronyn, as it was later in New York, and heading the university cast were Jessica Tandy and Akim Tamiroff. "Romeo and Juliet" was the succeeding production.

In an inter-campus exchange of the arts, the University of California group presented on its postage stamp stage at Berkeley the players of the institution's Los Angeles branch in a fine production of Molière's "The Miser," followed later in the season by the home campus Thespians in "Hamlet." The Straw Hat Theatre, which grew out of the same university's drama group, continued its musical revues in the suburban town of Lafayette, with seasonal tours into nearby fields.

Growth of the Summer theatre in contiguous areas had its significance in view of the increasingly slim metropolitan fare as touring companies became more hesitant about venturing this far West. Planned for the 1950 season at Stanford was a season of eight weeks at the campus Memorial Theatre, with a schedule of four plays, to be given on the stock principle. The adjacent city of Palo Alto offered rivalry for the same period at its Community Theatre, with a nine-week play festival, involving seven groups of the San Francisco peninsula area.

THE SEASON IN SOUTHERN CALIFORNIA

By Edwin Schallert

Drama Editor of the *Los Angeles Times*

RECESSION, which has afflicted much of the country theatrically, made itself emphatically felt in Southern California during the 1949-50 season. It hit touring attractions particularly. Most companies abandoned the long jump to the West Coast. Few projects of the traveling type originated even in the Pacific area. Self-dependence became the order of the day, once again within well-marked limitations.

Only the light opera organizations remained strong and sturdy in the big theatrical sphere. The Los Angeles Civic Light Opera Association not only brought out national companies of "Brigadoon," "Kiss Me, Kate" and "High Button Shoes," but also as an added event underwrote the special engagement of "Finian's Rainbow." That gave four visiting troupes as against one locally organized for "The Great Waltz," which belonged to the 1948-49 season.

The Spring of 1950 witnessed the western staging of "The Chocolate Soldier," with a company headed by Wilbur Evans, Marion Bell, Ralph Dumke, Kathy Barr, Donald Clarke, Hilda Kosta, and notably Salvatore Baccaloni, the buffo of the Metropolitan Opera Company. Then came a remarkable feature, the advent of "South Pacific," with Janet Blair and Richard Eastham in the Mary Martin and Ezio Pinza roles.

A sellout for a full ten weeks' season of "South Pacific" was indicated at the close of the theatrical year (circa June 1), an unprecedented record for the Civic Light Opera Association. This meant a potential audience of 250,000 or more people for this super attraction. Such a huge attendance forecast was regarded as contrasting strangely, if not almost miraculously, with the dour impression evoked through most of the theatrical season. Particularly so as people were apparently "buying" the name "South Pacific" rather than its stars, evidencing small regard for the fact that this was not the original company.

Opening notices were not all favorable to Miss Blair, though expectations were that she would greatly improve her interpretation during the run, and were generous to Eastham as well as other mem-

38

bers of the cast. Staging was on a notably high level, and the presentation generally met with enthusiasm, The amazing advance interest was attributed to the build-up because of familiarity of the
music through recordings and radio. Simultaneously the astonishing results, as heralded, inspired much thought about basic possibilities of the theatre in Southern California.

The success of "South Pacific" tied up with some other unusual
happenings during an otherwise dull season. At just about the same
time Michael and Marcella Cisney, who had operated the Laguna
Beach Summer Theatre in 1949, were scoring a surprise hit with their
production of "Light Up the Sky" at Las Palmas Theatre. The
cast in this Moss Hart comedy included Jean Parker, later replaced
by Nancy Kelly; Guy Madison, who gave way to Richard Crane;
Florence Bates, a special favorite; Tom Powers, Fred Clark, Hayden
Rorke and Muriel Maddox. Miss Parker and Madison had to leave
the cast only because of other engagements. Originally scheduled
for three weeks, the show went on for more than seven. It might
be remarked that the groundwork was laid for its popularity by performances in 1949 during the La Jolla Playhouse Summer season,
when Gregory Peck did the role later assigned to Madison and
Crane. It was rated first-class entertainment on both occasions.

As a footnote it might be added that whereas La Jolla seemed to
benefit the Cisneys from Laguna, they in turn may have helped in a
preliminary way the London play world. For from Laguna Jessie
Royce Landis, quite notably, and Reginald Denny went to London
for a much acclaimed presentation of Somerset Maugham's "Theatre." This was staged by the Cisneys as a particularly bright event
of their Summer, 1949, season.

Highlighting the early turn of the theatrical year was "A Streetcar Named Desire" with Judith Evelyn, Anthony Quinn, Russell
Hardie and Mary Welch. Miss Evelyn and Quinn enjoyed the ap-
plause of large audiences during a four-week engagement at the Biltmore Theatre. This remained practically the most distinguished
offering at the playhouse, which is the stopping-off place for visiting
organizations throughout the entire season. Frank Fay in "Harvey,"
which preceded "Streetcar"; Monty Woolley in "The Man Who
Came to Dinner"; Sarah Churchill, Jeffrey Lynn, Margaret Banner-
man, Hugh Reilly and Frances Tannehill in "The Philadelphia
Story"; Lloyd Nolan in "The Silver Whistle"; the Olsen and Johnson tryout of "Tsk! Tsk! Tsk! Paree"; Maurice Schwartz in repertory; "Oklahoma!" on its fourth or fifth visit; "John Loves Mary,"
with June Lockhart, Jimmy Lydon, Richard Denning, Donald Mac-

Bride and Hayden Rorke—these attractions kept the Biltmore lights glowing at intervals, but they were dark much of the time.

It could hardly be said that any of these offerings made new theatrical history, but they at least afforded a first opportunity to see Fay and Woolley in their original roles, while the other productions held varying interest. "Tsk! Tsk! Tsk! Paree" had to be staged with Marty May substituting for Ole Olsen, who was injured in an automobile accident just prior to this West Coast première. "Tsk! Tsk! Tsk! Paree" represented a blending of Olsen and Johnson's comedy routines with a musical entertainment previously given at El Capitan Theatre called "A la Carte," of which more anon, and that fact probably stood in the way of any great stir on the part of the public, added to the absence of a member of the famous comedy team. Olsen and Johnson made it known that they expected further to augment the production before its arrival in New York.

Not to be omitted among visiting attractions was Beatrice Lillie in "Inside U.S.A.," who proved herself as always one of the most popular of comediennes during four weeks at Philharmonic Auditorium. In her company were Lew Parker, Eric Victor, David Atkinson, Olga Lunick and Aileen Stanley, Jr.

The Pasadena Playhouse remains a fortress for the drama in Southern California, regardless of change, and it is particularly striking that twice during the season usual engagements of two weeks were extended. This happened with the Summer session comedy, "Strange Bedfellows," which was played for approximately five weeks, and again with "Two Blind Mice," which had a month's run.

The Playhouse presented the American première of "The Trial" from the novel by Franz Kafka. Jacqueline and Frank Sundstrom made the English translation from the stage adaptation by André Gide and Jean-Louis Barrault, and Sundstrom both acted in and directed the play. "The Trial" actually dates back some twenty years, and was appraised as a kind of psychological allegory. Its practical values seemed dubious.

Far less esoteric were "Edward, My Son" in its West Coast première; "This Happy Breed," "John Loves Mary," "Happy Birthday," "For Love or Money," "The Young and Fair," "The Two Mrs. Carrolls," "Evening Star," "The Heiress," "O Mistress Mine" and "Many Waters" on the Pasadena program. "Home is Tomorrow," by J. B. Priestley, was given during International Theatre Month with a cast headed by Edward Ashley and Jacqueline De Wit, and otherwise very professionally performed. It was essentially drama with a purpose, and as such far too discursive for popular

acceptance. "The Tempest" and "Cricket on the Hearth" represented the classics during the Pasadena season. The Summer festival of 1949 covered the work of California dramatists.

One new theatre made its bow during the season, and another was
released for plays after a long vaudeville tenure, namely, El Capitan,
where "Ken Murray's Blackouts" finally ended its run not long after
entering its eighth year. Horace Heidt with "The Kids Break
Thru" followed, still in the vaudeville mood, to be succeeded by the
musical, "A la Carte," presented by Ernst Matray, Maria Matray
and Edward Heyman, with Gale Robbins and Bill Shirley heading
the company. Frank Fontaine became the primary comedian during
the two months or so run. "A la Carte" was an attractive frame,
but lacked the zest of entertainment.

Later in the season Buddy Ebsen and Skeets Gallagher played an
engagement of some weeks in a revival of "Good-Night Ladies," in
which they enjoyed a big Chicago success. The farce had paid a
previous visit without them. Charlotte Greenwood, under the supervision of Russell Lewis and Howard Young, appeared in "I Remember Mama," previously staged at the Biltmore, with Kurt Katch as
her principal support.

Financed by motion picture capital to large extent, the new Century Theatre with capacity of a little less than 400, opened in January, 1950. John Claar, Peter Prouse, Roy Rowan and Del Sharbutt
introduced "The Fabulous Invalid," with a cast including Maria
Palmer, Harlan Howe, Edward Clark, Norman Rainey, Peter Prouse,
Roy Rowan and more than fifty others. It was a courageous undertaking for a new organization, and not happily rewarded. The
production was too demanding for all concerned. It was interesting
that they chose the Moss Hart-George S. Kaufman brochure for the
perennial qualities of the "legit" as their opening venture.

After that the Century housed mostly musical attractions, the
only one qualifying for this particular type of review being "Of All
Things" presented by Leighton Brill and William Trinz, and directed
by Keenan Wynn. It was in need of many script revisions before
it could essay Broadway, named as its final destination. Music was
by Maurice Engleman, and lyrics and sketches were credited to Alan
Alch, the dances to Eugene Loring. The show lost its feminine star,
Anne Triola, on the eve of the opening, and her duties were taken
over by three other members of the cast, with Mara Lynn faring
the best and Bunny Bishop winning some laurels. Tom Noonan
and Pete Marshall among the comedians were effective.

Central Staging made rather sound progress, with Eighteen Actors,
Inc. as a new entrant. This is composed of a rather professional

assemblage including as members Dana Andrews, Robert Preston, Ralph Freud, Morri Ankrum, Leona Roberts, Charles Lane, Cyrus Kendall, Catherine Craig, Jean Inness, Byron Foulger, Peggy Converse, Victor Jory, Joan Wheeler, Mary Todd and various others. The group gave noteworthy performances of "The Father," "A Doll's House" and "The Play's the Thing" at its own small theatre in the Pasadena area, and was elected to present "A Doll's House" as part of the Ojai Valley late Spring festival.

The Circle Theatre split into two groups during the year, the new one taking the name The Players Ring, and launching its own theatre with "Street Scene," directed by Mabel Albertson. Second event was "Androcles and the Lion" with Thornton Wilder's "The Long Christmas Dinner" as a curtain raiser.

The Circle Theatre specialized most of the year in producing plays with professional actors, including Sydney Chaplin and William Schallert, its executives. Apart from "Major Barbara," given with a cast headed by Diana Douglas, Ron Rondell, Alexander Gerry and Kathleen Freeman, and a revival of "Sherlock Holmes," the company sponsored the first Los Angeles presentation of "Kitty Doone," as revised by its author, Aben Kandel, with Ellanora Reeves, Allan Nixon and Sydney Chaplin as major principals, and also introduced "The Son" in a new William Saroyan version of a play that he originally wrote about ten years ago, with Schallert in the title role. At the close of the season the group was looking into possibilities for a larger theatre, and contemplating the production of "The School for Scandal" with Marie Wilson as the star.

Generally speaking, these arena theatres enjoy marked success with even limited capacity, and are more and more attracting professionals.

Another unique establishment is "The Stage" as conducted by Eugenie Leontovich. She offered "Dear Virtue," with Betsy Blair and Richard Stapley heading the cast in this adaptation by Madeline Blackmore of "Pamela," by Samuel Richardson. Charles Laughton joined forces with her before the close of the season in a planned production of "The Cherry Orchard."

Far less successful were experiments in playgiving with normal staging that originated in Southern California, except for the Summer theatres.

A rundown of shows could go on indefinitely. "Winter Kill" by Steve Fisher was offered with Robert Alda as principal. The author was also represented by "Blood in the Streets." "Anna Lucasta" was given with Lois Andrews featured. Buddy Ebsen brought "Honest John" to the stage with Lynne Carter and William Talman as his aides. "Behold the Day," by Lewis Allan and Michael Blankfort, about the conflict in Israel, held some appeal. A really noteworthy production was "Strange Bedfellows," which inaugurated the stay of the Cisneys and James Doolittle at Las Palmas, with Barbara Britton heading the cast as she did at Laguna Beach, but its popularity was probably diminished by the long Pasadena Playhouse run. "The Respectful Prostitute," featuring Lynne Sherman and Hurd Hatfield, and "Hope is a Thing with Feathers," with Will Geer, played at both the Coronet and Las Palmas. And that is but a portion of the experimental ventures, most of which did not prove notably profitable.

Institutional is the Greek Theatre, headed by Gene Mann, with its light operas. "Show Boat" returned Charles Winninger to his original Cap'n Andy role during the season, with Charles Fredericks, Evelyn Wyckoff, Collette Lyons, Sammy White, Caleb Peterson and others in its cast. Gertrude Niesen was a sensational hit in "Annie Get Your Gun." John Raitt, Lucille Norman and Sterling Halloway were in "The New Moon." "Girl Crazy" and "Carmen Jones" filled out the season.

The La Jolla Playhouse, Inc., headed by Mel Ferrer, Gregory Peck and Dorothy McGuire, came out in the black in its third year, a matter of great jubilation, and had a heavy advance sale for its 1950 season. The Laguna Playhouse enjoyed success, and the Holiday Stage at Tustin pursued its way, but most of the other Summer enterprises had faded. An interesting experimental showhouse, New Horizons Theatre, was completed at Pacific Palisades for year-round presentations. Call Board, Geller Workshop, Bliss Hayden, Ben Hard, and the newer Orchard Gables were among the most active little theatres. The Bard organization operated the Key Theatre in San Fernando Valley for a time.

An effort was made to revive "The Mission Play" in San Gabriel, but not too happily. "The Pilgrimage Play" remained a Summer event in its twenty-second season. The Turnabout puppet and live show, with Elsa Lanchester, entered its ninth year, and "The Drunkard" at the Theatre Mart its seventeenth. "Ramona," the historic pageant, was presented as usual at Hemet, Calif., and the Padua Hills Players entertained, as is their wont, throughout the year with their famous Latin-American divertissements. The Orpheum reintroduced vaudeville during the season, and Earl Carroll's Theatre Restaurant ceased operations, probably as a sequel to the death of its noted entrepreneur.

"The Drunkard" had two rivals during the year, particularly worth-while being "The Banker's Daughter," old-time melodrama set to music by Sol Kaplan. Howard da Silva, Morris Carnovsky, Lloyd Bridges and Helen Ford headed the cast at the outset. Henry Myers and Edward Eliscu were identified with the new stage adaptation. It was presented at the Globe Theatre, formerly a night club operated by Slapsie Maxie Rosenbloom. The show had hit elements.

The other entrant was "Will the Mail Train Run Tonight?" performed at The Golden Spike Theatre, formerly a recreational center for service men. This had less good fortune.

As always in latter years the spread of Southern California show-giving activities is terrific. The question is whether it is just a recurrent malady, or is it leading somewhere?

THE COCKTAIL PARTY *

A Comedy in Three Acts

BY T. S. ELIOT

CONTENTION and controversy are most precious elements in the theatre, and the play that is blessed with them is sure of a vigorous life. The reason for this is that the pleasure of playgoing is derived only in small part—say a tenth—in the actual attendance upon a performance; the other nine-tenths comes afterward in talking about it and remembering it—in arguing pro or con. Too few plays are worth arguing about, and so, for that matter, are too few books, restaurants, movies and motor cars, for they are so comfortably and uninterestingly standardized.

When T. S. Eliot's "The Cocktail Party" arrived at Henry Miller's Theatre in January, 1950, the New York theatre came alive. The play opened on a Saturday night, which meant that the notices would not be printed until Monday—and that the reviewers, released from the grip of the nightly deadline, would have more time to ponder. Ponder they did, and the controversy was off to a good start. Some of the writers confessed bafflement; to others the play was as clear and tasty as a good consommé; some boldly used the word "masterpiece," which is the biggest word in the critical arsenal and, like the A-bomb, is to be used only after the profoundest of consideration.

When the text of "The Cocktail Party" was published in the U. S. by Harcourt, Brace and Company, the controversy spread to the literary world, and the biggest guns in the book business boomed about it. Some reviewers warned that the work should not be taken too seriously; one, indeed, said flatly that it was a practical joke. Others had for it an unqualified enthusiasm. Joseph Wood Krutch, who has high standing as a literary critic and a drama critic as well, summarized his opinion by stating, "It introduces a genuinely new note into writing for the contemporary theatre." "The Cocktail Party" became a best seller among books—a pinnacle that plays rarely achieve. In recent years the only other drama to get into the

---

best-seller class has been Eugene O'Neill's "The Iceman Cometh."

T. S. Eliot, a High Church Englishman who was born in Missouri, is considered by many to be the greatest living poet writing in English. He has found the modern theatre to be a challenge to the modern poet, and has written three plays. His first, "Murder in the Cathedral," a historical drama about Thomas à Becket, was an artistic novelty but not a commercial success in New York. His second, "The Family Reunion," had considerable success in England, but has not been viewed locally.

For his third go at the stage Eliot set himself his stiffest task— to write as a poet would write about contemporary people, contemporary affairs and contemporary problems. As he once spoke about his own problem, the poet must write so skillfully that poetry seems like common speech except at such moments as the dramatist chooses to heighten an effect by using the sonorities and cadences of recognizable dramatic verse. It would seem that his first task is to make an audience forget it is listening to poetry and to persuade it to accept the people of the drama and their speech; then, having caught the audience, to persuade it to accept the emotional grandeur of verse as something simple, unstrained and perfectly natural. In our native theatre Maxwell Anderson has often jousted with the same problem. Like Eliot in "Murder in the Cathedral," Anderson has found that history—or at least the heroics of kings and queens of another time—is the easiest setting for a verse-play. And, like Eliot, Anderson has succeeded in fitting this form to the world of contemporary thought, as in "Winterset."

"The Cocktail Party" was presented at the Edinburgh Festival for five days in August, 1949, by Henry Sherek. Skipping London, it was brought with the original company to New York by Mr. Sherek and Gilbert Miller. The play was directed by E. Martin Browne, who had staged Eliot's other dramas. By now it is evident that nobody expected "The Cocktail Party" to be more than a *succès d'estime*. The players expected to be back in London in a few weeks. The author told Foster Hailey, New York *Times* correspondent in London, that he was surprised that the play was a success. He also was surprised that some people were apparently finding it difficult to understand, and that some were reading into it moral or political ideas he had not put into it.

It certainly is simple and gay enough on this particular early evening in the drawing room of the Chamberlaynes' London flat. It is an assemblage one might have found in one of Noel Coward's places —well-bred and well-off. The host, Edward Chamberlayne, is handsome, personable, approaching middle age, a successful barrister—

and somehow more distrait than a perfect cocktail host should allow himself to appear. One of the guests, Julia Shuttlethwaite, is sharp-eyed, baldly inquisitive and given to gossip. Then there are Celia Coplestone, an attractive girl; Peter Quilpe, a young writer; Alexander MacColgie Gibbs, a man-about-the-world, and an Unidentified Guest whom nobody seems to know.

Apparently Alex has just finished telling a story, and Julia has missed the point of it. Peter suggests that he tell it all over again, but Alex demurs. Celia tactfully suggests that it's Julia's turn to tell something—perhaps the one she told the other day about Lady Klootz and the wedding cake. "I don't believe everyone here knows it," urges Celia. "You don't know it, do you?" she asks the Unidentified Guest, and he admits he does not know it.

CELIA

Here's one new listener for you, Julia;
And I don't believe that Edward knows it.

EDWARD

I may have heard it, but I don't remember it.

CELIA

And Julia's the only person to tell it.
She's such a good mimic.

JULIA

Am I a good mimic?

PETER

You *are* a good mimic. You never miss anything.

ALEX

She never misses anything unless she wants to.

CELIA

Especially the Lithuanian accent.

JULIA

Lithuanian? Lady Klootz?

PETER

I thought she was Belgian.

ALEX

Her father belonged to a Baltic family—
One of the *oldest* Baltic families
With a branch in Sweden and one in Denmark.
There were several very lovely daughters:
I wonder what's become of them now.

JULIA

Lady Klootz was very lovely, once upon a time.
What a life she led! I used to say to her: "Greta!
You have too much vitality." But she enjoyed herself.
        (*To the* UNIDENTIFIED GUEST.)
Did *you* know Lady Klootz?

UNIDENTIFIED GUEST
No, I never met her.

CELIA

Go on with the story about the wedding cake.

JULIA

Well, but it really isn't my story.
I heard it first from Delia Verinder
Who was there when it happened.
        (*To the* UNIDENTIFIED GUEST.)
                    Do *you* know Delia Verinder?

UNIDENTIFIED GUEST
No, I don't know her.

JULIA
                Well, one can't be too careful
Before one tells a story.

ALEX
                Delia Verinder?
Was she the one who had three brothers?

JULIA

How many brothers? Two, I think.

ALEX

No, there were three, but you wouldn't know the third one:
They kept him rather quiet.

JULIA
Oh, you mean *that* one.

ALEX
He was feeble-minded.

JULIA
Oh, not feeble-minded:
He was only harmless.

ALEX
Well then, harmless.

JULIA
He was very clever at repairing clocks;
And he had a remarkable sense of hearing—
The only man I ever met who could hear the cry of bats.

PETER
Hear the cry of bats?

JULIA
He could hear the cry of bats.

CELIA
But how do you know he could hear the cry of bats?

JULIA
Because he said so. And I believed him.

CELIA
But if he was so . . . harmless, how could you believe him?
He might have imagined it.

JULIA
My darling Celia,
You needn't be so skeptical. I stayed there once
At their castle in the North. How he suffered!
They had to find an island for him
Where there were no bats.

ALEX
And is he still there?
Julia is really a mine of information.

CELIA

There isn't much that Julia doesn't know.

PETER

Go on with the story about the wedding cake.
(EDWARD *leaves the room.*)

JULIA

No, we'll wait until Edward comes back into the room.
Now I want to relax.   Are there any more cocktails?

PETER

But do go on.   Edward wasn't listening anyway.

JULIA

No, he wasn't listening, but he's such a strain—
Edward without Lavinia! He's quite impossible!
Leaving it to me to keep things going.
What a host! And nothing fit to eat!
The only reason for a cocktail party
For a gluttonous old woman like me
Is a really nice tit-bit.   I can drink at home.
(EDWARD *returns with a tray.*)
Edward, give me another of those delicious olives.
What's that?   Potato crisps?   No, I can't endure them.
Well, I started to tell you about Lady Klootz.
It was at the Vincewell wedding.   Oh, so many years ago!
(*To the* UNIDENTIFIED GUEST.)
Did *you* know the Vincewells?

UNIDENTIFIED GUEST
No, I don't know the Vincewells.

JULIA

Oh, they're both dead now.   But I wanted to know.
If they'd been friends of yours, I couldn't tell the story.

But, as so often happens—as so happily happens at cocktail parties—the story never gets told, for people fly off on conversational
tangents.   Mention of the Vincewells reminds Peter that he met a
Tony Vincewell last year in California—and then he has to tell what
he was doing there—which was making a film—or trying to.   They
made the picture, but didn't use his scenario.

Julia has a go at Edward. She wishes he would sit down and pretend he is just another guest at his wife Lavinia's party. There are so many questions she wants to ask him, now that Lavinia is away—"And this is the first time I've seen you without Lavinia except for the time she got locked in the lavatory and couldn't get out." Celia politely inquires if Lavinia will be away for some time, and Edward answers rather fumblingly that he doesn't know—that if her aunt is very ill she may be gone some time.

Julia has detected the false note and asks if it is Lavinia's Aunt Laura. No, not that one; this one is rather a recluse. Julia probes for her name and address, and Edward evades. Julia gives up—for the moment—by informing Edward that he is to dine alone with her on Friday and talk to her about everything. She has already chosen the people he is to meet.

"But you asked me to dine with you alone."

What Julia meant was without Lavinia. And now she prepares to bucket off. In a burst of warm leavetaking she invites everybody else to dinner, too, then takes it back by remembering that her housekeeper might give notice at so many extra guests. The others think it is time to go, too, and there is considerable maneuvering. Peter would like to walk along with Celia, but Celia evades by saying she must take a taxi. Julia commandeers Peter and they are the first to leave. Next go Alex and Celia. The Unidentified Guest has made no particular move toward departure, and Edward urges him to stay and finish the cocktails—or have whisky, if he prefers. The Guest prefers gin with a drop of water in it.

Edward tries to apologize for the party and explain about it. He had tried to put it off, but he couldn't reach everybody in time. It was only that dreadful old woman who mattered—but she always turns up when she's least wanted. Edward answers a ring of the doorbell—and there is the dreadful old woman. She had forgotten her umbrella, and it was lucky it was raining because it reminded her of her umbrella. When she has gone again the Guest makes a move to leave.

He is a remarkable fellow, this Guest. He is so sure of himself, yet he is not impudent, and is so clever at not saying who he is or whom he knows. Edward urges him to stay; the fact is that he wants to talk to somebody and he finds it easier to talk to somebody he does not know. The fact also is that Lavinia has left him.

UNIDENTIFIED GUEST

Your wife has left you?

EDWARD
                Without warning, of course;
Just when she'd arranged a cocktail party.
She'd gone when I came in, this afternoon.
She left a note to say that she was leaving me;
But I don't know where she's gone.

UNIDENTIFIED GUEST
                        This is an occasion.
May I take another drink?

EDWARD
Whisky?

UNIDENTIFIED GUEST
                    Gin.

EDWARD
Anything in it?

UNIDENTIFIED GUEST
                    Nothing but water.
And I recommend you the same prescription . . .
Let me prepare it for you, if I may . . .
Strong . . . but sip it slowly . . . and drink it sitting down.
Breathe deeply, and adopt a relaxed position.
There we are. Now for a few questions.
How long married?

EDWARD
Five years.

UNIDENTIFIED GUEST
                    Children?

EDWARD
No.

UNIDENTIFIED GUEST
                    Then look at the brighter side.
You say you don't know where she's gone?

EDWARD
                        No, I do not.

UNIDENTIFIED GUEST

Do you know who the man is?

EDWARD

There was no other man—

None that I know of.

UNIDENTIFIED GUEST

Or another woman

Of whom she thought she had cause to be jealous?

EDWARD

She had nothing to complain of in my behavior.

UNIDENTIFIED GUEST

Then no doubt it's all for the best.

With another man, she might have made a mistake

And want to come back to you. If another woman,

She might decide to be forgiving

And gain an advantage. If there's no other woman

And no other man, then the reason may be deeper

And you've ground for hope that she won't come back at all.

If another man, then you'd want to re-marry

To prove to the world that somebody wanted you;

If another woman, you might have to marry her—

You might even imagine that you wanted to marry her.

EDWARD

But I want my wife back.

UNIDENTIFIED GUEST

That's the natural reaction.

It's embarrassing, and inconvenient.

It was inconvenient, having to lie about it

Because you can't tell the truth on the telephone.

It will all take time that you can't well spare;

But I put it to you . . .

EDWARD

Don't put it to me.

UNIDENTIFIED GUEST

Then I suggest . . .

EDWARD

And please don't suggest.
I have often used these terms in examining witnesses,
So I don't like them.   May I put it to *you?*
I know that I invited this conversation:
But I don't know who you are.   This is not what I expected.
I only wanted to relieve my mind
By telling someone what I'd been concealing.
I don't think I want to know who you are;
But, at the same time, unless you know my wife
A good deal better than I thought, or unless you know
A good deal more about us than appears—
I think your speculations rather offensive.

The stranger is impervious to Edward's annoyance.   After all, it was Edward who wanted the luxury of an intimate disclosure to a stranger, and now he should know that "to approach the stranger is to invite the unexpected, to release a new force, or let the genie out of the bottle."   Does Edward love his wife?

In a way this is a facer.   Why, they took each other for granted . . . were used to each other.   And her going away like this is a mystery—it's unfinished.

The stranger agrees, and agrees that nobody likes to be left with a mystery.   But there is more to it than that: there is a loss of one's own personality.   He advises Edward to take this opportunity and find out what he really is and what he feels, and to do nothing else but wait.

Edward thinks waiting would be impossible—doing nothing would be impossible.   It makes him ridiculous.   He can't answer questions about his wife because he doesn't know what to say.   It would be humiliating.   The Unidentified Guest, whose wisdom is growing in profundity, observes that this would be all to the good—that surviving humiliation is an experience of incalculable value.

Edward continues to protest that he must have his wife back—to find out who she is and who he is.   "I want to see her again—here."

"You shall see her again—here."   There is something uncanny in the man's assurance as he lays down the terms: Edward must ask her no questions as to where she has been.   Edward agrees, and the stranger declares, "In twenty-four hours she will come to you here."

There is a ring at the bell again, and, of course, it is Julia—this time looking for her glasses.   She has Peter with her.   As she begins poking around, Edward's odd visitor begins a song:

As I was drinkin' gin and water,
    And me bein' the One Eyed Riley,
Who came in but the landlord's daughter
    And she took my heart entirely.

And with a jaunty flourish of leavetaking he finishes:

Tooryooly toory-iley
    What's the matter with One Eyed Riley?

Edward is weary of Julia, of the stranger, of everybody. He wishes Julia would go away and stay away, and he gruffly fends off all her questions about the stranger. As for her glasses, he suggests that she look in her bag—which she does, and there they are. Once again she is off, and Edward hopes Peter is, too, but Peter wants to stay for a private talk. He hopes that Edward hadn't noticed the situation at the party—and indeed Edward hasn't.

It's about Celia—himself and Celia, the young man confides hopefully in the older. He is, obviously, in love with the girl, and they seem to have much in common. They both are artists; she has written poetry and he has written a novel, and they both are much interested in the cinema—in the art of the film. Peter is just warming to his subject, or confession, when in walks Alex. Julia must have left the door off the latch. Good old Alex has come to take Edward out to dine.

But Edward does not want to go out to dine. He wants to stay in and be alone. Very well, then, Alex will prepare him a nice little dinner for one, for Alex admits he is rather a famous cook. In spite of Edward's protestations that there is nothing in the kitchen, Alex has his way; his specialty is concocting a toothsome meal out of nothing. Peter's narrative is resumed, but is interrupted now and then by Alex appearing from the kitchen to ask where the double boiler is or to complain that there is no curry powder.

Peter met Celia here in this apartment about a year ago.

"At one of Lavinia's amateur Thursdays?" asks Edward.

"A Thursday. Why do you say amateur?"

Edward meant Lavinia's amateur attempts at starting a salon. Peter, the novelist, was to be one of Lavinia's discoveries. Celia's role was to provide society and fashion. "Lavinia always had the ambition to establish herself in two worlds at once—but she herself had to be the link between them. That is why, I think, her Thursdays were a failure."

Well, a few days after the first meeting, Peter saw Celia alone at a concert and he was alone, so he joined her. And they both began going to concerts and to look at pictures together, and have tea, and dine once or twice. Peter had begun to think that Celia really cared about him—and then something puzzling happened. Celia faded—into some other picture—like a film effect. She doesn't want to see him, makes implausible excuses and seems preoccupied with some secret excitement.

Edward takes these disclosures lightly, which the young man does not, and wryly congratulates him on a timely escape. He advises him to go back to California and wait.

PETER

But I must see Celia.

EDWARD

Will it be the same Celia?
Better be content with the Celia you remember.
Remember! I say it's already a memory.

PETER

But I must see Celia at least to make her tell me
What has happened, in her terms. Until I know that
I shan't know the truth about even the memory.
Did we really share these interests? Did we really feel the same
When we heard certain music? Or looked at certain pictures?
There was something real. But what is the reality . . .

(*The telephone rings.*)

EDWARD

Excuse me a moment.
(*Into telephone.*) Hello! . . . I can't talk now . . .
Yes, there is . . . Well then, I'll ring you
As soon as I can.

I'm sorry. You were saying?

PETER

I was saying, what is the reality
Of experience between two unreal people?
If I can only hold to the memory
I can bear any future. But I must find out
The truth about the past, for the sake of the memory.

EDWARD

There's no memory you can wrap in camphor
But the moths will get in. So you want to see Celia.

I don't know why I should be taking all this trouble
To protect you from the fool you are.
What do you want me to do?

PETER
          See Celia for me.
You know her in a different way from me
And you are so much older.

EDWARD
          So much older?

PETER
Yes, I'm sure that she would listen to you
As someone disinterested.

EDWARD
          Well, I will see Celia.

PETER
Thank you, Edward. It's very good of you.
(*Enter* ALEX, *with his jacket on.*)

ALEX
Oh, Edward! I've prepared you such a treat!
I really think that of all my triumphs
This is the greatest. To make something out of nothing!
Never, even when traveling in Albania,
Have I made such a supper out of so few materials
As I found in your refrigerator. But of course
I was lucky to find half-a-dozen eggs.

EDWARD
What! You used all those eggs! Lavinia's aunt
Has just sent them from the country.

ALEX
                Ah, so the aunt
Really exists. A substantial proof.

EDWARD
No, no . . . I mean, this is another aunt.

ALEX

I understand.   The real aunt.   But you'll be grateful.
There are very few peasants in Montenegro
Who can have the dish that you'll be eating, nowadays.

EDWARD

But what about my breakfast?

ALEX

Don't worry about breakfast.
All you should want is a cup of black coffee
And a little dry toast.   I've left it simmering.
Don't leave it longer than another ten minutes.
Now I'll be going, and I'll take Peter with me.

PETER

Edward, I've taken too much of your time,
And you want to be alone.   Give my love to Lavinia
When she comes back . . . but, if you don't mind,
I'd rather you didn't tell *her* what I've told you.

EDWARD

I shall not say anything about it to Lavinia.

PETER

Thank you, Edward.   Good night.

EDWARD

Good night, Peter,
And good night, Alex.   Oh, and if you don't mind,
Please *shut the door after you,* so it latches.

ALEX

Remember, Edward, not more than ten minutes,
Twenty minutes, and my work will be ruined.

(*Exeunt* ALEX *and* PETER.)

(EDWARD *picks up the telephone, and dials a number.   There is no reply.*)

The curtain falls.

Scene II

Edward has managed fifteen minutes of solitude and now he is playing Patience—but he is interrupted by another ring of the door-bell. It is Celia. "I said I would telephone as soon as I could: and I tried to get you a moment ago." The girl explains that she could not understand his manner on the telephone, although she could understand what had happened; she felt she must see him. "Tell me it's all right, and then I'll go." Edward protests that she can't understand what has happened when he doesn't himself—and to try to understand it he wants to be alone.

It looks simple enough to Celia: Lavinia has left him, and that should settle their difficulties. On the contrary, he tells her, it has brought to light the real difficulties—and, moreover, Lavinia is coming back. This sounds to the girl as if Lavinia had set a trap for them.

The telephone again. It is the ever-solicitous Alex, wondering if Edward has enjoyed his repast, and Edward tells a polite lie and says he has. He desperately fends off Alex's offer to bring over some cheese or prunes or something; then he explains to Celia about the meal that was left cooking, and she hurries to the kitchen to investigate. Edward returns to his Patience, but only for the move of a card, for the doorbell rings repeatedly. It is dear Julia, bursting with an inspiration—and at this moment Celia comes from the kitchen with a charred saucepan.

Julia takes in the situation with aplomb; obviously Celia has had the same inspiration she has had—that Edward must be fed, when all that is wrong with him is that he is fed up.

Julia determines that she shall take her turn in the kitchen and Celia shall stay and talk with Edward. Swiftly the girl returns to her questioning. Edward *thinks* Lavinia is coming back, but doesn't know? No, he doesn't, but he believes it. That man who was here had said he would bring her back tomorrow. . . .

Celia remembers the man, confesses she was rather afraid of him; and now she could believe he was the Devil and had bewitched Edward. This colloquy is punctuated by a pop from the kitchen and halted by Julia's return with a tray with three glasses of champagne. There was nothing fit to eat in the kitchen, but she found a half-bottle of champagne and would propose a toast—to Lavinia's aunt. Edward flatly refuses Julia's invitation to come home with her to eat, but Celia accepts—if she can have ten minutes with Edward

When they are alone the girl demands what the man did to persuade Edward to ask for the return of Lavinia. Edward, though puzzled, has retained the clear impression that the stranger had argued the opposite—that it was all for the best that Lavinia had gone. It was he, Edward, who had done the persuading. "That's the Devil's method!" she exclaims.

The girl tries to fit her lover's action into some pattern of reason. Vanity? Surrender to fatigue? Panic? Inability to face trouble? He denies them all—and they all were advanced by a man whose name he does not know, but whom he calls Riley because that was a name in a song the stranger sang.

Now Celia thinks she has the answer: Edward is not—well, not mad, but on the edge of a nervous breakdown. She has heard of a very great doctor whose name *is* Reilly, and if Edward would only consult with him . . . No, he says despondently, it wouldn't work. The girl makes one great, heartfelt plea: If she goes now, will he assure her that he does not mean to have Lavinia back and that everything is right? He answers this in a more or less customary manner: It won't work. It has been wonderful, and he is grateful, and she is a very rare person . . . but it all wasn't fair to her; there could be no future.

CELIA

What had I thought that the future could be?
I abandoned the future before we began,
And after that I lived in a present
Where time was meaningless, a private world of *ours,*
Where the word "happiness" had a different meaning
Or so it seemed.

EDWARD
I have heard of that experience.

CELIA
A dream. I was happy in it till today,
And then, when Julia asked about Lavinia
And it came to me that Lavinia had left you
And that you would be free—then I suddenly discovered
That the dream was not enough; that I wanted something more
And I waited, and wanted to run to tell you.
Perhaps the dream was better. It seemed the real reality,
And if this is reality, it is very like a dream.
Perhaps it was I who betrayed my own dream
All the while; and to find I wanted
This world as well as that . . . well, it's humiliating.

EDWARD

There is no reason why you should feel humiliated . . .

CELIA

Oh, don't think that *you* can humiliate me!
Humiliation—it's something I've done to myself.
I am not sure even that you seem real enough
To humiliate me. I suppose that most women
Would feel degraded to find that a man
With whom they thought they had shared something wonderful
Had taken them only as a passing diversion.
Oh, I dare say that you deceived yourself;
But that's what it was, no doubt.

EDWARD

I *didn't* take you as a passing diversion.
If you want to speak of passing diversions
How did you take Peter?

CELIA

Peter? Peter who?

Peter Quilpe, he tells her, and he tells her of Peter's visit in tones of cynical righteousness. The girl denounces this as a cruel subterfuge to justify himself, and protests there never was anything between herself and the young novelist except that she thought he had talent, saw that he was lonely, and thought she could help him. And as time went on she found him less interesting. All that matters is that Edward thinks he wants Lavinia. Well, he had better have her.

EDWARD

It's not like that.

It is not that I am in love with Lavinia.
I don't think I was ever really in love with her.
If I have ever been in love—and I think that I have—
I have never been in love with anyone but you,
And perhaps I still am. But this can't go on.
It never could have been . . . a permanent thing:
You should have a man . . . nearer your own age.

CELIA

I don't think I care for advice from you, Edward.
You are not entitled to take any interest
Now, in *my* future. I only hope you're competent

To manage your own. But if you are not in love
And never have been in love with Lavinia,
What is it that you want?

EDWARD

I am not sure.
The one thing of which I am relatively certain
Is, that only since this morning
I have met myself as a middle-aged man
Beginning to know what it is to feel old.
That is the worst moment, when you feel that you have lost
The desire for all that was most desirable,
And before you are contented with what you can desire;
Before you know what is left to be desired;
And you go on wishing that you could desire
What desire has left behind. But you cannot understand.
How could *you* understand what it is to feel old?

CELIA

But I want to understand you. I could understand.
And, Edward, please believe that whatever happens
I shall not loathe you. I shall only feel sorry for you.
It's only myself I am in danger of hating.
But what will your life be? I cannot bear to think of it.
Oh, Edward! Can you be happy with Lavinia?

EDWARD

No—not happy: or, if there is any happiness,
Only the happiness of knowing
That the misery does not feed on the ruin of loveliness,
That the tedium is not the residue of ecstasy.
I see that my life was determined long ago
And that the struggle to escape from it
Is only a make-believe, a pretense
That what is, is not, or could be changed.
The self that can say "I want this—or want that"—
The self that wills—he is a feeble creature;
He has to come to terms in the end
With the obstinate, the tougher self; who does not speak,
Who never talks, who cannot argue;
And who in some men may be the *guardian*—
But in men like me, the dull, the implacable,
The indomitable spirit of mediocrity.

The willing self can contrive the disaster
Of this unwilling partnership—but can only flourish
In submission to the rule of the stronger partner.

CELIA

I am not sure, Edward, that I understand you;
And yet I understand as I never did before.
I think—I believe—you are being yourself
As you never were before, with me.
Twice you have changed since I have been looking at you.
I looked at your face: and I thought that I knew
And loved every contour; and as I looked
It withered, as if I had unwrapped a mummy.
I listened to your voice, that had always thrilled me,
And it became another voice—no, not a voice:
What I heard was only the noise of an insect,
Dry, endless, meaningless, inhuman—
You might have made it by scraping your legs together—
Or however grasshoppers do it. I looked,
And listened for your heart, your blood;
And saw only a beetle the size of a man
With nothing more inside it than what comes out
When you tread on a beetle.

EDWARD
              Perhaps that is what I am.
Tread on me, if you like.

CELIA
             No, I won't tread on you.
That is not what you are. It is only what was left
Of what I had thought you were. I see another person,
I see you as a person whom I never saw before.
The man I saw before, he was only a projection—
I see that now—of something that I wanted—
No, not *wanted*—something I aspired to—
Something that I desperately wanted to exist.
It must happen somewhere—but what, and where is it?
And I ask you to forgive me.

EDWARD
           You . . . ask me to forgive *you!*

CELIA

Yes, for two things. First . . .

(*The telephone rings.*)

Nor does Edward ever learn what those two things were, for it is Julia on the phone again; Julia thinks she must have left her glasses in the kitchen. While she holds on, Edward goes to the kitchen and discovers that for once Julia was right. He brings in the glasses —and the remainder of a full bottle, not a half-bottle, of his own champagne. He proposes a final drink with Celia, and the girl proposes a toast to "the Guardians. It may be that even Julia is a guardian. Perhaps she is *my* guardian. Give me the spectacles. Good night, Edward."

As Celia leaves, he remembers Julia still is on the wire. He tells her he has found the glasses and that Celia is bringing them now.

The curtain falls.

SCENE III

Late in the afternoon of the next day Edward admits to his apartment the Unidentified Guest, who has come to remind him that he has made a decision, and it is a serious matter to bring someone back from the dead. This seems a somewhat dramatic figure of speech to Edward, since it was only yesterday that his wife left him.

UNIDENTIFIED GUEST

Ah, but we die to each other daily.
What we know of other people
Is only our memory of the moments
During which we knew them. And they have changed since then.
To pretend that they and we are the same
Is a useful and convenient social convention
Which must sometimes be broken. We must also remember
That at every meeting we are meeting a stranger.

EDWARD

So you want me to greet my wife as a stranger?
That will not be easy.

UNIDENTIFIED GUEST
It is very difficult.

But it is perhaps still more difficult

To keep up the pretense that you are not strangers.
The affectionate ghosts: the grandmother,
The lively bachelor uncle at the Christmas party,
The beloved nursemaid—those who enfolded
Your childhood years in comfort, mirth, security—
If they returned, would it not be embarrassing?
What would you say to them, or they to you
After the first ten minutes?   You would find it difficult
To treat them as strangers, but still more difficult
To pretend that you were not strange to each other.

EDWARD

You can hardly expect me to obliterate
The last five years.

UNIDENTIFIED GUEST

I ask you to forget nothing.
To try to forget is to try to conceal.

EDWARD

There are certainly things I should like to forget.

UNIDENTIFIED GUEST

And persons also.   But you must not forget them.
You must face them all, but meet them as strangers.

EDWARD

Then I myself must also be a stranger.

UNIDENTIFIED GUEST

And to yourself as well.   But remember,
When you see your wife, you must ask no questions
And give no explanations.   I have said the same to her.
Don't strangle each other with knotted memories.
Now I shall go.

EDWARD

Stop! Will you come back with her?

UNIDENTIFIED GUEST

No, I shall not come with her.

EDWARD

I don't know why,
But I think I should like you to bring her yourself.

UNIDENTIFIED GUEST

Yes, I know you would. And for definite reasons
Which I am not prepared to explain to you
I must ask you not to speak of me to her;
And she will not mention me to you.

EDWARD

I promise.

UNIDENTIFIED GUEST

And now you must await your visitors.

EDWARD

Visitors? What visitors?

UNIDENTIFIED GUEST

Whoever comes. The strangers.
As for myself, I shall take the precaution
Of leaving by the service staircase.

EDWARD

May I ask one question?

UNIDENTIFIED GUEST

You may ask it.

EDWARD

Who are you?

UNIDENTIFIED GUEST

I also am a stranger.

The first of the visitors is, to Edward's great surprise, Celia. The
girl explains that Lavinia has asked her to come—not directly, but
she had telegraphed Julia to come and bring Celia with her. Julia
will be up soon. Edward is distraught at being alone with the mistress with whom he had toasted a farewell last night, but Celia has
found her sense of humor. Edward looks to her like a little boy
who has been sent for by the headmaster. She seems almost happy
in her laughter; at last she can see Edward as a human being, and
she hopes he can see her as one too.

The next arrival is Peter, who also has been summoned by Lavinia.
Not directly, but she'd wired Alex to bring him. Alex is on his way
up. Peter has the impression that it is to be yesterday's cocktail
party all over again with the hostess present. Peter announces that

he is returning to California; Alex has put him in touch with a man out there and the deal has already been settled.

The third visitor does not have to ring the bell, for it is Lavinia and she has her latchkey. She is a cool, handsome blonde. She greets Celia and Peter pleasantly and says she did not expect to find them here. But the telegram! they protest. She knows of no telegrams. Edward denies having sent them, and Lavinia decides, "This is some of Julia's mischief."

Edward makes conversation by telling his wife that Peter is going to America and that Celia has said she is going away too. Lavinia takes it for granted that the young people are going together, and congratulates them. Celia corrects this misunderstanding, and says that, now that she may be going away somewhere, she would like to say good-by—as friends.

Lavinia boxes cleverly, saying she has always thought Celia was one of her dearest friends—at least in so far as a girl can be a friend of a woman so much older than herself. The girl, direct and honest, will not be put off. "I should like you to remember me as someone who wants you and Edward to be happy." Lavinia avers that they will manage somehow, as in the past, and the girl protests, "Oh, not as in the past!"

The bell again; this time Julia. She is sorry to be late, but the telegram was unexpected. And how is the dear aunt? Lavinia's puzzlement is increasing; telegrams? Aunt? She has sent no wires from Essex because she hasn't been in Essex. Alex increases the mystery when he arrives by also mentioning a message from Essex. He would like to pursue this mystery, but Julia unexpectedly suggests that they abandon inquisitiveness and leave Lavinia and Edward alone; Lavinia must be quite worn out after her anxiety about her aunt. . . .

Peter goes for a taxi, and Celia takes her leave. Julia gets Alex moving, and Edward maliciously inquires, "Are you sure you haven't left anything, Julia?" But before they all go, Lavinia tries in vain for the answer to the riddle of the telegrams. "Somebody is always interfering. . . . I don't feel free . . . and yet I started it . . ." she says, in puzzlement.

When they are at last alone, husband and wife exchange rather strained but purposefully pleasant greetings. Each knows that he is to ask no questions and give no explanations—but at least they can talk about the party. Lavinia apologizes for having let Edward down; he explains that he telephoned everyone he knew was coming, but couldn't get everyone. Lavinia thinks it is odd that those who came were those who were here a moment ago; and she thinks also that Julia has an instinct for finding awkward situations. And what did Edward tell them?

"I invented an aunt who was ill in the country."

"Really, Edward! You had better have told the truth: nothing less than the truth could deceive Julia."

In not much more than the same period of time, Lavinia has made the same discovery that Celia made: she finds that she has taken Edward much too seriously, and now she can see how absurd he is. She has found that she spent five years with a man who has no sense of humor, and the effect upon her was that she lost all sense of humor herself. That's what came of always giving in to him.

EDWARD

I was unaware that you'd always given in to me.
It struck me very differently. As we're on the subject,
I thought it was I who had given in to *you*.

LAVINIA

I know what you mean by giving in to *me:*
You mean, leaving all the practical decisions
That you should have made yourself. I remember—
Oh, I ought to have realized what was coming—
When we were planning our honeymoon,
I couldn't make you say where you wanted to go . . .

EDWARD

But I wanted *you* to make that decision.

LAVINIA

But how could I tell where I wanted to go
Unless you suggested some other place first?
And I remember that finally in desperation
I said: "I suppose you'd as soon go to Peacehaven"—
And you said "I don't mind."

EDWARD
Of course I didn't mind.

I meant it as a compliment.

LAVINIA
You meant it as a compliment!

EDWARD

It's just that way of taking things that makes you so exasperating.

LAVINIA

You were so considerate, people said;
And you thought you were unselfish. It was only passivity;
You only wanted to be bolstered, encouraged . . .

EDWARD

Encouraged? To what?

LAVINIA

To think well of yourself.
You know it was I who made you work at the Bar . . .

EDWARD

You nagged me because I didn't get enough work
And said that I ought to meet more people:
But when the briefs began to come in
And they didn't come through any of *your* friends—
You suddenly found it inconvenient
That I should be always too busy or too tired
To be of use to you socially . . .

LAVINIA

I *never* complained.

EDWARD

No; and it was perfectly infuriating,
The way you *didn't* complain . . .

LAVINIA

It was you who complained
Of seeing nobody but solicitors and clients . . .

EDWARD

And you were never very sympathetic.

LAVINIA

Well, but I tried to do something about it.
That was why I took so much trouble
To have those Thursdays, to give you the chance
Of talking to intellectual people . . .

EDWARD

You would have given me about as much opportunity
If you had hired me as your butler:
Some of your guests may have thought I *was* the butler.

LAVINIA

And on several occasions, when somebody was coming
Whom I particularly wanted you to meet,
You didn't arrive until just as they were leaving.

EDWARD

Well, at least, *they* can't have thought I was the butler.

LAVINIA

Everything I tried only made matters worse,
And the moment you were offered something that you wanted
You wanted something else.   I shall treat you very differently
In future.

EDWARD

Thank you for the warning.   But tell me,
Since this is how you see me, why did you come back?

LAVINIA

Frankly, I don't know.   I was warned of the danger,
Yet something, or somebody, compelled me to come.
And why did you want me?

EDWARD

I don't know either.
You say you were trying to "encourage" me:
Then why did you always make me feel insignificant?
I may not have known what life I wanted,
But it wasn't the life you chose for me.
You wanted your successful to be *successful*,
You wanted me to supply a public background
For your kind of public life.   You wished to be a hostess
For whom my career would be a support.
Well, I tried to be accommodating.   But in future,
I shall behave, I assure you, very differently.

It is almost the same old war between husband and wife.   The
acrimony becomes sharper, the anger deeper as the debate continues.
But one senses a change, because their viewpoints are changing
almost momentarily.   They are seeing themselves and each other
differently.   Edward senses the change: They are back in the same
trap, but now they can fight each other instead of each taking his
corner of the cage.   As the heat of argument finally subsides, Edward
discloses some of his inner torment by saying he cannot walk out
of his prison.   Hell, he has discovered, is oneself.   There is nothing

to escape from, and nothing to escape to. It was only yesterday that this damnation took place, and now he must live with it forever.

"I think you are on the edge of a nervous breakdown!" Thus again does Lavinia agree with Celia. And she, too, knows of a doctor who could help. . . .

Edward firmly announces that, if there are to be any doctors, he will do the choosing. And in the future she is going to find him a different person. Slyly she inquires if this difference has anything to do with Celia going off to California—with Peter. It is a well-placed and hurtful thrust, and it opens Edward's mind to new miseries. Having made her thrust and her point, Lavinia turns practical and says she will find some eggs in the kitchen, but they will have to go out for dinner. Will Edward get the porter to fetch up her luggage?

CURTAIN

ACT II

The setting is Sir Henry Harcourt-Reilly's consulting room in London. The place has a business-like look about it—and so does Sir Henry as he summons his nurse-secretary from an outer office by pressing an electric button. He is the Unidentified Guest who was at the cocktail party. Briskly he gives the nurse-secretary a run-down of the morning's affairs: when the first appointment arrives at 11 A.M. he is to be shown into the small waiting room and Sir Henry will see him at once. The second, due at 11:15, is to be asked to wait in the other room, as usual. She is usually punctual. She will wait until Sir Henry rings three times. The third patient is to go into the small room, and not be announced until the others have gone. Several weeks have passed since Edward and Lavinia have had their self-revelatory reunion.

The nurse-secretary says Mr. Gibbs has arrived, and Alex is shown in to make a report: he had no difficulty in persuading Edward to seek this consultation; in fact, Edward was impatient at having to wait four days for an appointment. "It was necessary to delay his appointment to lower his resistance," says Sir Henry, who seems to think of everything. Under questioning, Alex reveals that Edward trusted his judgment implicitly—thinks he's the sort of well-informed person who would know the right doctor as well as the right shops. "Besides, he was ready to consult any doctor recommended by any-one except his wife." One more thing: Edward has been staying at his club. When the nurse-secretary announces an arrival on the

house telephone, Alex departs by a side door and the service staircase.

When Edward is shown in he recognizes and stops and stares at
the man he has come to consult. Sir Henry imperturbably invites
him to sit down, but Edward's mind is racing as pieces of the puzzle
fall together. He reproaches himself for having taken Alex's recom-
mendation, but Alex is so plausible and his recommendations of
shops have always been satisfactory. . . . Edward makes a move
to leave, but Sir Henry assumes command. "You are not going
away, so you might as well sit down."

Edward's suspicion focuses on his wife. Did she invite Sir Henry
as a guest to the party—or did she send him? Reilly says neither
was the case—Mrs. Chamberlayne did not know he was coming, but
Reilly knew Edward would be there and who would be with him.

REILLY
You have reason to believe that you are very ill?

EDWARD
I should have thought a doctor could see that for himself.
Or at least that he would inquire about the symptoms.
Two people advised me recently,
Almost in the same words, that I ought to see a doctor.
They said—again, in almost the same words—
That I was on the edge of a nervous breakdown.
I didn't know it then myself—but if they saw it
I should have thought that a doctor could see it.

REILLY
"Nervous breakdown" is a term I never use:
It can mean almost anything.

EDWARD
                              And since then, I have realized
That mine is a very unusual case.

REILLY
All cases are unique, and very similar to others.

EDWARD
Is there a sanatorium to which you send such patients
As myself, under your personal observation?

REILLY

You are very impetuous, Mr. Chamberlayne.
There are several kinds of sanatoria
For several kinds of patient. And there are also patients
For whom a sanatorium is the worst place possible.
We must first find out what is wrong with you
Before we decide what to do with you.

EDWARD

I doubt if you have ever had a case like mine:
I have ceased to believe in my own personality.

REILLY

Oh, dear yes; this is serious. A very common malady.
Very prevalent indeed.

EDWARD

I remember, in my childhood . . .

REILLY

I always begin from the immediate situation
And then go back as far as I find necessary.
You see, your memories of childhood—
I mean, in your present state of mind—
Would be largely fictitious; and as for your dreams,
You would produce amazing dreams, to oblige me.
I could make you dream any kind of dream I suggested,
And it would only go to flatter your vanity
With the temporary stimulus of feeling interesting.

EDWARD

But I am obsessed by the thought of my own insignificance.

REILLY

Precisely. And I could make you feel important,
And you would imagine it a marvelous cure;
And you would go on, doing such amount of mischief
As lay within your power—until you came to grief.
Half of the harm that is done in this world
Is due to people who want to feel important.
They don't mean to do harm—but the harm does not interest them.
Or they do not see it, or they justify it
Because they are absorbed in the endless struggle
To think well of themselves.

The consultation continues, with Edward pouring out his tale of what his wife has done to him and with Sir Henry appearing not to be very much absorbed. At last Edward wonders aloud if Sir Henry has understood a word he has been saying, and the consultant suavely yet drily explains that he learns a lot merely by observing, "and letting you talk as long as you please, and taking note of what you do not say."

Edward, feeling that he can no longer act for himself, submits himself as a patient. "And now will you send me to the sanatorium?" He can't go home again, and the club won't let him keep a room more than seven days, and he hasn't the courage to go to a hotel. Is it far to go?

"You might say, a long journey," replies Sir Henry. But first, before he treats a patient like Edward, he must know more about him than the patient himself can tell. Often, patients are only pieces of a total situation which must be explored; the single patient who is ill by himself is an exception. It happens that he has another patient in a similar situation, and proposes an introduction.

Reilly pushes the button on his desk three times. Edward bridles; he will not discuss his case before another patient. He will go to a hotel—but, before he can move, Lavinia is admitted. The surprise of the one is as great as that of the other. Lavinia is indignant, and Edward calls it a dishonorable trick—to which Sir Henry replies, "Honesty before honor, Mr. Chamberlayne."

Lavinia supposes that the physician intends to send her husband to the same sanatorium she went to, and Sir Henry blandly informs her that she was not at a sanatorium at all— just a kind of hotel for people who imagine that they need a respite from everyday life. "The people who need my sort of sanatorium are not easily deceived."

Edward scoffs at the idea of his wife wanting a sanatorium—she who is stronger than a battleship. It's *he* who needs one, but he he is not going there. To this Sir Henry agrees. "You are much too ill," he says. They both are too ill. For instance, one of the symptoms qualifying a patient for Sir Henry's establishment is an honest mind.

LAVINIA

No one can say my husband has an honest mind.

EDWARD

And I could not honestly say that of *you*, Lavinia.

REILLY

I congratulate you both on your perspicacity,
But this does not bring us to the heart of the matter.
I do not trouble myself with the common cheat,
Or with the insuperably, innocently dull:
My patients such as you are the self-deceivers
Taking infinite pains, exhausting their energy,
Yet never quite successful. You have both of you pretended
To be consulting me; both, tried to impose upon me
Your own diagnosis, and prescribe your own cure.
But when you put yourselves into hands like mine
You surrender a great deal more than you meant to.
This is the consequence of trying to lie to me.

LAVINIA

I did not come here to be insulted.

REILLY

You have come where the word "insult" has no meaning;
And you must put up with that. All that you have told me—
Both of you—was true enough: you described your feelings—
Or some of them—omitting the important facts.
Let me take your husband first.
                    (*To* EDWARD.)
                              You were lying to me
By concealing your relations with Miss Coplestone.

EDWARD

This is monstrous! My wife knew nothing about it.

LAVINIA

Really, Edward! Even if I'd been blind
There were plenty of people to let me know about it.
I wonder if there was anyone who didn't know.

REILLY

There was one, in fact. But you, Mrs. Chamberlayne,
Tried to make me believe that it was this discovery
Precipitated what you called your nervous breakdown.

LAVINIA

But it's true! I was completely prostrated;
Even if I have made a partial recovery.

REILLY

Certainly, you were completely prostrated,
And certainly, you have somewhat recovered.
But you failed to mention that the cause of your distress
Was the defection of your lover—who suddenly,
For the first time in his life, fell in love with someone,
And with someone of whom you had reason to be jealous.

EDWARD

Really, Lavinia! This is very interesting.
You seem to have been much more successful at concealment
Than I was. Now I wonder who it could have been.

LAVINIA

Well, tell him if you like.

REILLY

A young man named Peter.

EDWARD

Peter? Peter who?

REILLY

Mr. Peter Quilpe

Was a frequent guest.

EDWARD

Peter Quilpe!

Peter Quilpe! Really Lavinia!
I congratulate you. You could not have chosen
Anyone I was less likely to suspect.
And then he came to *me* to confide about Celia!
I have never heard anything so utterly ludicrous:
This is the best joke that ever happened.

LAVINIA

I never knew you had such a sense of humor.

REILLY

It is the first more hopeful symptom.

LAVINIA

How did you know all this?

REILLY
That I cannot disclose.
I have my own method of collecting information
About my patients. You must not ask me to reveal it—
That is a matter of professional etiquette.

LAVINIA
I have not noticed much professional etiquette
About your behavior today.

REILLY
A point well taken.
But permit me to remark that my revelations
About each of you, to one another,
Have not been of anything that you confided to me.
The information I have exchanged between you
Was all obtained from outside sources.
Mrs. Chamberlayne, when you came to me two months ago
I was dissatisfied with your explanation
Of your obvious symptoms of emotional strain
And so I made enquiries.

Now the cards are on the table, and now Sir Henry proceeds to analyze and prescribe.

Edward and Lavinia have much in common and are exceptionally well-suited to each other.

When Edward thought his wife had left him, he discovered to his surprise and consternation that he was not really in love with Celia. This injured his vanity and made him suspect he was incapable of loving.

As for Lavinia, when she discovered that Peter had fallen in love with Celia, she had been shocked. She had wanted to be loved, and then she began to fear that no one *could* love her. Here they are—a man who finds himself incapable of loving and a woman who finds that no man can love her.

It strikes Lavinia that this much in common might be just enough to make them loathe each other.

No, counsels Sir Henry. See it rather as the bond which holds them together.

"Then what can we do when we can go neither back nor forward? Edward! What can we do?"

Sir Henry interposes that, although Lavinia may not know the meaning of what she has just said, she has answered her own question. Edward gets his meaning. "We must make the best of a bad job."

Sir Henry concurs—but points out that, except for the saints—such as those who go to the sanatorium—the best of a bad job is all any of us make of it. If they forget the phrase, it will alter the condition.

Husband and wife begin to make plans. Lavinia will take Edward to a hotel in the New Forest, or leave him at the club. . . .

It seems to Edward that he might as well go home, and Lavinia proposes that they be economical and share a taxi.

They depart, with Sir Henry's benediction, "Go in peace. And work out your salvation with diligence." His bill will be sent along.

Julia pops in, reports that she has brought Celia, and that Celia is ready to make a decision—but is doubtful that Sir Henry will take her seriously. Julia pops out by the side door, and Celia is admitted. After a moment the girl recognizes the Unidentified Guest, and he explains that he had been at the party at Julia's request—which makes it even more perplexing to Celia, since she now is here at Julia's request.

"I suppose most people, when they come to see you, are obviously ill, or can give good reasons for wanting to see you. I can't," the young woman says frankly. She feels perfectly well and could lead an active life—if there's anything to work for.

Sir Henry suggests that she describe her present state of mind. First, she replies, she has an awareness of solitude. It's not just the ending of one relationship, or having found that it never existed; it's a revelation about her relationship with *everybody*. It no longer seems worth while to *speak* to anyone. She can't even face returning to her family in the country.

And the second symptom is stranger still: She has a sense of sin. Not in the ordinary sense of being immoral. She doesn't feel immoral. It might be wicked to hurt other people knowingly, but she hasn't hurt *her* and wasn't taking away from her anything she wanted. And everything seemed so right at the time! Now she knows it was all a mistake, but she can't see why a mistake should make one feel sinful. She must have some kind of hallucination; she is frightened by a fear that is more real than anything she believed in.

REILLY

What is more real than anything you believed in?

CELIA

It's not the feeling of anything I've ever *done,*
Which I might get away from, or of anything in me
I could get rid of—but of emptiness, of failure
Towards someone, or something, outside of myself;
And I feel I must . . . *atone*—is that the word?
Can you treat a patient for such a state of mind?

REILLY

What had you believed were your relations with this man?

CELIA

Oh, you'd guessed that, had you? That's clever of you.
No, perhaps I made it obvious. You don't need to know
About him, do you?

REILLY

          No.

CELIA

                Perhaps I'm only typical.

REILLY

There are different types. Some are rarer than others.

CELIA

Oh, I thought that I was giving him so much!
And he to me—and the giving and the taking
Seemed so right: not in terms of calculation
Of what was good for the persons we had been
But for the new person, *us.* If I could feel
As I did then, even now it would seem right.
And then I found we were only strangers
And that there had been neither giving nor taking
But that we had merely made use of each other
Each for his purpose. That's horrible. Can we only love
Something created by our own imagination?
Are we all in fact unloving and unlovable?
Then one *is* alone, and if one is alone
Then lover and belovèd are equally unreal
And the dreamer is no more real than his dreams.

REILLY

And this man. What does he now seem like, to you?

CELIA

Like a child who has wandered into a forest
Playing with an imaginary playmate
And suddenly discovers he is only a child
Lost in a forest, wanting to go home.

REILLY

Compassion may be already a clue
Towards finding your own way out of the forest.

CELIA

But even if I find my way out of the forest
I shall be left with the inconsolable memory
Of the treasure I went into the forest to find
And never found, and which was not there
And perhaps is not anywhere. But if not anywhere,
Why do I feel guilty at not having found it?

REILLY

Disillusion can become itself an illusion
If we rest in it.

CELIA
                    I cannot argue.
It's not that I'm afraid of being hurt again:
Nothing again can either hurt or heal.
I have thought at moments that the ecstasy is real
Although those who experience it may have no reality.
For what happened is remembered like a dream
In which one is exalted by intensity of loving
In the spirit, a vibration of delight
Without desire, for desire is fulfilled
In the delight of loving. A state one does not know
When awake. But what, or whom I loved,
Or what in me was loving, I do not know.
And if that is all meaningless, I want to be cured
Of a craving for something I cannot find
And of the shame of never finding it.
Can you cure me?

Sir Henry assures Celia that the condition is curable—but the form of treatment must be her own choice; he cannot choose for her. He can reconcile her to "the human condition" of giving and taking, being tolerant of self and others, the normal life of two people contented with parting in the morning, rejoining in the evening—two people who do not understand each other, breeding children they don't understand and who will never understand them. . . . A good life in a world of violence, stupidity and greed.

This prospect leaves Celia cold. It seems like a betrayal of herself; it would be dishonest for her, now, to try to make a life with *any*body.

There is another way, pursues Sir Henry—an unknown way which requires faith—the kind of faith which issues from despair. A blind journey, destination unknown. A terrifying journey.

Celia forthrightly chooses the second way. She supposes it will be lonely, but he assures her it is no lonelier than the first way.

"So what am I to do?" she asks.

"You will go to the sanatorium," he replies.

To her this is an anti-climax. She knows people who have been to his sanatorium and have returned as . . . normal people. Sir Henry assures her that her friends have not been to the place he has in mind for her; those who go to her place do not come back as her friends did—nor do they stay there, either, as in a prison. In this place, people choose; nothing is forced on them. Some return, in a physical sense; no one vanishes; very often they lead active lives in the world.

Celia is ready to go—tonight. Reilly advises her to go home and get ready; a car will come for her at nine o'clock. He writes out an address for her to give to her friends. She needs to take nothing with her; everything will be provided and she will have no expenses. Celia asks about his fee.

"For a case like yours there is no fee."

The girl departs with his benediction, "Go in peace, my daughter. Work out your salvation with diligence." He dials the house telephone and says, "You can come in now." In comes Julia. Reilly tells her he is confident of Celia, but is worried about the other two. He may have been wrong to send them back; he has taken a great risk. Julia thinks the Chamberlaynes will be all right; it is Celia *she* is worried about.

REILLY

But when I said just now
That she would go far, you agreed with me.

JULIA

Oh yes, she will go far. And we know where she is going.
But what do we know of the errors of the journey?

You and I don't know the process by which the human is
Transhumanized: what do we know
Of the kind of suffering they must undergo
On the way of illumination?

REILLY
Will she be frightened
By the first appearance of projected spirits?

JULIA
Henry, you simply do not understand innocence.
She will be afraid of nothing; she will not even know
That there is anything there to be afraid of.
She is too humble. She will pass between the scolding hills,
Through the valley of derision, like a child sent on an errand
In eagerness and patience. Yet she must suffer.

REILLY
When I express confidence in anything
You always raise doubts; when I am apprehensive
Then you see no reason for anything but confidence.

JULIA
That's one way in which I am so useful to you.
You ought to be grateful.

REILLY
And when I say to one like her,
"Work out your salvation with diligence," I do not understand
What I myself am saying.

JULIA
You must accept your limitations.
—But how much longer will Alex keep us waiting?

REILLY
He should be here by now. I'll speak to Miss Baraway.
(*Takes up house-telephone.*)
Miss Barraway, when Mr. Gibbs arrives . . .
Oh, very good.
(*To* JULIA.)
He's on his way up.
(*Into telephone.*)
You may bring the tray in now, Miss Barraway.
(*Enter* ALEX.)

THE COCKTAIL PARTY

ALEX

Well! Well! and how have we got on?

JULIA

Everything is in order.

ALEX

The Chamberlaynes have chosen?

REILLY

They accept their destiny.

ALEX

And *she* has made the choice?

REILLY

She will be fetched this evening.
(NURSE-SECRETARY *enters with a tray, a decanter and three glasses, and exits.* REILLY *pours drinks.*)
And now we are ready to proceed to the libation.

ALEX

The words for the building of the hearth.
(*They raise their glasses.*)

REILLY

Let them build the hearth
Under the protection of the stars.

ALEX

Let them place a chair each side of it.

JULIA

May the holy ones watch over the roof,
May the Moon herself influence the bed.
(*They drink.*)

ALEX

The words for those who go upon a journey.

REILLY

Protector of travelers
Bless the road.

ALEX

Watch over her in the desert
Watch over her in the mountain
Watch over her in the labyrinth
Watch over her by the quicksand.

JULIA

Protect her from the Voices
Protect her from the Visions
Protect her in the tumult
Protect her in the silence.

(*They drink.*)

REILLY

There is one for whom the words cannot be spoken.

ALEX

They cannot be spoken yet.

JULIA

You mean Peter Quilpe.

REILLY

He has not yet come to where the words are valid.

JULIA

Shall we ever speak them?

ALEX

Others, perhaps, will speak them.
You know, I have connections—even in California.

The curtain falls.

ACT III

The Chamberlaynes are getting ready for another party. They have come far, for it is now two years since they and Celia had their consultations with Sir Henry. A caterer's man is arranging a buffet table, and Lavinia is supervising in a housewifely manner. When all is arranged for a 6:30 P.M. beginning, the man withdraws.

Edward lets himself in and expresses the hope that he is in good time and that Lavinia has not been worrying. She has not. She did ring up his chambers and was told that he had already left, but all she rang up for was to reassure him—

"That you hadn't run away?" he finishes for her, smiling.

She protests lightly that this is unfair. They have given *several* parties the last two years and she has been at all of them.

"I like the dress you're wearing," says Edward. A compliment. And *before* a party, too, when a woman needs one! They discuss the party. Too many people invited, of course. But one couldn't have two parties instead, because the people invited to one would suspect that the other was more important. Anyhow, they won't all come, because the Gunnings are giving a party, too. But consider the Gunning parties: the guests will get just enough to make them thirsty and come to the Chamberlaynes roaring for drink. One can only hope that those who come early will be going to the Gunnings afterward and will make room for those who are coming from the Gunnings.

Nobody is coming for half an hour, and Edward suggests that Lavinia stretch out on the sofa. She will if he sits beside her. On the sofa they contemplate the end of the party and what is to follow—a holiday in a remote house. . . .

The bell sounds; the caterer's man announces Mrs. Shuttlethwaite. As Julia comes in, Alex is seen passing behind her and going directly toward the kitchen. Julia babbles like the old party-going Julia. She is early, but she is going to the Gunnings' and wants to stock up here because she is ravenous and dying of thirst. And she has a surprise—she has brought Alex, who got in only this morning from one of his mysterious expeditions.

Alex appears. This time, he says, he comes from the East— from Kinkanja, an island that they won't have heard of yet. He had been staying with the Governor and inspecting local conditions.

"Monkey nuts?" inquires Julia.

"That was a nearer guess than you think. No, not monkey nuts. But it had to do with monkeys—"

The monkeys have been creating unrest among the natives. They are destructive, but they cannot be exterminated because the majority of the natives, who are heathen, hold monkeys in veneration and do not want them killed. So the heathen blame the Government for the damage the monkeys do.

But some of the tribes are Christian converts and they have a different view. They trap the monkeys and eat them. Alex, indeed, invented several new recipes for the Christian natives. Well, the Christians protect their crops from the monkeys and prosper exceedingly.

Recently foreign agitators have been stirring trouble. They have been convincing the heathen that slaughtering monkeys has put a curse on them, and this curse can be removed only by slaughtering the Christians. This is being done, and some of the heathen are even eating Christians.

"And have any of the English residents been murdered?" asks Edward.

They have. But they are not usually eaten. When the natives have done with a European he is no longer fit to eat.

And now Alex thinks he ought to tell about someone they know —or knew. At this moment Peter, another surprise guest, appears. He has just flown over from New York. He is working for Pan-Am-Eagle, and the others wonder what *that* might be. "Alex knows," says Peter. "Did you see my last picture, Alex?"

"I knew about it, but I didn't see it. There is no cinema in Kinkanja."

Peters avers that Pan-Am-Eagle should look into such a state of affairs. The young man explains that Alex knows all about Pan-Am-Eagle—it was he who introduced Peter to the great Bela Szogody, his boss. Bela has sent Peter over to look at Boltwell— not to stay with the Duke, but to observe the place. They are making a film of English life and they want to use Boltwell because of its state of decay. It is the most decayed noble mansion in England, and Pan-Am-Eagle plans to reproduce it in California. Peter has come over because he has written the script and is helping the casting director look for some typical English faces.

Julia suggests that Peter engage them all. "We're all very typical."

Another surprise, as the caterer's man announces Sir Henry Harcourt-Reilly. It has become a chummy gathering. Julia still playfully pleads with Peter for a movie job, but he says there is one person he wanted to ask about—a person who really wanted to get into films and he always thought she could make a success of it—Celia Coplestone. He has been looking for her and can't find her in the telephone directory.

JULIA

Not in the directory,
Or in any directory. You can tell them now, Alex.

LAVINIA

What does Julia mean?

ALEX
I was about to speak of her
When you came in, Peter. I'm afraid you can't have Celia.

PETER
Oh . . . Is she married?

ALEX
Not married, but dead.

LAVINIA
Celia?

ALEX
Dead.

PETER
Dead. That knocks the bottom out of it.

EDWARD
Celia dead!

JULIA
You had better tell them, Alex,
The news that you bring back from Kinkanja.

LAVINIA
Kinkanja? What was Celia doing in Kinkanja?
We heard that she had joined some nursing order . . .

ALEX
She had joined an order. A very austere one.
And as she already had experience of nursing . . .

LAVINIA
Yes, she had been a V.A.D. I remember.

ALEX
She was directed to Kinkanja,
Where there are various endemic diseases
Besides, of course, those brought by Europeans,
And where the conditions are favorable to plague.

EDWARD
Go on.

ALEX

It seems that there were three of them—
Three sisters at this station, in a Christian village;
And half the natives were dying of pestilence.
They must have been overworked for weeks.

EDWARD

And then?

ALEX

And then, the insurrection broke out
Among the heathen, of which I was telling you.
They knew of it, but would not leave the dying natives.
Eventually, two of them escaped:
One died in the jungle, and the other
Will never be fit for normal life again.
But Celia Coplestone, she was taken.
When our people got there, they questioned the villagers—
Those who survived.   And then they found her body,
Or at least, they found the traces of it.

EDWARD

But before that . . .

ALEX

It was difficult to tell.
But from what we know of local practices
It would seem that she must have been crucified
Very near an ant-hill.

The listeners are shocked, and Peter is numbed. For two years
he has been thinking about Celia. He had tried to forget about
her, but could not. He never thought of anything like this, and
he cannot understand. . . .

"You understand your *métier*," suggests Sir Henry.

Peter has no pride in his *métier*. He once thought he had revolutionary ideas, and now here he is making a second-rate film.
He had hoped for something better, with Celia alive, for he wanted
it for Celia—wanted to do something for her. And now it is worthless.

Lavinia comforts him out of her own experience. "You've only
just begun. I mean, this only brings you to the point at which
you *must* begin." Edward agrees, and Julia counsels, "Celia chose
a road that led her to Kinkanja; you have chosen one that leads

you to Boltwell—and you've got to go there." Which reminds Peter that he has a car waiting, and he leaves.

"That young man is very intelligent," Sir Henry observes. "He should go far—along his own lines."

Lavinia turns to Sir Henry. What struck her was that his face showed no surprise or horror at the way in which Celia died. Indeed, his expression seemed to have been one of satisfaction. He was interested, yes, but not in the details.

Alex submits an interesting detail: When the village was reoccupied, the natives erected a shrine for Celia where they brought offerings of fruit, flowers, fowls and even suckling pigs. They thought that by so doing they might insure themselves against further misfortune—a nice problem for the Bishop to wrestle with.

Reilly is interested in what Lavinia has said; he must be very transparent or she very perceptive. He explains:

—When I first met Miss Coplestone, in this room,
I saw the image, standing behind her chair,
Of a Celia Coplestone whose face showed the astonishment
Of the first five minutes after a violent death.
If this strains your credulity, Mrs. Chamberlayne,
I ask you only to entertain the suggestion
That a sudden intuition, in certain minds,
May tend to express itself at once in a picture.
That happens to me, sometimes. So it was obvious
That here was a woman under sentence of death.
That was her destiny. The only question
Then was, what sort of death? *I* could not know;
Because it was for her to choose the way of life
To lead to death, and, without knowing the end
Yet choose the form of death. We know the death she chose.
I did not know that she would die in this way,
She did not know. So all that I could do
Was to direct her in the way of preparation.
As for Miss Coplestone, because you think her death was waste
You blame yourselves, and because you blame yourselves
You think her life was wasted. It was triumphant.
But I am no more responsible for the triumph—
And just as responsible for her death as you are.

Julia comes up with a reminder: Celia chose a way which led to crucifixion; Peter chose a way that takes him to Boltwell; the Chamberlaynes have chosen a cocktail party and their guests may be arriving at any moment. Alex steps out of the room, and Sir Henry agrees that Julia is right, and it is also right that the Chamberlaynes should be giving a party. Edward explains to his wife that he believes Sir Henry means that every moment is a fresh beginning, and that Julia means that life is only keeping on—and that somehow the two ideas fit together.

Lavinia, however, is still upset over what she has heard about Celia, and does not want to see these people. "It is your appointed burden," Reilly counsels—and he is sure the party will be a success. Alex re-enters, followed by the caterer's man with a tray and five glasses. "I took the liberty of bringing a bottle of my own champagne," he explains—and he proposes a toast.

"To the Guardians," toasts Edward, absently.

Alex submits, "To one particular Guardian, whom you have forgotten. I give you—Lavinia's aunt!" They chorus "Lavinia's aunt!" and drink. Julia bustles Sir Henry and Alex out of the apartment and toward the Gunnings'.

. . .And now for the party.

LAVINIA
I wish it would begin.

EDWARD
There's the doorbell.

LAVINIA
Oh, I'm glad. It's begun.

CURTAIN

THE MEMBER OF THE WEDDING *

A Play in Three Acts

By Carson McCullers

IN Philadelphia nobody had much hope for "The Member of the Wedding." Witnesses of tryout performances conceded that it was beautifully staged and beautifully acted, but they felt that it was not long for this world—that it could not cope with the rigors of Broadway commerce. It was predicted that it would get good notices and die at the box office in about a week. When the play opened at the Empire Theatre in New York it *did* get good notices —yet many reviewers included a "but" in their estimates, and "but" is one of the deadliest words in a reviewer's vocabulary. The play, said the butters—including the editor of this volume— was extraordinarily sensitive, beautifully staged by Harold Clurman, magnificently acted by Ethel Waters, Julie Harris and 7-year-old Brandon de Wilde; but it was not exactly a play, not having the polished form of the ideally constructed drama.

Mrs. McCullers is a novelist and she never had any great leaning toward the theatre. She wrote "The Member of the Wedding" as a novel and thought no further about it until someone suggested it might make a play. A dramatist undertook an adaptation of the novel, and the resulting play so disturbed young Mrs. McCullers that she decided she would make her own stage version. Concerning the result she wrote for *Theatre Arts* the following observations:

" 'The Member of the Wedding' is unconventional because it is not a *literal* kind of play. It is an *inward* play and the conflicts are inward conflicts. The antagonist is not personified, but is a human condition of life; the sense of moral isolation. In this respect 'The Member of the Wedding' has an affinity with classical plays—which we are not used to in the modern theatre where the protagonist and antagonist are present in palpable conflict on the stage. The play has other abstract values; it is concerned with the weight of time,

---

the hazard of human existence, bolts of chance. The reactions of the characters to these abstract phenomena projects the movement of the play. Some observers who fail to apprehend this modus operandi felt the play to be fragmentary because they did not account for this aesthetic concept. . . . Some observers have wondered if any drama as unconventional as this should be called a play. I cannot comment on that. I only know that 'The Member of the Wedding' is a vision that a number of artists have realized with fidelity and love."

The lights come slowly up, revealing part of a Southern back yard and a kitchen. There is a scuppernong arbor in the yard, and hanging from it is a sheet used as a make-believe stage curtain. The kitchen has a center table and chairs, and a small coal heating stove. The back of the kitchen opens on the yard, and on the other side of the room are two doors—one leading to a small inner room, the other into the front hall. It is August, 1945. Berenice Sadie Brown, a large, comfortable Negro woman with a patch over one eye, is working in the kitchen. Out in the yard is a family group. One of them, Frankie Addams, is a gangling girl of 12, wearing shorts and a sombrero. She is standing in the arbor gazing adoringly at her brother, Jarvis, a GI in uniform, and Jarvis' fiancee, Janice, a young and pretty girl. Also present are Frankie's father, a man about 40 with a somewhat old-fashioned look, who runs a jewelry store in his small town, and Frankie's cousin from next door, John Henry, a bespectacled young man of 7.

Jarvis hasn't been home for some time, and now he is observing how the arbor seems to have shrunk from what it used to be when he was a child, and how Frankie has grown. "I think maybe we ought to tie a brick to your head," he tells his sister. It is a playful remark, but it hurts the self-conscious Frankie. Janice heals the wound by saying she had had the biggest portion of her growth by the time she was 13, and probably Frankie won't grow much more.

Frankie wails, "But I'm just twelve. When I think of all the growing years ahead of me, I get scared." Berenice brings out a tray of drinks—lemonade for John Henry and Frankie, and something with liquor for the others. Frankie hands the drinks around, then perches on the ground and gazes adoringly at her brother and his fiancee. It was such a surprise when she heard about their going to get married . . . but a nice surprise. Berenice adds, "Frankie's been bending my ears ever since your letter came, Jarvis. Going on about weddings, brides, grooms and what not."

The girl has been sipping her drink and notes that it tastes sharp and hot. Jarvis has been thinking his drink tasted mighty sissy—so he and his sister exchange glasses. The girl wonders aloud if she's drunk. In fact, she thinks she is. She begins to stagger around in an imitation of drunkenness and calls upon all to watch. Suddenly she turns a handspring, just as a blare of music comes from a gramophone at a children's clubhouse near the Addams yard. "It must be nice having your club house so near," says Janice.

"I'm not a member now," Frankie reveals. "But they are holding an election this afternoon, and maybe I'll be elected."

John Henry's mother comes into the yard and is introduced to Janice. Her name is Mrs. West, but she is Aunt Pet to the Addams family. Amiably she asks, "Berenice, what have you and Frankie been doing to my John Henry? He sticks over here in your kitchen morning, noon and night."

Berenice explains, "We enjoys him. We just talks and passes the time of day. Occasionally plays cards." Berenice calls the lad Candy. "Candy don't bother nobody." At the moment Candy is in the arbor, barefoot, stepping on grapes because they are so squelchy. Janice notices the curtain on the arbor and says to Frankie, "Jarvis told me how you used to write plays and act them out here in the arbor. What kind of shows do you have?"

FRANKIE—Oh, crook shows and cowboy shows. This summer I've had some cold shows—about Esquimos and explorers—on account of the hot weather.

JANICE—Did you ever have romances?

FRANKIE—Naw. (*With bravado.*) I had crook shows for the most part. You see I never believed in love until now. (*Her look lingers on* JANICE *and* JARVIS. *She hugs* JANICE *and* JARVIS, *bending over them from back of the bench.*)

MRS. WEST—Frankie and this little friend of hers gave a performance of "The Vagabond King" out here last spring.

JOHN HENRY (*spreads out arms and imitates heroine from memory and sings in high childish voice*)—Never hope to bind me. Never hope to know. (*Speaking.*) Frankie was the king-boy. I sold the tickets.

MRS. WEST—Yes, I have always said that Frankie has talent.

FRANKIE—Aw, I'm afraid I don't have much talent.

JOHN HENRY—Frankie can laugh and kill people good. She can die, too.

FRANKIE (*with some pride*)—Yeah, I guess I die all right.

FATHER—Frankie rounds up John Henry and those smaller children, but by the time she dresses them in the costumes, they're worn out and won't act in the show.

JARVIS (*looks at watch*)—Well, it's time we shove off for Winter Hill—Frankie's land of icebergs and snow—where the temperature goes up to 102. (*Takes* JANICE's *hand. He gets up and gazes around yard and arbor fondly. Pulls her up and stands with arm around her, gazing around him at arbor and yard.*) It carries me back—this smell of mashed grapes and dust. I remember all the endless summer afternoons of my childhood. It does carry me back.

FRANKIE—Me, too. It carries me back, too.

FATHER (*puts arm around* JANICE: *shakes* JARVIS' *hand*)—Merciful heavens! It seems I have two Methuselahs in my family! Does it carry you back to your childhood, too, John Henry?

JOHN HENRY—Yes, Uncle Royal.

FATHER—Son, this visit was a real pleasure. Janice, I'm mighty pleased to see my boy has such lucky judgment in choosing a wife.

FRANKIE—I hate to think you have to go. I'm just now realizing you're here.

JARVIS—We'll be back in two days. The wedding is Sunday.

(*The family moves to around house toward front street.* JOHN HENRY *enters kitchen through back door. There are the sounds of good-bys from the front yard.*)

JOHN HENRY—Frankie was drunk. She drank a liquor drink.

BERENICE—She just made out like she was drunk—pretended.

JOHN HENRY—She said, "Look, Papa, how drunk I am." and she couldn't walk.

(*Sounds of good-bys clearer.*)

FRANKIE'S VOICE—Good-by, Jarvis. Good-by, Janice.

JARVIS' VOICE—See you Sunday.

FATHER'S VOICE—Drive carefully, son. Good-by, Janice.

JANICE—Good-by and thanks, Mr. Addams. Good-by, Frankie darling.

VOICES (*all*)—Good-by! Good-by!

JOHN HENRY—They are going now to Winter Hill.

(*Sound of front door opening, steps in hall.* FRANKIE *enters through hall.*)

FRANKIE—Oh, I can't understand it! The way it all just suddenly happened.

BERENICE—Happened? Happened?

FRANKIE—I have never been so puzzled.

BERENICE—Puzzled about what?

FRANKIE—The whole thing. They are so beautiful.

BERENICE (*pause*)—I believe the sun done fried your brains.

JOHN HENRY (*whispering*)—Me, too.

BERENICE—Look here at me. You jealous.

FRANKIE—Jealous?

BERENICE—Jealous because your brother's going to be married.

FRANKIE (*slowly*)—No. I just never saw any people like them. When they walked in the house today it was so queer.

BERENICE—You jealous. Go and behold yourself in the mirror. I can see from the color of your eyes.

FRANKIE (*goes to the mirror and stares. She draws up her left shoulder, shakes her head, and turns away, with feeling*)—Oh! They were the two prettiest people I ever saw. I just can't understand how it happened.

BERENICE—Whatever ails you—actin' so queer.

FRANKIE—I don't know. I bet they have a good time every minute of the day.

JOHN HENRY—Less us have a good time.

FRANKIE—Us have a good time? Us? (*She rises and walks around the table.*)

BERENICE—Come on. Less have a game of three-handed bridge. (*They sit down to the table, shuffle, deal, etc.*)

The game is desultory, with Frankie dreaming aloud of where her brother has been—Oregon, Alaska, and now Winter Hill. She and John Henry quarrel about who has the right to bid spades. Berenice, who hasn't had any luck all week, looks at the children's hands and sees that their cards aren't good, either. The three of them are alone at their game, for Mr. Addams has gone back to his store.

Frankie has won the bid and when she leads a trump John Henry hesitates to follow suit, saying, "The only spade I got is a king and I don't want to play my king under Frankie's ace. And I'm not going to do it, either." In disgust Frankie throws in her hand. Figuring there is something wrong with the deck, Berenice counts and finds the deck is short. John Henry has been cutting the pictures out of the face cards because they're cute.

"We'll just have to put him out of the game. He's entirely too young," Frankie announces, and John Henry begins to whimper.

"We can't put him out," Berenice points out. "We gotta have a third to play. Besides, by the last count he owes me close to three million dollars."

Frankie is sick unto death, according to her own diagnosis. She sweeps the cards from the table and exclaims, "I wish they'd taken me to Winter Hill this afternoon! I wish tomorrow was Sunday instead of Saturday! I wish I was somebody else except me!"

There is the sound of children playing in the neighboring yard, and John Henry is all for joining them but Frankie is not. "Just a crowd of ugly silly children," she pronounces. Soon several girls around 13 and 14, dressed in clean frocks, file slowly across the Addams yard and Frankie runs out of the kitchen to greet them. "Am I a member?" she asks. No, she is informed, she is not. Everybody voted for Mary Littlejohn. Frankie is amazed. "You mean the girl who moved in next door? That pasty fat girl with those tacky pigtails? The one who plays the piano all day?" That's the one, all right; the club thinks she is talented.

Frankie blazes into wild fury and orders the girls out of the yard. "Son of a bitches!" she rails at them, and, plunging into the house, cries, "Why didn't you elect me?" The girl is too angry to be crushed—but she is badly hurt. She thinks maybe the club has been spreading it all over town that she smells bad because once when she had boils she had to use a bitter smelling ointment. Still muttering about "the son of a bitches" she fetches a bottle of perfume from the house and generously sprays it on herself, Berenice and the boy.

Berenice tries to calm the girl down, pointing out that the club girls are older than she is, and suggesting that Frankie round up a club of her own and be the president. There are plenty of children in the neighborhood—but Frankie doesn't want to be president of all those little leftover people. John Henry is not too much interested in Frankie's crisis. He has taken a large doll from a kitchen chair—a doll Frankie has given him—and is playing with it. Now he puts down the doll and calmly rummages through Berenice's pocketbook on the table. "I'm looking for your new glass eye," he explains. He finds it, and notices also that Berenice has two nickels and a dime. He hands her the eye, and, turning her back, Berenice removes her patch and inserts the orb. She doesn't wear it much yet because she isn't used to it. It's a blue eye, and John Henry likes it better than Berenice's brown one. Berenice observes that green-eyed people, like Frankie, are apt to be jealous—and Frankie certainly is something or other, for she is still mooning about her brother and Janice. "J. A.," she cogitates— Janice and Jarvis will have the same initials when they are married. "If only my name was Jane. Jasmine or Jane," she muses, pacing around the kitchen table. Then inspiration strikes: she will name herself F. Jasmine Addams! And oh, if only she hadn't got this close crew haircut, with the wedding coming up. She looks at herself in the kitchen mirror. From somewhere near the house comes the sound of Negro singing as Frankie, stepping back from the mirror and slumping her shoulders, exclaims, "Oh, I am so worried about being so tall! I'm twelve and five-sixths years old and already five feet five and three-fourths inches tall. If I keep on growing like this until I'm twenty-one, I figure I will be nearly ten feet tall!"

Berenice soothes her, saying that when she fills out she will do very well—but Frankie wants to do very well by next Sunday, and Berenice suggests that cleaning up for a change might help, including scrubbing the elbows. Frankie's fury now turns upon John Henry, and she orders him to go home. "I'm sick and tired of you, you little midget!" The disconsolate lad departs, taking his doll, and Frankie, taking a carving knife from the table drawer, begins hacking at a splinter in her foot. Berenice suggests that a needle would be better, but the girl goes on hacking—and suddenly is almost weeping. Not from pain, for the digging doesn't hurt, but from remembering what fine times she used to have, dressing up in costumes, or shopping, or playing with Evelyn Owen—who has moved to Florida. Suddenly she inquires, "How old were you, Berenice, when you married your first husband?"

"I was thirteen years old."

"You never loved any of your four husbands but Ludie."

"Ludie Maxwell Freeman was my only true husband. The other ones were just scraps."

Now Frankie's interest leaps to her cat; pouring milk into a saucer, she calls "Charles, Charles. . . . If only I just knew where he is gone."

Berenice explains he has gone off to hunt a lady friend, and Frankie thinks this is odd; why doesn't he bring his lady friend home? She'd be only too glad to have a family of cats. "I ought to notify the police force." With this girl, the thought is immediately father of the deed, and she goes to the inner room where the phone is and *does* call the police. Charles, she tells them, is almost Persian with short hair and a lovely color of gray. "My name is Miss F. Jasmine Addams," she announces.

This throws Berenice into a fit of giggling at the picture of the Milledgville police force going about town calling Charles. Then Frankie, pacing the room, returns to her obsession: "I expect Janice and Jarvis are almost to Winter Hill by now."

BERENICE—Sit down. You make me nervous.

FRANKIE—Jarvis talked about Granny. He remembers her very good. But when I try to remember Granny, it is like her face is changing—like a face seen under water. Jarvis remembers Mother too, and I don't remember her at all.

BERENICE—Naturally! Your mother died the day that you were born.

FRANKIE (*standing with one foot on seat of chair, leaning over chair back, laughing*)—Did you hear what Jarvis said?

BERENICE—What?

FRANKIE (*after laughing more*)—They were talking about whether to vote for C. MacDonald. And Jarvis said, "Why I wouldn't vote for that scoundrel if he was running to be dog catcher." I never heard anything so witty in my life. (*After silence during which* BERENICE *watches* FRANKIE, *but does not smile.*) And you know what Janice remarked. When Jarvis mentioned about how much I've grown, she said she didn't think I looked so terribly big. She said she got the major portion of her growth before she was thirteen. She said I was the right height and had acting talent and ought to go to Hollywood. She did.

BERENICE—O.K. All right! She did!

FRANKIE—She said she thought I was a lovely size and would probably not grow any taller. She said all fashion models and movie stars—

BERENICE—She did not. I heard her from the window. She only remarked that you probably had already got your growth. But she didn't go on and on like that or mention Hollywood.

FRANKIE—She said to me—

BERENICE—She said to you! This is a serious fault with you, Frankie. Somebody just makes a loose remark and then you cozen it in your mind until nobody would recognize it. Your Aunt Pet happened to mention to Clorina that you had sweet manners and Clorina passed it on to you. For what it was worth. The next thing I know you are going all around and bragging how Mrs. West thought you had the finest manners in town and ought to go to Hollywood, and I don't know what all you didn't say. And that is a serious fault.

FRANKIE—Aw, quit preaching at me.

BERENICE—I ain't preaching. It's the solemn truth and you know it.

FRANKIE—I admit it a little. (*She sits down to table and puts forehead on palms of hands. Pause and then softly:*) What I need to know is this. Do you think I made a good impression?

BERENICE—Impression?

FRANKIE—Yes.

BERENICE—Well, how would I know?

FRANKIE—I mean how did I act? What did I do?

BERENICE—Why you didn't do anything to speak of.

FRANKIE—Nothing?

BERENICE—No. You just watched the pair of them like they were ghosts. Then when they talked about the wedding, them ears of yours stiffened out the size of cabbage leaves—

FRANKIE (*raising hand to ear*)—They didn't.

BERENICE—They did.

FRANKIE—Someday you going to look down and find that big fat tongue of yours pulled out by the roots and laying there before you on the table.

BERENICE—Quit talking so rude.

FRANKIE (*after pause*)—I'm so scared I didn't make a good impression.

BERENICE—What of it. I got a date with T. T. and he's supposed to pick me up here. I wish him and Honey would come on. You make me nervous.

(FRANKIE *sits miserably, her shoulders hunched. Then with a sudden gesture she bangs her forehead on the table. Her fists are clenched and she is sobbing.*)

BERENICE—Come on. Don't act like that.

FRANKIE (*her voice is muffled*)—They were so pretty. They must have such a good time. And they went away and left me.

BERENICE—Sit up. Behave yourself.

FRANKIE—They came and went away, and left me with this feeling.

BERENICE—Hosee! I bet I know something. (*Begins tapping with heel: One, two, three—bang. After a pause in which rhythm is established she begins singing.*) Frankie's got a crush! Frankie's got a crush! Frankie's got a crush on the *wedding*.

Frankie becomes violently angry and Berenice continues her taunts. She snatches the carving knife and Berenice, in alarm, orders her to lay it down. "Make me," the girl challenges—and taking aim, she throws the knife at the door to the inner room. It sticks and she boasts, "I used to be the best knife thrower in town." She is warned that she may try that stunt once too often. "You are not fit to live in a house," says the angry Berenice.

That's all right with Frankie. She won't be living here much longer anyway. She is going to run away right after the wedding— "and I swear to Jesus by my two eyes that I'm never coming back here any more."

Berenice takes the girl by the shoulders to calm her down just as two Negroes, T. T. Williams and Honey Camden Brown, come into the yard to take Berenice to town. They are trailed by John Henry. T. T. is very fat and about 50; Honey is slender, natty and about 20, and is carrying a horn. John Henry is natty, too, having been cleaned up and dressed for the afternoon in a white suit. T. T. talks about a recent adventure of Honey's: Honey, who is Berenice's foster brother, got in a ruckus in front of the Blue Moon café and police cracked him on the head. Honey adds details: He was walking along when a drunk soldier came out of the Blue Moon and ran into him, and then gave him a push. So Honey pushed back, and a white M.P. came up and slammed him with his stick.

John Henry would like to hear Honey blow his horn, but Honey is not in the mood; so the boy takes it, tries to blow, but only manages to slobber into it, and Honey snatches the instrument back roughly. Berenice warns her foster brother sharply, and he exclaims, "You ain't mad because John Henry is a little boy. It's because he is a white boy." Honey lifts John Henry and presents some coins, asking, "Which would you rather have—the nigger money or the white money?" In John Henry's simple soul there is no race problem, and there also is sound instinct, for he says immediately, "I rather have the dime. . . . Much obliged." And he goes back home.

The afternoon has almost ended and the light grows dim. Berenice suggests that her visitors have a quickie before they start, and Frankie, feeling excluded, goes into the yard. When Berenice is ready to leave, she calls to Frankie that if her father doesn't come home by good dark she can go over and play with John Henry, and she should forget all that foolishness they were talking about. Frankie maintains she isn't afraid of the dark and she will get John Henry to come over and spend the night. When Berenice, T. T. and Honey have gone, the girl calls her little cousin and suggests that he spend the night—sleep out in the yard in her Indian teepee. John Henry calls back that he doesn't want to.

FRANKIE (*angrily*)—Fool Jackass! Suit yourself! I only asked you because you looked so ugly and so lonesome.

JOHN HENRY (*skipping toward arbor*)—Why, I'm not a bit lonesome.

FRANKIE (*looks at house*)—I wonder when that Papa of mine is coming home. He always comes home by dark. I don't want to go into that empty ugly house all by myself.

JOHN HENRY—Me neither.

FRANKIE (*standing with outstretched arms, and looking around her*)—I think something is wrong. It is too quiet. I have a peculiar warning in my bones. I bet you a hundred dollars it's going to storm.

JOHN HENRY—I don't want to spend the night with you.

FRANKIE—A terrible terrible dog day storm. Or maybe even a cyclone.

JOHN HENRY—Huh.

FRANKIE—I bet Jarvis and Janice are now at Winter Hill. I see them just as plain as I see you. Plainer. Something is wrong. It is too quiet.

(*A clear horn begins to play in distance, a blues tune.*)

JOHN HENRY—Frankie?

FRANKIE—Hush! It sounds like Honey. (*The tune becomes jazzy and spangling, then the first blues tune is repeated. Suddenly while still unfinished the music stops. FRANKIE waits tensely.*) He has stopped to bang the spit out of his horn. In a second he will finish. (*After wait.*) Please, Honey, go on finish!

JOHN HENRY (*softly*)—He done quit now.

FRANKIE (*moving restlessly*)—I told Berenice that I was leavin' town for good and she did not believe me. Sometimes I honestly think she is the biggest fool that ever drew breath. You try to impress something on a big fool like that, and it's just like talking to a block of cement. I kept on telling and telling and telling her. I told her I had to leave this town for good because it is inevitable. Inevitable.

(*Father enters kitchen from up right calling: "Frankie, Frankie."*)

FATHER (*calling from the kitchen door*)—Frankie, Frankie.

FRANKIE—Yes, Papa.

FATHER (*opens back door*)—You had supper?

FRANKIE—I'm not hungry.

FATHER—Was a little later than I intended fixing a timepiece for a railroad man. (*Goes back through kitchen and into hall calling: "Don't leave the yard!"*)

JOHN HENRY—You want me to get the week-end bag?

FRANKIE—Don't bother me, John Henry. I'm thinking.

JOHN HENRY—What you thinking about?

FRANKIE—About the wedding. About my brother and the bride. Everything's been so sudden today. I never believed before about the fact that the earth turns at the rate of about a thousand miles a day. I didn't understand why it was that if you jumped up in the air you wouldn't land in Selma or Fairview or somewhere else instead of the same back yard. But now it seems to me I feel the world going around very fast. (FRANKIE *begins turning around in circles with her arms outstretched.* JOHN HENRY *copies her.* *They both turn.*) I feel it turning and it makes me dizzy.

JOHN HENRY—I'll stay and spend the night with you.

FRANKIE (*suddenly stopping*)—No. I just now thought of something.

JOHN HENRY—You just a little while ago was begging me.

FRANKIE—I know where I'm going.

(*Sounds of children playing in distance.*)

JOHN HENRY—Let's go play with the children, Frankie.

FRANKIE—I tell you I know where I'm going. It's like I've known it all my life. Tomorrow I will tell everybody.

JOHN HENRY—Where?

FRANKIE (*dreamily*)—After the wedding I'm going with them to Winter Hill. I'm going off with them after the wedding.

JOHN HENRY—You serious?

FRANKIE—Hush, just now I realized something. The trouble with me is that for a long time I have been just an I person. All other people can say "we." When Berenice says "we" she means her lodge and church and colored people. Soldiers can say "we" and mean the army. All people belong to a "we" except me.

JOHN HENRY—What are we going to do?

FRANKIE—Not to belong to a "we" makes you too lonesome. Until this afternoon, I didn't have a "we," but now after seeing Janice and Jarvis I suddenly realize something.

JOHN HENRY—What?

FRANKIE—I know that the bride and my brother are the "we" of me. So I'm going with them and joining with the wedding. This coming Sunday when my brother and the bride leave this town, I'm going with the two of them to Winter Hill. And after that to whatever place that they will ever go. (*Pause.*) I love the two of them so much and we belong to be together. I love the two of them so much because they are the *we* of me.

The curtain falls.

ACT II

It is afternoon of the next day and Frankie and Berenice are in the kitchen, with Berenice cooking and lecturing Frankie. The girl has been gone since morning, and her father was mad when she didn't come home to dinner this noon. Frankie, excited and elated, tells of all she has done. She walked up and down Main Street, stopped in every store, bought her wedding dress and her silver shoes. She went around by the mills—all over the complete town, and talked to nearly everybody in it.

"What for, pray tell me?"

"I was telling everybody about the wedding and my plans."

While Berenice creams batter for cookies, Frankie tells about all the people—all the strangers and people she knows—she has talked to about the wedding. Berenice comments, "I honestly believe you have turned crazy on us." Frankie says everybody but Papa believes she is going, and he just didn't pay any attention when she told him at the store. He just told her to charge her wedding clothes at MacDougal's and sat there with his nose to the grindstone. And now Frankie brings out a suitcase and instructs Berenice that everything good of hers must be washed and ironed so she can pack them.

The Negro woman is worried about Frankie and tries gently to dampen her enthusiasm. Jarvis and Janice won't want her along, for two's company and three's a crowd. And how about Noah and the Ark? He admitted the creatures only two by two. But Frankie refuses to listen; "They will take me," she says confidently.

"And if they don't?"

It is a sickening suggestion to the girl. "If they don't," she announces, "I will kill myself. . . . I will shoot myself in the side of the head with the pistol that Papa keeps under his handkerchiefs with Mother's picture in the bureau drawer."

The girl is a growing wonder to Berenice. She has known about people falling in love—even ugly people—but never in all her days did she ever hear of anybody falling in love with a wedding. "And," she says, "thinking it all over, I have come to a conclusion. What you ought to be thinking about is a beau. A nice little white boy beau."

Frankie, who does not want one, asks if she means a beau like the soldier she talked with this morning, who wanted to come on the wedding trip too. But Berenice is not talking about soldiers; she means somebody like little old Barney next door, who is Frankie's age. Frankie explodes, "You are the biggest crazy in this town."

John Henry, who has been watching the cooking and listening, wants to know how many beaus Berenice caught, and she ducks the question. Frankie opines that Berenice had better quit worrying about beaus and be content with T. T. Inside the house a piano tuner begins work, getting the Addams piano ready to play the wedding march. The sound makes Frankie sad—and jittery, too, and Berenice suggests they could turn on the radio and drown it out.

FRANKIE—I don't want the radio on. (*Goes into interior room and takes off dress. Speaks from inner room.*) But I advise you to keep the radio on after I leave. Someday you will very likely hear us speak over the radio.

BERENICE—Speak about what, pray tell me.

FRANKIE—I don't know exactly what about. But probably some eye witness account about something. We will be asked to speak.

BERENICE—I don't follow you. What are we going to eye witness? And who will ask us to speak?

JOHN HENRY (*excitedly*)—What Frankie? Who is speaking on the radio?

FRANKIE—When I said *we*, you thought I meant you and me and John Henry West, to speak over the world radio. I have never heard of anything so funny since I was born.

JOHN HENRY (*climbs up to kneel on seat of chair*)—Who? What?

FRANKIE—Ha! Ha! Ho! Ho! Ho! (FRANKIE *goes around punching things with fist, and shadow boxing.* BERENICE *raises right hand for peace. Then suddenly they all stop.* FRANKIE *goes to window and* JOHN HENRY *hurries to window also and stands on tiptoe with hands on sill.* BERENICE *turns head to see what has happened. The piano is still. Three young* GIRLS *in clean dresses are passing before the arbor.* FRANKIE *watches them silently at window.*)

JOHN HENRY (*softly*)—The club of girls.

FRANKIE—What do you son of a bitches mean crossing my yard. How many times must I tell you not to set foot on my Papa's property?

BERENICE—Just ignore them and make like you don't see them pass.

FRANKIE—Don't mention those crooks to me.

(T. T. *and* HONEY *approach by way of back yard.* HONEY *is whistling a blues tune.*)

BERENICE—Why don't you show me the new dress. I'm anxious to see what you selected. (*Exit* FRANKIE *into interior room.* T. T. *knocks on door. He and* HONEY *enter.*) Why, T. T., what you doing around here this time of day?

T. T.—Good afternoon, Miss Berenice. I'm here on a sad mission.

BERENICE (*startled*)—What's wrong?

T. T.—It's about Sis Laura Thompson. She suddenly had a stroke and died.

BERENICE—What! Why, she was by here just yesterday. We

just ate her peas. They in my stomach right now, and her lyin'
dead on the cooling board this minute. The Lord works in strange
ways.

T. T.—Passed away at dawn this morning.

FRANKIE (*puts head in doorway*)—Who is it that's dead?

BERENICE—Sis Laura, Sugar. That old vegetable lady.

FRANKIE (*unseen—from interior room*)—Just to think—she
passed by yesterday.

T. T.—Miss Berenice, I'm going around to take up a donation
for the funeeal. The polict people say Sis Laura claim has lapsed.

BERENICE—Well, here's fifty cents. The poor old soul.

T. T.—She was brisk as a chipmunk to the last. The Lord had
appointed the time for her. I hope I go that way.

FRANKIE (*from interior room*)—I've got something to show you
all. Shut your eyes and don't open them until I tell you. (*Enters
room dressed in orange satin evening dress with silver shoes and
stockings.*) These are the wedding clothes. (BERENICE, T. T. *and*
JOHN HENRY *stare.*)

JOHN HENRY—Oh, how pretty!

FRANKIE—Now tell me your honest opinion. (*Pause.*) What's
the matter. Don't you like it, Berenice?

BERENICE—No. It don't do.

FRANKIE—What do you mean? It don't do.

BERENICE—Exactly that. It just don't do. (BERENICE *shakes
head while* FRANKIE *looks at dress.*)

FRANKIE—But I don't see what you mean. What is wrong?

BERENICE—Well, if you don't see it I can't explain it to you.
Look there at your head to begin with. (FRANKIE *goes to mirror.*)
You had all your hair shaved off like a convict and now you tie this
ribbon around this head without any hair. Just looks peculiar.

FRANKIE—But I'm going to wash and try to stretch my hair
tonight.

BERENICE—Stretch your hair! How you going to stretch your
hair? And look at them elbows. Here you got on a grown woman's
evening dress. And that brown crust on your elbows. The two
things just don't mix. (FRANKIE, *embarrassed, covers elbows with
her hand.* BERENICE *still shaking her head.*) Take it back down
to the store.

T. T.—The dress is too growny looking.

FRANKIE—I can't take it back. It's bargain basement.

BERENICE—Very well then. Come here. Let me see what I
can do.

FRANKIE (*going to* BERENICE, *who works with dress*)—I think you're just not accustomed to seeing anybody dressed up.

BERENICE—I'm not accustomed to seein' a human Christmas tree in August.

Mr. Addams arrives home, and the first thing he does is scold his daughter for not coming home to dinner. He has not seemed to notice Frankie particularly, though, until she demands that he look at her dress. "I thought it was a show costume," he says, and then, turning to Honey and T. T., asks if either could do a little porter work at his store next Wednesday. T. T. says regretfully and politely that he has another job that day, but Honey just snaps a rough, "I ain't got the time." This arouses Mr. Addams, who proclaims angrily, "I'll be glad when the war is over and you biggety, worthless niggers get back to work. And furthermore, you *sir* me, hear me?" Honey pronounces a grudging "Yes—sir" and Mr. Addams returns to his store. At another scolding from Berenice, Honey mutters that he has a real good nigger razor for folks that call him nigger. He is tensed up, and he begs his foster sister for a dollar. Relenting, she takes out some change and offers him thirty cents—enough for two beers—and Honey departs. So does T. T., to do some more "donation visiting." Frankie muses upon death; she only knows six dead people, not counting her mother, who died when she was born. She enumerates them, and John Henry points out that she forgot Ludie Maxwell Freeman—but Frankie won't count Ludie because he died just before she was born. "Do you think very frequently about Ludie?" she asks Berenice.

"You know I do. I think about the five years when me and Ludie was together and all the bad times I seen since. It leaves you too lonesome afterward . . . and you take up with too many sorry men to try to get over the feeling."

Frankie opines that T. T. is not a sorry man, and asks when Berenice is going to marry him. "I ain't going to." Berenice sincerely respects and regards T. T. because he doesn't make her shiver, and that is all. Speaking of shivering, Frankie has something queer to tell. She was passing an alley between two stores, and out of the corner of her eye she saw a dark double shape—and it was just as if Janice and Jarvis were right there, instead of almost a hundred miles away. When she looked again she saw it was just two colored boys—but it gave her such a queer feeling.

Berenice is all attention. It's the most remarkable thing she ever heard of, as if Frankie had been reading her mind. "You mean right here in the corner of your eye. You suddenly see something there. And this cold shiver run all the way down you. And you whirl around. And you stand there facing Jesus knows what. But not Ludie, not what you want. And for a minute you feel like you'd been dropped down a wall. . . . Yes, that is the way it is when you are in love. A thing known and not spoken."

Frankie says she never did believe in love and never put any of it into her shows.

BERENICE (*squares shoulders*)—Now I am here to tell you I was happy. There was no human woman in all the world more happy than I was in them days. And that includes everybody. You listening to me, John Henry? It includes all queens and millionaires and first ladies of the land. And I mean it includes people of all color. You hear me, Frankie? No human woman in all the world was happier than Berenice Sadie Brown.

FRANKIE—The five years you were married to Ludie.

BERENICE—From that autumn morning when I first met him on the road in front of Cambells Filling Station until the very night he died, November, the year 1933.

FRANKIE—The very year and the very month I was born.

BERENICE—The coldest November I ever seen. Every morning there was frost and puddles were crusted with ice. The sunshine was pale yellow like it is in wintertime. Sounds carried far away, and I remember a hound dog that used to howl toward sundown! And everything I seen come to me as a kind of sign.

FRANKIE—I think it is a kind of sign I was born the same year and the same month he died.

BERENICE—And it was a Thursday towards six o'clock. About this time of day. Only November. I remember I went to the passage and opened the front door. Dark was coming on; the old hound was howling far away. And I go back in the room and lay down on Ludie's bed. I lay myself down over Ludie's with my arms spread out and my face on his face. And I pray that the Lord would contage my strength to him. And I ask the Lord let it be anybody, but not let it be Ludie. And I lay there and pray for a long time. Until night.

JOHN HENRY—How? (*In a higher, wailing voice.*) How, Berenice?

BERENICE—That night he died. I tell you he died.. Ludie! Ludie Freeman! Ludie Maxwell Freeman died! (BERENICE *hums.*)

FRANKIE (*after pause*)—It seems to me I feel sadder about Ludie than any other dead person. Although I never knew him. I know I ought to cry sometimes about my mother, or anyhow Granny. But it looks like I can't. But Ludie—maybe it was because I was born so soon after Ludie died. But you were starting out to tell some kind of a warning.

BERENICE (*looking puzzled for a moment*)—Warning? Oh, yes! I was going to tell you how this thing we was talking about applies to me. (*As* BERENICE *begins to talk* FRANKIE *goes to shelf above refrigerator and brings back to the table a fig bar.*) It was the April of the following year that I went one Sunday to the church where the congregation was strange to me. I had my forehead down on the top of the pew in front of me, and my eyes were open—not peeping around in secret, mind you, but just open. When suddenly this shiver ran all the way through me. I had caught sight of something from the corner of my eye. And I looked slowly to the left. There on the pew, just six inches from my eyes, was this *thumb*.

FRANKIE—What thumb?

BERENICE—Now I have to tell you. There was only one small portion of Ludie Freeman which was not pretty. Every other part about him was handsome and pretty as anyone would wish. All except this right thumb. This one thumb had a mashed chewed appearance that was not pretty. You understand?

FRANKIE—You mean you suddenly saw Ludie's thumb when you were praying?

BERENICE—I mean I see *this* thumb. And as I knelt there just staring at this thumb, I begun to pray in earnest. I prayed out loud! Lord, Manifest! Lord, Manifest!

FRANKIE—And did He—Manifest?

BERENICE—Manifest, my foot! (*Spitting.*) You know who that thumb belonged to?

FRANKIE—Who?

BERENICE—Why, Jamie Beale. That big old no-good Jamie Beale. It was the first time I ever laid eyes on him.

FRANKIE—Is that why you married him? Because he had a mashed thumb like Ludie's?

BERENICE—Lord only knows. I don't. I guess I felt drawn to him on account of that thumb. And then one thing led to another. First thing I know I had married him.

FRANKIE—Well, I think that was silly. To marry him just because of that thumb.

BERENICE—I'm not trying to dispute you. I'm just telling you what actually happened. And the very same thing occurred in the case of Henry Johnson.

FRANKIE—You mean to sit there and tell me Henry Johnson had one of those mashed thumbs, too?

BERENICE—No. It was not the thumb this time. It was the coat.

Frankie and John Henry listen in amazement as Berenice tells how she needed money for Ludie's funeral, so she pawned many things and sold her coat and Ludie's coat. Then, one evening, she saw this shape coming down the street—so much like Ludie that she almost dropped dead right there. It was only Henry Johnson —but he had chanced to buy Ludie's coat. And that is how Berenice happened to marry Henry Johnson. This, she says solemnly, should be a warning to Frankie. "I loved Ludie. . . . Therefore I had to go and copy myself forever afterward. What I did was to marry off little pieces of Ludie whenever I come across them. It was just my misfortune they all turned out to be the wrong pieces." Continuing, she warns Frankie, "You think you are going to break into that wedding."

Berenice gives John Henry a piece of dough to make a cookie man with, and Frankie goes and gets the evening paper. Scanning it, she says, "I see where we dropped a new bomb. They call it the atom bomb." This is of mild interest, but much less than Frankie's plan to take two baths tonight. One long soaking bath, a scrub with a brush to get the crust off her elbows; then a second bath. Berenice applauds the project, picks up the paper and strains in the fading light from the window to see what's in it, and Frankie goes back to chattering about an old subject—changing her name. Berenice snorts, "Suppose I would suddenly up and call myself Mrs. Eleanor Roosevelt. And you would begin naming yourself Joe Louis. And John Henry here tried to pawn off as Henry Ford."

That isn't what Frankie means; she just wants a name she prefers, like F. Jasmine. Berenice is against it, because if people went around changing the whole world would go crazy. Things accumulate around a name—one thing after another happens to you.

FRANKIE—Until yesterday, nothing ever happened to me.

(JOHN HENRY *crosses to the door and puts on* BERENICE's *hat and shoes and takes pocketbook and crosses around the table twice.*)

BERENICE—John Henry, take off my hat and my shoes and put up my pocketbook. Thank you very much.

(JOHN HENRY *does so.*)

FRANKIE—Listen, Berenice. Doesn't it strike you as strange that I am I and you are you. Like when you are walking down a street and you meet somebody. And you are you. And he is him. Yet when you look at each other, the eyes make a connection. Then you go off one way. And he goes off another way. You go off into different parts of town, and maybe you never see each other again. Not in your whole life. Do you see what I mean?

BERENICE—Not exactly.

FRANKIE—That's not what I meant to say anyway. There are all these people here in town I don't even know by sight or name. And we pass along side each other and don't have any connection. And they don't know me and I don't know them. And now I'm leaving town and there are all these people I will never know.

BERENICE—But who do you want to know?

FRANKIE—Everybody. Everybody in the world.

BERENICE—Why, I wish you would listen to that. How about people like Willie Rhodes. How about them Germans? How about them Japanese? (FRANKIE *knocks her head against the door jamb and looks up at the ceiling.*)

FRANKIE—That's not what I mean. That's not what I'm talking about.

BERENICE—Well, what *is* you talking about?

(*Children's* VOICE *calls off: "Batter up! Batter up!"*)

JOHN HENRY (*in a low voice*)—Less play out, Frankie.

FRANKIE—No. You go. (*After pause.*) This is what I mean. (BERENICE *waits, and when* FRANKIE *does not speak again, says:*)

BERENICE—What on earth is wrong with you?

FRANKIE (*long pause, then suddenly with hysteria*)—Boyoman! Manoboy! When we leave Winter Hill we're going to more places than you ever thought about or even knew existed. Just where we will go first I don't know, and it don't matter. Because after we go to that place we're going on to another. Alaska, China, Iceland, South America. Traveling on trains. Letting her rip on motorcycles. Flying around all over the world in aeroplanes. Here today and gone tomorrow. All over the world. It's the damn truth. Boyoman! (FRANKIE *runs around the table.*)

BERENICE—Frankie!

FRANKIE—And talking of things happening. Things will happen so fast we won't hardly have time to realize them. Captain Jarvis Addams wins highest medals and is decorated by the President. Miss F. Jasmine Addams breaks all records. Mrs. Janice Addams elected Miss United Nations in beauty contest. One thing after another happening so fast we don't hardly notice them.

BERENICE—Hold still, Fool.

FRANKIE (*during next lines her excitement grows more and more intense*)—And we will meet them. Everybody. We will just walk

up to people and know them right away. We will be walking down
a dark road and see a lighted house and knock on the door and
strangers will rush to meet us and say: Come in! Come in! We will
know decorated aviators and New York people and movie stars.
We will have thousands and thousands of friends. And we will
belong to so many clubs that we can't even keep track of all of them.
We will be member of the whole world. Boyoman! Manoboy!
(FRANKIE *has been running round and round the table in wild excitement and when she passes the next time* BERENICE *catches her
slip so quickly that she is caught up with a jerk.*)

BERENICE—*Is* you gone raving wild? (BERENICE *pulls* FRANKIE
closer and puts her arm around her waist.) Sit here in my lap and
rest a minute. (FRANKIE *sits in* BERENICE'S *lap.* JOHN HENRY
comes close and jealously pinches FRANKIE.) Leave Frankie alone.
She ain't bothered you.

JOHN HENRY—I'm sick.

BERENICE—Now you, you ain't. Be quiet and don't grudge your
cousin a little bit of love.

JOHN HENRY—Old mean bossy Frankie. (JOHN HENRY *hits*
FRANKIE.)

BERENICE—What she doing so mean right now. She just laying
here worn out. (*They continue sitting.* FRANKIE *is relaxed now.*)

FRANKIE—Today I went to the Blue Moon—this place that all
the soldiers is so fond of and I met a soldier—redheaded boy.

BERENICE—What is all this talk about the Blue Moon and soldiers?

FRANKIE—Berenice, you treat me like a child. When I see all
these soldiers milling around town I always wonder where they come
from and where they are going.

BERENICE—They were born and they going to die.

FRANKIE—There are so many things about the world I do not
understand.

BERENICE—If you did understand you would be God. Didn't
you know that?

FRANKIE—Maybe so. (*She stares and stretches herself on* BERE-
NICE'S *lap, her long legs sprawled out beneath the kitchen table.*)
Anyway after the wedding I won't have to worry about a thing
anymore.

Frankie's tension has eased in the mothering embrace of the
Negro woman. John Henry climbs the back rungs of Berenice's
chair, hugs her head, and begins to sing a spiritual:

> *"I sing because I'm happy,*
> *I sing because I'm free,*
> *For His eye is on the sparrow*
> *And I know he watches me. . . ."*

Berenice picks up the song: "Why should I feel discouraged . . ." Soon Frankie joins in. When they come to the final, "And I know He watches me," Berenice gently comments, "Frankie, you got the sharpest set of human bones I ever felt."

The curtain falls.

ACT III

Scene I

The wedding day. In the kitchen Berenice is in her apron, and T. T., who has come to help, is in a white coat. There are sounds of congratulations from the front of the house, for the ceremony has just finished. Even so, it could be a happier day for Berenice, for there is not only the problem of Frankie, but trouble about Honey as well. "I wish Honey was here," she says. "I'm so worried about him since what you told me."

T. T. replies, "He was in a bad way when I saw him this morning."

"Honey Camden don't have too large a share of judgment as it is, but when he gets high on them reefers he's got no more judgment than a four-year-old child. Remember that time he swung at the police and nearly got his eyes beat out? . . . I've got two people scouring Sugarville to find him. . . . God," she concludes fervently, "you took Ludie but please watch over my Honey Camden. He's all the family I got."

Frankie comes back and says it was such a pretty wedding she wanted to cry. No, she hasn't told them about her plans yet. She knows she'll have to hurry and do it, for the newlyweds are going to leave right after the refreshments—but every time she tries to tell them something happens to her throat and different words come out. And she is so embarrassed about her evening dress. Oh, why didn't she listen to Berenice!

John Henry comes in with a bundle of fine loot—several costumes Frankie gave him when she was packing her suitcase, and a sea shell, too. Berenice warns him that Frankie may be asking for them back tomorrow. T. T. carries a tray of sandwiches to the wedding guests, and returns to report that everybody is compliment-

ing Berenice's wedding cake. Frankie goes to make one more try
at breaking her news, but returns in a moment holding a punch cup.
She didn't get the chance because too many people were around.
Somehow the words just die.

Frankie loves the two of them so much—but Janice put her arms
around her and said she always wanted a little sister, and asked for
the third time what grade she was in. And Jarvis, when she tried
to tell him, picked her up by the elbows and swung her and said,
"Frankie the lankie the alaga Frankie, the tee legged, toe legged,
bow legged Frankie." And then he gave her a dollar bill.

Again she goes to try to tell Janice and Jarvis. John Henry, who
has been spying, comes back with a report that the bride and groom
are leaving. Mr. Addams is taking their suitcases to the car.
Frankie comes running back to the interior room, snatches her suitcase, kisses Berenice and bids all a good-by. Even the kitchen:
"Farewell, old ugly kitchen." She hurries to the front, and in a
moment there is a sound of disturbances. Although Frankie is
speaking loudly, her voice seems to be getting farther away. In the
kitchen they hear her cry, "That's what I am telling you," and her
father's shouted answer, "Now be reasonable, Frankie." Again
the girl screams, "I have to go. Take me! Take me!" John Henry
gallops in with an eye-witness report—Frankie is in the wedding
car and they can't get her out. He goes for another look and reports that now his father and Frankie's father are trying to drag
her away from the steering wheel. Finally Mr. Addams comes into
the kitchen with the sobbing Frankie in tow. "You take charge of
her," he orders Berenice. Then, softening, he puts his hand on his
daughter's head, asking, "What makes you want to leave your old
papa like this? You've got Janice and Jarvis all upset on their
wedding day."

"I love them so!"

The bride and groom come in to tell Frankie good-by. Janice
says that when they've found a place to live they want Frankie to
come for a nice visit. "Won't you tell us good-by now?"

"We," says Frankie passionately. "When you say we, you only
mean you and Jarvis. And I am not included!" She buries her
head and sobs. Finally the newlyweds break away and Frankie
gazes at their departing figures with a look of wonder and misery.
Falling on her knees she begs, "Take me!" Gently Berenice lifts
her back to a chair and soothingly says that school will begin in only
three weeks, and Frankie will find another bosom friend like Evelyn
Owen.

John Henry suddenly announces that he is sick; his head hurts.

Berenice cuts him off, thinking it is a play for attention, and continues to work on Frankie. She suggests a party soon, and Frankie could call the society editor and get it written up in the paper.

The girl shows a trace of interest. She remembers that when her bike ran into an automobile the paper had spelled her name Frankie instead of correctly. But soon she returns to her tears. Mr. Addams returns with his daughter's suitcase, and he, too, wants to help. He offers to let Frankie come to the store tomorrow and polish silver or play with the old watch springs. Frankie, eyeing her suitcase, will not be appeased. If she can't go with the bride and her brother, she is going to leave town anyhow. She will hop a train to New York, or hitch rides to Hollywood and get a job. "If worse comes to worse, I can act in comedies. Or I could dress up like a boy and join the merchant marines." Suddenly she grabs the suitcase and runs, and John Henry calls, "Uncle Royal, Frankie's got your pistol in the suitcase."

T. T. and Mr. Addams run in pursuit, John Henry following. The wind has begun to rise ominously. Berenice, alone, shudders at the slam of a door, the sound of thunder and the flash of lightning. John Henry comes back, also afraid of thunder, and is taken into Berenice's lap. He tells her his father and Uncle Royal are chasing Frankie in his father's car. He repeats that he has a headache and is sick, but again she thinks he is fooling. The lights go out, and she lights a candle.

"I'm scared," says the boy. "Where's Honey?"

"Jesus knows. I'm scared, too. With Honey snow-crazy and loose like this—and Frankie run off with a suitcase and her Papa's pistol. I feel like every nerve has been picked out of me."

John Henry offers a little comfort in his turn. He strokes Berenice, holds out his sea shell and asks, "You want to listen to the ocean?"

The curtain falls.

SCENE II

It is 4 A.M., but there still are signs of the wedding in the kitchen —glasses and the punch bowl on the drainboard. There is a faint glow in the yard. Berenice and Mr. Addams are alone in the kitchen, and he is saying that he never believed in corporal punishment and never spanked Frankie, but when he lays his hands on her—

"She'll show up soon," says Berenice. "But I know how you feel. What with worrying about Honey Camden, John Henry's sickness and Frankie, I've never lived through such an anxious night." Mr. Addams goes next door to get the latest news on John Henry, and Berenice sees Frankie crossing the yard to the arbor. She rushes out, exclaiming, "You ought to be skinned alive!" She shakes a story out of the girl. Frankie confesses that when she was running around in the dark, scary streets, she realized her plans were child plans that would not work. She hid in the alley behind Papa's store and was going to shoot herself—took out the gun and figured on counting up to three and pulling the trigger. But when she counted up to two she changed her mind.

Honey Camden appears suddenly from a hiding place in the arbor and Berenice embraces him. "Shush," he warns. "The law is after me. Mr. Wilson wouldn't serve me so I drew a razor on him."

"You kill him?"

"Didn't have no time to find out. I been runnin' all night."

Berenice finds her purse, gives Honey six dollars, and tells him to go to Fork Falls and then to Atlanta. She weeps.

"Don't you dare cry," says Honey. "I know now all my days have been leading up to this minute. No more 'boy this—boy that' —no bowing, no scraping. For the first time I'm free and it makes me happy." He begins to laugh hysterically, and leaves, still laughing.

Mrs. West comes into the yard to find out what the noise was, and to remind people that John Henry is critically ill. The doctors say he has meningitis. Berenice promises there will be no more noise, and confesses that she didn't believe John Henry yesterday afternoon when he said he had a headache, and Mrs. West goes home.

Frankie embraces Berenice, saying, "The wedding, Honey, John Henry—so much has happened that my brain can't hardly gather it in. Now for the first time I realize that the world is certainly— a sudden place."

"Sometimes sudden," Berenice replies, "but when you are waiting like this it seems so slow."

The curtain falls.

SCENE III

It is sunset on a day in November; the elm tree is bare and the arbor is withered. The kitchen is neat and bare and all the furniture has been removed, except for a chair Berenice is sitting in, with an old suitcase and a doll at her feet. Frankie comes in—but she is not Frankie any more; she is Frances. The house seems so hollow to her with the furniture packed. "I wish you hadn't given quit notice just because Papa and I are moving into a new house with Uncle Eustace and Aunt Pet out in Limewood," she says.

Berenice replies that she respects and admires Mrs. West but she'd never get used to working for her. Frances chatters about Mary Littlejohn and the progress she is making at the piano, but Berenice sniffs at Mary's being lumpy and white. Frances gives a short answer and the Negro woman, stroking a battered fox fur she is wearing, checks herself. "Let's not fuss and quarrel this last afternoon."

Frances agrees—and says, besides, it isn't our last afternoon, for she will come and see Berenice often.

"No you won't, baby. You'll have other things to do. Your road is already strange to me."

Frances pats Berenice on the shoulder, and notices the fur—the fox fur that Ludie had given. "Somehow this little fur looks so sad. . . ."

It has every right to be sad, according to Berenice. Honey gone, and John Henry, her little boy, gone.

FRANCES—It's peculiar—the way it all happened so fast. First Honey caught and hanging himself in the jail. Then later in that same week, John Henry died and then I met Mary. As the irony of fate would have it, we first got to know each other in front of the lipstick and cosmetics counter at Woolworth's. And it was the week of the fair.

BERENICE—The most beautiful September I ever seen. Countless white and yellow butterflies flying around them autumn flowers —Honey dead and John Henry suffering like he did and daisies, golden weather, butterflies—such strange death weather.

FRANCES—I never believed John Henry would die. (*After long pause—looks out window.*) Don't it seem quiet to you in here? (*Longer pause.*) When I was a little child I believed that out under the arbor at night there would come three ghosts and one of the ghosts wore a silver ring. (*Whispering.*) Occasionally when it gets so quiet like this I have a strange feeling. It's like John Henry is hovering somewhere in this kitchen—solemn looking and ghost gray.

BOY'S VOICE (*from neighboring yard*)—Frankie, Frankie.

FRANCES' VOICE (*calling to* BARNEY)—Yes, Barney. Clock stopped. (*Shakes clock.*)

BARNEY—Is Mary there?

FRANCES (*aside to* BERENICE)—It's Barney MacKean. (*In a*

sweet voice.) Not yet. I'm meeting her at 5:00. Come on in, Barney, won't you?

BARNEY—Just a minute.

FRANCES (*to* BERENICE)—Barney puts me in mind of a Greek god.

BERENICE—What? Barney puts you in mind of a what?

FRANCES—Of a Greek god. Mary remarked that Barney reminded her of a Greek god.

BERENICE—It looks like I can't understand a thing you say no more.

FRANCES—You know, those old timey Greeks worship those Greek gods.

BERENICE—But what has that got to do with Barney MacKean?

FRANCES—On account of the figure.

BARNEY MACKEAN, *a boy of 13, wearing a football suit, bright sweater and cleated shoes, runs up back steps into kitchen.*)

BERENICE—Hi, Greek god, Barney. This afternoon I saw your initials chalked down on the front sidewalk M.L. loves B.M.

BARNEY—If I could find out who wrote it, I would rub it out with their faces. Did you do it, Frankie?

FRANCES (*drawing up with sudden dignity*)—I wouldn't do a kid thing like that. I even resent you asking me. (*Repeats in pleased undertone.*) Resent you asking me.

BARNEY—Mary can't stand me anyhow.

FRANCES—Yes she can stand you. I am her most intimate friend. I ought to know. As a matter of fact, she's told me several lovely compliments about you. Mary and I are riding on the moving van to our new house. Would you like to go?

BARNEY—Sure.

FRANCES—O.K. You will have to ride back with the furniture 'cause Mary and I are riding on the front seat with the driver. We had a letter from Jarvis and Janice this afternoon. Jarvis is with the Occupation Forces in Germany and they took a vacation trip to Luxembourg. (*Repeats in a pleased voice.*) Luxembourg. Berenice, don't you think that's a lovely name?

BERENICE—It's kind of a pretty name, but it reminds me of soapy water.

FRANCES—Mary and I will most likely pass through Luxembourg when we are going around the world together.

BERENICE *sits in kitchen alone. Picks up doll, looks at it and hums first two lines of "I Sing Because I'm Happy." Piano plays the scale offstage.*)

CURTAIN

THE INNOCENTS *

A Play in Two Acts

By William Archibald

Based on "The Turn of the Screw," by Henry James

THERE is no accurate record of how many persons have made or tried to make dramatizations of Henry James' odd little horror tale, "The Turn of the Screw"—but it is certain that a great many attempts have been made and abandoned. James, who suffered disappointment as a dramatist, never tried it. Among those who have recently jousted with the story is Mel Dinelli, an experienced practitioner in fabricating movie scenarios of the suspense variety. Mr. Dinelli took a crack at fitting the tale to films and gave it up. He was represented on Broadway during the season with a suspense drama of his own, "The Man."

William Archibald, 31, who came to the United States from his native British West Indies in 1937, had first read "The Turn of the Screw" in St. Mary's College and Agricultural College, Trinidad. He formed the habit of re-reading it, and "for his own amusement" started a film scenario. "The sheer craftsmanship awed me," he wrote in *Theatre Arts*. "It seemed that James must have written it backwards and forwards until, like the secretion of a spider, his ink had made a superb web of words which would entangle the reader and kill him if he were at all susceptible to fright." When he started to work on "The Innocents" in 1948 (a task which took him through eight complete revisions), he read Edmund Wilson's famous essay, "The Ambiguity of Henry James," in which Wilson maintained that the governess was insane and the ghosts did not exist. Archibald then read all he could on James, including the James notebooks, and came to a different conclusion. To him the ghosts are real and they inhabit the souls of two children. "The children," says Mr. Archibald, "were my method of creating supports for this play of suspension. I used them to charm the audience and veil the direction; but, as though making them their own enemies, I also used them (more than Henry James did) to create their own destruction—or, more correctly, to allow it. . . . This transference of tragedy from the governess to the children is, I believe, the greatest difference between the book and the play."

The time is about 1880 and the scene is the drawing room of an old country house in England. The room is large and high ceilinged. A French window which rises up and up, and which is framed in dark curtains, opens on a garden. The garden itself suggests spaces and also suggests hiding places among trees and shrubs. The sky is apparent in all its changes of weather. The room contains the elegance of space. A staircase winds away without a visible landing. (This setting, as realized by Jo Mielziner, was acclaimed as best of the season in *Variety's* poll of the drama critics.)

It is 4:30 on a sunlit afternoon. Flora, a neatly dressed little girl of 8, is at the piano, accompanying herself as she sings a song, "O bring me a bonnet. . . ." She stops her song and turns quickly as Mrs. Grose, who is about 60 and who wears the starched apron and frilly cap of a housekeeper, enters the room. It is quickly apparent that Flora is an unusual child; she is, when she wants to be, unusually well-mannered; her speech is almost eerily precise . . . and yet one senses in her a quality of independence, or perhaps rebelliousness, that makes her more than ordinary for one of her age.

Mrs. Grose is excited, for the new governess is about to arrive. Mrs. Grose has made everything spotless, including Flora, and now she is worried because Flora's dress looks rumpled. "Now sit down and don't muss yourself," she orders.

Flora looks at her coolly as she rises from the piano bench and says, "There'd be less chance of that if I remain standing, don't you think? When will she get here, Mrs. Grose?"

She is told the carriage will bring her soon. Flora has more questions as the housekeeper dusts things which already are immaculate: Will her uncle be coming? Is she pretty? Does she need another governess? Will Miles like her? It is unlikely that the uncle will be coming, for he is too busy; Mrs. Grose expects that the new governess will be pretty (but Flora sensibly comments that she might be ugly), and Mrs. Grose is sure that Master Miles will like her when he comes home from school for the holidays some time from now.

About her brother Miles, Flora says, "He might be. Mightn't he, Mrs. Grose? Before that?"

The housekeeper can see no reason why he should be, and then, embracing the little girl with gentle quickness, she exclaims, "Oh,

Miss Flora, lamb! You miss him, don't you?" Flora returns the embrace charmingly and replies that, although she is not lonely, she would like it if her brother were *always* here.

Flora speculates on what sort of governess is arriving. It would be interesting, for instance, if she'd let Flora get all dirty and then put her to bed without a bath—or if she didn't make her study her books. "Perhaps we'll spend the time with conversations, or, if we feel like it on a particular day, we might just sit and stare at each other—lots of people do—"

Mrs. Grose thinks there is small chance of sitting and staring without talking, with Flora around, and the child has a reasonable explanation of that: Things pop into her head, and there doesn't seem much sense in leaving them there. Right now, for instance, she is standing still and looking at the ceiling, and she declares she feels quite small when she is not moving. And why do people run past tall trees? Flora, wandering toward the window and looking out, feels so small at the moment that she could crawl under the carpet and be completely flat.

"She's walking," Flora announces. Miss Giddens is approaching the house through the garden and she is carrying only a *little* bag. Wouldn't she have a trunk if she's going to stay? Mrs. Grose explains that the carriage went to fetch her, and doubtless the carriage will be bringing her trunk. The housekeeper pushes open the window and stands at the threshold, primping herself, to await the new governess.

Miss Giddens, coming in from the garden, is a young and pretty woman, dressed for traveling. Her face is aglow from the walk and from the beauty of the gardens. She has walked from the gate so she could see it all, and she is happy about it; the carriage has taken her trunk to the back.

Mrs. Grose introduces Flora, and Flora drops a curtsey. Mrs. Grose flusters off into the kitchen, saying she will fetch tea. The governess and the child size each other up for a moment; then Flora invites Miss Giddens to take off her hat and sit down.

"I hope you like your room," says Flora. "If you don't, you may choose another. There are thirty-five—most of them closed—and think of it! one hundred and forty windows! . . . Shall we go into the garden and count them?"

Miss Giddens laughingly puts the child off, saying that Mrs. Grose would be alone with her tea, and she *did* say she would like some. Flora, the realist, catches Miss Giddens on that one, saying, "*You* didn't. *She* said she'd get it." Flora goes on to say that there are several ways of walking, if you don't walk on the drive.

"You mean hopping and skipping?"

Flora is amazed. "I've never had a governess who did *that*."

"Well," explains Miss Giddens, "we're each a little different."
With that, Flora's smile disappears and she inquires, so oddly that
Miss Giddens doesn't know what to say for a moment, "Different?"

The new governess asks Flora's age, and Miles'. Miles is 12.
Mrs. Grose brings in the tea things and Miss Giddens invites her to
sit with her on the love seat, for there are things she would like to
ask.

"Things, Miss?" queries the housekeeper. Miss Giddens explains
that she means the habits of the house, and Mrs. Grose sits down.
Flora declines tea. "And I was so afraid!" says Miss Giddens—
and to the questioning Flora she explains she was timid and couldn't
make up her mind for days about accepting this post. She has a
large family, but she wouldn't ask any of them for advice. Miss
Giddens thinks it would be well to have Flora out of the way for a
while so she can get down to business with the housekeeper, and she
suggests that Flora take a walk in the garden.

The new governess observes the child out there and comments,
"Poor child, she looks so lonely out there. . . ." Mrs. Grose reassures her: Flora is most independent and would just as soon wan-
der off by herself; but to Miss Giddens, who has a large family,
Flora *must* be lonely. And the garden—it is so quiet and peaceful,
with its thick trees walling off the paths. "As I walked under them
I had a feeling of solitude—and yet, I also felt that I was not completely alone—" She turns to the room, examines each detail, and
exclaims, "How awful if it were an ugly one! I was almost afraid
it might be!"

Mrs. Grose is puzzled. "Might be, Miss?"

Miss Giddens explains that it was about the uncle. His house
on Harley Street was—well, the uncle had been so brief with her.
He said he didn't want to be bothered with letters about the children—seemed to make this the most important part of his terms.
Under no condition was she to bother him. Doesn't he love the
children?

Mrs. Grose is sure he does, in his own fashion. He has been the
children's guardian since their parents died soon after Flora's birth.
He is not a young man and never has enjoyed good health; he is
studious and is always wrapped up in his work—but he *does* keep
this house on especially for the children and *is* doing all that can be
expected.

Miss Giddens begins to understand. After all, Miles and Flora
aren't his children, and he seemed much more interested in his Chi-

nese paintings—some of which, she notes, are here in this room. "But I couldn't help being angry when he spoke to me about not bothering him about the children . . . I'm afraid *that* is why he engaged me—because I stood up to him. I was caught. I showed how much I loved children—and that I would do *anything* to make them happy. . . . When he pays us a visit—"

"I don't expect he will, Miss," says Mrs. Grose. "He's been here only once or twice that I can bring to mind. Though there were times in the months just passed when—" The housekeeper breaks off.

"When *what*, Mrs. Grose?"

"When *he* should have been the one to shoulder the—"

"The what, Mrs. Grose?"

The housekeeper suddenly drops it. "Bygones is bygones." Miss Giddens asks what sort of person the last governess was.

MRS. GROSE—She was also young and pretty, Miss, even as you—

MISS GIDDENS (*smiling with embarrassment*)—He doesn't mind them being young and pretty?

MRS. GROSE (*turning to her vehemently*)—Oh, no, it was the way he liked everyone! (*Flushing.*) I mean—why should the master mind?

MISS GIDDENS—But of whom did you speak *first?*

MRS. GROSE (*blankly*)—Why, of *him.*

MISS GIDDENS—Of the master?

MRS. GROSE—Of who else? (*They search each other's faces.*)

MISS GIDDENS (*casually*)—Mrs. Grose, was she—my predecessor —careful, particular—in her work?

MRS. GROSE (*against her will*)—About some things, yes—

MISS GIDDENS—But not about all?

MRS. GROSE—Well, Miss, she's passed on. I won't tell tales.

MISS GIDDENS (*quickly*)—I understand your feelings but— Did she die here?

MRS. GROSE—No, she went away. (FLORA *appears at window.*)

MISS GIDDENS—Went *away?* To die? She was taken ill, you mean—and went home?

MRS. GROSE—She was not taken ill so far as *appeared* in this house. She—she left it to go home, she said, for a short holiday. At the very moment I was expecting her back I heard from the master that she was dead.

MISS GIDDENS—But of what? (*The two women stare at each other. From the French window comes a last ray of sunlight.*)

FLORA (*in a small, clear voice*)—Miss Giddens, aren't you coming for a walk? (*The stage darkens slowly.*)

SCENE II

Three hours later. A pale moonlight comes through the windows. Miss Giddens is on the love seat, with Flora, in a long white nightgown, sleepily beside her. On the table before the love seat is a lighted candle. Flora leans against the shoulder of her new governess as Miss Giddens continues to read from a book, softly, "In the wintertime, when deep snow lay on the ground, a poor boy was forced to go out on a sledge to fetch wood. When he had gathered it together and packed it, he wished, as he was frozen cold, not to go home at once but to light a fire and warm himself a little—"

Flora, the realist, asks how he would light it, and Miss Giddens fumbles for an answer about a flint. The reading continues, about the boy finding a tiny golden key, and then an iron chest, and wonderful things in the chest. Flora wonders if he was a little boy like Miles and is told he might even have *been* Miles. She also wants to know what was in the chest. When Miss Giddens refuses to reveal the secret ahead of time, Flora announces that in the mean time she will just *imagine* things.

Suddenly the governess closes the book and shivers as though a sudden draught had entered the room. "Aren't you cold, dear?" Flora, snuggling closer, says, "No. I'm half asleep, I think. Shall I stay in your room tonight?"

"If you'd like to."

"Mrs. Grose wanted to give you a larger room—but I said, 'She'll only be there when she's asleep and big rooms have a way of growing bigger at night.' Mrs. Grose says they *don't*, but that's because *she* doesn't like the dark and won't open her eyes."

The shadow of a man appears against the silk curtains of the window, and, as if the man were approaching, grows larger until it fills the window space. Flora yawns, then giggles at a notion she has just had—about there being some way to sleep in several rooms at once. Miss Giddens laughs nervously, and the shadow recedes as though the man were stepping away. Flora chatters about how startled Mrs. Grose was at the idea of sleeping in several rooms, and about something she did about the rooms in the attic—and suddenly the governess rises from the seat, a puzzled frown on her face.

Flora inquires angelically, "Why, what's the matter, Miss Giddens, dear?"

Smiling quickly, the governess replies, "Nothing. What about the attic rooms?"

"They are empty, but you can see everything that once was in them!"

Miss Giddens has been looking toward the window and listens absently as Flora describes how the things can be seen because everything has left a mark—and if you look closely you can see the carpet though it's been rolled up and put away. Flora seems to be watching Miss Giddens rather closely as she relates that Mrs. Grose has locked up all those rooms and several more.

Miss Giddens is preoccupied, and Flora breaks in on her by asking her to tell a story out of her head, with Flora and Mrs. Grose and Miles and herself in it. "Come along, then," says Miss Giddens, taking the child by the hand. They start for the stair and the governess fumbles for a beginning: "Once upon a time—once upon a time there —was a ship called *Bly*—"

"That's the name of this house—I know."

At the foot of the stair the governess pauses and looks up to the ceiling as though she hears something there. Then, as they go up, she tells more about the ship, which had long corridors and empty rooms and an old square tower, and a crew named Flora and Mrs. Grose and Miss Giddens—and, yes, still another—and *his* name was Miles. They continue off beyond the curving steps, and as Miss Giddens says *Miles* a thin vibration comes from far away—more a trembling than a sound—and with it the shadow fills the window, blocking out the moon.

The stage darkens.

Scene III

The next morning is clear and beautiful. The window is open and the garden, green and cool, is almost in the room. Mrs. Grose, who has been polishing furniture, puts two letters on the desk. She does not notice Flora, who has come halfway down the stair and now is sitting quietly, chin in hands, watching. She startles the housekeeper by inquiring where Miss Giddens is. Miss Giddens is out picking flowers—and Flora should go back up to her schoolroom. But Flora has finished her work already; the task set for her was too easy. She asks, "Are you dusting the ship?" Mrs. Grose doesn't understand until the child tells her that Miss Giddens says Bly is a ship—and she thinks Miss Giddens was seasick. Anyhow, she was very restless. Mrs. Grose laughs, and Flora, laughing, too, goes in search of Miss Giddens. In a moment Miss Giddens returns alone; obviously Flora has missed her. She has forgotten the flowers. She tells the housekeeper that she was standing where the path ends close to the woods, and was about to pick the flowers, when suddenly she felt she was being stared at. She turned and saw a man staring at her—a stranger, but he stood there casually as though he belonged here. It wasn't the gardener or his boy. He just stood there, fifty feet away, and his eyes were bold and insolent. He made Miss Giddens feel as though *she* were the intruder. Then he went away, casually. He might still be in the garden or the woods —and now Miss Giddens feels angry and a trifle ill. . . .

The governess pulls herself together and takes up the letters. The first is from her youngest sister, and it includes a snapshot of the family, which Miss Giddens proudly shows the housekeeper. The second letter has been forwarded, unopened, by this odd uncle; it had been addressed to the uncle and is from Miles' school, and on the back of the envelope the uncle has written, "Whatever it is, deal with it. Don't bother me with it. Not a word."

Miss Giddens opens the letter and is at a loss how to deal with it —for it states that Miles has been dismissed from school and sent home. There are no details, except the information that it is impossible to keep Miles because he is an injury to the others. He will arrive on the coach this afternoon.

Mrs. Grose has never known Miles to be bad, really.

Miss Giddens' thoughts return to the man in the garden. She sways as though about to fall, then starts to climb the stairs. Mrs. Grose suddenly remembers where Flora is, and tells the governess that the girl is not upstairs but in the garden. Both women, frightened, run through the window and begin calling, in diminishing voices, "Flora! Flora!"

A moment passes. Flora comes into the room, not from the garden, but from another part of the house. She listens to the women calling her and stands silently looking out the window.

The stage darkens.

SCENE IV

The same day is drawing to a close. The window is still open and the lamps are not lighted, but it is only a golden afterglow of sunlight which illumines the room. From the garden Flora cries, "We're here, Mrs. Grose! Miles is back!" The child runs into the room, calling through a door for Mrs. Grose to come quickly and see how tall Miles has grown. Then she dashes back into the garden, calling, "Where are you, Miles? Don't hide from me, now!"

Mrs. Grose comes into the room just as Miss Giddens appears at the window. The governess explains that Miles has run off amongst the trees in the garden. In reply to questioning, she says the boy doesn't seem to be bothered and has said nothing. In the carriage he was all smiles and unconcerned. Miss Giddens *does* think he's charming, but somehow she expected him to be uneasy, or at least say something about his school. She figures that if she is going to learn anything, she will have to get it out of Miles.

At this moment the boy appears at the window. He is handsome, with a remarkably innocent face and a gentlemanly, proud bearing. With a great smile of welcome he goes to Mrs. Grose and she embraces him. Flora abandons her garden hunt and finds Miles in the room.

Miss Giddens has made up her mind to get the upper hand by being firm from the start. When the sunlight fades she sharply suggests that Flora go with Mrs. Grose and get a taper for lighting the lamps, and that Mrs. Grose see to supper. Flora suggests that they all have supper together and Miss Giddens acquiesces. But when Flora and the housekeeper have gone, Miss Giddens seems filled with indecision. She puts her hat on the desk, opens the desk drawer and closes it, then, affecting casualness, says, "Well, Miles, don't you want to tell me something." The boy smiles charmingly at her and inquires, blandly, "Something?"

The governess gets no further, for Flora, bubbling and impish, returns with a lighted taper. There is an intimate companionship between the boy and the girl, and as they light the desk lamp they seem to ignore her, and she catches herself moving out of their way as they approach the desk. They talk with relish about the Mrs. Grose's pudding, which Flora has seen. When the lamp has been lighted and the taper blown out, the children go to the staircase. Miss Giddens, once more firm, says, "Miles."

On the first step the boy turns, all smiles, and says, "I *should* wash my hands for supper, shouldn't I?"

The defeated governess angrily sits at the desk, takes a letter from the drawer, rapidly reads through it, and with sudden decision begins to write a letter of her own. She is still at it when Miles comes down the staircase and says, "Flora's hiding. When she's hidden, I'm to find her." The governess keeps on with her writing and the boy looks out into the garden, now completely dark. It must be nice out there, he comments; he isn't afraid of the dark— everything's the same at night as it is by day. Miss Giddens is taken aback by his coolness, and confesses that some times *she* is afraid of the dark—just timid, she supposes. She is finding it difficult to retain her anger against Miles. Flora calls that she is hid, and he goes up the stairs to find her. On the way he says, "I'm glad you're here, Miss Giddens. I'm sure we'll get along splendidly together."

Mrs. Grose brings in Miles' bag and books, and Miss Giddens confesses that she has changed her mind about Miles. She has been stupid, to be angry with him. She will give him a chance to tell about school voluntarily, and she won't write to the school until then. Nor will she write to the uncle. She is going to handle the matter herself, and is confident Miles will help her. He is an intelligent boy. Mrs. Grose, close to tears, embraces Miss Giddens and returns to the kitchen.

Abovestairs, Flora has been caught and is shrieking with laughter. Miss Giddens calls to her not to get excited. Flora, coming on the staircase, says she can't help it—her brother was so clever finding her and now he is hiding. She can hear him rustling, which means he is pretending to hide under the bed; but he'll be somewhere else and she'll *never* find him. Miss Giddens laughs, and Flora solicitously asks if she is feeling better now. The question is disturbing.

Now Miles is hidden, and Flora runs off—but cries almost immediately, "I've found you!" Miss Giddens crosses toward the stair from her desk, and at the foot comes to a sudden stop. She does not turn, but she is fully aware of the man at the window, staring in from the garden. His face is close to the glass. Slowly she turns to face him. She does not cry out or move until the man steps backward into the darkness. Then she runs to the window, opens it, and goes out into the garden after him. There is absolute silence for a long moment. Mrs. Grose enters, comes to an abrupt stop and covers her mouth to stifle a scream—for Miss Giddens has reappeared in the window and stands there, framed, with blank terror on her features. "He was here—again,." she gasps. "He stared in at the window—just as he did in the garden this afternoon. He stared—only this time he looked right past me as though he were looking for someone else."

Shrill laughter is heard upstairs as the children play in their room. Miss Giddens looks up, and Mrs. Grose asks if she fears for the children. What is the man like?

He is no one Miss Giddens has seen before. He has very red hair, close and curling. A long, pale face. Dark, arched eyebrows. Sharp, strange, small, very fixed eyes. . . .

Mrs. Grose stares at the governess with a horror which grows as the description continues—wide mouth, thin lips, tall, erect, well dressed but certainly not a gentleman—Mrs. Grose gasps, "A gentleman? Not he!"

"You know him?"

Mrs. Grose's answer is almost a whisper. "Quint." She explains. Peter Quint—the valet when the master was here. When the master left, Quint was alone here—in charge.

"And then?"

"He went."

"Went where?"

"God knows where. He died."

Laughter sounds from above as Miss Giddens seeks to grasp Mrs. Grose's queer statement.

The stage darkens quickly.

Scene V

The next morning is bleak and rainy and the light from the dripping garden is cold and gray. Miles and Flora are at the desk working hard on some task set them by their governess. Miss Giddens is on the love seat, working at a frame of embroidery. Every now and then she looks into one corner or another of the room, and every stab of her needle shows her tenseness—a tenseness not eased by the thin scratching of slate pencils. Flora goes to the window and would like very much to go out, but is commanded sharply to sit down.

Back at her work again, the girl sees Miss Giddens put her hand to her head. She complains about Miles' pencil squeaking and he says he can't help it. Flora thought he was doing it on purpose— so she tries to make *hers* squeak and the pencil snaps in two. "Oh, *dear,*" Flora frets, and the distracted Miss Giddens snaps, "*Now,* what's the matter?" The governess reaches into a box beside her for another pencil and Flora comes to get it. She is sweet and solicitous. Does Miss Giddens' head hurt? "Oh, Miles—*poor* Miss Giddens," she sympathizes.

Flora sits beside the governess, takes her hand and announces, "Miles, I do believe Miss Giddens has a fever!" The boy, all solicitude, offers to fetch tea or a plaster. Miss Giddens, though nearer tears, laughs and says she is not ill. It is just the rain—and tiring her eyes with the embroidery.

Flora, the realist, queries, "Then why do you bother about it if you don't like it?"

Trying to laugh again, Miss Giddens explains that the embroidery is her task for the day, just like their spelling and geography. "Though nothing seems to be getting finished."

Miles knows what's the matter—it's the rain. He knows, because when he wakes up and finds the sun isn't out he is all turned around. Flora knows, too. When it rains she gets the funny feeling that *something* is going to happen, but nothing ever does. "It's so disappointing—what with having to stay in—"

Miss Giddens announces flatly, "Well, you're *not* going out." Miles chides his sister for keeping on at the governess like that and reminds her, in almost cherubic fashion, that they must do what Miss Giddens wishes. Miss Giddens is almost breaking down, and Flora puts her arm around her shoulder and says, "I'm being naughty, aren't I?"

Such behavior conquers Miss Giddens. She confesses she has been a grumpy old governess and the children stoutly deny it— "Though," says Miles, "I wouldn't wonder if she were." Flora agrees, "Nor would I—with *everything* so horrible."

Miss Giddens is hardly able to breathe as she asks what the child means, but is relieved when Flora answers reasonably enough that she means the rain and the squeaky pencil and her naughtiness. Miss Giddens, her forebodings lightened, announces that all three have worked enough and suggests that they play. Flora can choose the game.

"Hide-and-seek," Flora chooses—and Miss Giddens startles the girl by almost screaming "No!" Downcast, Flora weeps, and Miss Giddens apologizes. It wouldn't be good to play hide-and-seek just after Mrs. Grose has dusted and tidied all morning. The dispirited Flora says Miss Giddens can choose a game, then—but Miles steps in and proposes one. It is "dressing up." Miss Giddens approves enthusiastically and offers Flora her handkerchief to use as part of a costume.

Miles takes Flora's hand and they go to the stairway. Miss Giddens falteringly asks where they are going and they reply that they are going to dress up, of course.

"I'll—I'll go with you," the governess announces. But the children object, pointing out quite reasonably that if Miss Giddens went with them there would be no surprise. Reluctantly they are permitted to go on up—and Miss Giddens stand in the middle of the room, unable to move. When Mrs. Grose comes in a moment later, Miss Giddens says, almost inaudibly, "I let them go, I let them go—"

MRS. GROSE—Where, Miss?

MISS GIDDENS—Up there— (*All the bleakness of the garden seems to come indoors.* MISS GIDDENS *covers her face with her hands. Her voice comes wearily.*) I let them go— All morning

I kept them with me. Now—I've let them go—

MRS. GROSE—Couldn't you stop them?

MISS GIDDENS—How? What reason could I give them? I see a man at the window— I ask you who it is. You tell me who it *was*—that he is dead— (*Violently.*) Last night it was as though a nightmare possessed me! It was a nightmare, I told myself—it would pass, it must pass! All the things I would have asked you had I been able— I couldn't come to you even when the children were in bed. I couldn't allow myself to think further—it was a nightmare! I told myself it would pass! But it is no longer dark —it is daylight. And I *know* it. A man, something that was a man, looked in at me *from its grave!* (*Her voice never rises above a harsh whisper.*) Should I call them now? What shall I say to them?

MRS. GROSE—Miss, I—

MISS GIDDENS (*without interruption*)—I can't go up after them! I made Flora cry because I wouldn't let her play hide-and-seek. Because I thought of them hiding—and of how I would go through the rooms and find each one empty! I would call to them—they wouldn't answer. They would be up there alone. What would come at them —first from one room and then—from another? *Why* has he come back? (*Her words die away. She stares through the dimness at* MRS. GROSE. *Little but their faces can be seen, so feeble is the light from the garden . . . so strange at morning . . . so much more, this dimness, than that loss of light that comes from a cloud passing over the sun.* MISS GIDDENS *moves, slowly, across to* MRS. GROSE *until she is but a step from her.*) MRS. Grose—How did he die?

MRS. GROSE—Quint? Quint died early one morning . . . on the road from the village. They said at the inquest that he had slipped on the icy slope. He had been drinking. There was a wound on his head . . . from falling, they said. But I saw him. It was I who found him. The wound was terrible. He had died in pain . . . such pain, Miss! . . . It was there in his face. His eyes were still opened. It wasn't an accident. I knew it couldn't be . . . for there were things in his life that would have accounted for violence done him. . . .

MISS GIDDENS—What things?

MRS. GROSE (*numbly, as though beaten*)—Disorders—secret disorders—vices I don't guess at—

Silence crowds the room. Then Miss Giddens recalls that the children have never mentioned Quint, and it seems odd. The housekeeper warns her not to try them. Miss Giddens asks if Quint and Miles were together often and Mrs. Grose, bursting with disgust, explodes, "It wasn't *him!* It was Quint's own fancy! To spoil him! Quint was much too free!"

Mrs. Grose elaborates on the picture of Quint. Quint was too free with everyone—but the master never knew it because he hated complaints. So Quint fancied himself the master—even over the children, who were in charge of a governess. Quint gave all the orders.

Miss Giddens is struck with an overwhelming thought. "Why has he come back? Not . . . not . . ." But whatever she was going to say is stopped by the appearance of the children on the stair. Flora is dressed in what might have been a heavily brocaded curtain for a gown and wears a pincushion on her head. The curtain makes a long train on the stair. Behind her is Miles, with a sheet wound round his head as a turban. He lifts his sister's train and they majestically descend. At the foot of the stair they bow low to each other and cross to the piano. Miles lights the candelabra there and Flora invites Miss Giddens and Mrs. Grose to take the love seat. Miles sits at the piano to play and Flora arranges herself for a song.

The child's song is a sweet nursery affair about a merry king with handsome daughters two. It is sung with a lovely childlike effect. When she has finished, Flora formally announces that now she will play and Miles will sing. Miles, bowing to the audience, takes the candelabra, holds it before him, and sings:

> *What shall I sing*
> *to my Lord from my window?*
> *What shall I sing?*
> *For my Lord will not stay—*
> *What shall I sing?*
> *For my Lord will not listen—*
> *For my Lord is away—*
> *Where shall I go?*
>
> *Whom shall I love*
> *when the moon is arisen?*
> *Gone is my Lord*
> *and the grave is His prison—*

Miles begins to move slowly toward the window, and the two women watch him, frozen. A strange, low vibration begins, a dis-

cord of sound as though something is trying to enter the room—
soft but persistent. Miles continues:

> What shall I say
>   when my Lord comes a-calling?
> What shall I say
>   when he knocks on my door?
> What shall I say
>   when His feet enter softly
> Leaving the marks
>   of His grave on my floor?
>
> Then I shall sing
>   and my Lord He will listen—
> Then I shall sing
>   and my Lord will not leave—

Miles reaches the window, candelabra before him.

> Enter! My Lord! Come from thy prison!
> Come from thy grave
> For the moon is arisen!

Miles throws open the window and the silk curtain blows into
the room. He steps beyond the threshold and remains there, the
candles guttering. The vibration rises with the wind.

Miss Giddens gasps, "Mrs. Grose! He knows! He *knows!*"

Flora, looking up from the piano with a puzzled frown mixed
with a strange half-smile on her face, asks softly, "Knows *what*,
Miss Giddens?"

The curtain falls.

ACT II

Night has fallen. Upstairs Flora is singing. In the drawing
room one lamp is lighted. Mrs. Grose is standing by the piano,
looking up and listening. She hears Flora laugh at the end of her
song and ask, "Isn't that a lovely song, Miss Giddens?" And she
hears the governess reply, "It is. Now go to sleep—and don't pull
the covers off."

Flora is not to be abandoned. First she asks Miss Giddens to
see what it is dripping outside her window, and is assured it is
rain. Then she claims she has a beetle on her neck. Miss Giddens
will not be taken in, and soon she appears on the stair—but Flora

is behind her, now asking if the box with the golden key has been opened yet. Finally the child is driven off to bed and Miss Giddens comes the rest of the way down.

Mrs. Grose has something on her mind. She tells the governess that she thinks it is time to get in touch with the uncle and tell him, no matter what his instructions were.

"Tell him what?"

This stumps Mrs. Grose, but she still urges Miss Giddens to write and ask the uncle to come.

"And have him laugh at me?"

Then the children must be taken away, says Mrs. Grose—but that isn't practical, either, because sooner or later they would have to return home. The governess suggests that perhaps it is her own imagination from which the children should be protected, and perhaps things would be better if she left. Mrs. Grose, frightened, says, "You can't leave, Miss!"

Miss Giddens would like to know more about Quint—about what kind of effect he had upon Miles. Mrs. Grose instinctively tries to protect Miles, for always she believes him innocent. She disclaims ever having seen anything wicked in the boy—just restlessness to be with Quint and ask him questions; the kind of thing any boy without a father might do. And Quint encouraged the boy—took him away from his lessons for hours. Mrs. Grose remembers that she always heard Miles' questions, but never Quint's answers, for the man always kept his voice low. The housekeeper begins to sob as she repeats that there was nothing wicked in Master Miles.

Miss Giddens sees through Mrs. Grose's protectiveness and demands, "Couldn't he have corrupted Miles? And couldn't Miles have deceived you with pretended innocence?" As the governess asks aloud about whatever were the things that Quint told the boy, horror seizes her—horror and confusion. She doesn't know whether she is wrong. She asks if she can sit in Mrs. Grose's room for a while, and as the women go out Miss Giddens blows out the lamp on the desk.

A faint, gray moonlight comes in from the garden; then a soft music which diminishes until only the loud ticking of a clock can be heard—a clock measuring the passage of time. The chime of two is heard. From the landing a small whiteness passes down the stairs, into the room and across the window. From the piano comes a run of notes. Then a match is struck and Flora is seen lighting a candle on the candelabra. She takes the candle with her to the middle of the room; she is in her nightgown. Miles, in a long white nightshirt, comes down and they sit on the floor. Miles is

intent on something that he creates on the floor in front of him—
something that is soon recognizable as a house of cards. Flora
stands watching him. After the paper walls have risen, Flora bends
over and blows them down and the children laugh softly. It is one
of those delicious children's games played in forbidden hours.

Miles whispers that there is cake in the pantry, and when Flora
nods he moves silently to get some. Flora kneels before the cards,
shifting them with one hand and holding the candle above her head
with the other. She examines one card closely, and as she does the
figure of a woman appears on the staircase—a tall and rigid woman
dressed in black. Flora returns the card to the pack, rises, slowly
turns, faces the figure on the stair—and stretches her hand toward
it. A deep moan comes from the figure, and as the moan dies away
Miss Giddens enters from Mrs. Grose's room. She is carrying a
lighted candle. She stares directly at the figure on the stair, then
at Flora . . . and the figure moves into shadow and is no longer
seen.

Flora has noticed Miss Giddens, but she continues playing with
the cards and singing softly. Miss Giddens, her voice thin, calls,
"Who is it!" Flora drops her candle, as though startled, and exclaims that she has burnt her finger. Miss Giddens keeps repeating,
"Who is it! Who is it!"

"It is I," says Flora, and she adds, giggling, that Miles will be
surprised when he comes from the pantry. Again Miss Giddens demands, "Who is it!" The girl gently reminds her that it is she,
Flora, and that she and Miles have been naughty. The governess
asks who it was just now on the staircase and Flora, as though bewildered, says, "There? There's no one there—" She looks as
though she were about to cry and says she is frightened.

Miss Giddens counters, "You're *not* frightened!" When Miles
comes in with a plate of cake Flora rather pleasedly informs him
they have been caught, and the boy asks if Miss Giddens is angry.
Miss Giddens pays no heed to the children and still gazes at the
stair. Flora whispers to her brother that she thinks Miss Giddens
is still half asleep, and perhaps they had better get to bed—without the cake. Miles puts the plate on the desk and the children cross
the room to the stair and begin to go up. Miss Giddens stares at
them as though she does not see them, and when they reach the top
they smile at her and bid her, "Good night, Miss Giddens, dear."

In a moment the governess numbly asks once again, "Who was
it?" She goes to the stair and stops at the foot. She looks at the
window and sees nothing there but the pale moonlight. She goes
to the scattered cards, puts her candlestick on the floor, kneels and

whispers, "Who was it?" She rises slowly, goes to the window and stands looking out to the garden. Then, soundlessly, she draws the curtain cord, cutting off the light, shutting herself in with the candlelight and the deep shadows of the room.

"Was it—?" She shakes her head, quickly, as though something had caught in her hair. Now, in a thin monotone, like a woman talking in her sleep, she speaks broken sentences, and her body passes through all the extremes of terror, from utmost rigidity to spasmodic tremblings. "I-I-I must sleep. . . . I must write. . . . What shall I write? . . . I must sleep. . . . I can't think. . . . I must write." Running to the stair she asks, "Who was it?" Her body becomes rigid. "Was it she?" Back in the middle of the room, she sags to her knees. "What were they doing here?" She picks up a card as though seeing it for the first time. "Do they know. What is it? What is it?"

She crouches and covers her head with her arms. Her hair touches the floor and she is silent. Flora moves silently and swiftly down and to the window, where she slips behind the curtains. Miss Giddens lifts her head as though listening; then, lifting herself from the floor she goes to the window—and quickly and sharply pulls the cord. Flora is standing quietly . . . facing into the garden. She smiles up at the governess and says, "Why, I thought I saw you walking in the garden." She slips by and runs up the stair as Miss Giddens pushes the window open. The moonlight is brilliant, but a cold white; it floods the room and throws the governess' shadow far behind her. She steps backward into the room as the shadow of someone in the garden follows her. In the middle of the room she stops, frozen—and Miles appears at the window, barefoot and in his nightshirt. Miss Giddens whispers, "How did you get into the garden?"

He smilingly answers, "Through my window."

MISS GIDDENS—And why did you go out— What were you doing there—

MILES—If I tell you, will you understand? I did it to have you do this.

MISS GIDDENS—Do what?

MILES—Think me, for a change, bad. When I'm bad I *am* bad. (*He laughs softly.*)

MISS GIDDENS—And—how did you know I would find out—

MILES—Oh, I planned that with Flora. She was to get up and look out—and you were to find her. And you did, didn't you?

MISS GIDDENS—You didn't think that I might be displeased.

MILES—Oh, yes. How otherwise should I have been bad enough? Are you angry?

MISS GIDDENS—Your feet are wet. You might catch cold. You must go to bed. (*She does not move as* MILES *starts toward the stair.*)

MILES (*stopping near her*)—Why don't you stop it?

MISS GIDDENS—Stop what, Miles?

MILES—What you are doing.

MISS GIDDENS—*What am I doing, Miles*—

MILES (*although he does not raise his voice, there is a new sharpness in it*)—For one thing, your meddling. You can't stop me going out if I choose to. You're just a governess. Wouldn't it be better if you remembered that? (*He moves toward the stair and his voice is now charming and casual. He laughs softly, charmingly.*) It is difficult, isn't it? This whole situation? Couldn't you write my uncle? . . . You can't, can you? He so *hates* being bothered— (*He stops and looks at her for a moment.*) Oh, it isn't that I mind being with you and Mrs. Grose and Flora— I rather like it—and I do like *you*— But is it the best thing? Being with a governess all the time? (*Then, very softly, casually.*) A boy wants other things, you know— (*He exits beyond bend of staircase.* MISS GIDDENS *remains in the strained, staring position she has taken. Her shadow flickers in the candlelight—then, as though her body imitates the quivering of her shadow, she begins to tremble. Her mouth opens . . . no sound comes from her. She remains thus, caught with a palpitation of terror. Then, as though awakening from a nightmare, she screams.*)

MISS GIDDENS—Mrs. Grose! (*As she screams the clock chimes the quarter hour, and with this sound she moves—running toward a door.*) Mrs. Grose! (*As her screams die away a silence falls. . . then the sound of the clock's ticking seems to swell. She turns from the door. Her movements are mechanical as though she feels the need of movement without reason. In the candlelight, she is a figure dwarfed by shadow without substance.* MRS. GROSE *enters, carrying a candle. Her hair is in two braids, a shawl is about her shoulders. She wears a nightgown and slippers. As she enters* MISS GIDDENS' *words come pouring out, not waiting for an answer.*) Why have you kept it from me! *What* have you kept from me? You must tell me—Miss Jessel—why did she leave? And—Miles— (*going close to* MRS. GROSE.) I'll make you tell me!

MRS. GROSE (*deep emotion beneath her bewilderment*)—What has she to do with Master Miles?

MISS GIDDENS—*What* have you kept from me?

MRS. GROSE—Nothing— I promise you—nothing that could
concern you—

MISS GIDDENS—Why did she leave?

MRS. GROSE (*against her will*)—I thank heaven she left—

The housekeeper declares Miss Jessel couldn't have stayed. When
she left Mrs. Grose wouldn't see her. Here she was with two children and not caring—only thinking of herself and of *him*. Using
the house—any room—this very room—sitting together and laughing loudly. And at night, toward morning, the silence was always
broken by her weeping. She would walk through the halls calling
his name. He did what he wished with her. And then they heard
she had killed herself.

Miss Giddens, shocked, thinks Mrs. Grose should have taken the
children away—but the children weren't in her charge. Suppose the
children knew what was going on; suppose they used the children
to hide what was between them. . . . It is Mrs. Grose's turn to
be shocked and she shouts, "No!" Miss Giddens persists: They
made the children lie to Mrs. Grose. What did they tell them,
show them, make them do? As if in a dream, the governess muses,
"She was here—up there—a woman—Miss Jessel—her eyes fixed
on Flora—fixed with a fury of intention, as though to get hold
of her—to share with the child the torments she suffers. She's come
back! You don't believe me— Then ask Flora! No, she'll lie!"

Mrs. Grose protests, "How *can* you?" but Miss Giddens is not
to be stopped. "And Miles— You should have heard him! Reminding me to keep my place. Not to *meddle*. In *what?* . . . .
He was not a child! I felt obscene!"

This is too much for the housekeeper. She seizes the hysterical
young woman by the shoulders and commands her to stop. Miss
Giddens' voice turns piteous and pleading. "Help me. . . . I am
so tired. . . . Stay with me. . . ." Mrs. Grose takes her arm
gently, but almost fearfully.

The curtain falls slowly.

SCENE II

The following afternoon is Sunday. It is a gray, rainless day.
The curtains are open but the window is closed, and now and again
the light brightens as clouds move momentarily away from the sun.
It is half past one and Miss Giddens is coming downstairs. Mrs.
Grose has been in the garden and she pulls open the window and
enters. Mrs. Grose is uneasy, but she greets the governess and

apologizes for having let her sleep so long.

"I was not sleeping. I was writing a letter." Miss Giddens' voice is flat and unemotional. "I have written to their uncle. I am resigning from this post—"

Mrs. Grose breaks in in protest; Miss Giddens can't leave now. The older woman is assured that Miss Giddens will wait for the uncle's answer and until she leaves will do her best. The governess is told that the children are in the garden, and she harshly orders Mrs. Grose to tell them to come in. Mrs. Grose is taken aback at the tone of the order, but she starts to obey; however, Flora already is at the window, dressed for Sunday and carrying a hymnal. Mrs. Grose continues out. Flora chatters about the soloist at church, and how squeaky she and Miles thought her voice was. Flora bids Miss Giddens a pleasant good afternoon—and then the little one and the older one size each other up. Miss Giddens starts to say something to Flora, but the child suddenly kneels on the floor with an exclamation of pleasure and picks up a dead beetle. Her governess orders her to throw it outdoors, but Flora begs to keep it. Before there is time for reply she flits to and up the stairs, announcing that she will put it with her handkerchiefs and ribbons; and as she goes she chants an improvised song, "Beetles don't decay, you know—they get drier and drier like a twig. Beetles don't decay."

Again a strange panic seizes Miss Giddens and she calls after the child. Flora carols that she won't be long. Then, from her room, she cries, "Oh, Miss Giddens!" and the chilled Miss Giddens finds herself unable to move. But Flora's exclamation was simply over finding another beetle on her bed, and she makes up another song about "Bettles on Sunday." Having tucked her prizes among her ribbons, she returns downstairs and prattles gruesomely about beetles. Once Mrs. Grose gave her some porridge and she ate all of it—and the last spoonful had a beetle in it! "I chewed on it and I chewed on it and it tasted like twigs." Seemingly the child's story will never end, but suddenly Miss Giddens kneels and pulls her close. She is weeping.

Most tenderly Flora leads her governess to the love seat and tries to comfort her, telling her not to worry about a thing. When Miles and Mrs. Grose come in they will sing a song or play a quiet Sunday game. Flora, looking out the window, can see the other two; Mrs. Grose is chasing Miles and he is running away from her and throwing leaves at her. A strange, subtle sadness creeps into the girl's voice as she says, "They're having fun—but so are we. . . .

I'd rather be here with you." Forlornly, she takes scissors from the desk and begins cutting a picture out of a book, talking half to herself and half to Miss Giddens. Outside, Mrs. Grose can be heard calling Miles.

Flora, still chattering, wonders if they may go to the pond tomorrow. There is a little boat there. Miles used to go there. In a tight voice Miss Giddens asks, "Alone?"

"Oh, no. And he told me he saw a hand waving on the bottom, but Mrs. Grose said stuff and nonsense."

Suddenly sitting up, her back rigid, Miss Gidden asks, "With whom did Miles go?" Flora just stares at her. The light seeps away and she exclaims, "Oh, dear! I know it's going to rain again! I must cover my beetles, poor things!" And, singing her beetle song, she scampers upstairs.

Miss Giddens' eyes turn to a shadowy corner of the room—and there stands a woman as though she has just entered. It is a rigid figure, its head tilted toward the staircase on which Flora now reappears, slowly. Flora is sad about her beetles, which are getting colder and colder, and she sings a dirge about them as she descends. The breathless Mrs. Grose appears in the window to say that she can't find Miles. Miss Giddens, rising from the love seat and forcing herself not to scream, declares, "She's there—she's there!" Mrs. Grose comes in a step, halts, and stares at the figure. Her hand covers her mouth. Miss Giddens cries, "Flora!"

The child, on the last stair, answers a polite "Yes?"

"Look," gasps the governess, pointing.

Flora, her eyes fixed on Miss Giddens, says, "I don't see anything—"

"There! There! There! You *see* her! You see her as well as you see me!"

Flora acts puzzled. "I don't—I don't see anyone—*really*— truly—" Then, screaming, she runs to Mrs. Grose and cries, "I'm frightened!" Mrs. Grose takes the girl in her arms and comforts her, saying, "She isn't there. Nobody's there. How can she be? She's dead and buried!"

Flora turns toward Miss Giddens, her face distorted with hatred, and she spits, "I see nothing! I never have! You're cruel! Wicked! I hate you! I hate you! I hate you!" She buries her head against Mrs. Grose and begs to be taken away—taken away from Miss Giddens, who is cruel and wicked.

The curtain falls slowly.

Scene III

Twilight has fallen on this Sunday afternoon. It has rained some, and now a sulphurous light seems to divide the room into shadow and substance. Mrs. Grose is dressed for traveling and has a coat over her arm; she is caught by the agitation of departure. She calls out the window for Miss Giddens—but Miss Giddens, hidden in the shadow, is right here, in the love seat. Mrs. Grose says the carriage is waiting and everything is packed, and they must leave.

"And Miss Flora? Where is she?" Flora is in Mrs. Grose's room, dressed and waiting. She will come down—just as they leave. The child is frightened as long as she is in this house.

"Frightened? That is anger, Mrs. Grose." Miss Giddens knows all of Flora's tricks and is not impressed—even when she hears that Flora made Mrs. Grose lock her in the bedroom. Mrs. Grose is sure Miss Giddens is wrong, thinking what she does about Flora, and she will realize it when they are gone. Mrs. Grose looks at the coat she is carrying; it is Miles'. "Where is he?" she asks.

"He is in the garden. He is hiding. He's been hiding ever since he came back from church. He won't come to you."

Mrs. Grose, bewildered, suggests that Miss Giddens call him, and the governess startles her by saying, calmly, "He is not going. He is staying here with me."

"Why?"

"I think it best. . . . You must take Miss Flora to her uncle."

Mrs. Grose cannot understand and the governess tries to explain: Miles must stay here and be faced with it. Mrs. Grose makes one last attempt, running to the window and calling for Miles, but Miss Giddens is confident he will not come. When the carriage has left, Miles will think everybody has gone and will return to the house—and then Miss Giddens can face him with it.

Violently, Mrs. Grose declares that, whatever she has seen, and however much evil she believes there is in this house, the children are not evil and they should be taken away. "You can take Flora . . . she is young," says Miss Giddens. "But Miles? He must end it here. It isn't easy for me. . . . I almost ran from it. All that was base in Quint lives in Miles. He lives with the memory, the longing, for all that Quint taught him. I must free him of it. Even if I must *hurt* him."

Mrs. Grose warns that no child could survive such terrors. Miss Giddens remains firm, and repeats her instructions to take Flora to her uncle, and to deliver a letter she has written. She opens the desk drawer to take out the letter—and cannot find it. She is sure she put it there. Without emotion she tells the housekeeper that she will just have to tell the uncle—and Miss Giddens is confident that Mrs. Grose will tell the truth—or as much of it as she understands. "And now, you must go."

Slowly, Mrs. Grose moves out, praying, "God help you. God help you both."

Miss Giddens resumes the love seat and sits there, her face expressionless. A low music is heard—a sonorous, slow-moving passage of time. Twilight fades. Carriage wheels are heard to pass. A clock whirs, preparatory to chiming, and finally chimes. Miles, dimly seen, comes through the window, starts to climb the stairs, then stops and inquires matter-of-factly, "Why are you sitting in the dark, Miss Giddens? I knew you'd still be here."

She lights the lamp and Miles strides around the room as though he were master of the house, hands in pockets. "Well, here we are. The two of us alone. I hope you don't mind?"

Miss Giddens does mind, for she is afraid, but she does not show it to Miles. She asks what Miles was doing in the garden, and why it was that he didn't come when she called. The boy seems amazed; he *saw* Miss Giddens, but didn't hear her say anything, and thought she wanted to be alone. In fact, *he* called *her* and she didn't answer. Miles asks a question for a change: why aren't they with Flora and Mrs. Grose?

Miss Giddens, almost crying, pleads, "Ah, Miles, you won't come out with it yourself—how, then, can I?" She tries to persuade the lad that she is not cruel—that she has stayed here to help him—and won't he let her help? The boy stares long at her with a sneering smile on his face, then demands, "Why don't you stop pretending?"

Stiffly, Miss Giddens rises, picks a tray of food from the desk and offers it to the boy. At first he says he is not hungry; then he says he has never eaten in here—it isn't a dining room, and what would Mrs. Grose think? But he does sit at a table with food before him at Miss Giddens' command, and she takes up her embroidery.

The figure of Quint appears at the window, eyes on Miles' back. A high vibration is heard as Miles stiffens, fully aware of what is behind him. As he begins to turn his head he notices the governess looking up at him; she has not noticed Quint, so with a sudden sweep of his hand he knocks his plate to the floor. Quint disappears. Miles explains to Miss Giddens that he was just being naughty again. Then, in an almost peevish tone, he wishes he could go away.

"To another school?"

"I don't think I should suit *any* school—"

Miss Giddens has more questions: What was the real reason Miles went out in the garden when he was supposed to be in bed? It wasn't just the naughtiness he claimed, she is certain. And didn't he take a letter from her desk? He admits taking the letter—and reading it—and burning it.

"Did you take other things? Is that what you did at school?" Miles replies no, he didn't steal at school. A low vibration is heard momentarily, then Miles, looking as though he were in pain, says, vaguely, "I—well—I said things—" He doesn't remember whom he said them to—just a few boys he liked. And the boys repeated them to *their* friends, and finally the masters heard. Miles supposes the things were too bad for the masters to write in the letter to his uncle.

"Where did you first hear these things?" she asks—and they both seem to freeze at the question. Miles stammers that he made them up, but Miss Giddens knows it's a lie—and he knows she knows it. "Who told you to say them?" He vaguely answers that they came into his head, and says he would like to go to bed now. She holds him, persisting, "What were they? These things you said?"

MILES (*still smiling*)—You know so much—can't you guess, then?

MISS GIDDENS—Shall I tell you who it was that said them?

MILES (*quickly*)—It was a boy—a boy at school—that's all. I won't say them again—I promise—

MISS GIDDENS—Shall I tell you his name?

MILES (*moving slowly toward staircase*)—What does it matter? It wasn't anything.

MISS GIDDENS—It wasn't a boy at school!

MILES (*looking at her sharply*)—You can't get away with this, you know. I know why you're doing this!

MISS GIDDENS—What did *he* say to you when you went walking by the pond?

MILES (*desperately*)—This afternoon? Why, no one was there. Who would be there?

MISS GIDDENS—Not this afternoon!

MILES—When then? Yesterday?

MISS GIDDENS—Not yesterday. Before I came here—to live in this house.

MILES—I was at school!

MISS GIDDENS—And before that? (*The vibrations grow sharper, stronger.*)

MILES (*his head thrust out*)—I know why you're asking me all these questions! You're afraid! That's why!

MISS GIDDENS—And not only the things you said—things you've done!—and what you *might* do—

MILES—Oh, yes, I might! You're afraid—that's why you try to make me admit something—

MISS GIDDENS—Miles!

MILES—You're in it and you won't stop at anything, will you?

MISS GIDDENS—Miles! I want to help you! Let me help you!

MILES—You keep saying that. But there's nothing you can do, is there? Because I know Flora isn't ill. You frightened her because you didn't know what else to do!

MISS GIDDENS (*moving toward him*)—Miles!

MILES (*retreating backward to staircase*)—But *I'm* not a baby! What *are* you going to do? What will you say to my uncle? He'll laugh at you! (*The vibration grows all the while.*) I'll tell him! I'll tell him what you're like. He'll believe me. I'll tell him that you're vile—he won't believe what *you* say! Because you're dirty! Dirty! Dirty!

MISS GIDDENS—You've never stopped seeing him, have you?

MILES—Don't ask me, Miss Giddens!

MISS GIDDENS—You still want to be with him, don't you, Miles?

MILES (*before he can stop himself—a terrible scream*)—He's dead! (*As the boy screams, the figure of* QUINT *appears at the window. All the musical vibrations stop, but a low thumping is heard—a sound as that of a heart, low and in a broken rhythm.*)

MISS GIDDENS (*now with a desperate pleading*)—Who, Miles! His *name!* Give me his name!

MILES—He's dead. He's dead.

MISS GIDDENS—Give me his name.

MILES (*crying*)—He'll hurt me! Stop it, Miss Giddens!

MISS GIDDENS—Reject him, for he is here, now!

MILES—Miss Giddens, you don't know, you don't know!

MISS GIDDENS—Reject him or he'll destroy you. I'm here to help you.

MILES (*clinging to her*)—You can't. Don't you see. You *can't!* You don't understand. He'll hurt me. You can't help.

MISS GIDDENS—You will be free. Confess. His name!

MILES (*breaking away—with a tremendous directness*)—Quint! Peter Quint!

MISS GIDDENS—Now, Miles, Now.

For a moment there is absolute silence; then there is a sound like a heart quickening its beat. With a tremendous shudder Miles forces himself to turn to the window, and he screams, "Leave me! Leave me! Ah—leave me!" As he screams, Quint's arms rise, as though to touch the boy across the distance, and Miles begins to crumple. He spins around, tries to cry out, and falls. The sound of a heart stops, and Quint slowly steps back into the darkness.

Miss Giddens kneels, cradles the boy in her arms, a feeling of great release within her. She comforts him gently, saying Quint is gone, and they're alone, and nothing can hurt him any more. Then she looks down closely at the boy and releases his body, horror on her face. As Miles' body falls back a thin, shrieking sound is heard and the silk curtains blow into the room. Dried leaves swirl across the threshold. Miss Giddens kneels and says, "You are free —Miles—you're free. You're free—" Great sobs break out of her.

CURTAIN

LOST IN THE STARS *

A Musical Play in Two Acts

LIBRETTO BY MAXWELL ANDERSON; MUSIC BY KURT WEILL

Based on a novel by Alan Paton, "Cry, the Beloved Country"

THE musical part of the theatre, which is rather insultingly called
Tin Pan Alley, consists mostly of teams of twos or threes: a man
who writes the music, another who writes the words to go with the
music, and perhaps a third who writes the book, or libretto. There
were Bolton, Wodehouse and Kern, and De Sylva, Brown and Henderson. There were George and Ira Gershwin, and Richard Rodgers
and Lorenz Hart, to write the songs for whatever plot-makers came
to hand. There have been few exceptions like George M. Cohan,
Noel Coward, Gian-Carlo Menotti (and Richard Wagner!), able to
write all the words and all the music necessary for a theatrical production with songs. The most illustrious of all lyric theatre teams
was the firm of W. S. Gilbert and Arthur Sullivan. In recent Broadway seasons the most illustrious have been Richard Rodgers and
Oscar Hammerstein II, and Maxwell Anderson and Kurt Weill—
with Mr. Anderson doing the double duty of being book-writer and
lyric-writer. The first of the Anderson-Weill collaborations was
"Knickerbocker Holiday," in which Walter Huston sang the un-
forgettable "September Song."
One might think that teamwork requires men of similar type,
background and outlook, but this is not so. Gilbert and Sullivan,
whose work was such a beautiful blend, were vastly different as persons, and their quarrels have become history. Different, too, were
Anderson and Weill. Maxwell Anderson is a big, brooding, extremely serious American who is the son of a preacher. Kurt Weill
was a small German pixy, gay, humorous and the son of a cantor.
There is no record of Anderson and Weill ever quarreling. When

Kurt Weill died during the Broadway run of "Lost in the Stars," Anderson was crushed; he had lost his most cherished friend. At the time of Weill's death the two were deep in a new project—the making of a musical play, tentatively titled "Twain on the River," based on Mark Twain's tales of Huck Finn, Tom Sawyer and life on the Mississippi.

Anderson and Weill never wanted to write a show just to write another show. They wanted to "say" something. "Knickerbocker Holiday" was early New York history. "Twain on the River" was to capture a time and a place in the American scene. They both were drawn to Alan Paton's long novel, "Cry, the Beloved Country," because it said something about race relations and because it had the fascinating folk background of South Africa. Probably no other team but the son of the preacher and the son of the cantor would have been inspired to make a musical theatre piece of so sweeping a work of fiction. They managed it, in eighteen scenes—scenes that blend and intermingle on the stage with a minimum of mechanical interference.

As the lights come up one sees in the background the Ixopo hills. From the orchestra pit a broad flight of stairs, almost as broad as the stage itself, leads to the stage. On these banks a group of singers sit, so placed that they are not in the way of the action, but they can comment on it or walk up and take part in it at any time. As the lights grow brighter the small, cheap but clean sitting room in the home of Stephen Kumalo comes into view. Stephen lives near St. Mark's Church, near Ndotsheni, Natal, South Africa. At the moment there is nobody in the room, so the Leader of the singers tells something of this land we are in, and is urged to continue by the Answerer:

LEADER—

There is a lovely road
that runs from Ixopo into the hills.
These hills
are grass covered and rolling, and they are lovely
beyond any singing of it.
About you
there is grass and bracken, and you may hear
the forlorn crying of the titihoya bird.
The grass of the veld is rich and matted.
You cannot see the soil.
The grass holds the rain and mist,
and they seep into the ground, feeding

the streams in every clove.
The clove is cool and green and lovely beyond any singing of it.

ANSWERER—But sing now about the lower hills.
LEADER—

Where you stand the grass is rich and matted—
but the rich green hills break down.
They fall to the valley below—
and, falling, change.
For they grow red and bare;
they cannot hold the rain and mist;
the streams run dry in the clove.
Too many cattle feed on the grass;
it is not kept or guarded or cared for,
It no longer keeps men, guards men, cares for men.
The titihoya cries here no more.

ANSWERER—Yes, wherever the hills have broken down and the red clay shows through, there poor people live and dig ever more desperately into the failing earth.
LEADER—

The great red hills stand desolate,
and the earth has torn away like flesh.
These are the valleys
of old men and old women,
of mothers and children.
The men are away.
The young men and the girls are away.
The soil cannot keep them any more.

Stephen Kumalo enters his room and sits at the table. He is a middle-aged black man with an air of great gentleness and dignity. He is followed by his wife, Grace, who has the same gentleness, and a small Zulu child, Nita, who has come to bring Stephen a letter. She addresses him by the respectful salutation, *umfundisi.* She has brought the letter from the store, where the white man gave it to her.
"That was good of you," he thanks the little girl gravely. "Go well, small one." She starts to leave, but her reluctance is apparent, and Stephen remembers that she may be hungry and tells her she will find a little bowl on the kitchen table with a spoon beside it. Nita makes for the kitchen with grave and polite thanks.
The arrival of a letter in the Kumalo household is no ordinary

event, and Stephen fingers it thoughtfully while his wife looks over his shoulder. They note that the envelope is postmarked Johannesburg and dated August 9, 1949. It is addressed to "Reverend Stephen Kumalo, St. Mark's Church"—and from this inscription and the handwriting they know it cannot be from their son, who is one of those whom "the soil cannot keep any more." Stephen speculates: Their son Absalom is in Johannesburg, so the letter might at least be news of him; and Stephen's sister Gertrude and his brother John are there—but then they have never written before. . . .

The way to find out about a letter is to open it and read it. In this case Grace does the reading, aloud, for her eyes are better than her husband's. The letter is from brother John, and it is crude and shocking to the gentle couple. Saluting his brother as an "old faker in Christ," John has written about Gertrude. "She says she came looking for a husband who ran away from her. Maybe so. Anyway she's found plenty husbands, and the stories about the kind of house she keeps are not good for my business, because it's known here who she is." John suggests that Stephen do something about it.

"He's an evil man," says Grace, but Stephen will not agree. John may really believe his brother is a faker, because John is one himself, and this is understandable to Stephen. The one who worries him is not John, but Gertrude.

Grace thinks of a plan. If Stephen went to Johannesburg he could find Gertrude . . . and their son Absalom, too.

"It's many hundreds of miles," her husband points out. "Where would I find the money?"

There is St. Chad's money—Absalom's money—the money they saved for their son to go to St. Chad's school. Grace argues there is no need of saving it longer, for now Absalom will never go to the school; when people go to Johannesburg they do not come back.

Stephen counters, "But Absalom will! Absalom went to Johannesburg for one purpose—to earn money for his education! When he returns he will bring twelve pounds of his own to put with the twelve we have saved. . . ."

Grace is more realistic. Absalom has been gone for a year. He has been in the mines—and no young man could work in the mines and not change. "Take the money—use it!" she implores.

STEPHEN—Do you know what you are saying? If I take his school money and use it to bring Gertrude back, then I have given

up Absalom! I have said by this action that he will not make a
place for himself, that we shall not see him nor be proud of him
again, and he is only a drop in the great river of blacks that pours
into the earth and is seen no more! I will not say this! I will
not think it!

GRACE—I love him as much as you, but why has he not written
to us? If there's nothing wrong he could have written.

STEPHEN—O mother of little faith! A letter can be lost so
easily! We must not cease to believe in him. We must love him,
and not doubt him. There's a great gulf between people, Grace,
between husband and wife, between parents and child, between
neighbor and neighbor. Even when you live in the same house
it's deep and wide, except for the love between us. But when there
is love, then distance doesn't matter at all—distance or silence or
years.

Stephen continues in song:

> *How many miles*
> *To the heart of a child?*
> *Thousands of miles, thousands of miles.*
> *When he lay on your breast*
> *He looked up and smiled*
> *Across tens of thousands,*
> *Thousands of miles.*
> *Each lives alone*
> *In a world of dark,*
> *Crossing the skies*
> *In a lonely arc,*
> *Save when love leaps out like a leaping spark*
> *Over thousands, thousands of miles.*
>
> *Not miles, or walls, or length of days,*
> *Nor the cold doubt of midnight can hold us apart,*
> *For swifter than wings of the morning*
> *The pathways of the heart!*
> *How many miles*
> *To the heart of a son?*
> *Thousands of miles, thousands of miles. . . .*

Nita returns to say thanks for the bowl of food.

"Go well, my child," says Stephen, and she replies, "Stay well,
umfundisi." When the lass has gone Grace renews her appeal for
Stephen to take the money and go to Johannesburg, and he gives

in because she wishes it so much. It is too late to take the train today, but he could go at noon tomorrow.

Next day, at the station at Carrisbrooke, the white station master announces that the train for Johannesburg will arrive in five minutes. A group of Zulus has come to the station to say farewell to one of their number, who has been called to work in the mines. They chant "Farewell. Go well. . . . White man go to Johannesburg—he come back, he come back. Black man go to Johannesburg—never come back, never come back!" Their friend who is going protests that he will fool them; he will come back.

Also come to the station is James Jarvis, an Englishman about 55. With him are his son, Arthur, and his grandson, Edward. The boy is disconsolate at having to go back to school. His father is going with him—back to work. Stephen comes, carrying a little black bag, and with him is his wife. Arthur has not seen Stephen for a year, and now he goes to greet him—but is halted by his father. "In our village," Jarvis reminds his son, "one does not go out of his way to speak to a black." But Arthur will not be deterred, saying, "I have friends among the Zulus. And my friends are my friends." He offers his hand to Stephen, greeting him as Mr. Kumalo. Stephen explains that he is going to Johannesburg—his first long journey, and a happy one—to see his son.

Jarvis is profoundly offended at Arthur's action. Arthur has hurt him—and damaged him in the eyes of those who stand here. Sternly he tells his son that, even if what he does in Johannesburg is his own affair, he must avoid affronting him here in the future; otherwise, he is not sure that he wants Arthur to come back another time.

The chorus begins to imitate the approaching train, "Clink, clink, clickety," and the passengers move to go aboard. A chorister imitates a locomotive whistle, and the lights fade as the singers chant, "Black man go to Johannesburg . . ."

One of Stephen's stops in the big city will, of course, be his brother John's tobacco shop, which also is a political headquarters of sorts. At the moment John is conferring with some of his Zulu and Bantu lieutenants. He is telling them that they won't get equal suffrage, social equality or any other kind of equality—but the natives are not to be told this. They are to be told to be patient. "And in ten years, gentlemen," John concludes, "our League will own Johannesburg."

Stephen has found the shop, and is leading a small Zulu boy,

Alex, by the hand. John greets him as "our old gospel bird" and asks the news: Is Gertrude going back with Stephen?

STEPHEN—She allows the child to go with me. But she stays here.

JOHN—Brother, I want our sister out of this town. There's a limit to the number of bastard nephews a respectable tradesman can have.

STEPHEN—I asked her to come with me. She would not. And she said, "John won't put me away anywhere. He would have to find me first, and he won't find me."

JOHN—You have failed with her.

STEPHEN—Yes.

JOHN—Take her son, then, and go back to your hills and your sheet-iron chapel and your rusty god. I thought you might rid me of the woman. If you can't do that I have no further use for you.

STEPHEN—Honest and straightforward, aren't you, John? I'll go, but first there are two things I must ask. I have no room to stay in—

JOHN—There's no room here.

STEPHEN—Don't be afraid. I can pay for a room.

JOHN—Perhaps I can find you one, then. What else?

STEPHEN—My son Absalom. Did you see him while he was here?

JOHN—How much have you heard from Absalom?

STEPHEN—Four letters—from the mines—nearly a year ago. He was well, and working hard.

JOHN—I see. Well—your son left the mines and went about with my son Matthew for a while. They both stayed here. But your Absalom was not a good influence on Matthew.

STEPHEN—John!

JOHN—I had to tell them to get out.

STEPHEN—You sent them away?

JOHN—Yes.

STEPHEN—Do you know—where they went?

JOHN—Yes, I've written it somewhere.

STEPHEN—I hoped you would know. That makes it all easy. Now I thank my God—I thank my *Tixo*—

JOHN—You can leave your God out of it. He's not interested. 14 Krause Street, Doornfontein Textiles Company.

STEPHEN—Doornfontein Textiles Company, 14 Krause Street.

JOHN—That's it. And now you want a place to stay. (*He writes an address.*) You think I am a hard man.

STEPHEN—Brother, you have helped me. We do what we can.

JOHN—Brother, you're right. We do what we can. I hope you know what you do. You're the white man's dog, trained to bark and keep us in order. You know that.

STEPHEN—No, brother, I do not know it.

JOHN—They pile up mountains of gold, and they pay our sons three shillings a day, and out of this wage take a heavy tax. Is that fair?

STEPHEN—No, brother, it is not fair.

JOHN—Then why do you wear their Anglican clothes and read their Testament?

STEPHEN—Because all men do evil, I among them—and I wish all men to do better, I among them.

JOHN (*giving* STEPHEN *the address*)—Yes, blessed are the chicken-hearted. This will give you a place to sleep. It's expensive and it's in Shanty Town and it's not pleasant. Such are the customs of our city.

STEPHEN—I shan't mind. Good-by, John. (*He puts out his hand.*)

JOHN (*taking it*)—Good-by. You old faker in Christ.

STEPHEN—The same John! (*He starts out.*) 14 Krause Street. . . .

Stephen has left little Alex in Shanty Town and now he plods patiently in search of his son. The foreman at the Textiles Company remembers Absalom Kumalo and his cousin, Matthew—but they left some months ago. When they were working here they lived with a Mrs. Mkize in Alexandra. But they are not at Mrs. Mkize's; they have been gone some months, she tells Stephen when he finds his way to her door. She is obviously afraid—afraid to talk, until Stephen explains that he is Absalom's father. "Then it would be better if you followed him no further," she advises. Reluctantly she tells of the boys' friendship with a taxi driver, and how they brought things to her house in the middle of the night— watches, clothing, money. And then one day they left in haste. "I think they were near to being discovered. Oh, follow him no further!"

The dogged Stephen obtains the name and address of the taxi driver, and finds the man. "They were picked up for something they'd done, and one of them went to jail for a while," the taxi- man informs Stephen. Absalom was the one who went to jail, but he is on parole now.

"Where would he be?"

"You could ask the parole officer at the government building."
It is four or five miles away, this building, and it is getting late—
but Stephen plods on; he finds the parole officer, whose name is
Eland, and from him he learns facts: Absalom was paroled, partly
because of good behavior and his youth, but mainly because there
was a girl who was pregnant by him. They are not married, but
the girl seemed fond of him, and they are living now in Pimville,
which is among the shacks some miles away. Eland offers to take
Stephen there—but tomorrow, not tonight.

So Stephen goes back to Alex in a tiny, squalid room. The boy
asks if he must live there. No, he is told, he will live in Ndotsheni,
where there are hills and valleys and trees and streams. He will
live in Stephen's house, and the boy is full of questions about it.
What color is it? Does Stephen have a wife? Alex doesn't like
his mother, for she hits him and then he hits her. Why is the
house gray? Is the water good, or must it be boiled? Stephen
sings of the house:

> *There's a little gray house*
> *In a one-street town,*
> *And the door stands open,*
> *And the steps run down;*
> *And you prop up the window*
> *With a stick on the sill,*
> *And you carry spring water*
> *From the bottom of the hill;*
> *And the white star-of-Bethlehem*
> *Grows in the yard,*
> *And I can't really describe it*
> *But I'm trying hard;*
>
> *It's not much to tell about,*
> *It's not much to picture out,*
> *And the only thing special is*
> *It's home.*

The boy slips off into pleasant sleep as Stephen continues his
song about the little gray house and the woman who is in it, waiting
for them. . . .

In another part of Shanty Town is a dive, from which strange
harmonies emanate. Linda, a gaudily dressed girl, is on a table
singing a song, "Who'll buy my juicy rutabagas, who'll buy my
yellow corn?" As the verse continues it is obvious that she is offering

something besides garden produce. A man and a girl are dancing, and others who are listening include Matthew Kumalo, Johannes Pafuri, two girls named Rose and Sutty, and Absalom. Absalom sits alone, and is moody.

As Linda finishes her song Johannes exclaims that *he* will buy, and she falls into his arms. Matthew is inspired to turn the party into a mock court session, with himself as the judge. He orders Linda arrested for not having a license and sentences her to twenty years. Johannes attacks "his lordship" for having a dirty wig and faulty logic, and Matthew pronounces him in contempt. Matthew is a bit drunk. Tiring after a while of his burlesque of British justice ("Justice is when the black woman cooks and the white woman has breakfast in bed"), he orders most of the crowd to go outside and wait. Only Johannes and Absalom are left with him, and Matthew gets down to cases by inquiring, "Now to begin with —how do we get in?"

The house is never locked, Johannes explains. The man who lives there has some theory—says if anybody wants what he's got he can come and take it.

"Then why would we need a gun?" Absalom asks.

Matthew says nobody ever knows when he's going to need a gun—and, since Absalom already has one, they might as well have it along.

Absalom is not enthusiastic. Johannes has said there won't be anybody there; the white man has gone on a trip and the servants get home late every night. Absalom thinks it would be better without the gun. "Well, I don't, see?" says Matthew firmly. "And if you don't bring it you're not in on this at all. I'm going to get to those new gold fields! . . . Now if you want to help us raise the money to get there, you're in; you come along! But if you're scared to carry that cheap revolver of yours you're of no use to us. So bring it or stay home." Matthew and Johannes go outside to get rid of the girls, leaving Absalom to think the ultimatum over.

Into the dive comes Irina, a young and pretty Zulu girl, who calls timidly to Absalom. She has come to tell him something— something about the parole officer. The officer came to the cabin asking for him, and Irina had to lie—said Absalom was at work. And surely now Absalom must be at the factory tomorrow, for the parole officer will be there.

Absalom's mind suddenly is made up. He will not be at the factory, or anywhere where he can be found. "We'll live in a better place than Shanty Town." He speaks bitterly of the life they face there—Irina would have her baby, and another, and he'd keep on at the factory, and they'd live in the same shack until, perhaps, they'd be four in a room, or even ten. "I love you, Irina. I want you to have something better than that." He tells of the new gold fields, where, if you go there as a free man and not in a labor gang, you can sometimes get ahead . . .

Irina is miserable with foreboding. She begs Absalom to come home with her, but he refuses. He tells her to wait for him, and when he has something and is something he will come.

IRINA—Where will you get money to go to the mines?

ABSALOM—We'll get it.

IRINA—You won't steal again?

ABSALOM—We'll get it.

IRINA—Oh, Absalom, Absalom, if you were caught once more they could keep you from me a whole lifetime! Come home with me, Absalom, come home with me!

ABSALOM—Oh, God damn this world! (*He kisses her.*) Yes, I'll come with you. (*They start out as* MATTHEW, *followed by* JOHANNES, *re-enters.*)

MATTHEW—Where are you going, Absalom? (*He sees* IRINA.) It's his cook! It's his little cookie!

ABSALOM—I'm out of it.

MATTHEW—She gives the orders, huh? . . . You could be rich, you know—

ABSALOM—I'm on parole. You're not.

MATTHEW—One more black boy loose in a gold field, they'd never locate you.

ABSALOM—But even if we make money in the gold fields, we still have to come back here. And they'll get me.

MATTHEW—Why would they? You'll change your name, you'll be wearing new clothes, you'll have cash in your pocket, you can walk up and buy a shack of your own. There won't be any Absalom Kumalo. There'll be a new man! A man—not somebody's dumb ox!

ABSALOM—He's right, Irina—wait for me. It'll take a little time, but wait for me.

IRINA—Please—

ABSALOM—Go now, Irina. I'll be back.

IRINA—Oh, Absalom—

ABSALOM—Go, Irina!

IRINA—Yes, I'll go. (*She goes out.*)

MATTHEW—That's more like it!

JOHANNES—You know what I heard? I heard there's sometimes loose gold you can pan out of a river if you get there before the land's all fenced.

MATTHEW—Some places you can take just a kitchen pan and wash the dirt around in it and there's gold at the bottom.

JOHANNES—It's that way beyond Rigval clove.

MATTHEW—And then, by God, we'll live like men! Johannes, you bring along that machinery you talked about?

JOHANNES—I've got it where I can pick it up quick.

MATTHEW—Then pick it up, and pick up your feet! This is the best time.

Two days later, and Irina is in her hut in Shanty Town, and beyond the hut one may see the great buildings of the city. Eland, the parole officer, has returned, bringing Stephen with him. Stephen has wanted to meet Irina, and they will go on from here to the factory. "Absalom's there, of course?"

"No, sir. . . . I lied to you. . . . He's gone, I don't know where."

Eland, a conscientious officer, feels like a failure. Stephen asks if he can be alone with the girl a moment, and Eland goes outside. Gently Stephen questions the girl, and trustingly and sweetly she replies. Then his questions get sharper and his voice harder and angrier.

"Do you have a family?"

"I have no one."

"But you lived somewhere—before you met Absalom."

"I lived in Sophiatown."

"Alone?"

Irina picks nervously at the back of a chair and answers hesitantly, "Nobody lives alone in Sophiatown."

He suggests, "You lived with your first—husband?"

"Yes, with my first."

"How many have there been?"

"Three."

"And now," he says contemptuously, "you will seek a fourth."

"No. I wait for Absalom."

Stephen is contemptuous in his disbelief. "I think you would do anything! You would go to anyone! I am an old man, Absalom's father, but you would come to me if I asked you!"

The girl cries terrified denials, but Stephen will not relent. If she was with others, why not with him? "Would you be willing?" he asks, and then repeats the question insistently. Irina begins to break, and when he savagely orders her to speak she falters, "I could be willing."

"Yes," he sneers, "you are a woman who would go to anyone." Irina is confused, and she breaks in a passion of crying. Why did Stephen come? How would she know what he thinks—or wants? All she knows is that she is to have a child—and Absalom is gone—and she loves him. "I want only Absalom. He brought me only trouble—but I love him!"

Stephen's anger vanishes. "I was wrong," he says. "I should not have put you to such a test." He asks her to forgive him and says he will go now to search for his son. If he finds him he will come to tell her, and if Absalom comes back to her, Irina should tell Stephen. He writes his address and leaves it with her, and the girl, alone, sings of "Trouble Man":

Since you came first to me,
Dear one, glad one,
You bring all the worst to me,
Near one, sad one;
There's trouble in your coming,
Trouble in your laughter,
There's trouble in your going,
And trouble after.

.   .   .   .   .

Trouble man, trouble man, walking out there,
Maybe in a strange place, God knows where,
Maybe in a strange town, hurrying and walking,
Listen to my blood and my bones here talking,
Listen to the blood in my hands and feet,
Finding you out on a far, strange street;
Finding the footprints out where you ran,
Asking, "Aren't you coming home, trouble man?
Trouble man! Trouble man! Trouble man! Trouble man!"
Saying, "All day long you don't catch me weeping,
But, oh, God help me when it comes time for sleeping,
When it comes time for sleeping here alone!"
Trouble man! Trouble man!

Back, now, for a short and terrible moment of the evening when Matthew, Johannes and Absalom left Irina in the dive. . . .

It is the kitchen of Arthur Jarvis' home. The three young men, with handkerchiefs over their faces, have entered it, and Absalom is carrying a revolver. They are discovered by a servant who demands what they want. "We want money and clothes," Johannes demands—and the servant recognizes his voice. "I know you! You cannot do such a thing!" The servant runs to the door, crying for his master, and Johannes strikes him down with an iron bar. Arthur Jarvis runs into the doorway, and Absalom fires his gun. As the stage darkens the chorus chants a song of "Murder in Parkwold!"

And now, for some time, justice has been at work. James Jarvis is at the desk in the library of his son's home, and Eland, the parole officer, has come to him with news. Johannes Pafuri, who used to be a houseboy in this house, has been arrested and identified by the servant who was struck that night in the kitchen.

"I suppose he could be guilty," says Jarvis. "Not that it would help to fix the guilt. Our son is dead. Arthur is dead and punishment will not bring him back. . . . One thing I hope the police will remember: no man is to be punished unless guilty."

Eland replies that the police will make very certain before they act.

JARVIS—I differed sharply with my son concerning our policy toward the blacks, but in this I want what he would have wanted—that the guilty feel the penalty—no man else. I had quarelled with my son, I suppose you know that. I wish we'd had a chance to patch up that quarrel.

ELAND—I'm sure it wasn't serious.

JARVIS—Yes. It was serious. Over Negro equality. (*He rises.*) And the irony of it, that an advocate of Negro equality should have been killed by a Negro. There's only one course with them—a strong hand and a firm policy. They understand nothing but discipline, respect nothing else.

ELAND—There are good and bad among them.

JARVIS—Are there? At this moment I wonder.

ELAND—We can know them only by their actions. There was a man who came into this house with a pistol, came with intent to steal, and ended by committing murder. Let us find this one man and see that he is punished. Let us not blame the whole race.

JARVIS—You think he will be found?

ELAND—He will be found.

JARVIS—May he suffer as we suffer. As my wife suffers now.

ELAND—There's something I wanted to ask you, Mr. Jarvis. If you'd rather not stay in this house—

JARVIS—I want to stay here. This is where he worked. He was here when he heard the cry from the kitchen and ran to help.

ELAND—He will be a great loss to us. To our country and to me personally. As parole officer—well, many times I'd have given up in despair except for him.

JARVIS—And yet they killed him. What would he have said about a crime like this?

ELAND—He would have said, "They live in such poverty and fear. They see no way out of their poverty or their fear and they grow desperate."

JARVIS—Yes. (*He sits.*) It sounds like him.

The parole officer leaves the elder man alone, and as the library darkens the chant of "Murder in Parkwold!" is heard again. And along a street in Shanty Town there is fear. At the sound of a warning whistle, several groups of Zulus who have been reading newspapers vanish into the houses and the houses go dark. A white man and woman, obviously fearful, show relief when a police officer walks down the street and escorts them on their way. There is a chorus of whites and blacks which tells of fear—the whites afraid because the blacks are so many and they are so few; the blacks fear the whip, the guard, the loss of a house, the mines, prison. . . .
Together, whites and blacks sing:

Fear of the few for the many,
Fear of the many for the few.

Eland has sent for Stephen and has told him that Absalom is in prison. "It's not proved, of course—but the charge is that he killed Arthur Jarvis." The old man cannot believe what he has heard, and Eland must repeat it, gently. The officer takes Stephen to Absalom's cell, where the boy is sitting on a stool. "My father!" he cries.

Says Stephen, "I have searched in every place for you—and I find you here. Why have they charged you with this terrible crime?" Absalom does not answer, and his father entreats, "Answer me, my child." Still there is no answer. To Stephen there is no question of his son's innocence, and he reassures the boy. "The courts are just, and when they have found that you did not kill it will be only a light punishment. And when it ends you will come back to Ndotsheni and be content in our quietness. For you were a boy without guile and without anger. . . . The hills are as beautiful as ever, Absalom. You will be happy there again."

Finally Absalom brings himself to say what he must: "I shall never come home."

"Why, my son?"

"Because I am guilty."

"Of what, my son?"

Absalom pauses, for it is hard to say it. Then, "I killed the white man."

This, to the old man, is incomprehensible. A guard comes to end the interview, and tells Stephen he may pay other visits at certain hours on certain days. Dazedly, Stephen turns to go, saying, "Stay well, my child." "Go well, my father," replies Absalom.

Stephen returns to his Shanty Town room and Alex. The boy is still awake, although it is very late; he is happy and excited about the shoes Stephen has bought him, and he wants to chatter; but the old man begs him to be still, for there is a letter to write.

"Who do you write to, Uncle Stephen?"

"I write to my wife in Ndotsheni. To the mother at home. O, *Tixo, Tixo!* O God of all lost people and of those who go toward death, tell me what to say to her! How can I say this to the mother, O my *Tixo?* That he has done this thing! That I cannot bring him home! That he will perhaps never, never come home!"

Stephen sings "Lost in the Stars":

(EDITOR'S NOTE: Mr. Anderson and Mr. Weill wrote this song several years ago, before Mr. Paton's novel was written. They thought it fitted the adaptation so well that they not only included it, but also made its title the title of their musical play.)

> *Before Lord God made the sea and the land*
> *He held all the stars in the palm of his hand,*
> *And they ran through his fingers like grains of sand,*
> *And one little star fell alone.*
>
> *Then the Lord God hunted through the wide night air*
> *For the little dark star on the wind down there—*
> *And he stated and promised he'd take special care*
> *So it wouldn't get lost again.*
>
> *Now a man don't mind if the stars grow dim*
> *And the clouds blow over and darken him,*
> *So long as the Lord God's watching over them,*
> *Keeping track how it all goes on.*
>
> *But I've been walking through the night and the day*
> *Till my eyes get weary and my head turns gray,*
> *And sometimes it seems maybe God's gone away,*
> *Forgetting the promise that we heard him say—*
> *And we're lost out here in the stars—*

Little stars, big stars,
Blowing through the night,
And we're lost out here in the stars.

The curtain falls.

ACT II

Stephen is in the tobacco shop of his brother John—John the cynic, John the practical, who has hired a good lawyer, a white man's lawyer. He is trying to reassure Stephen, and says that there is no evidence against Matthew, Absalom and Johannes except one shaky identification. Stephen is not so sure; the boys *were* there and they will have to tell the truth.

John—The truth! Why would they tell the truth in a court? Do they want to get themselves hanged? No, if they all say they know nothing about it, they'll get off, as sure as God's got whiskers.

Stephen—But in a court there is a plea—guilty or not guilty.

John—Yes. They'll plead not guilty. Everybody does.

Stephen—But Absalom says he will plead guilty.

John—Good God! Why?

Stephen—Because he is guilty.

John—Look, Stephen, if they don't all tell the same story, anything can happen to them. Surely you see that. Let them prove the boys guilty if they can. It's not up to the defense to hand 'em their case on a platter.

Stephen—I haven't told Absalom what to say. But he says he will not lie again. That he's done his last evil, and from now on he won't tell a lie or do any wrong. And so he will tell them that he was there. And that he shot Arthur Jarvis.

John—Will he tell them Matthew was there—and Johannes?

Stephen—Yes.

John—Well—that changes everything. You better fix that, brother, and fix it fast, or I give you my word we'll fix Absalom. Talk to him, brother.

Stephen—I have. He will plead guilty.

John—A man who pleads guilty to murder receives the punishment of the first degree—and that's hanging by your neck with a sack over your head. They don't fool about that.

Stephen—He has already made a confession. He has admitted the whole charge.

John—He can deny that. He can say he was out of his mind—anything.

STEPHEN—And Matthew and Johannes will plead not guilty?

JOHN—Of course they will. That's part of the game. This is what happens in a court, Stephen. The defendant may be guilty as hell but he goes in and pleads not guilty and his lawyer tries to make the evidence look as if he's not guilty. The prosecution may be weak as hell but it goes in and tries to make things look as if the defendant's guilty as a hyena. Each one tries to foul up the witnesses on the other side and make his own witnesses look good. If the defense piles up the most points, why fine, the old sheep-face of a judge says he's not guilty. If the prosecution piles up the most points, why old sheep-face says hang him up. It's a game. Truth has nothing to do with it. Now if Absalom pleads guilty it would make it look bad for all three—but don't let him do it, brother, because I'm going to get Matthew out of this, and anything Absalom says is going to be used against him. By me, if necessary. So talk to him, Stephen, talk to him as you never talked to anybody before. He doesn't want to die—and you don't want him to die. If you want him to live, tell him to plead not guilty.

What John has said is a new torture for the gentle soul of Stephen Kumalo, a profound problem in ethics and religion. He debates it in a song, "The Soliloquy." Must his boy tell a lie and live—or speak the truth and die? How can he advise Absalom? He, who always told his boy to speak truly. Can he go to Absalom now and advise him to tell no truth in the court? "I must find some other way—some other hope," he concludes. "My son did not mean to kill his son, did not mean to kill."

Perhaps this other way, this other hope, lies with another father —the father of the murdered man. Stephen goes timidly to the well-kept residence in Johannesburg where James Jarvis now is living and knocks at the door. Jarvis himself answers, and tells this black minister who has called that the servants are away today. "I wish to see you," Stephen falters. His body fails him; his cane clatters to the ground, his hat falls off and he sinks to the step. Jarvis, concerned, offers water, or food if the visitor is hungry. Stephen rallies and stands erect, retrieving his cane. Jarvis picks the old man's hat from the ground and hands it to him. "Thank you, sir. I am sorry. I shall go now," says Stephen.

Jarvis interposes, "But you said you wished to see me."

"I have no words to say it."

"I wish to help whenever I can. Is it so heavy a thing?"

"It is the heaviest thing of all my years. . . . It is also the heaviest thing of all your years."

Jarvis has an inkling of what Stephen is trying to say, even before Stephen comes out with it: "It was my son that killed your son." Stephen begs for Jarvis' help—perhaps his intercession in court. He has had the truth from Absalom—and the boy may die for this truthtelling. Yet the lad never meant to kill; the revolver was in his hand and when he heard someone coming he was frightened.

JARVIS—Have you thought what it is for me that my son is dead?

STEPHEN—I have tried. I have thought of—my son—

JARVIS—Have you thought what it is for his mother? His mother will die of this. It's in her face.

STEPHEN—I know. I can see the face of my son's mother. Forgive me, umnumzana—I know what this is to you. But—if he were only to live—even shut up—even far from us.

JARVIS—I try to be just. I know what it is to lose a son. But —I say again—one does not try to influence a court. And even if the judge were merciful, mercy can be pitiless. If your son went free ten thousand others might be misled into the death he escaped. Better that one be punished where punishment is deserved —and the ten thousand be warned.

STEPHEN—I think he did not mean evil, umnumzana. And to die—when he is loved—

JARVIS—I know about death.

STEPHEN—If I could take him back to his home, umnumzana! Away from Johannesburg. He grew up in Ndotsheni. Among the hills. There was no evil in him then. From our house we could see up through the clove to your great house. You were kind to the folk who worked the little farms. Be kind again. A terrible thing has befallen my people. We are lost. Not many have found their way to the Christ, and those who have not are lost. My son was lost. This would not have happened if there were not the gold mines, and the great city your people have built, and the little hope we have.

JARVIS—Umfundisi, there are two races in South Africa. One is capable of mastery and self-control—the other is not. One is born to govern, the other to be governed. One is capable of culture and the arts of civilization—the other is not. The difference between us is greater than that I live on a hill and you live in the valley. If my son had killed your son I would not have come to you for mercy. Nor to the judge. Whether it were my son or yours, I would have said, let him answer the law!

STEPHEN—You—you could save him—

JARVIS—You have neither heard nor understood me! There is only a handful of whites in South Africa to control the great tide of blacks—and the blacks have no control of their own! They have no mind to it—and no mind for it! It's their way to run and evade and lie and strike down in the dark! Those who will not keep order must be kept in order! Those who lift their hands to kill must know that the penalty for death is death!

STEPHEN (*humbly*)—Umnumzana—I read my Testament carefully. Jesus has not said this.

JARVIS—No, he has not, but where there is government it's true. Have you more to say to me?

STEPHEN—No, umnumzana.

Stephen has gone. Next he comes to the hut of Irina, where the girl is hanging some clothes on a line and singing a song, "Stay Well":

(EDITOR'S NOTE: Lyrically and musically, "Stay Well" is widely considered the loveliest of the songs in "Lost in the Stars." For this play, Kurt Weill provided music of great range, much of it melodious, some of it with the beat and rhythm of the South African tribes. As was his practice, Mr. Weill himself wrote the orchestrations for his songs and choruses, and they added to the richness of his work. They may be heard in a phonograph album of "Lost in the Stars.")

> *If I tell truth to you,*
>   *My love, my own,*
> *Grief is your gift to me,*
>   *Grief alone,*
> *Wild passion at midnight,*
>   *Wild anger at dawn,*
> *Yet when you're absent*
>   *I weep you gone.*

> *Stay well, O keeper of my love,*
> *Go well, throughout all your days,*
> *Your star be my luckiest star above*
> *Your ways the luckiest ways.*
> *Since unto you my one love is given,*
> *And since with you it will remain,*
> *Though you bring fear of hell, despair of heaven,*
> *Stay well, come well to my door again.*

Stephen has come to tell Irina that the trial will begin tomorrow and to ask if she wants to be there. She does, for then she can see Absalom. She asks hopefully if he might go free and Stephen replies, "I wish I could say yes. He says he will plead guilty. He says he will speak the truth. If he does I think he will stay in the prison. For a long time."

Irina muses on that phrase, "for a long time." She decides, "I would wait."

Stephen continues, "He has asked me—would you wish to marry him in the prison—so your child will have his name?"

The answer is simply, "Yes." . . .

A courtroom. The judge is seated. Absalom and Matthew are in the prisoner's dock. And in the courtroom are all those concerned with the case or related to the prisoners; in addition there are many Zulu spectators. The whites are on the other side of the room from the Zulus. Johannes Pafuri is in the witness box, and Burton, the defense lawyer John Kumalo has hired, is questioning him.

Johannes is denying that he was in Arthur Jarvis' house when the man was killed. He was at Mrs. Ndela's house. He knows he was there at eleven o'clock, because he and others had been dancing until shortly before then at another place. And he was not alone at Mrs. Ndela's; Matthew and the girls Linda and Rose were with him.

Matthew is called to the box, and his denial is precisely the same. The lawyer then asks, "Do you know Absalom Kumalo?" Matthew replies that he does.

"Was he with you on this evening?"

"No, sir."

Lawyer Burton's next witness will be Absalom, but before he calls the boy he addresses the court: "I wish to explain that his plea of guilty is his own choice, and that I have not attempted to influence him in any way."

Absalom's answers are brief and direct. He was in the kitchen of Arthur Jarvis on the night of October 8. Matthew Kumalo and Johannes Pafuri were with him. They had gone there to steal. Johannes had said the house would be empty at this time. Absalom tells of the servant having discovered them and crying out for his master. "Then a white man came into the doorway. I was frightened. I fired the revolver. The white man fell. Matthew said, 'We must go.' So we all went quickly." Absalom wandered about looking for a place to hide.

The judge takes over the questioning, learning that Absalom had bought the revolver from "a man." It had two bullets in it, and Absalom had fired one at a tree. "And," pursues the judge, "when Matthew Kumalo and Johannes Pafuri say they were not with you at the time of the murder they are lying?"

"Yes, they are lying."

Absalom does not know where they went. He went to a plantation and buried the revolver.

"And what did you do next?"

"I prayed there." Absalom, continuing his answers to the judge, relates how the police brought Johannes to where he was, and how he had told the police it was he, not Johannes, who had killed the white man.

"And every word you have said is true?"

"Every word is true."

"There is no lie in it?"

"There is no lie in it," replies the boy, "for I said to myself, I shall not lie any more, all the rest of my days, nor do anything more that is evil."

The lights dim in the courtroom and the chorus sings of a man who has killed being again in this place. "And are the terms of justice clearly met? Not yet, no, not quite yet."

But the terms of justice *have* been met when the lights of the courtroom come up again. The judge begins to state the verdict of his "assessors" and himself, carefully reviewing the legal aspects of the evidence. It seems quite possible, he admits, that Matthew and Johannes are guilty with Absalom. Their alibis are obviously doubtful. "And yet," he says, "after long and thoughtful consideration, my assessors and I have come to the conclusion that the guilt of Matthew and Johannes is not sufficiently established. There remains the case of Absalom Kumalo. . . . His guilt is not established in the testimony alone, but that testimony, taken together with his confession, leads us inescapably to the conclusion that he is guilty.

"Matthew Kumalo and Johannes Pafuri, you are discharged and may step down." The young men move into the group of spectators and are joined by Linda and Rose, as the judge continues:

"Absalom Kumalo, have you anything to say before I pronounce sentence?"

Absalom answers, "I have only this to say, that I killed this man, but I did not mean to kill him, only I was afraid."

The judge puts a little black cap on his head and pronounces sentence: Absalom is to be hanged by the neck until he is dead, and may the Lord have mercy on his soul. First to arise in the courtroom is the stricken Irina, next the stricken Stephen. Stephen goes to his son, who is stunned and motionless, and on the way encounters Jarvis. Jarvis wordlessly steps aside and lets Stephen pass.

Absalom is returned to his cell. Some time afterward, Stephen takes Irina to him, and here, with the boy within the bars and the other two without, the Reverend Stephen Kumalo conducts the marriage service and commands the young people "to live together after God's ordinance in the holy estate of Matrimony."

When he has finished, Stephen says, "And now you are man and wife, my son and my daughter. Irina will come with me to Ndotsheni, Absalom. We shall care for your child as if it were our own."

Absalom does not want to say good-by to Irina now. He must go to Pretoria. There will be an appeal. "But it will not help," the boy predicts with growing terror. "I am afraid. I am afraid of the hanging."

"Be of courage, my son."

Absalom cries, "It's no help to be of courage! *O Tixo, Tixo*, I am afraid of the rope and the hanging!" Irina sinks to her knees in prayer, and a guard comes to tell the visitors it is time to go. "Where *I* go," calls Absalom, "there will be no wife or child or father or mother!"

Time has passed—time for the appeal, time for Stephen to take Irina and little Alex to his home, time for young Edward to have another holiday from school and to return to his grandfather's house.

Alex is a happy lad. He is playing with a Negro boy and girl near Stephen Kumalo's chapel. He has fashioned a crude toy, a digging machine, and is singing a song about Big Mole:

> *Big Mole was a digger of the fastest kind;*
> *He'd dig in the earth like you think in your mind;*
> *When Big Mole came to the side of a hill*
> *Instead of going over he'd start in to drill.*
> *He promised his mother a well in the town*
> *And he brought boiling water from a thousand feet down!*
>
> *Down, down, down, down,*
> *Three mile, four mile, five mile down;*
> *He can go through rock, he can go through coal;*
> *Whenever you come to an oversize hole*
> *Down at the bottom is Big Black Mole!*
> *Big Black Mole, Big Black Mole!*

Young Edward Jarvis has come upon the three Negroes and stands listening, enchanted, as Alex continues the fanciful tale of Big

Mole, who once was put to work in a mine and chunked out a city six mile in the ground—who dug so well, in fact, that he broke right into the ceiling of hell and looked the old devil spang in the eye and defied him.

Edward gives the youngsters a pleasant "Hi." Alex calls a return "Hi" but the other two Negroes run off. Edward says he likes Alex's big voice, and explains he is waiting for his grandfather to come along. He admires the digging machine, too. "What's your name?" he asks.

"Alex."

"Mine's Edward. I guess your uncle's the umfundisi here." Edward admits he knows some Zulu words that his father taught him and would like to know more—for instance, how to say, "The English boy is dying for water." "Only," says Edward, "I'd rather have milk out of the fridge."

"Fridge" is a new word to Alex, until Edward explains it means refrigerator. "We have no milk," says Alex. "Nobody has milk in Ndotsheni." He offers to get Edward some water, but the white boy says never mind and turns his attention to the toy. "You've got a real idea here," he says. "If you had something heavy on the string and it had a point on it, and it kept dropping on the ground, it would really dig."

This discussion of mechanical improvement is cut short by James Jarvis's arrival. Alex is afraid of this man, and he runs off. "Goodby, Alex," Edward calls. The Negro boy stops and calls, "Good-by —Edward!"

Jarvis is immensely offended at his grandson and tells him sternly that he must never be seen talking with this boy again. Edward protests, "But I like him. He's bright and nice." Jarvis sits on the ground, head in hands, a sad, tired and puzzled man. He no longer knows why a man should work for gain, or for love of his child, or why any child should obey. "But I do know this," he concludes, perhaps more to himself than to his grandson, "there are some things that I cannot bear to look on."

Someone begins to play the organ in the chapel. Inside the chapel parishioners have gathered and Stephen and Grace enter. Jarvis can see it all from where he sits on a step outside. He can hear, too, as the minister addresses his people.

STEPHEN—My son Absalom will die tomorrow morning on the scaffold for a murder to which he confessed, and of which he was guilty. You all know of this. The man he killed was known to

you, too. He was Arthur Jarvis. He was born in the hills above
our little town. There was a brightness upon him even as a child.
As a man he was a friend of our race, a friend of all men, a man all
men could be proud of. And my son—killed him. And the mother
of Arthur Jarvis is dead of grief for her son. My people, if I stay
here now I become a hindrance to you, and not a help. I must go.

PARISHIONERS—You cannot go, umfundisi! You cannot go! No,
umfundisi!

STEPHEN—This is a poor village, Ndotsheni, and it grows poorer.
In the past when our little church was in desperate need we have
sometimes turned to Arthur Jarvis, and he has helped us. He will
not help here again. And no one will help you while I remain here,
for the man who slew him was my son. I must go for still another
reason, my dear people. When I began to serve my God and my
church I had a sure faith that the God of our world ordered things
well for men. I had a sure faith that though there was good and
evil I knew which was good, and God knew it—and that men were
better in their hearts for choosing good and not evil. Something
has shaken this in me. I am not sure of my faith. I am lost. I am
not sure now. I am not sure that we are not all lost. And a leader
should not be lost. He should know the way, and so I resign my
place.

A PARISHIONER—Umfundisi, if you have lost your faith, I too
have lost my faith.

PARISHIONERS—Yes.

McRAE—Where does a man go, and what does he do when his
faith is gone?

STEPHEN—I don't know.

PARISHIONERS—Oh, Stephen, you have always helped us. Please
stay!

STEPHEN—If I keep my place, and this black thing has happened
to my son and is said, little by little the few who still worship here
will shrink away, the rusty roof will leak more, the floor will break
till there is none, the windows will go—they will be thrown at and
broken and will go—and the unpainted sides of this chapel I have
loved will stand empty, roofless—and I shall live in despair beside it,
knowing that I have done this thing to you and to my church by
remaining. (STEPHEN *starts to go—they all reach out to him and
he pauses.*)

VILLAGER (*sings "A Bird of Passage"*)

> *Lord of the heart, look down upon*
> *Our earthly pilgrimage,*

> *Look down upon us where we walk*
> *From bright dawn to old age,*
> *Give light not shed by any sun.*

PARISHIONERS—Lord of the heart!
MAN—Not read on any page.
CHORUS—Lord of the heart!

> *A bird of passage out of night*
> *Flies in at a lighted door,*
> *Flies through and on in its darkened flight*
> *And then is seen no more.*

(STEPHEN *stands for a moment at the pulpit, then turns and goes out.*)

> *This is the life of men on earth:*
> *Out of darkness we come at birth*
> *Into a lamplit room, and then—*

EDWARD (*speaking through the music*)—What is it, Grandfather?
CHORUS (*sings*)—

> *Go forward into dark again,*
> *Go forward into dark again.*

Time can never be stilled. It is before daylight the next morning and Stephen is sitting at the table in the sitting room of his home— that room in which, at a time which now seems so long ago, a polite little girl brought the Reverend Kumalo a letter which had been mailed from the big city. Stephen cannot help watching a clock on a shelf, and the chorus says ominously, "Four o'clock, it will soon be four."

Irina comes from the kitchen and reports, "She has fallen asleep. She meant to sit and watch with you at this hour, and she has been awake till only now—but now she sleeps."

He asks Irina to go back and sit beside Grace, if she can, and adds with deep affection, "My daughter, I'm glad he found you and not some other." When Irina has returned to the kitchen Stephen talks to himself: "If they would kill me instead, Absalom would make a good man. But it will never be. He is waiting now. Sleep, O mother. Sleep sound. Soon Absalom will sleep."

Jarvis appears in the sitting room doorway and knocks. "May I come in?" Stephen does not know the reason for the visit at this hour, but he courteously invites the white man in. Jarvis explains, directly: "I stood outside your church yesterday and heard what you said to your people, and what they said to you. I want you to know that I will help you with the roof and with the painting—and whatever must be done. I will do whatever my son would have done."

Stephen stammers his thanks, then, looking at the clock, falters, "It's hard for me to think of the church or of—in a quarter of an hour my son is to die."

Jarvis knows. He hasn't been able to sleep, either, thinking about it. He knows his presence is painful, and yet—may he stay for a moment?

STEPHEN—If you wish.

JARVIS—Stephen Kumalo, my wife is dead. My son is dead. I live in a house with a child who knows me only as an old man. I have thought many times I would be better dead. I thought myself alone in this desolation that used to be my home. But when I heard you yesterday I knew that your grief and mine were the same. I know now that of all the men who live near this great valley you are the one I would want for a friend. And—I have been walking about—and came and knocked here now—because I wanted to sit with you in this hour—

STEPHEN—You want to sit with me?

JARVIS—Yes, if I may.

STEPHEN—Mr. Jarvis, you know that you can give me only charity. If you were seen to touch my hand, this town, this whole valley, would turn against you.

JARVIS—I've finished with that. I haven't come here lightly. I shall take your hand wherever I like, before whom I like. I shall come and worship in your church if I wish to worship. May I sit here with you?

STEPHEN—Yes, umnumzana. (JARVIS *starts to sit.*) This is not a good chair. (*He brings another chair and places it.* JARVIS *sits.*) It's almost the hour. O God—O *Tixo*—it is almost now.

JARVIS—But there will be a tomorrow, Stephen. Edward will come tomorrow to see Alex. He wants to come and play.

STEPHEN—I shall be gone. I shall never see this place again. Nor the path where Absalom ran to meet me—nor the hills where he played and came late to supper—nor the room where he slept—never, never again.

JARVIS—You must stay in Ndotsheni.

STEPHEN—If I stayed, do you know what I would preach here? That good can come from evil, and evil from good! That no man knows surely what is evil or what is good! That if there is a God

He is hidden and has not spoken to men! That we are all lost here, black and white, rich and poor, the fools and the wise! Lost and hopeless and condemned on this rock that goes 'round the sun without meaning!

JARVIS—Not hopeless, Stephen, and not without meaning. For even out of the horror of this crime some things have come that are gain and not loss. My son's words to me and my understanding of my son. And your words in the chapel, and my understanding of those words—and your son's face in the courtroom when he said he would not lie any more or do any evil. I shall never forget that.

STEPHEN—You think well of my son?

JARVIS—I tried not to. But you and I have never had to face what Absalom faced there. A man can hardly do better than he did when he stood before the judge. Stay in Ndotsheni, Stephen, stay with those who cried out to you in the chapel. You have something to give them that nobody else can give them. And you can be proud of Absalom.

STEPHEN—And he is forgiven, and I am forgiven?

JARVIS—Let us forgive each other.

STEPHEN—Umnumzana—umnumzana!

JARVIS—Let us be neighbors. Let us be friends.

STEPHEN—Umnumzana—before the clock strikes—I shall stay in Ndotsheni. You are welcome in this house. I have a friend.

JARVIS—I have a friend. (*The clock strikes four.* STEPHEN *sits and buries his head in his hands.* JARVIS *goes to him, puts an arm around him.*)

CHORUS (*sings*)—

> *Each lives alone in a world of dark,*
> *Crossing the skies in a lonely arc,*
> *Save when love leaps out like a leaping spark*
> *Over thousands, thousands of miles!*

CURTAIN

COME BACK, LITTLE SHEBA *

A Play in Two Acts

By William Inge

THE Theatre Guild is making intelligent and profitable use of the Country Playhouse at Westport, Conn., as a Summer tryout base. During its fifteen years of operation, the Playhouse has built a large audience—in 1950 the theatre was 85 per cent subscribed for when the doors opened—which seems to prefer new productions to stock revivals. Lawrence Langner, co-director of the Guild, operates the Country Playhouse with his wife, Armina Marshall, and John C. Wilson. Langner says the theatre gives the Guild and other New York managements an opportunity to test the works of new authors and works of more or less experimental nature comparatively easily and inexpensively—and the promising ones can be brought to Broadway at a fairly reasonable production cost. One of the recent successes cradled in Westport was Robert E. McEnroe's "The Silver Whistle."

A success of the 1949 Summer season was "Come Back, Little Sheba," by a new dramatist, William Inge (pronounced Inje). It was brought to New York by the Guild February 15, 1950, and has run well into the 1950-51 season, even though critical approval was not complete. The drama got one vote as the best play of the season in the balloting of the Critics Circle. The principal actors, Shirley Booth and Sidney Blackmer, won many citations and medals, including Antoinette Perry "Tonys" from the American Theatre Wing. Mr. Blackmer and Miss Booth, in the roles of Doc and Lola, a long-married couple, do their acting in the downstairs part of an old house in a semi-respectable neighborhood of a mid-Western city—Mr. Inge's own St. Louis, perhaps. One can see two rooms of the house, the living room and the kitchen, with a stairway and a door between. Another door leads from the living room to a ground-floor bedroom, which is rented out. The living room conveys the atmosphere of the Twenties, and is decorated with a cheap pretense at niceness and respectability; but it is cluttered, even dirty. The house next door shuts out direct sunlight, but the kitchen does get some sun mornings. In the living room the davenport is littered; in the kitchen last night's supper dishes are still on the table, and one of the chairs has Doc's coat draped over the back.

Doc is the first one up this morning, and he comes down and straightens up a bit in the kitchen. He takes a roll from a paper bag on the drainboard, puts it on a plate, lights the oven, loads a pan with the dirty dishes, puts them in the sink and turns on the water. He pauses at the table to say a silent prayer, then tucks a towel in his vest for an apron. This obviously is a long-established routine with Doc, and Doc is a nice-looking, routine man in his forties. He is soon joined by Marie, the young girl of 18 or 19 who rents the downstairs bedroom. Marie's hair is piled in curls on her head, and she wears a dainty negligee and smart, feathery mules. Her greeting to Doc—"Hi!"—has the cheerfulness of youth, and he returns a friendly, "Well, well, how is our star boarder this morning? Want your breakfast now?" Marie will just have her fruit juice and drink it while she dresses, and have the rest later. She is up a little early because she must go to the library and check out some books before somebody else gets them.

Doc—Yes, you want to study hard, Marie, learn to be a fine artist some day. Paint lots of beautiful pictures. I remember a picture my mother had over the mantelpiece at home, a picture of a cathedral in a sunset, one of those big cathedrals in Europe somewhere. Made you feel religious just to look at it.

Marie—These books aren't for art, they're for biology. I have an exam.

Doc—Biology? Why do they make you take biology?

Marie (laughs)—It's required. Didn't you have to take biology when you were in college?

Doc—Well . . . yes, but I was preparing to study medicine, so of course I had to take biology and things like that. You see—I was going to be a real doctor then—only I left college my third year.

Marie—What's the matter? Didn't you like the pre-med course?

Doc—Yes, of course . . . I had to give it up.

Marie—Why?

Doc (goes to stove with roll on plate—evasive)—I'll put your sweet roll in now, Marie, so it will be nice and warm for you when you want it.

Marie—Dr. Delaney, you're so nice to your wife, and you're so nice to me, as a matter of fact, you're so nice to everyone. I hope my husband is as nice as you are. Most husbands would never think of getting their own breakfast.

Doc (*very pleased with this*)— . . . uh . . . you might as well sit down now and . . . yes, sit here and I'll serve you your breakfast now, Marie, and we can eat it together, the two of us.

MARIE (*a light little laugh as she starts dancing away from him*)— No, I like to bathe first and feel that I'm all fresh and clean to start the day. I'm going to hop into the tub now. See you later. (*She goes upstairs.*)

Doc (*the words appeal to him*)—Yes, fresh and clean— (*Doc shows disappointment but goes on in businesslike way setting his breakfast on the table.*)

MARIE (*offstage*)—Mrs. Delaney.

LOLA (*offstage*)—'Mornin', honey. (*Then* LOLA *comes downstairs. She is a contrast to* DOC's *neat cleanliness, and* MARIE's. *Over a nightdress she wears a lumpy kimono. Her eyes are dim with a morning expression of disillusionment, as though she had had a beautiful dream during the night and found on waking none of it was true. On her feet are worn dirty comfies.*)

LOLA (*with some self-pity*)—I can't sleep late like I used to. It used to be I could sleep till noon if I wanted to, but I can't any more. I don't know why.

Doc—Habits change. Here's your fruit juice.

LOLA (*taking it*)—I oughta be gettin' your breakfast, Doc, instead of you gettin' mine.

Doc—I have to get up anyway, Baby.

LOLA (*sadly*)—I had another dream last night.

Doc (*pours coffee*)—About Little Sheba?

LOLA (*with sudden animation*)—It was just as real. I dreamt I put her on a leash and we walked downtown—to do some shopping. All the people on the street turned around to admire her, and I felt so proud. Then we started to walk, and the blocks started going by so fast that Little Sheba couldn't keep up with me. Suddenly, I looked around and Little Sheba was gone. Isn't that funny? I looked everywhere for her but I couldn't find her. And I stood there feeling sort of afraid. Do you suppose that means anything?

Doc—Dreams are funny.

LOLA—Do you suppose it means Little Sheba is going to come back?

Doc—I don't know, Baby.

LOLA (*petulant*)—I miss her so, Doc. She was such a cute little puppy. Wasn't she cute?

Doc (*smiles with the reminiscence*)—Yes, she was cute.

Lola—Remember how white and fluffy she used to be after I gave her a bath? And how her little hind-end wagged from side to side when she walked?

Doc—I remember.

Lola—She was such a cute little puppy. I hated to see her grow old, didn't you, Doc?

Doc—Yah. Little Sheba should have stayed young forever. Some things should never grow old. That's what it amounts to, I guess.

Lola—She's been gone for such a long time. What do you suppose ever happened to her?

Doc—You can't ever tell.

Lola—Do you suppose she got run over by a car? Or do you think that old Mrs. Coffman next door poisoned her? I wouldn't be a bit surprised.

Doc—No, Baby. She just disappeared. That's all we know.

Lola—Just vanished one day . . . vanished into thin air.

Doc—I told you I'd find you another one, Baby.

Lola—You couldn't ever find another puppy as cute as Little Sheba.

Doc (*back to reality*)—Want an egg?

Lola—No. Just this coffee. Have you said your prayer, Doc?

Doc—Yes, Baby.

Lola—And did you ask God to be with you—all through the day, and keep you strong?

Doc—Yes, Baby.

Lola—Then God will be with you, Docky. He's been with you almost a year now and I'm so proud of you.

Doc (*preening a little*)—Sometimes I feel sorta proud of myself.

Lola—Say your prayer, Doc. I like to hear it.

Doc (*matter-of-factly*)—God grant me the serenity to accept the things I cannot change, courage to change the things I can, and wisdom always to tell the difference.

Lola—That's nice. That's so pretty. When I think of the way you used to drink, always getting into fights, we had so much trouble. I was so scared! I never knew what was going to happen.

Doc—That was a long time ago, Baby.

Lola—I know it, Daddy. I know how you're going to be when you come home now.

Doc is rewarded with a light kiss—and well he might be, for he will have been sober a year next month, and he can skip meetings for a while now. Tonight, however, he can't take his wife to a movie because he is going out on some Twelfth Step work with Ed Anderson. The Twelfth Step is the final one in Alcoholics Anonymous: "After you learn to stay dry yourself, then you go out and help other guys that need it. . . . Most alcoholics are disappointed men. They need courage." Tonight's man is somebody who was picked up on Skid Row and is in the City Hospital, and Doc dreads the visit. "They put alcoholics right in with the crazy people. It's horrible. . . ."

Doc suggests that Lola go to the movies with Marie, but Lola figures the girl will be having a date with Turk—and this Doc disapproves of, for Marie is too nice a girl to be going out with a guy like Turk. The easygoing Lola is more tolerant; she has seen Marie kissing the boy like he was Rudolph Valentino—a statement which rouses Doc to a flash of angry disbelief. He likes to think that people like Marie are clean and decent.

The girl comes in, dressed, for her breakfast roll and coffee. Doc is about ready to go to the office and suggests that they walk to the corner together, but she says Turk is coming by; Lola won't walk with him either because she isn't even dressed. "If you get hungry," she offers, "come home and I'll have something for you." So, donning his coat, Doc departs the front way, and in the living room finds Marie's scarf on his hat on a chair. He fingers the scarf a moment, fondly.

Lola gets a more becoming smock out of a closet and dons it. Marie, killing time till Turk comes, admires the smock—then remembers something important: "I'm expecting a telegram this morning. Would you leave it on my dresser for me?"

"Not bad news, I hope."

"Oh, no! It's from Bruce."

The girl's boy friends are one of Lola's liveliest interests, so she knows who Bruce is—the one in Cincinnati. "Is he coming to see you?"

Marie's "I guess so" is not too enthusiastic. She would rather talk about Turk. Turk was saying just the other night what good sports Lola and Doc were. Lola likes Turk, too; he reminds her of a boy she used to know in high school. "Where did you ever meet him?"

"In art class."

"Turk take art?"

This is funny to Marie. "No, it was in a life class. He was modeling. Lots of the athletes do that. It pays them a dollar an hour. . . . I've got some corrections to make in some of my drawings. Is it all right if I bring Turk home to pose for me?"

Lola is agreeable; more than that, she remembers that Doc will be gone tonight, and the youngsters can have the living room then, too, if they want it. Lola switches to the subject of Bruce, about whom she wants to hear more.

"Well," says Marie, "he comes from one of the best families in Cincinnati. And they have a great big house. And they have a maid, too. And he's got a wonderful personality. He makes three hundred dollars a month."

"Do you like him as well as Turk?"

Marie says something evasive about Bruce being dependable and a gentleman. Almost pinned down by another question from Lola, the girl says maybe she will marry Bruce after she graduates from college and he feels he can support a wife and children. She is going to have lots and lots of children.

Lola had wanted children, too. "When I lost my baby and found out I couldn't have any more, I didn't know what to do with myself. I wanted to get a job, but Doc wouldn't hear of it." Doc had been rich—inherited $25,000 from his mother. But it took him a lot to get his office started and . . . then he got sick. Doc is good to her *now*, though, and Marie agrees, "Oh, Doc's a peach."

LOLA—I used to be pretty, something like you. (*She gets her picture from table.*) I was Beauty Queen of the senior class in high school. My dad was awful strict, though. Once he caught me holding hands with that good-looking Dutch McCoy. Dad sent Dutch home, and wouldn't let me go out after supper for a whole month. Daddy would never let me go out with boys much. Just because I was pretty. He was afraid all the boys would get the wrong idea—*you* know. I never had any fun at all until I met Doc.

MARIE—Sometimes I'm glad I didn't know my father. Mom always let me do pretty much as I please.

LOLA—Doc was the first boy my dad ever let me go out with. We got married that spring.

MARIE—What did your father think of that?

LOLA—We came right to the city then. And, well, Doc gave up his pre-med course and went to Chiropractor School instead.

MARIE—You must have been married awful young.

LOLA—Oh, yes. Eighteen.

MARIE—That must have made your father really mad.

LOLA—Yes, it did. I never went home after that, but my mother comes down here from Green Valley to visit me sometimes.

TURK (*bursts into the front room from outside. He is a big, husky, good-looking boy, 19 or 20. He has the openness, the gen-*

erosity, vigor and health of youth. He's had a little time in the service, but he is not what one would call disciplined. He wears faded dungarees and a T-shirt. He always enters unannounced. He hollers for MARIE)—Hey, Marie! Ready?

MARIE—Just a minute, Turk. (*She runs into her bedroom.*)

LOLA—I'll entertain him until you're ready. (*She is by nature coy and kittenish with any attractive man. Picks up papers—stuffs them under table.*) The house is such a mess, Turk! I bet you think I'm an awful housekeeper. Some day I'll surprise you. But you're like one of the family now. My, you're an early caller.

TURK—Gotta get to the library. Haven't cracked a book for a biology exam and Marie's gotta help me.

LOLA (*unconsciously admiring his stature and physique and looking him over*)—My, I'd think you'd be chilly running around in just that thin little shirt.

TURK—Me? I go like this in the middle of winter.

LOLA—Well, you're a big husky man.

TURK—Oh, I'm a brute, *I* am.

LOLA—You should be out in Hollywood making those Tarzan movies.

TURK—I had enough of that place when I was in the Navy.

LOLA—That so?

TURK (*calling*)—Hey, Marie, hurry up.

MARIE—Oh, be patient, Turk.

TURK—She doesn't realize how busy I am. I'll only have a half hour to study at most. I gotta report to the coach at 10:30.

LOLA—What are you in training for now?

TURK—Spring track. They got me throwing the javelin.

LOLA—The javelin? What's that?

TURK (*laughs at her ignorance*)—It's a big, long lance. (*Assumes the magnificent position.*) You hold it like this, erect—then you let go and it goes singing through the air, and lands yards away, if you're any good at it, and sticks in the ground, quivering like an arrow. I won the State championship last year.

LOLA (*she has watched as though fascinated*)—My!

Marie has readied herself, and the youngsters depart; Lola calls after them to remind them they can have the living room tonight if they want it—to play the radio and dance "or anything you want." Alone, Lola looks sad and vacant. Slowly she walks to the front porch and calls, "Little Sheba! Come, little She-ba. Come back . . . come back, Little Sheba!" After a few moments she returns wearily to the house; now the morning has caught up with her.

The dishes depress her, and clearly she is bored to death. The ring of the telephone promises a reprieve—but it is only somebody who has a wrong number. She hears the postman, and runs to the door to meet him, for here is another reprieve.

She invites the postman in to rest his feet and have a glass of water . . . and before the poor man can get away she has told him almost everything, eagerly, hurriedly. Postmen get good exercise. Her husband is a doctor—a *chiro*practor, and the only exercise he gets is rubbing people's backbones. He has strong hands but a poor digestion. He's an Alcoholics Anonymous, and is proud of it. Hasn't touched a drop in almost a year, and all the time they have had a quart of whiskey in the pantry for company. Liquor transforms alcoholics. The postman should have seen Doc before he gave it up. Lost all his patients and just wanted to stay drunk all day long. But he's got his patients all back and is just doing fine. . . .

The postman finally manages to escape, and Lola, alone, turns on the radio and faces the dishes again. When they are done she notices Mrs. Coffman out in the adjoining yard hanging up baby clothes and calls, "My, you're a busy woman this morning, Mrs. Coffman." Mrs. Coffman, sticking her head in for a moment, replies in a German accent, "I don't have it as easy as you. When you got seven kids to look after, you got no time to sit around the house, Mrs. Delaney." They talk for a moment or two, but Mrs. Coffman can't take the time to come in for a cup of coffee, and soon Lola is is alone again.

But not for long. The milkman arrives, and she opens the back door and detains him. "I think I'm going to want a few specials today. Can you come in a minute?" She orders cottage cheese, and coffee cream, and buttermilk. "My husband has liked buttermilk ever since he stopped drinking. My husband's an alcoholic."

The milkman would like very much to get away—until Lola catches him where he is vulnerable. "You're a husky young man. You oughta be out in Hollywood making those Tarzan movies." Now the milkman has to remain and tell her about how he keeps fit with bar bell exercises and doing forty push-ups every morning. He even shows Lola what a push-up is. He lets her feel his shoulder muscles. He'd stay even longer, letting Lola admire him, but his partner on the milk truck is getting impatient and sounds the horn.

Lola is alone once more—but this time it is not so bad, for she has noticed the clock and hurries to turn up the radio. The introduction is a tom-tom beat, and a dramatic voice begins with "'TA-BOOoooo!'" and continues with an unctuous invitation to come along to an enchanted and pagan land. Lola settles enchantedly on the davenport as the program begins—and is brought up to reality by the call of a Western Union boy at the door. He has a telegram for Miss Marie Buckholder. Lola, taking it, cannot resist steaming it open in the kitchen—just as Marie and Turk burst into the living room. Lola hides the telegram in the pocket of her smock.

The girl and boy have come to do their art work. "You can change in there, Turk," says Marie, indicating her bedroom.

"Change?" asks Lola.

"He's gotta take off his clothes."

The mystified woman is told about life classes. Women pose naked, Marie informs her, but men are always more proper, and Turk will pose in his track suit. Soon Turk emerges, and Lola fetches him a broom which he can use as a javelin for his pose. Marie sets to work, and Lola hovers around, admiring it, as long as she dares. Then she goes to the kitchen to make coffee and Turk steals a kiss just as Doc comes up on the porch, home for a snack. He tries to size up the art situation, but Marie and Turk seem too busy to speak. In the kitchen, Lola tells him about the life class and Turk's brief clothes. Doc doesn't think a young girl like Marie should be drawing things like that—drawing bodies right in a classroom.

Marie has finished her sketching and orders Turk to dress. Lola still is fascinated by art. "You know what Marie said, Doc? She said that the women pose naked but the men don't." It isn't news to Doc and he dismisses it. Then she tells him a secret: Bruce is coming—the boy friend from Cincinnati. And Lola is going to get out the best china and cook him and Marie the best meal they ever sat down to.

"When did she get the news?"

"The telegram came this morning."

"That's fine. That Bruce sounds to me just like the fellow for her. I think I'll go and congratulate her."

Lola is trapped—for Marie hasn't seen the message yet. She gets out of the jam, though, by pointing out that talking about Bruce might embarrass Turk. Turk certainly does not seem embarrassed at the moment, for he has emerged from the bedroom, dressed, and is making advances to Marie. But Doc, in the kitchen, is angry. He doesn't like the way Lola is always sticking up for Turk. The young man in question manages to seize the girl and kiss her passionately just as Doc, his voice raised, says to his wife, "If anything happens to that girl I'll never forgive you."

The curtain falls.

Scene II

The same evening, after supper. There has been an almost miraculous transformation of the house—rooms clean, new lamp shades, fresh curtains, junk disposed of, kitchen enamel gleaming. Lola has had a busy afternoon, and now, while Doc does the dishes, she putters around putting on finishing touches. "You know what?" she offers. "Mrs. Coffman says I could come over and pick all the lilacs I wanted for my centerpiece tomorrow. Isn't that nice? I don't think she poisoned Little Sheba, do you?"

Doc takes pains to admire the looks of the house, then asks where Marie is.

"I don't know, Doc. I haven't seen her since she left here this morning with Turk."

He growls, "Marie's too nice to be wasting her time with him." He goes into the living room, for it is almost time for Fibber McGee and Molly. Lola goes across to Mrs. Coffman's to borrow some silver polish, and Doc, alone, turns on the radio. He snaps off several noisy programs, finally locates a soprano solo of Schubert's "Ave Maria." He may have heard it before, but now it is new to him, and is lovely. The music has expressed some ideal of beauty he never fully realized . . . but the spell is broken when Lola slams in from the back door, all energy in spite of a hard afternoon's work—or perhaps because of it. Since it is not time yet for Fibber McGee, Lola suggests some peppy music and her husband obligingly locates a dance band. Bored himself, he takes a pack of cards off the radio and shuffles them, absently, but very deftly. "Do me one of your card tricks," Lola suggests.

This is a bore, for Lola has seen all his tricks dozens of times, but Doc, being nice, obliges with one, and Lola admires it as though she has never seen it before. She begs him to tell the secret of the trick and he teasingly refuses. Lola, now listening to the radio, starts dancing alone and reminisces about the dances they used to go to, and the time she and Charlie Kettlekamp won the Charleston contest. Doc has picked up the evening newspaper and her chatter is annoying, but she keeps it up. She teases him about how jealous he got every time they went out any place and she even looked at another boy. "There was never anything between Charlie and me; there never was."

Doc is listening with only half an ear as she talks of all the boys who asked her for dates. It was a long time ago. . . . He turns off the radio.

Lola (*in the same tone of reverie*)—I was pretty then, wasn't I, Doc? Remember the first time you kissed me? You were scared as a young girl, I believe, Doc; you trembled so. (*She is being very soft and delicate. Caught in the reverie, he chokes a little and cannot answer.*) We'd been going together all year and you were always so shy. Then for the first time you grabbed me and kissed me. Tears came to your eyes, Doc, and you said you'd love me forever and ever. Remember? You said . . . if I didn't marry you, you wanted to die. . . . I remember 'cause it scared me for anyone to say a thing like that.

Doc (*in a repressed tone*)—Yes, Baby.

Lola—And when the evening came on, we stretched out on the cool grass and you kissed me all night long.

Doc (*opens doors*)—Baby, you've got to forget those things. That was twenty years ago.

Lola—I'll soon be forty. Those years have just vanished—vanished into thin air.

Doc—Yes.

Lola—Just disappeared—like Little Sheba. Maybe you're sorry you married me now. You didn't know I was going to get old and fat and sloppy. . . .

Doc—Oh, Baby!

Lola—It's the truth. That's what I am. But I didn't know it, either. Are you sorry you married me, Doc?

Doc—Of course not.

Lola—I mean, are you sorry you *had* to marry me?

Doc (*goes to porch*)—We were never going to talk about that, Baby.

Lola (*following* Doc *out*)—You *were* the first one, Daddy, the *only* one. I'd just die if you didn't believe that.

Doc (*tenderly*)—I know, Baby.

Lola—You were so nice and so proper, Doc; I thought nothing we could do together could ever be wrong—or make us unhappy. Do you think we did wrong, Doc?

Doc—No, Baby, of course I don't.

Lola—I don't think anyone knows about it except my folks, do you?

Doc—Of course not, Baby.

Lola (*follows him in*)—I wish the baby had lived, Doc. I don't think that woman knew her business, do you, Doc?

Doc—I guess not.

Lola—If we'd gone to a doctor, she would have lived, don't you think?

Doc—Perhaps.

Lola—A doctor wouldn't have known we'd just got married, would he? Why were we so afraid?

Doc (*sits on couch*)—We were just kids. Kids don't know how to look after things.

Lola (*sits on couch*)—If we'd had the baby she'd be a young girl now; then may be you'd have *saved* your money, Doc, and she could be going to college—like Marie.

Doc—Baby, what's done is done.

Lola—It must make you feel bad at times to think you had to give up being a doctor and to think you don't have any money like you used to.

Doc—No . . . no, Baby. We should never feel bad about what's past. What's in the past can't be helped. You . . . you've got to forget it and live for the present. If you can't forget the past, you stay in it and never get out. I might be a big M.D. today, instead of a chiropractor; we might have had a family to raise and be with us now; I might still have a lot of money if I'd used my head and invested it carefully, instead of gettin' drunk every night. We might have a nice house, and comforts, and friends. But we don't have any of those things. So what! We gotta keep on living, don't we? I can't stop just 'cause I made a few mistakes. I gotta keep goin' . . . somehow.

Lola—Sure, Daddy.

Doc (*sighs and wipes brow*)—I . . . I wish you wouldn't ask me questions like that, Baby. Let's not talk about it any more. I gotta keep goin', and not let things upset me, or . . . or . . . *I* saw enough at the City Hospital to keep me sober for a long time.

Lola asks what time Doc will be home tonight, and he says about eleven; she is beginning to feel lonesome already. He promises that some time soon he will take her out to a good dinner at the Windermere and they will dance between courses. He kinda hates to go to night clubs since he stopped drinking. Lola is eager and pleased, and says she has about forty dollars saved in the kitchen. "I'll have plenty of money the first of the month," he assures her. Lola, inspired, turns on the radio, finds a dance program, seizes her husband and begins to dance. Soon he is dancing vigorously—but it winds him and he stops. Lola, still wound up, does a solo Charleston and Marie bursts in upon them and asks if Mrs. Delaney is trying to do a jig. She doesn't mean her remark to be cruel, but Lola abruptly stops her dancing and, almost ready to cry, goes to the kitchen.

Marie notices the fine appearance of the living room and Doc asks
if she thinks her boy friend will like it. He means Bruce, but
Marie doesn't. On her way to her bedroom she blows a kiss to Doc
and replies, "You know how men are. Turk never notices things
like that."

Lola returns, dabbing at her eyes, and in a moment Marie bounces
out of her room with the telegram. "When did it come?"

Lola, looking nervously at Doc, answers, "It came about an hour
ago, honey." Marie reads the message. Bruce will arrive by air
tomorrow at 5 P.M. Love. Lola, still nervous, pretends surprise at
the news. "Isn't it nice I got the house all cleaned? Marie, you
bring Bruce to dinner with us tomorrow night. It'll be a sort of
wedding present."

The front bell rings. It's Turk. "Don't tell *him*," whispers
Marie, as Lola and Doc retire to the kitchen. Turk immediately
stalks the girl and kisses her, but Marie warns him to stop because
"they" are in the kitchen, and the boy subsides with a book.

Doc is displeased with his wife about the telegram. "Why didn't
you give it to her when it came?" Lola alibis about Turk posing
in the morning, and Doc admonishes her that it isn't nice to open
other people's mail. Lola sees no harm in it; she sealed the envelope back and Marie won't know the difference. Doc gives up
and gets ready to go on his Twelfth Step assignment, and Lola is
contrite. She suggests that on his way out Doc might entertain
Marie and Turk with a few card tricks, and he is willing—but Lola,
peeking into the living room, sees the youngsters spooning behind
a book and in a secretive voice giggles, "I guess they wouldn't be
interested now. Come and look, Daddy." Shocked and angry, he
refuses, and scolds his wife for snooping. Lola can't see any harm
in it. "You watch young people make love in the movies, don't
you?" He gives up again.

Marie and Turk seek the privacy of the porch while Doc reproves
his wife for encouraging that sort of thing—and for liking Turk.
"I say he's no good. Marie's sweet and innocent. I think I oughta
run him outa the house." His voice has risen and she shushes him.
Bruce is coming and Turk won't be around any longer, she predicts.
"All right," he says. "I better go."

His wife offers to walk with him a way and runs upstairs for a
sweater. Turk's laugh is heard from the porch. Doc sees the
whiskey bottle and reaches for it. Marie giggles. Doc, repressing
himself, turns his back on the bottle, and when Lola comes down
they depart to the bus line. Turk observes, "He hates my guts."

The boy thinks Doc is jealous, but Marie assures him Doc has never made a pass at her. He's just nice.

Turk, getting down to business, suggests a snuggle, but Marie is in a withholding mood. He calls her bluff by pretending to go home, and they sit on the couch. He mimicks her: "Oh, no, Turk. Not tonight, Turk. I want to talk about philosophy. . . . When all the time you know that if I went outa here without givin' you a good lovin' up you'd be sore as hell. . . . Wouldn't you?"

MARIE (*she has to admit to herself it's true; she chuckles*)—Oh . . . Turk . . .

TURK—It's true, isn't it?

MARIE—Maybe.

TURK—How about tonight, lovely; going to be lonesome?

MARIE—Turk, you're in training.

TURK—What of it? I can throw that old javelin any old time, *any* old time. C'mon, Baby, we've got by with it before, haven't we?

MARIE—I'm not so sure.

TURK—What do you mean?

MARIE—Sometimes I think Mrs. Delaney knows.

TURK—Well, bring her along. I'll take care of her, too, if it'll keep her quiet.

MARIE (*a pretense of being shocked*)—Turk!

TURK—What makes you think so?

MARIE—Women just sense those things. She asks so many questions.

TURK—She ever *say* anything?

MARIE—No.

TURK—Now *you're* imagining things.

MARIE—Maybe.

TURK—Well, stop it.

MARIE—O.K.

TURK (*follows* MARIE)—Honey, I know I talk awful rough around you at times; I never was a very gentlemanly bastard, but you really don't mind it . . . do you? (*She only smiles mischievously.*) Anyway, you know I'm nuts about you.

MARIE (*smug*)—Are you? (*Now they engage in a little rough-house, he cuffing her like an affectionate bear, she responding with "Stop it," "Turk, that hurt," etc. And she slaps him playfully. Then they laugh together at their own pretense. Now* LOLA *enters the back way very quietly, tiptoeing through the dark kitchen, standing by the doorway where she can peek at them. There is a quiet,*

*satisfied smile on her face. She watches every move they make,
alertly.*)

TURK—Now, Miss Buckholder, what is your opinion of the psychodynamic pressure of living in the atomic age?

MARIE—Turk, don't make fun of me.

TURK—Tonight?

MARIE (*her eyes dance as she puts him off just a little longer*)—
Well.

TURK—Tonight will never come again.   O.K.?

MARIE—Tonight will never come again. . . . (*They embrace and
start to dance.*)   Let's go out somewhere first and have a few beers.
We can't come back till they're asleep.

TURK—O.K.   (*They dance slowly out the door.   Then* LOLA
*moves quietly into the living room and out onto the porch.   There
she can be heard calling plaintively in a lost voice.*)

LOLA—Little Sheba . . . Come back . . . Come back, Little
Sheba.   Come back.

The curtain falls.

ACT II

It is the next morning, and about what it was yesterday morning,
with Doc nearly ready to go, but sitting meditatively and scarcely
listening to his wife's chatter.   She seems to be talking about Marie
and Turk dancing last night and then going out together. . . . She
chuckles as though the faults of youth were as blameless as the uncontrollable actions of a puppy.

Doc doesn't want to hear any more about it.   He didn't sleep
well last night; doesn't feel good.   He asks, "What time did Marie
come home last night?"

"I don't know, Doc.   I went to bed early and went right to sleep.
Why? . . . You musta slept if you didn't hear her."

"I heard her.   It was after midnight."

"Then what did you ask me for?"

"I wasn't sure it was her. . . . I thought I heard a man's voice.
I thought I heard someone laughing.   A man's laugh. . . . I guess
I was just hearing things."

He gets up to go and Lola, accepting a kiss, asks if he can get
home a little early and help entertain Bruce.   They are going to
have a lovely dinner.   Doc says he will be early, and goes into the
living room.   Marie's scarf is on the chair again, and, as before,
he picks it up and fondles it.   Then, barely audible, comes the

sound of Turk's laughter, and Doc's body stiffens. It is a sickening fact he must face. He has been fighting the truth, maybe suspecting all along that he was deceiving himself, and now he looks as though he might vomit. With a blank look on his face he stumbles into the table above the sofa. Lola calls, "Haven't you gone yet, Docky?" As she comes to the doorway he drops the scarf, takes his hat, braces himself and goes out.

Mrs. Coffman calls "Anybody home?" from the kitchen door and Lola goes back to greet her. Marie's door opens a fraction and the girl's head appears for an instant; then she ducks back to whisper to Turk that the coast is clear. Meanwhile, Mrs. Coffman is almost overcome with admiration at what Lola has done in the kitchen, and Lola boasts that she has fixed the living room up a little, too.

"I must see it," announces Mrs. Coffman, and Turk, who has been sneaking out, barely has time to make it back to Marie's room. Mrs. Coffman says seeing the house so clean makes her ashamed, and she's got to go home and work herself.

When Marie hears the back screen door slam she comes out and guards the living room-kitchen door, to keep Lola in the kitchen, and Turk slips out the front. As soon as she thinks it is safe she says a playful "Boo!" at Lola. It is Saturday and the girl could have slept late, but she wants to help with the dinner preparations.

Turk, however, has not gone unseen—for Doc returns and they meet at the front door. There is a moment of blind embarrassment, and then Turk, muttering an unintelligible apology, scurries out. At first Doc is merely mystified and is trying to figure things out when Marie encounters him on her way back to the bedroom. She is startled, for she thought he had gone. She falters, "Why . . . why . . . how long have you been here, Doc?"

"Just got here this minute." Lola hears him. He explains weakly that he just thought he might feel better if he had a glass of soda water. He makes it in the kitchen and stands at the drainboard, sipping . . . and thinking. In the living room the women are setting the table—setting it with the Irish linen cloth Doc's mother gave them when they got married, and the silver and Haviland china, too. Next come the napkins and they are upstairs. Lola and Marie go up to get them and Doc listens cannily as he looks cautiously at the whiskey bottle on the pantry shelf. After a brief struggle with himself he grabs the bottle, then wonders how he can get out with it. He solves this by taking his trench coat out of the pantry closet and draping it over his prize. He is again ready to go as his wife and Marie come down. "Get home early as you can," Lola reminds him, and he answers, "Yes, Baby."

When he has gone, Lola admires her table for a moment and then her expression changes to one of puzzlement as she muses aloud, "Now that's funny. Why did Doc take his raincoat? It's a beautiful day. There isn't a cloud in sight."

The curtain falls.

Scene II

Everything is ready for the party, for it is 5:30. The women, dressed in their best, are still primping the table and lighting the tapers. Lola is a little worried that Doc isn't home yet—but she is just dying to meet Bruce. "I feel sorta bad I never got to do anything nice for Turk," she says.

Marie, carefully prying, asks if Doc ever said anything about Turk and her. Doc hasn't.

"Aren't you being kind of mean to Turk?"

"He may be sore for a little while, but he'll get over it."

Lola asks, "Won't he feel bad?"

"He's had his eye on a pretty little Spanish girl in history class for a long time," Marie explains. "I like Turk, but he's not the marrying kind."

Wonder and disillusionment are like a physical blow to the romantic older woman, and she sinks abruptly to the arm of the couch. The doorbell rings and Marie answers it, for it is Bruce, a nice-looking young man who says, "How are you, sweetheart?" Marie introduces him to Lola and informs him, "Mrs. Delaney has fixed the grandest dinner for us."

Bruce objects affably. This was to be his treat. He has a big expense account now, and he thought they could all go down to the hotel for dinner and celebrate with a few cocktails first.

"Oh, we can have cocktails, too," says Lola, brightly. She goes to the kitchen and starts looking for the bottle. While Bruce is kissing Marie for the first time, asking if they've got to stay here the whole evening, and telling about getting a raise, Lola is becoming more and more frantic in her search. Presently she hurries into the living room and suggests that the kids entertain themselves for a while—turn on the radio and get some dance music—while she works in the kitchen. "I'll shut the door so . . . so I won't disturb you."

With the door closed, Lola swiftly dials a number and asks if Doc is there. Well, then, is Ed Anderson there? Apparently Ed isn't either, and she leaves a message for him to call right away if he comes in. She explains, "You see, he sponsored Doc in the club and helped him . . . you know. . . ."

She returns to the living room and announces they will go ahead without Doc. Doc got held up at the office. And now Lola will be the butler and serve the dinner for the two lovebirds alone. When the phone rings she rushes to it, closing the door behind her. It is Ed, and Ed hasn't seen Doc. She tells him about the missing bottle. "And you let me know when you find out anything," she implores.

Lola gets some tomato juice glasses from the ice box, brings them in, and begins serving. She says she really isn't hungry—and she's sorry there isn't time for cocktails. She turns up the radio and a Viennese waltz comes on as

The curtain falls.

SCENE III

It is about 5:30 the next morning. The remains of the dinner still clutter the table. Lola, who has been sleeping on the davenport, slowly comes awake. Her pretty dress is wrinkled now, her coiffure is awry, and one stocking has twisted loose and fallen around her ankle. When she is sufficiently awake to realize what has been happening—or not happening—she rushes to the phone and calls Ed Anderson again. "I'm scared," she quavers. "I'm awful scared. Will you come right over? . . . Thanks, Mr. Anderson."

In the kitchen she warms leftover coffee and takes it into the living room to sip it. Very quietly Doc comes in the back door and carefully places a big bottle of whiskey on the pantry shelf. Then, without making a sound, he hangs up his raincoat, puts his suit coat on the back of the usual chair and starts upstairs. But Lola, hearing him, calls, and he walks in from the kitchen. He is staggering drunk, but is managing for a moment to appear matter-of-fact and sober. His eyes, however, are blurred like ink pots, and his gasping wife is too frightened to talk. He gives her a casual good morning and she manages to ask if he is all right.

"The morning paper here? I wanta see the morning paper."

"Doc, we don't get a morning paper. You know that."

His anger rises. "Oh, then, I suppose I am drunk or something." Lola scampers to get last night's paper from the console table and takes it to him. He has trouble unfolding it, but when he manages he puts it in front of his face so as not to be seen. After a few minutes' silence Lola cautiously inquires, "Doc, are you all right?" Of course he is. "Where you been?"

Doc snarls, "What's it your business where I been? I been to London to see the Queen. What do you think of that? . . . Just let me alone. That's all I ask. I'm all right."

Lola is whimpering now as she tells of the big dinner. "Where's Marie?" he demands, threateningly. Marie was out with Bruce and didn't come in last night," she tells him, and he sneers, "I suppose you tucked them in bed together and peeked through the keyhole and applauded."

LOLA—Oh, Doc!

Doc—You and Marie are both a couple of sluts.

LOLA—Doc, please don't talk like that.

Doc—What are you good for? You can't even get up in the morning and cook my breakfast.

LOLA (*mumbling*)—I will, Doc. I will after this.

Doc—You won't even sweep the floors, till some bozo comes along to make love to Marie, and then you fix things up like Buckingham Palace or a Chinese whorehouse with perfume on the lamp-bulbs, and flowers, and the gold-trimmed china *my mother* gave us. We're not going to use these any more. My mother didn't buy those dishes for whores to eat off of. (*He jerks the cloth off the table, sending the dishes rattling to the floor.*)

LOLA—Doc! Look what you done.

Doc—Look what I *did*, not *done*. I'm going to get me a drink. (*Goes to kitchen.*)

LOLA—Oh, no, Doc! You know what it does to you!

Doc—You're damn right I know what it does to me. It makes me willing to come home here and look at you, you two-ton old heifer. (*Takes a long swallow.*) There! And pretty soon I'm going to have another, then another.

LOLA (*with dread*)—Oh, Doc! (LOLA *takes phone.* DOC *sees this, rushes for the butcher-knife from kitchen-cabinet drawer. Not finding it, he gets a hatchet from the back porch.*) Mr. Anderson? Come quick, Mr. Anderson. He's back. He's *back!* He's got a hatchet!

Doc—God damn you! Get away from that telephone. (*He chases her into living room where she gets the couch between them.*) That's right, phone! Tell the world I'm drunk. Tell the whole damn world. Scream your head off, you fat slut. Holler till all the neighbors think I'm beatin' hell outuv you. Where's Bruce now—under Marie's bed? You got all fresh and pretty for him, didn't you? Combed your hair for once—you even washed the back of your neck and put on a girdle. You were willing to harness all that fat into one bundle.

LOLA (*about to faint under the weight of the crushing accusations*) —Doc, don't say any more. . . . I'd rather you hit me with an ax, Doc. . . . Honest I would. But I can't stand to hear you talk like that.

Doc—I oughta hack off all that fat, and then wait for Marie and chop off those pretty ankles she's always dancing around on . . . then start lookin' for Turk and fix him too.

LOLA—Daddy, you're talking crazy!

Doc—I'm making sense for the first time in my life. You didn't know I knew about it, did you? But I saw him coming outa there, I saw him. You knew about it all the time and thought you were hidin' something . . .

LOLA—Daddy, I didn't know anything about it at all. Honest, Daddy.

Doc—Then *you're* the one that's crazy, if you think I didn't know. You were running a regular house, weren't you? It's probably been going on for years, ever since we were married. (*He lunges for her. She breaks for kitchen. They struggle in front of sink.*)

LOLA—Doc, it's not so; it's not so. You gotta believe me, Doc.

Doc—You're lyin'. But none a that's gonna happen any more. I'm gonna fix you now, once and for all. . . .

LOLA—Doc . . . don't do that to me. (LOLA, *in a frenzy of fear, clutches him around the neck, holding arm with ax by his side.*) Remember, Doc. It's *me*, Lola! You said I was the prettiest girl you ever saw. Remember, Doc! It's me! Lola!

Doc (*the memory has overpowered him. He collapses, slowly mumbling*)—Lola . . . my pretty Lola. (*He passes out on the floor.* LOLA *stands now, as though in a trance. Quietly* MRS. COFFMAN *comes creeping in through the back way.*)

Mrs. Coffman has heard the screams and has come to help. Seeing the prostrate Doc, she can guess what has happened. Lola tells her some men are coming, and begs her to stay until they arrive. The good woman begins straightening up, righting a chair, hanging up the telephone. She has just picked up the hatchet when Ed Anderson and Elmo Huston hurry in unannounced. They are neatly dressed business men approaching middle age, and being experienced AA's they know what to do. They consult over Doc as objectively as a pair of surgeons.

The hatchet business is bad, and Elmo doesn't think Doc should be left here. They try to rouse their patient but he only mutters thickly as they seat him at the kitchen table, and his head falls forward. While Mrs. Coffman warms the coffee the men offer Doc food and he brushes them away.

"City Hospital, Ed?" asks Elmo.

"I guess that's what it will have to be." Elmo calls the hospital quietly, without Lola quite realizing what is up. When the coffee is hot the men force Doc to drink some, and it brings him to enough to ask dazedly what is going on.

"We're taking you with us, Doc," says Ed.

The hell they are, says Doc. Just a little slip. Give him a few days to sober up and he'll be all right.

As if he were talking to a deaf man, Ed shouts, "Wanta go to the City Hospital, Doc?" The question has a terrible and sobering effect, and Doc, looking furtively for possible escape, pleads that the hospital is a torture chamber and his friends wouldn't do this to him. Inexorably the men lift him to his feet and he looks so pleadingly at Lola that she hides her face in her hands. "Honey! Honey!" he sobs.

Suddenly he wrenches loose and bolts into the living room, but is captured there. He begs Lola not to let them take him to the hospital, and she asks the men if there is any place else. Ed reminds her that private sanitariums are expensive.

"I got forty dollars in the kitchen."

"That won't be near enough."

Doc continues his struggles and Ed, losing all patience, tells him it's either the City Hospital or—worse—the City Jail; for he must get sober.

Doc seems to give in. He will go if they give him another drink— and since, in his case, another little drink won't do any harm, or several little ones, they give him a huge glass of the whiskey Mrs. Coffman brings and he downs it swiftly. His captors start off with him, and assure Lola that he will be home again as good as new in a few days. Doc thinks of another stall: he wants a glass of water— and suddenly he twists away. But in an instant he is recaptured and is dragged out, kicking and screaming and begging for some-body to stop them.

In the sudden quiet of the house Mrs. Coffman speaks softly. "Get busy, Lady. Get busy and forget it." She goes back home. Lola, in a big chair, is too exhausted to move, and at first she can-not weep; then the tears come, slowly and softly. In a few mo-ments Marie and Bruce, bright and merry, appear and Marie tells the joyful news. They danced all night, and then drove out to the lake and saw the sun rise, and Bruce gave her a ring, and they are engaged. Plans are all made for Marie to quit school and fly with Bruce to Cincinnati, where she will visit Bruce's mother before going to her own home. Could Mrs. Delaney throw her things into a big box and send it to Marie at home?

They have a taxi waiting, and hurry into Marie's room to snatch a few things. Alone, Lola dials the long distance operator and gives a number. In a moment Marie and Bruce are back in the room, and Marie is saying nice things about hating to leave, but planning to visit once in a while. Bruce thanks Lola for the dinner. As they depart, Marie calls, "Tell Doc good-by for me, will you, and remember I think you're both a coupla peaches."

Pretty soon the long distance call comes through and the beaten Lola says: "Hello. Hello, Mom. It's Lola, Mom. How are you? Mom, Doc's sick again. Do you think Dad would let me come home for a while? I'm awfully unhappy, Mom. Do you think . . . just till I made up my mind? . . . All right. No, I guess it wouldn't do any good for you to come here . . . I . . . I'll let you know what I decide to do. That's all, Mom. Thanks. Tell Daddy hello."

She hangs up, utterly disconsolate, and

The curtain falls.

Scene IV

It is morning, a week later. Lola has solaced herself with work and the house is neat again. Mrs. Coffman calls to offer to take Lola to the games at the Stadium. She has a box lunch ready and she is taking all her kids—and there is a ticket for Lola, too.

Lola declines, even though she knows that Turk is one of the big stars and will be competing with athletes from all the colleges in the Spring relays. "Doc may be coming home today," she explains.

Mrs. Coffman leaves, and the milkman comes in with a load of extra orders. Again Lola explains, "I think my husband's coming home."

Lola is putting things in the ice box when Doc appears, carrying the little suitcase she packed and sent him. His quiet manner and serious demeanor are the same as before—but Lola, shocked by his sudden appearance, can't help showing her fright. "Docky!" she exclaims. Obviously, her fear pains him, and he is not at ease. He assures her he is all right and begs, "Please don't stand there like that . . . like I was gonna . . . gonna . . ." She tries to relax and he asks if there is any news. She mentions Marie—but then she has told him about it over the phone.

Doc—It . . . it's good to be home.

Lola—Is it, Daddy?

Doc—Yah. (*Beginning to choke up, just a little.*)

Lola—Did everything go all right . . . I mean . . . did they treat you well and . . .

Doc (*now loses control of his feelings. Tears in his eyes, he all but lunges at her, gripping her arms, drilling his head into her bosom*)—Honey, don't ever leave me. *Please* don't ever leave me. If you do, they'd have to keep me down at that place all the time. I don't know what I said to you or what I did, I can't remember hardly anything. But please forgive me . . . please . . . please . . . And I'll try to make everything up.

Lola (*there is surprise on her face and new contentment. She becomes almost angelic in demeanor. Tenderly she places a soft hand on his head*)—Daddy! Why, of course I'll never leave you. (*A smile of satisfaction.*) You're all I've got. You're all I ever had. (*Very tenderly he kisses her.*)

Doc—I . . . I feel better . . . already.

Lola (*almost gay*)—So do I. Have you had your breakfast?

Doc—No. The food there was terrible. When they told me I could go this morning, I decided to wait and fix myself breakfast here.

Lola (*happily*)—Come on out in the kitchen and I'll get you a nice, big breakfast. I'll scramble some eggs and . . . You see I've got the place all cleaned up just the way you like it. (*Doc goes to kitchen.*) Now you sit down here and I'll get your fruit juice. (*He sits and she gets fruit juice from refrigerator.*) I've got bacon this morning, too. My, it's expensive now. And I'll light the oven, and make you some toast, and here's some orange marmalade, and . . .

Doc (*with a new feeling of control*)—Fruit juice. I'll need lots of fruit juice for a while. The doctor said it would restore the vitamins. You see, that damn whiskey kills all the vitamins in your system, eats up all the sugar in your kidneys. They came around every morning and shot vitamins in my arm. Oh, it didn't hurt. And the doctor told me to drink a quart of fruit juice every day. And you better get some candy bars for me at the grocery this morning. Doctor said to eat lots of candy, try to replace the sugar.

Lola—I'll do that, Doc. Here's another glass of this pineapple juice now. I'll get some candy bars first thing.

Doc—The doctor said I should have a hobby. Said I should go

out more. That's all that's wrong with me. I thought maybe I'd
go hunting once in a while.

LOLA—Yes, Doc. And bring home lots of good things to eat.

DOC—I'll get a big bird dog, too. Would you like a sad-looking
old bird dog around the house?

LOLA—Of course, I would. (*All her life and energy have been
restored.*) You know what, Doc? I had another dream last night.

It is the same Lola, the same life—no, not quite the same. The
dream she chatters about is more elaborate and exciting than usual.
And it is Lola who is at the stove fixing breakfast.

CURTAIN

THE HAPPY TIME *

A Comedy in Three Acts

BY SAMUEL TAYLOR

A GOOD many people, including Robert Fontaine, thought that Robert Fontaine's novel, "The Happy Time," would make a play. In 1945 the author and his wife made a dramatization of it. Leland Hayward saw this dramatization, liked it, took an option and said, as all managers always do, "This needs work."

The Fontaines rewrote their play six times, but by then Hayward's interest had waned—and so had theirs. Several other producers took options, according to Mr. Fontaine's article about the play in the *Saturday Evening Post,* and they all wanted rewrites. Then one day Hayward telephoned and asked if Fontaine would let a man named Samuel Taylor try a rewrite, and this was agreed on.

Mr. Taylor had come to New York from California and had got his first job—that of a playreader—through the help of the late Sidney Howard. In his playreading job Taylor found the opportunity to rewrite a script, "What a Life," which had been kicking around producers' offices for several seasons. This comedy, produced by George Abbott, was a hit; it established Ezra Stone as a comedian, and from it stemmed the long radio series, "The Aldrich Family"—written by Taylor, of course.

Taylor had been occupied for several years in writing radio comedies and television plays when the chance to dramatize "The Happy Time" came to him. He declined to look at any of the previous stage treatments, preferring the original novel as his source. He took the book to Maine, wrote the play in three months and dedicated it to the memory of his benefactor, Sidney Howard. Rodgers and Hammerstein produced it.

The scene is the living room of a house in Ottawa and the time is in the 1920's. The room is inexpensive, cheerful, bright—a happy room, neat and well lived in. It belongs to some people named

Bonnard, who are French but not French Canadians—a distinction which may seem academic but has validity.

One could enter the room through a wide arch in its center, framed by portieres. Another arch leads to the dining room. On the other side is a staircase to the floor above; a few steps up, where the stairs turn, there is a landing, and the landing is lighted by a small window of many-colored glass which looks out on the front porch and the street.

The room is vaguely Victorian, but its contents are mostly Bonnard and hint at the constant struggle of one woman among many men to bring Scotch feminine order out of French masculine chaos. There is a player-piano; the sofa is comfortable; the round center table, covered with a fringed cloth, holds a bowl of fruit and nuts; another table, against a wall, holds many bottles of wine, cognac, absinthe and benedictine, and there are shelves of glasses above it. In the wall by the staircase is a bay window, and beneath it a long window seat with a hinged cover.

Now the room is filled with pleasant sound, for Bibi is pumping the player-piano and Papa is playing "La Petite Tonkinoise" on a violin. They have not dressed since they got up. Bibi, who is in his nightgown, is twelve—a lad with a thin, dark, sensitive face. His father, Jacques Bonnard, is in his middle thirties, and if he were not clad in an old horse-blanket of a bathrobe he might appear gay and debonair.

Maman is both amused and annoyed at the musicians, for they have been at it since six o'clock this morning and are not yet dressed for breakfast. She comes from the dining room, carrying napkins, napkin rings and a fringed runner for the top of the piano. Maman is a Scot among Frenchmen, and she protests that it will be lunch by the time they get breakfast. Her hair and skin are light, and she shows a steady good humor—and firmness, too, yet a quiet resignation that has come with thirteen years of happy, comfortable failure.

"To have a piano moved into the house at six o'clock in the morning!" she expostulates.

"But it's my birthday," Bibi points out, and his father adds reasonably that a birthday present must be a surprise. The boy dreams of the future. "It will be wonderful when Papa teaches me to play the piano with the hands instead of the feet. Then I can play in his vaudeville orchestra with him and see the show every day!"

Maman vows that this will happen only when she is too old and weak to prevent it. She shoos Bibi upstairs to dress, and turns on her husband with a cold, practical question: "How much?" Papa tries to evade, but is forced to admit it was eighty-five dollars. He

got the piano from a friend, and the friend says he can take his
whole life to pay for it. He draws his wife to him and argues that,
although one should have money in the bank, a bank can't play
"Tales of the Vienna Woods." To clinch the argument he kisses
her warmly.

"Jacques! Not in your pajamas!" she protests laughingly.

"Is it a new rule?"

A third Bonnard, another version of the first two, comes down—
Grandpa. He is dressed—very dapper and very precisely except for
wine spots here and there: high, stiff collar, dark suit, spats. His
pointed mustache is tightly waxed, and he has tried to conceal his
bald spot by brushing gray hair up over it. As Grandpa gives the
greetings of the morning a canary is heard from the dining room.
Papa heads upstairs to dress and in passing inquires of Grandpa,
"How goes with the new love, the widow La Touche?"

"One makes progress. Last night it is discovered she wears a
wig." And to Maman, after Papa has gone: "This piano will bring
you much joy, Suzanne."

MAMAN—Yes. . . . (*She chuckles as she spreads the fringed
runner across the top of the piano.*) You have three sons, and they
are all mad.

GRANDPA—When all the world is mad, one understands no one
is mad.

MAMAN—I am not mad.

GRANDPA—No, you are Scotch. But there is hope for you, eh?
The Scotch does not show so much, now. You have become French
in the kitchen; soon, with the years, the transformation will be complete.

MAMAN (*ironically*)—It is a transformation devoutly to be
wished.

GRANDPA—You quote?

MAMAN—Shakespeare.

GRANDPA—Ah, there was an Englishman with glands. (*She
throws him a quick, shocked glance, looking around instinctively to
see if BIBI is anywhere near. Then she approaches the old man,
with quiet resolve.*)

MAMAN—Grandpa, there's something I'd like to ask you.

GRANDPA—It is of eternal significance?

MAMAN—Yes. I think so.

GRANDPA—Eh bien, you may speak.

MAMAN (*directly, gently, with a nice smile*)—Now that you've
come to live with us, I want you to be careful of what you say in

front of Bibi and how you talk to him. (GRANDPA *looks up, surprised, then accepts the rebuke calmly and sincerely.*)

GRANDPA—Ah—something has been said that troubles you. I am sorry.

MAMAN—It's just that Bibi is so young and he's so strongly influenced by the men of this family. He adores you; he takes in everything you say. And you talk to him as though he were another adult.

GRANDPA—There is no other way to talk to a child.

MAMAN—Why do men always say that? It sounds so broadminded, and it's such nonsense! You treat a child as a child. If you don't, you get him in trouble.

GRANDPA (*nods cheerfully*)—Eh bien, after breakfast I will play marbles with him. (*He starts across to the liquor table to get a box of candy.*)

MAMAN—Ah, you know what I mean. After all, it's been a long time since you lived with a child.

GRANDPA—It has been a long time since I lived with anyone.

MAMAN (*gently*)—Are you sorry we made you come live with us? Do you miss living alone?

GRANDPA (*with a small smile*)—At my age, wherever one lives, one lives alone. (*He takes the box of candy as* BIBI *comes rushing in from the dining room.*)

BIBI—Grandpa! Thank you very much for the canary! We've got the cage hanging in the dining room!

GRANDPA—You are welcome, Bibi. I hope it will sing for you for many years. (*He offers the boy the box of candy.*)

BIBI (*taking a chocolate*)—And I got new ice skates and the piano and a stuffed owl from Uncle Louis . . .

MAMAN (*with a sudden start*)—Grandpa! Don't give Bibi chocolates before breakfast.

GRANDPA—You said breakfast will be late; even a child must keep up his strength.

MAMAN—They have cognac centers! (PAPA *has appeared on his way downstairs, carrying his violin case.*)

PAPA—No, Papa. Bibi, put it back.

BIBI (*politely, as he does*)—I'm not hungry, Grandpa.

PAPA (*shaking his head at* GRANDPA, *amused*)—You have the stomach of an ostrich.

BIBI—Ah! Uncle Desmonde has not yet seen the piano! Or the canary! (*He calls, as he starts for the stairs.*) Uncle Desmonde! Uncle Desmonde! (GRANDPA *leaps from the rocker.*)

GRANDPA—Wait! Bibi! Do not wake your Uncle Desmonde!

BIBI (*stopping short*)—Huh?

PAPA—Why not?

GRANDPA—He sleeps.

MAMAN—Your Grandpa is right, Bibi. Uncle Desmonde only has a week's vacation before he goes back on the road. Let him sleep.

GRANDPA (*sinking back into the rocker*)—Oui, it would be impossible to wake him, anyway. I looked in his room just now; if he slept more soundly, he would be dead.

MAMAN—I don't know how he could sleep, with that piano going since six o'clock this morning. Bibi, go up and finish dressing.

BIBI—Oui, Maman. (*To* PAPA, *as he starts.*) When will we let the canary out of the cage?

PAPA—A little later.

MAMAN (*startled*)—What?

PAPA—Just for a few minutes. So he can fly a little. He is our guest.

MAMAN—Jacques, you're not going to let that bird out of his cage!

PAPA—For a few minutes. Is this too much to ask? (*He takes her by the shoulders, and grins down at her wickedly.*) Believe me, my love, this bird, in his song, which I understand completely, has expressed a desire to live his own life. It is a desire that must be respected.

BIBI (*wide-eyed, but suspicious*)—How do you know, Papa? How do you know what the canary wishes?

PAPA (*his eyes twinkling as he glances at* MAMAN)—Tell the boy. Inform him. (*He takes a cigar from a box on the table, sits down, and lights it.*)

BIBI—Tell me, Maman!

MAMAN (*with a tight-lipped smile*)—Your father, it seems, understands the language of birds. When I first met him, he was playing in an orchestra in a summer hotel. The first day we met, he told me that he had been speaking to a lark, who wished us to visit him in the woods.

BIBI—Ah!

GRANDPA (*impressed, he looks over at* PAPA)—This is how it happened?

PAPA (*modestly*)—This is how it began.

GRANDPA (*to* MAMAN, *who stands on display, embarrassed, and yet trying to keep from laughing*)—And you! The bird's wish was granted? You went into the woods with him? (*Blushing, she tries to shrug it off.*) You cannot be all Scotch.

Once more Maman tries to shoo son and husband up to finish dressing, when the front door slams and a young man in a crumpled dinner jacket swings gaily into the room—Uncle Desmonde, youngest of the three Bonnard brothers, and the handsomest. Desmonde had hoped to get in unnoticed, but now he puts a good face on it as Maman looks accusingly at Grandpa.

Desmonde will tell what he has been doing—yes, even in front of Bibi, for it is for all ears. Last evening he took a young lady of amazing charm to a dinner of many fine courses at the Château Laurier, and then went to her house, where they fell into a conversation of the most intellectual nature. "We were, believe me, engrossed. And then, suddenly, we look up! Sacré bleu! The sun is shining in the window!

"And now, Suzanne, if you will excuse me . . . There is no need for breakfast. . . . The young lady was kind enough . . . I will go to bed. It is exhausting, such mental exertion." Maman cannot help smiling at his dead-pan expression, and Desmonde, hooting with laughter, kisses her. As he goes up Bibi runs after him, calling, "You did not tell us what you had for breakfast."

Maman is scandalized. Even if Bibi does not know now what this was all about, he will realize it some day. And the other Bonnard, Louis, next door, who is famous throughout Ottawa for the amount of white wine he drinks! Grandpa protests that Bibi and Louis are like children together, and Louis is so gentle. "Who knows how he would be if he were sober?"

As for Desmonde, Maman continues, it is time he married and settled down—Desmonde, with the most roving eye in Ottawa. "With everything else, does he have to be a traveling salesman? I shudder to think what is happening to women all over Canada!"

Bibi returns in a clatter, bearing a copy of *La Vie Parisienne* which Desmonde had borrowed from Papa and wearing two garters on his shirt sleeves to keep the cuffs up—a gift from his uncle, of course. In horror, Maman snatches them off. "Off some stranger's legs!" she cries.

"To Desmonde she was not a stranger," says Grandpa . . . and then he essays to soothe his daughter-in-law by explaining that they probably were caught as they were thrown from the stage of the Casino Burlesque—an innocent form of "le sport." But Bibi informs them that only one is from the Burlesque; the other was obtained privately. Maman, wailing in defeat, picks up the napkins and stalks into the dining-room.

PAPA—Bibi, in the world of men, one does not talk too much, tu comprends? It is enough to have the garters; one does not volunteer the information where they were obtained.

BIBI—Maman is mad?

PAPA—No, not really. She is insulted because the men have stuck together. But in matters of this sort, it is essential, Bibi. The men must stick together. You will understand when you are a man. (*He pats* BIBI *on the head, sticks the cigar in his mouth, plucks a flower from a vase, and goes to the kitchen to make his peace.* BIBI *turns to* GRANDPA *and sits on the edge of the rocker and they rock together quietly for a moment.*)

BIBI—When will I be a man?

GRANDPA—One cannot tell. Perhaps soon. It is a matter of the glands.

BIBI—Ah? These I do not yet have?

GRANDPA—No. And even when you have, Bibi, you will still not be a man. C'est à dire, a man such as a Bonnard must be.

BIBI—No? (*He has picked up the garters from* GRANDPA's *lap and toys with them idly.*)

GRANDPA—No. For this of the glands is purely technical. It is a law of nature called "la puberté" and is widespread among all animals, being the awakening of a natural appetite. It gives pleasure, like eating, but also gives children, which eating does not do. It is, enfin, a matter of the glands.

BIBI—But this other of being a man. How is it to be a man—like Papa?

GRANDPA—Ah, there! It is when you have the knowledge to use the glands and the heart and the mind, together, correctly. Tu comprends, Bibi? To be truly a man, one must know two things. One must know love, one must know truth.

BIBI (*thinking it over*)—Love—truth—it is difficult to know them?

GRANDPA—It is almost impossible.

BIBI—Oh. (*With childish ingenuity, he has formed the garters into a crown and now, as he considers the problem, he places the crown on his head and starts across the room, balancing it.*) But I will try.

GRANDPA—Bien. It is all one can do. (*He pops a chocolate into his mouth.*)

The lights dim, the curtain falls.

SCENE II

Six months have passed; it is early Spring, late in the afternoon, and Maman has been alone, sewing and softly singing an old Scottish ballad. She looks up when the front door slams, and sees Papa and Bibi coming home. Papa is wearing a black suit, a soft white shirt with a stiff collar and a black string bow tie. "I have a surprise," he announces—but his son lets him get no further. Bibi is still in short pants—and Bibi is overflowing with enthusiasm. He has been to the vaudeville theatre with Papa and is full of talk about the show. The trained seal took twelve bows, and Papa was so wonderful conducting the orchestra—but, better than that, Monsieur La Salle Dubois, the dancer, has taught Bibi and his father a soft-shoe dance.

And they do it for Maman, right there—a simple dance to the accompaniment of Bibi's singing "Carolina in the Morning." Papa nearly upsets the lamp on the table accidentally, but Maman agrees that it is a beautiful dance. "If your father could do that and play the violin at the same time, he would become famous." She beckons her son to her and measures the blouse she has been making against his youthful frame. Papa puts his hat away, lights a cigar and sits for a session with the evening paper, while Bibi scoops some cakes from the table and methodically stuffs them into his mouth. Maman, smiling a little wickedly at her son, remarks, "Sally was over here looking for you a while ago."

BIBI (*his mouth full, casually*)—Mmmmmm?
MAMAN—Sally O'Hare, from next door.
BIBI—Mmmmm.
PAPA—Bibi's beautiful American?
BIBI (*trying to say: "Mine?"*)—Mmmmmmm?
PAPA—What did she come to borrow this time?
MAMAN (*smiles*)—The vacuum cleaner. She said theirs was broken. Stand still, dear. As soon as she saw that Bibi wasn't here, she lost interest, but I made her take it anyway. Turn around, Bibi. (BIBI *does.*) Some day she's going to run out of things she can think of to borrow and then she'll have to admit it's just an excuse to see Bibi.

BIBI (*astounded, tries to say: "Me?"*)—Mmmmmmmmmmm?

MAMAN—Don't try to talk with your mouth full, dear.

PAPA—Our handsome son. A true Bonnard. The women come to borrow his vacuum cleaner.

MAMAN (*smiling at him*)—I know just how she feels.

BIBI (*swallowing the last cookie*)—Qu'est-ce que c'est of Sally?

MAMAN—Bibi, I hope you're nice to Sally.

BIBI—She wears braces on her teeth.

MAMAN—That's so she'll look pretty later on. I want you to be nice to her, dear. She's an American and she hasn't been in Canada long; she can't have many friends.

BIBI (*not particularly interested*)—Oui, she has friends. She has already her own gang at school. She says in America all the world is formed in gangs.

PAPA—C'est vrai. In America one lives dangerously. And you? You are in Sally's gang?

BIBI—Me? To let a girl be the leader? Pas possible!

PAPA—Ah, such is the sad fate of women. They can be leaders, or they can be loved—never both.

MAMAN—Let us weep.

BIBI—Maman is both. (*His parents look at him.*) In this house. (MAMAN *laughs.*)

PAPA—Ah, oui, it is true, Bibi. But we do not speak of it, tu comprends? It is our secret shame.

MAMAN (*turning* BIBI *so that his back is being fitted*)—Don't you believe it, Bibi. No poor, lorn female could be a leader in the house of the Bonnards. I am a slave to five men and it's a terrible hard life.

BIBI—Ah! (*He looks over his shoulder at his father.*) Vraiment?

PAPA—Oui. But it is at least something to be loved by five men.

MAMAN (*smiling*)—It is at *least*—something . . .

BIBI (*the subject is closed*)—This is for my Sunday best?

MAMAN—To go with your dark-blue pants. Do you like it?

BIBI—Oui. (*Then, matter-of-factly; he doesn't really care.*) Many boys in my class now come to school in long pants.

MAMAN—They are too young.

BIBI—It is true they look like small men. On the other hand, let us consider: I am almost as tall as Papa.

PAPA—Have a cigar?

BIBI (*refusing, with a shake of his head*)—Merci. I will wait until I am a man.

MAMAN (*teasing*)—And when will that be?

BIBI (*with a shrug*)—It is a matter of the glands. (PAPA *almost swallows his cigar.*)

MAMAN—Bibi! (*She looks at* PAPA, *who denies all responsibility.*)

BIBI—I said something?

MAMAN (*finished with the blouse*)—That is all. Please pick up your things.

BIBI—Mmm? (MAMAN *points to the floor before the window seat, where are strewn roller skates, ice skates, baseball bats, three broken hockey sticks, a stuffed owl, a gutless tennis racket and various other treasures.*)

MAMAN—We agreed that you could have the window seat for your things only if you would promise to keep them in there, not all over the floor.

BIBI—Ah! I was looking for something. (*He crosses over and starts gathering the things together.*) It was important. I wonder what it was.

MAMAN—Please put them away quickly; I want you to go upstairs and have a nap before supper. (*She turns to* PAPA.) What is the surprise?

Ah oui! Maman is no longer the poor, lorn female. Papa has obtained a maid. No, they have not just inherited a million in gold, but they have enough—and, besides, the girl needs help. She is one Mignonette Chappuis and she was crying backstage because she had just lost her job. So he told her she could come home here. "In this way we make two birds to sing with the same food. We help her and she helps you."

"What does she do?" Maman asks.

"She is an acrobat."

"Oh, dear Lord!"

If Papa is nothing else, he is persuasive. He continues his campaign, explaining that the girl isn't an acrobat, really. She was *with* the acrobats, being the one who stood at the side, cried "Et voilà!" and threw the handkerchief. He pantomimes tossing a kerchief, catching it and dusting himself under the armpits. Also, he has questioned the girl closely and she is a magnificent cook and she has a strong desire to wash, mop, dust, make the beds and serve the meals.

Smiling tenderly, Maman echoes, "Et voilà! And when she serves the meals, will she throw the napkins to us and cry, 'Et voilà!'?"—and in turn she demonstrates.

This girl, Papa continues, is really a singer, but she found no opportunity to sing. And she lost the job with the acrobats because—and Papa checks himself, for he becomes aware of Bibi leaning over the back of the sofa and taking in every word. "Everything is put away. Regard!" Bibi announces, and his mother tells him to go up for his nap. But first the boy must have a drink of water, and as he heads for the dining room he imparts the information, "She did not always cry 'Et voilà!' Sometimes she cried 'Hup!'" Papa bows in grateful acknowledgment, then looks at Maman hopelessly. "How can ears so unwashed hear so well?"

He continues with the story of Mignonette, whose job in the troupe was to provide certain services—"But also, the leader of the troupe, who is a very large man, begins to demand other services, which she declines to give. . . ."

Maman capitulates. "When will she arrive, your canary?"

"As soon as she has packed her bag."

Suddenly Maman is disturbed. What about Desmonde? A young and pretty girl . . . Papa reassures her; his brother is not a devil and will not attack her—and besides he is now on the road selling his wines and will not be back for several weeks.

Sounds of an altercation break out way out in the kitchen, and Bibi speeds in with the news, "It is Uncle Louis! He is coming with his water cooler! He comes the back way from their house next door, and Aunt Félice is after him, and she yells and he yells and she yells and he yells, and they come now!" And approach they do, with the argument going like this:

Louis—Sacré bleu! I will hear no more, tu comprends? No more!

Félice—You will hear it again and again! You are a walking wine keg for whom no one will mourn!

Louis—Do not be so holy! The king is not your cousin!

Félice—Give that to me!

Louis—Take care! The mustard is rising in my nose!

Félice—Ah, Sacré Bon Dieu! What shall I do?

Louis—Stop talking!

Félice—Of what good is it to talk to you? I preach in the desert!

Louis—Then stop talking!

Félice—It goes in one ear and out the other! (*And now, as they enter,* Louis *tries to end the argument with one last stentorian blast.*)

Maman, worried about the neighbors, is a good general; quickly she orders Bibi to start pumping the piano.

Louis—Fiche-moi la paix! (*But* Félice *cannot be silenced.*)

Félice—Regard yourself! Drunk! Dirty!

Louis (*trying to stare her down*)—You lose so many chances to be quiet! (*Whereupon the player-piano starts playing, and for a while will compete with the maledictions hurled so freely.* Uncle Louis *is the oldest of the three brothers; he is heavier and rounder and has lost the keenness and sharpness from years of drink and sloth. His nose is red and bulbous; the bags under his eyes have bags of their own. He is flabby and he is undoubtedly a drunkard; but he has luckily saved a few things to live with: warmth and kindness and compassion.* Félice *is small and dry and quick and hard; she has for twenty years earned a living for herself, her husband and her child. Still, it is possible, by looking carefully at these two, to find some small signs of affection here, born in adversity and reared in conflict.* Félice *is dressed in a brown house dress.* Louis *wears a vest but no coat; black string tie, carpet slippers. Clasped tightly to his breast is a small water cooler. He looks as though he would straight-arm anyone who made a pass at it.* Félice *is right on his heels.* Papa, *who has experienced these scenes before and does not like them, retires upstage.*)

Félice—Here is a husband for you! One who sleeps when he does not drink and drinks when he does not sleep! May I be cursed for the day I said I would marry you!

Louis—Et moi? Am I to be congratulated? Let me tell it to your whiskers . . . (*She reaches for the cooler; he blocks her off with his outstretched arm.*) Do not tempt me to break your arm!

Papa (*who can no longer stand the noise, yells at* Bibi)—Bibi, assez! Hold! Stop it! (*The piano stops.*) Why must we worry about the neighbors! *These* are the neighbors! And you two! You boil over like milk soup!

Maman—Bibi, I want you to go up and take a nap before supper.

Bibi—I'm not tired.

Maman—Marche! Vite! (*He marches up the stairs.*)

Louis—She would make the mountains fight, this one! Go, you are the cork in my cognac! (*He picks up a glass from the table, and with the water cooler firmly clasped, circles the table and lies down on the sofa. He places the cooler on the table at his elbow, and fills the glass.*)

Félice—*A man who drinks wine from a water cooler!*

Papa—Since he drinks it like water . . .

Félice—A man who has not let the thought of work disturb his slumbers in twenty years!

Louis—The husband and the wife must not both work. All the world knows: it is a matter of la politesse.

FÉLICE—La politesse!

LOUIS (*to* PAPA, *waving at the cooler*)—She stole this from me! Imagine to yourself a wife who steals! It is against nature, n'est-ce pas?

FÉLICE—You will listen to me, do you hear? You will arrange your ears and listen! You have a daughter, recall to yourself that you have a daughter, who is an angel from heaven, a pearl among women . . .

LOUIS (*tenderly*)—Ah, oui, Yvonne, ma princesse. . . .

FÉLICE—. . . and yet this sweet child, this tender blossom, cannot get an 'usband! Pourquoi?

LOUIS (*demanding*)—Pourquoi?

FÉLICE—Pourquoi! Her father drinks wine from a water cooler! (*And she makes another stab at the cooler.*)

LOUIS (*starts up with a magnificent gesture*)—Take care! This is war! (*And he wards her off successfully.*)

FÉLICE—Zut!

LOUIS (*sinking back with a sigh*)—Ah, I am a lonesome dove, to whom even the sweetest cherries are bitter.

FÉLICE—Listen to me. You will become sober, do you hear? I demand it.

LOUIS—I am sober now.

FÉLICE—You are drunk now. But you will become sober. Before you can come again into your own house and speak to your family, you will become sober. (*To the others.*) He sits, this one, and drinks wine and regards his navel, while his only child becomes an old maid. He has hallucinations! He sees butterflies! He lives in terror that a butterfly will attack him!

LOUIS (*vigorously, defending his faith*)—I have reason! To a man in my condition, the bite of a butterfly can be fatal!

FÉLICE—To a man in your condition, blowing his nose can be fatal! (*She starts out toward the dining room.*) You will not hear me speak again until you are sober.

Toward the end of the row Mignonette appears in the doorway— a beautiful French girl in her twenties, dark hair, large black eyes, tapering from fullness where fullness should be down to small feet and trim ankles. Her cheap coat and cloche hat look well on her. As Papa discovers her she explains that she rang the bell and knocked, and there was no answer but she heard voices. . . .

Ah, oui, there were voices! Papa presents Mignonette to Maman. Bibi comes downstairs a bit to have a look at the newcomer and just sits there quietly, listening, as Mignonette meets

Louis and is taken in by Maman's friendliness. She thinks the house is bee-oo-tee-ful. When Papa brings in the girl's suitcase she takes it and Maman leads her toward her room next to the kitchen, explaining that the only bathroom is upstairs and she will have to walk through the house. . . .

When the women return Mignonette still is saying that everything is so bee-oo-tee-ful. Papa excuses himself, intending to go up and rest a little before dinner. Uncle Louis, pouring himself a glass of wine as Mignonette watches him, puzzled, announces that he, too, must sleep—and he curls up on the sofa. Papa, swinging up the stairs, discovers Bibi and queries, "This is where you take your nap now?"

Maman calls her son down and introduces him to Mignonette. "Our little son . . . Doesn't pick up . . . Takes cookies . . . But really very good. We hope you will learn to love him."

Bibi has approached shyly, never taking his eyes off the girl. She exclaims, "What a bee-oo-tee-ful little boy!"—and, throwing her arms about him, encompasses him with warmth and softness he has never known before. She holds him close and kisses him heartily on the cheek. Maman has other things to show Mignonette, such as where the tablecloths are, and they go to the dining room.

Bibi stands alone, a shattered shell of a boy. His arms hang limp; his eyes are glazed; his mouth opens convulsively, seeking more air, but still there is not enough air, and he anxiously gulps. He tries to take a step and finds his ankles have turned to jelly. He looks slowly about the room, but nothing is familiar to him, everything is slightly out of focus. He feels his cheek, then the back of his neck, and then finally gives his pants a hitch.

Sally appears from the dining room and stops. She is holding a vacuum cleaner. Sally O'Hare is Bibi's age and has already entered puberty: the waistline has begun to indent, the bosom to obtrude. Sally is thin and quick and tense. Her hair is painfully straight. She wears bands on her teeth. She stands there, waiting for Bibi to notice her.

Finally Sally breaks in with, "I—I brought your mother's vacuum cleaner back. . . ." Bibi appears not to have heard. Sally continues: Who's the lady? Why did she kiss Bibi? She must be some kind of a relative. . . .

Bibi seems to regain consciousness. "Bee-oo-tee-ful!" he sighs— and Sally, with happy surprise, opens her mouth in a wide smile. "What? What did you say?"

Bibi has recovered, and crushes Sally by asking with natural curiosity if those bands on her teeth hurt. The girl kicks him in the shin and he screams with pain—just as Uncle Desmonde arrives, the dream of traveling salesmen right down to the checked vest and the cane.

"Ah, love!" booms Desmonde. Bibi runs to him and is lifted high, with Desmonde bellowing "Oho! . . . And this? This is your beautiful sweetheart?"

"I am not!" cries Sally, and she runs from the room. Bibi explains that it's only the girl from next door.

Desmonde's greetings have roused Uncle Louis, who explains his presence by saying that this time Félice has gone too far.

Bibi has news: They've got a maid named Mignonette. Desmonde is not overpowered by the news. He gives Bibi a copy of *La Vie Parisienne,* then samples some of Louis' wine from the cooler and opines that it's a bad year. Papa, who also has been aroused by the "ohos," speeds down the stair and is almost dismayed at seeing his younger brother. He would like to know why Desmonde has returned so soon, but the boulevardier is much more willing to tell those assembled how he captured the most ornate garter in the world—a truly gaudy thing which he pulls from his pocket. It is from the Casino Burlesque, and really an item for his collection.

At Papa's insistence, Desmonde diffidently explains that he has not lost his job. "The sales manager has lost his. He is dead. The sales manager has died, he has unscrewed his billiard table, the office has sent for me." And Desmonde plumps on the sofa beside Louis to continue the story of the garter. He caught the prize, snatched it from other hands, by spearing it with his cane. Occasionally he interrupts the tale of this triumph to give more business details to the insistent Papa. Desmonde has been offered the sales manager's job and has refused it; he likes to travel and will stay in Ottawa only until they find another sales manager. He does *not* want to marry and settle down.

Grandpa now appears on the staircase, dressed to the nines and as bright as a bowl of spring flowers—bright blue linen jacket, immaculate white trousers, sailor straw hat with a blue-and-white band tilted cockily, large imitation diamond in cravat, bright yellow cane. Desmonde gives a high moan of admiration, Papa exclaims "Mon Dieu" and Louis contributes an "Oh, la, la." "Ah, c'est beau," opines Bibi.

Grandpapa announces that he is going to faire l'amour with the Widow La Touche.

Roaring with laughter, Desmonde exclaims, "Oho! It will unscrew your billiard table!" Louis, too, is of the belief that it will entail certain death. "No, believe us," Papa expostulates, "it will stop your teeth from aching, permanently."

Grandpa jauntily belittles the warnings. "The one who knows of a better way to die, will he step forward? Allons!" And he dances out of the house with a flourish of his hat.

At Desmonde's request, Bibi takes his uncle's bag upstairs. Louis must go to the cellar for a refilling of his water cooler, and Papa goes back upstairs. Alone, Desmonde inspects the bottles on the liquor table, chooses one and pours a drink. While his back is turned, Mignonette enters from the dining room, her head bent low as she attempts to tie the straps of the small white apron she has put on. By the time she succeeds, she is at the center of the room and has not noticed Desmonde. But he, about to taste his drink, notices her with amazed admiration. She begins to dust; he stands, drinking and admiring; then she turns, catches sight of him and is startled. A moment; she nods; he nods. She hesitates, then goes back to her dusting, conscious all the while that his eyes are on her. He drifts down into the room, slowly, casually, but always somehow seeming accidentally to come up to her; and always, as he reaches her, she seems just to have finished dusting that particular object of furniture, and sees something in another part of the room that demands her attention. It is all completely casual; there is no sign of recognition; and yet both he and she are aware and it is somehow like game-stalking in slow motion; it is like a bullfight, with all the bullfight's grace; the handsome bull advancing, the pretty toreador flicking her cloth and dancing out of reach. But now the bull wins. Desmonde corners her downstage and as she rises from dusting the leg of the sofa, she finds herself facing him. A pause; he smiles.

DESMONDE—How are you called?

MIGNONETTE—Mignonette.

DESMONDE—Mignonette . . . (*There is a caress in his voice and a look in his eye, and they are both a little too obvious. He is turning it on.*) I am Desmonde . . . the brother. . . .

MIGNONETTE (*pleasantly impersonal*)—Ah, oui, there are many brothers. One has gone to the cellar, one is upstairs, Madame is in the kitchen. (*She smiles politely, nods and is about to try to break through, when* BIBI *comes clattering downstairs.*)

BIBI—Uncle Desmonde, I did not open your suitcase but . . . Ah! this is Mignonette.

DESMONDE—Yes, we have met. (*He lifts* BIBI *high in the air again, this time more to impress* MIGNONETTE.) Ah, Bibi, every time I come back, you have grown two more inches. Soon you will be the biggest of the Bonnards, eh?

BIBI (*from up there, to* MIGNONETTE)—Uncle Desmonde travels all over Canada; he sells wines; you will like him. (*She smiles.*) I did not open the suitcase; you have brought me a present?

DESMONDE (*bringing him down*)—It is there.

BIBI—And you have had many adventures.

DESMONDE—Oho! Such adventures! Let me tell you, Bibi, in Calgary, I saw a horse—(*This, too, is as much for* MIGNONETTE,)—such a horse, mon vieux, as I have never dreamed existed!

BIBI—And you rode him?

DESMONDE—I rode him—listen carefully, my pigeon—up the main street of Calgary! Through the doors of the chief hotel! Up to the bar! Where together we drank a bottle of wine!

BIBI—You and the horse?

DESMONDE—The horse and I!

BIBI—Mon Dieu!

DESMONDE—Oui!

BIBI (*to* MIGNONETTE)—Uncle Desmonde is one of the great horsemen of Canada!

DESMONDE—The greatest!

BIBI—In the war he was an officer of the Canadian Cavalry! He fought gloriously for His Majesty's Empire and killed many Germans and obtained all the medals! Show her, Uncle Desmonde! Show the medals! (UNCLE DESMONDE *obliges by unbuttoning and whipping back his coat, to expose the medals pinned to the lining. And they do make quite a glittering display; they have obviously been a selling point before.*)

MIGNONETTE (*dazzled*)—Ah!

DESMONDE (*modestly*)—It is nothing.

BIBI (*carrying on enthusiastically*)—Mignonette was with the vaudeville! She threw the handkerchief and cried et voilà! and hup!

DESMONDE—C'est vrai? An acrobat?

MIGNONETTE—Réellement, I am a chanteuse.

DESMONDE—Ah!

BIBI—But now, she has come to help Maman and she will stay forever, n'est-ce pas?

MIGNONETTE (*smiling*)—J'sais pas. May-be.

DESMONDE (*smiling at her, giving it all the charm*)—C'est bien. But it takes great courage to live in this house, eh, Bibi? Especially when Saint Louis of the Water Cooler has arrived and all the brothers Bonnard are together. And have you met Grandpa? (*She shakes her head.*) Ah, there is the white wolf to beware! It will demand great courage and great daring to live here, eh, Bibi? She will, perhaps, deserve a medal, eh?

BIBI (*laughing*)—Ah, oui!

DESMONDE—Bien! Let us give her a medal now, in advance! She has deserved it, merely by entering the front door! (*He starts to unpin a medal.*)

BIBI—You will give Mignonette a medal? Oh, yes! Oui! Mais oui!

DESMONDE—Regard it!

MIGNONETTE (*her eyes shining as he holds it up*)—Ah! It is bee-oo-tee-ful!

DESMONDE—Eh, bien! (*He maneuvers her downstage a bit; BIBI cannot see the following action. DESMONDE pins the medal on her breast, and after it is pinned, he gives its resting place a few loving pats. MIGNONETTE'S reaction is immediate and instinctive: she leaps back like a startled fawn, not angry, or insulted, not even sure the gesture was intentional, but quite startled. DESMONDE is smiling at her. BIBI is looking from one to the other, puzzled. And it is at this moment that PAPA comes downstairs and stops on the landing, sensing something. And again, at this moment, MAMAN enters from the dining room, her head down, tying an apron behind her, just as MIGNONETTE was, a few minutes ago. She looks up, sees the situation, and stops dead.*)

PAPA—Nom de Dieu!

DESMONDE—Ah, Suzanne! I am home!

MAMAN (*through tight lips*)—Name of a dark blue pig! (*BIBI abruptly crosses to his mother.*)

BIBI—Maman, I have changed my mind. (*He hitches his belt.*) I wish now to have long pants!

The curtain falls.

ACT II

By the evidence of the flowers in the living room, Spring is finally here—and so is Sally. She stands there, looking about. In one hand she holds a catcher's mask; with the other she adjusts the bands on her teeth. Casually she looks at something on the table— a new copy of *La Vie Parisienne*. The cover surprises her. What she sees inside surprises her even more, and she might go on being surprised, except that she hears the slam of the door and quickly drops the magazine.

Mignonette and Bibi come in and give Sally an "Allo." Bibi walks right past the girl to the table, where there is something which interests him—a platter of cold frogs' legs. Sally stammers, "I— I've got something. . . . Jimmy Bishop told me you couldn't get on his baseball team because you haven't got a catcher's mask. You can borrow mine, if you want to."

Bibi's eyes gleam as he takes the mask, admires it, tries it on.

Sally continues, "I looked for you to give it to you right after school, but I couldn't find you."

"I went to the movies with Mignonette." Still exultant, he tosses the mask on the window seat and marches upstairs, chewing on a frog's leg and leaving a greatly deflated Sally. Rather pitiably and desperately she asks Mignonette if *she* ever wore braces on her teeth. "No." Is her hair naturally wavy? "Oui."

Maman comes from the kitchen in search of Bibi, who will have to go to the store for some garlic. Desmonde, coming down, relays this information to his nephew, then samples a frog's leg. "Sally," suggests Maman, "how would you like to stay for dinner? I'm sure Bibi would like to have you."

This is a prospect, and Sally brightens. "A real French dinner," Maman tempts. "Something very special: kidneys." Sally is dubious.

Bibi bounces down to go on his errand. "Maman, we went to see 'The Son of the Sheik'! With Rudolph Valentino! Also Vilma Banky!" Maman thinks this must have been nice, but Desmonde appears upset. "Fah!" he says at Rudolph Valentino.

"Never have I seen such a wonderful movie!" bubbles Bibi.

"I think," explains Mignonette, "it is because never before has he held a girl's hand in a movie." The boy adds to the information this detail: Every time Valentino kissed Banky Mignonette squeezed his hand tight. Desmonde is disgusted, Mignonette is embarrassed . . . and Sally, boiling with rage and frustration, is close to tears. "I don't want to stay for dinner," she bawls. "I don't *like* kidneys!" And she speeds homeward, which is something Bibi can't understand since she even brought him something just now. He shrugs the problem off and is about to go for the garlic when he sees the magazine on the table. If Uncle Desmonde has finished with it, can he have it?

Desmonde is willing, but Maman is dead opposed until her son explains that he can trade it for many baseball pictures at school. Desmonde murmurs that to the pure all things are pure, and Maman gives in. The boy goes happily for the garlic, and Maman back to the kitchen. Desmonde, still miffed, observes to Mignonette,

"Everything has changed since Rudolph Valentino entered our life, eh?"

MIGNONETTE—Ah, oui . . . He is so bee-oo-tee-ful . . .

DESMONDE—Vas donc!

MIGNONETTE—And he does things with such an air!

DESMONDE—What things? Voyons! First, the eyes! (*He opens his eyes wide, as though he were seeing* MIGNONETTE *for the first time and finds it hard to believe that anyone could be so beautiful.*) Then he approaches on the toes. (*Raising his cloak before him, he takes long, careful, passionate steps to her, on his toes.*) This is to show good balance. (MIGNONETTE, *smiling quietly, holds her ground. He takes her gloves from her hand with a courtly nod and tosses them on the table, thus clearing for action.*) Now, since he wishes to show deep love, he wiggles the nose. It is no great trick to wiggle the nose; it demands only a seriousness of purpose.

MIGNONETTE—Oh? (*During this last, he has taken her by the hand, and put his right hand behind her back.*)

DESMONDE—And now, the smile of passion—(*He puts on Valentino's agonized smile. He is really doing a good job on Valentino.*) —and he bends the woman backwards. (*And he is doing a good job on* MIGNONETTE.) It is not difficult to bend a woman backwards; it demands only some small co-operation from the woman. And now, he kisses her. (MIGNONETTE *deftly slips out from under him, and stands free.*)

MIGNONETTE—Which also demands some small co-operation from the woman.

DESMONDE (*straightening up, insulted*)—Why then do we not have it?

MIGNONETTE—Perhaps because we do not deserve it.

DESMONDE—Pourquoi? Why does it always stop this way? I wish to know! I demand it!

MIGNONETTE (*shrugging*)—Many reasons. A man who is known all over Ottawa for his affairs, a man who collects the garters of all women. . . .

DESMONDE—Not all women; I have taste.

MIGNONETTE—You are welcome to it.

DESMONDE (*grinning broadly*)—Aha! So this is the eel under the rock! Do not be afraid, my little one; I will not steal a garter from you.

MIGNONETTE—No, you will not.

DESMONDE—From you I will steal something of greater significance. (*Her eyebrows shoot up, but she manages to retain a certain insouciance.*) Is there anything else? Allons! What else troubles you, my dove?

MIGNONETTE (*moving to the table, to gather the debris of the frogs' legs*)—Nothing. It is of no importance. It is not my business.

DESMONDE (*he's enjoying himself*)—What?

MIGNONETTE—That a man should refuse a good job here, because he wishes to travel about the country, living in hotels, eating bad food, making love to strange women: it is his business. . . .

DESMONDE (*breaking in*)—Ah, no! That I do not give up! Mais non! This traveling is something I enjoy, tu comprends? I do not give it up. For no one! Personne! I am young! I must live! Ah, but a few years from now, that is a different matter! I have shown you the picture of the house? (*She looks up, interested, and shakes her head. He comes down to the table, fishing out his wallet.*) No? Alons-y. My father, you understand, owns a house up the Gatineau, on the edge of the river. He has promised it to me, since he has come to live here, and there I will settle down some day. It is my dream. (*He has the picture out, and returns the wallet to his pocket.*) Voilà!

MIGNONETTE—When?

DESMONDE—Eh?

MIGNONETTE—When will you settle down?

He evades the question as he shows the picture. They are leaning on the table, their heads almost together, as he describes the river, the number of rooms, the woods, the apple trees by the house . . . "You have never been up the Gatineau, late in the Spring, to see the apple blossoms fall?" Her eyes are shining as she gently shakes her head. In a moment their lips meet—it is a long kiss and a gentle one. Desmonde would have another, but the girl straightens up—luckily enough, perhaps, for Bibi returns from his errand. Mignonette seizes the bag of garlic and the chance to escape and flies to the kitchen—flies right past Uncle Louis. Desmonde notices that Mignonette has left her gloves on the table. He picks them up and waves them after her—and then, deciding to keep them as souvenirs, pockets them.

Louis is groggy—from sleep as well as wine, for he has been snoozing in the cellar. He makes for the sofa as Bibi stands looking after the girl, lost in a fog of love, and Desmonde goes upstairs. Thoughtfully, the boy asks Louis, "A woman who has dimples in the face when she laughs . . . does she have dimples in other places, too?"

"To know that, one must ask her to remove her clothes, and laugh."

Bibi is full of important questions and Louis supplies drowsy answers. Does Valentino have a desire to see Banky with her clothes off? And what does he do? If only one could find a way. . . .

"Perhaps," Bibi cogitates . . . "it would be possible to remove all the night gowns—and hide them?" In his sleep Louis murmurs, "I do not think this is how Rudolph Valentino does it. . . ."

Bibi's idea is growing. Since the bedroom is there . . . and the bathroom is there . . . and she must walk at night . . . The boy steals toward Mignonette's room.

Louis cannot sleep long, for Papa comes excitedly in, carrying Grandpa. Grandpa is considerably mussed and he is beating his son with his cane and demanding to be put down. Papa's shouts for help and his father's objections to being carried rouse Louis and bring Maman running. Louis is deposed and Grandpa is dumped on the sofa. Papa explains that when he was coming home he saw Grandpa fall on the sidewalk a couple of blocks from the house— pouf! like a wounded sparrow. Papa has sent around the corner for Dr. Gagnon. Desmonde and Mignonette join the crowd. "First the doctor, then the priest," says Desmonde. "Now, my old goat, you pay for the pots you have broken."

In a moment the doctor is here—a tired and harassed man. His black suit is turning green with age. He sets his bag beside Papa's violin case and looks around inquiringly. The men point to Grandpa. "This is the one with lead in his wings, eh?" Grandpa belligerently asserts, "I have not sent for you."

In this crisis even Félice appears from next door and they all wait as Dr. Gagnon takes Grandpa's pulse. "The pulse is like the roller coaster at Rock Cliff Park," he announces. He asks that the patient's coat and shirt be removed—and it takes Papa and Desmonde together to manage the job. When the doctor asks for his bag, Louis at first absently hands him the violin case. When the mistake is rectified the doctor takes out a stethoscope and says he would like to hear Grandpa breathe. The old man snarls, "I will try to oblige."

After the breathing is heard the doctor wraps a blood-pressure apparatus about the old man's arm and begins pumping it. He stares at the gauge in amazement, tries again, stares again and utters a low moan. "By the rules, he is dead," he proclaims.

To Grandpa's utter horror, the doctor declares that the sick man must be kept in bed and put on a diet of wet toast, warm milk and an occasional mushed egg. "Better to die!" shouts Grandpa, and the physician replies, "That is a matter of taste." When the healer is gone, Desmonde sweeps his father into his arms and carries him kicking and cursing, upstairs, and Papa follows them up.

Félice returns home after a few cracks at Louis and his wine-bibbing, and after refusing Maman's suggestion that she take her husband back. Papa comes down to ask where the baking soda is, and Maman says there is some in the bathroom. Papa calls this information up to Desmonde, but Mignonette starts quickly for the stairs and says she will get it.

Papa stops her by taunting, "See how she runs when I speak the name of Desmonde." Half playfully he reminds her that he has warned against the snake in the grass, "the large snake with the mustache, that devours les jeunes femmes. And now, alas, he has devoured you, eh?"

Mignonette denies it. But, shyly, she speaks of seeing the picture of the house on the Gatineau, and Maman and Papa exchange despairing glances. It is obvious from both faces that Desmonde has sold that house many times before and has collected many a down payment, and Mignonette senses this. Papa tries to ease the situation by suggesting that perhaps this time Desmonde means it, and Maman hopefully agrees.

Mignonette is proud and she covers as best she can. She knows all about Desmonde, all right, and she makes no such mistakes. All they have is fun and no more. "We understand each other like thieves at the fair. Next week he goes back on the road, for me it is finished. C'est gai, mais c'est fini!" But her bravado fails, and she flees from the room.

Maman thinks it is high time Papa did something about an out-of-hand situation—Desmonde, Louis and Grandpa. "What will you do to protect your child? He's growing up! He can't watch these men do the things they do around here and not be affected by them."

To Papa, Bibi is the happiest boy in the world, and his father and brothers are not evil. One may drink and the others may look for girls, but there is no harm in this for Bibi. The boy won't imitate them.

Maman demands, "What makes you think he won't? Bibi's not blind! And if anything happens to Bibi, I'll never forgive you." She begins to weep and flies upstairs, with the agonized Papa after her.

Slowly Bibi's head comes around the center arch; when he is sure the room is clear he enters cautiously. He looks oddly misshapen, having grown large around the middle. Beneath his jacket hang edges of silk and lace—Mignonette's nightgowns. At the sound of Papa's voice upstairs, calling for Maman, the boy hides under the center table. But, since nobody comes down, he emerges in a moment and completes his mission, stuffing the nightgowns into the window seat.

The deed is done. Fully recovered, he goes to the piano and begins to pump a merry tune. Maman comes stalking down the stairs, carying a tablecloth. The sight of her small son innocently intent upon the music raises the cloud from her mind; she smiles as she goes to the dining room, and pats him lovingly on the head as she passes.

The curtain falls.

Scene II

It is the next afternoon and there is a great mystery in the house, and Maman and Félice are discussing it. Félice is sure Desmonde has stolen the nightgowns, but Maman is still hoping they are just mislaid.

Mignonette comes from above and she is quite sure. Desmonde has a locked trunk in his room—et voilà! A man who collects garters and girls will also collect nightgowns, no?

At this moment Louis descends the stairs and is somewhat of an apparition, for he is dressed in his only suit, is much more alive than usual and is impressively neat—except that he is still wearing his bedroom slippers and has forgotten to put on a necktie. To Félice he coldly announces, "It is understood you will remain in the kitchen. I do not wish women in the room when he comes." His wife reminds him that he has forgotten his tie, and Louis makes a dash for the stairs.

The "he" who is coming is one Alfred, and Alfred is coming to ask for the hand of Yvonne, Louis' and Félice's daughter. He is, for Yvonne, a catch, for he works.

Bibi arrives home from school—late and close to tears, but he won't admit to his mother that anything is wrong.

"You're tired," Maman ventures. "Mignonette tells me that she came into the living room last night, after midnight, and found you down here."

"Oui, Maman." And the boy adds in a low voice, "She was in her bathrobe." He explains that he was looking for something. Maman suggests that her son take a nap and warns him not to disturb Grandpa's sleep. She goes to the kitchen. Bibi sits on the edge of the sofa, lost in misery.

The front door slams—and in walks Grandpa, cheerily. In one hand he swings his cane; in the other a small, pretty basket with a handle. He holds it up for the boy to admire. "Regard it closely, Bibi. It is a messenger of love to the one the heart chooses. Observe." He goes to the liquor table, inspects it, then picks a bottle of absinthe, and comes down to the center table, on which is a large bowl of fruit. "This I will send ahead, to announce that I come. In this way, one prepares the heart." He places the bottle in the basket, and arranges fruit around it. "L'absinthe, the green parrot who speaks of love . . . this one knows the words and the mood . . . and fruit, for the quiet moments that come in the late evening . . . watch closely, Bibi, for the young know nothing of this; it is of the old world, where one understands life must be pleasant; it is to know the time, and the mood, and those things which fit the mood . . . 'Stay me with flagons, comfort me with apples: for I am sick of love. . . .'" He turns to display the filled basket. "Regard it!" Bibi smiles warmly. Grandpa looks at him closely, for the first time. "You are sad, Bibi?" Bibi tries to shrug it off. "For a reason?" No answer. Grandpa turns away. "Whatever it is, Bibi, when you are my age you will have forgotten it."

The troubled Bibi seeks help from his wise old grandfather. Why doesn't the Lord make people believe the truth? And what *is* the truth? "If I speak the truth and I am not believed and another speaks a lie and it is taken for the truth, then what is the truth?"

Grandpa's verdict is that the falseness can be ignored.

"But suppose they beat you with a strap."

The old philosopher explains that it is force which makes the false true and the truth false. Since no man can live with pain all his life, there are times when he might say black is white.

"It is wrong!" cries Bibi. He would tell his troubles to this old man, but doesn't want Maman or Papa to know, because they would blame Uncle Desmonde. "It is a matter of *La Vie Parisienne,* which I have taken to school. Someone copied a drawing from it and made a dirty picture. They say I did it."

"Who beat you?"

"The principal. And he will beat me again tomorrow, he says. And every day until I say I did it."

It pains Grandpa to say so, but his advice is to admit doing it and stop the beating. "Bibi, we will think more of this. I will send away the basket, and return. Do not worry." As he is leaving, Louis comes down again with his tie on and in his slippers, but carrying his shoes. He is in fine fettle as he announces to Bibi that Yvonne has found a fiancé.

Bibi accepts the news mournfully, but Louis continues to expand —and so do his feet, for his shoes hurt when he puts them on. He tells Bibi the scene which is about to occur—how the fiancé will arrive and be greeted; how they will talk of the world and the position of the pound sterling, and how he will explain his wealth and high social position. Alfred will be charmed by him—Alfred, who is, Louis believes, president of a bank in Ottawa. At least one bank. . . .

When the suitor does arrive, Bibi lets him in. Alfred is pale, slim, in his early twenties. He is dressed in a dark, stiff suit, his collar is very shiny and stiff, and he carries his hat. He is shy, scared and truly a gentle man. He says "Bon jour" and identifies himself. Louis introduces Bibi, then offers wine.

ALFRED—Non, merci, I have never tasted wine.

LOUIS (*stabbed to the heart*)—You have never tasted wine.

ALFRED—Non, but I have a great thirst. If it is permitted, I will take some water. (*And he heads for the water cooler.* BIBI *immediately makes a move to stop him, but* LOUIS *merely puts out a hand and completely covers his nephew's face. And then, with an innate sense of delicacy, he and* BIBI *turn their backs, so that they may not see what happens to* ALFRED *next, and busy themselves at the table.* ALFRED, *who has taken a glass from the table, pours a glassful of wine from the water cooler and gulps it down. His face reacts immediately to the strangeness of the taste, but then he realizes that, whatever it is, it is what he needs for the situation. He pours another glass, and gulps it down, then fills the glass again. The others have turned, now, and he stands, glass in hand, smiles at them, and gestures to the water cooler.*) Rusty pipes. (LOUIS *bows, takes two bottles of wine and a glass and returns to the center table.* ALFRED *comes back up.* LOUIS *raises his glass in a toast, they both drain their glasses and sit down. It is now three in a row for* ALFRED; *he is glad to sit down.*)

LOUIS—Eh, bien?

ALFRED—Monsieur, I am filled with love for your daughter. I have come to speak with you as one man to the next. I wish to discuss the matter from every side.

LOUIS—Proceed. (BIBI *has returned to the rocker, and half listens, half reflects on his own problem. Every once in a while* LOUIS *looks over and gives him a wink or a nod to make sure he realizes with what worldliness he is handling this situation.*)

ALFRED—As you know, I work in a bank.

LOUIS—Oui, all the world knows. (*A thought occurs to him.*) One bank?

ALFRED—One bank.

LOUIS—One bank. Ah, but you are young. Dites-moi, how is the pound sterling, these days? (ALFRED *looks bewildered.*) International trade. What is the situation with Swiss gold francs? What do you think of Canadian Pacific Railway? Is it expected to rise?

ALFRED (*scared*)—Monsieur—it is permitted? (*And at* LOUIS' *courtly nod, he hastens to the water cooler, and fills the glass with number four.*)

LOUIS (*as he does so*)—My brother, you know, plays sometimes the violin, chamber music, at one of the railway hotels, the Château Laurier, of course. A genius, my brother. We are all geniuses in this family. My brother's son here, we are also bringing up to be a genius. (ALFRED *has come back.*) Eh, bien, we speak of high finance.

ALFRED (*trying to get his feet organized*)—Me, I know nothing of this, Monsieur.

LOUIS—Eh?

ALFRED—I know nothing of international trade, Swiss francs, or geniuses. In the bank, I add up the checks, I add up also the coins; as for the Château Laurier, I cannot afford such an elegant place, I am a simple clerk.

LOUIS—A clerk?

ALFRED—Oui. (*He drains his glass.*)

LOUIS—I am unbuttoned. A clerk?

ALFRED—Oui. (*He heads for the cooler.*)

LOUIS—This is another pair of sleeves! A clerk?

ALFRED—Oui. A clerk. (*He pours number five.*)

LOUIS—How can a clerk afford automobiles, jewels, rare cheeses, fine wines?

ALFRED—Yvonne does not wish such things, Monsieur; neither do I. We wish to have only a small house with flowers and many babies.

LOUIS—I do not believe a pale clerk in a small bank can give her many babies.

ALFRED—It is not the size of the bank that counts in these cases. (*He looks around with amazement to see who could have said that, then drains his glass. Let us face it:* ALFRED *is drunk. And* LOUIS *has been way ahead of him.*)

LOUIS (*he is up, and has begun to pace*)—I do not like this kind of music. (*He stops, and scratches the end of his nose. Then, with great dignity.*) Tell me, my boy—about the salary.

ALFRED (*reciting*)—It amounts to fifteen dollars weekly, with a small increase each year until it reaches twenty-two. There, one understands, it is stabilized.

LOUIS—Ah. Mm. Yes. Stabilized, eh? At twenty-two dollars, eh? It does not rise beyond this?

ALFRED—Only in the case of a remarkable feat of some sort.

LOUIS—Ah, let us stick to reality. Twenty-two dollars, stabilized. (*He resumes his pacing.* ALFRED *has refilled his glass.* LOUIS *manages, somehow, to keep his glass full.*)

ALFRED—I will work hard. Perhaps I will find also another position; I will work in two places. Believe me, I will work hard for the love that blooms in my heart for Yvonne.

LOUIS—Stabilized. (*He stops short and points a menacing finger.*) Think of your children! (ALFRED, *about to drink, almost swallows the glass.*) You wish to live on fifteen to twenty-two dollars weekly. Very well. Children are born, no? Combien? How many, please? (ALFRED, *still trying to recover, merely waves.*) One? two? three? four? five? six? seven! They must be fed, they must be clothed, they will grow up, they will go to school, no?

ALFRED—Yes!

LOUIS—Good. They are through school now, and it is time for them to go to the University. McGill, perhaps, eh? Toronto? Queens? Good. (*Now he throws the bomb.*) But tell me, mon ami, how do you intend to send seven children to the University on twenty-two dollars a week?

ALFRED (*smiling, and waving a finger*)—Ah, but, Monsieur. . . .

LOUIS (*bringing his fist down on the table with triumphant crash*)—Stabilized!

ALFRED (*still smiling blearily, still waving his finger*)—Ah, but, Monsieur, I do not send the children to the University. (*And he turns to the cooler, gives it a loving pat, and refills his glass.*)

LOUIS (*aghast*)—Not? Not send the children to the University? This is hard cheese you make me eat. You *will* send them to the University!

ALFRED—Pas de chance! It is time they went to work!

LOUIS—Work? My grandchildren work? Tell me, mon ami, why did you have these children, if you could not afford to bring them up the equal of any man?

ALFRED (*mad, waving a finger in his face*)—I will not pay another cent for their education!

LOUIS—What have you done all these years with your money?

Do you spend your nights drinking and gambling, while your poor wife, now pale and thin, waits at home alone?

ALFRED—How alone? She has seven children!

LOUIS—They are at the University!

ALFRED—Non! Mais non! Mille fois non! They are out earning a living for their poor old papa, who has slaved all his life in the bank and now wishes to rest! These are my children!

LOUIS—These are my grandchildren! Sacré Bon Dieu! They must have an education!

ALFRED—Monsieur! Now you go too far! I am the father, I will decide! And if you speak one more word—ONE MORE WORD!—I will have no children at all!

LOUIS (horrified)—No children? You will have no children?

ALFRED—None! Not one! (With a sweep of his arm, LOUIS points to the door. ALFRED bows with great dignity, weaves to the table, puts on his hat and marches up to the center arch. There he bumps into PAPA, just entering, tips his hat and with the ramrod stiffness of the very drunk, strides out. The door slams. LOUIS sits, overcome.)

The row brings Félice and Maman running, and Bibi informs them that Alfred has gone. Papa puts down his violin case and kisses his wife as Louis dully explains, "He refuses to have children. And he will not send them to the University."

Félice is desolated, for this was her daughter's only chance. They must pray for Alfred's return, and if this happens Louis will apologize—apologize or go to work.

Maman is grim. She must speak to Papa inside, immediately, and Bibi must put away his skates and take his nap. Papa obeys, but Bibi lingers with his uncle and they make a disconsolate pair. It is, in fact, a grim household to which the ebullient Desmonde returns. Louis won't smile, Bibi won't smile—and, surprisingly, neither will Mignonette, who is grimmest of all. She demands of the puzzled Desmonde an answer to a question—something of hers is missing and does he know anything about it?

"Ah, you have discovered the loss! Oui, I have them."

Mignonette restrains an impulse to take a punch and coldly orders Desmonde to return them, but he declines. "I keep them to look at, since they remind me of you." So now the girl does sock him. Desmonde is dazed. Why such a fuss? They have holes in them. But if she wants them back that badly he will return them—and will even put them on her! This time he gets slapped harder than before, and Mignonette runs upstairs. Desmonde wonders aloud why a woman should come off the hinges because of a pair of gloves. He joins Bibi and Louis in their melancholy.

Papa, returning, is concerned about his son. "If you have broken your hockey stick, I will fix it," he comforts. "Whatever you have broken, my son, I will fix it." Such tenderness is too much for the boy and he bursts into tears, and Maman hurries in to comfort him. Soon the lad is telling them what happened at school, with some new details. Somebody, not Bibi, made a drawing from the magazine and made it worse by taking off all the clothes and draw-ing in the face of Miss Short, the geometry teacher.

Maman is concerned for her son and furious at her men—but Bibi defends the men. It is not their fault. It isn't Uncle Des-monde's fault for giving him the magazine. It's Sally O'Hare. "It is she who tells the teacher I have brought the magazine to school. And then, in the principal's office, they ask her if I drew the picture and she says yes, I drew it. It is a lie!"

The principal had laughed when Bibi denied drawing the picture —laughed and said he had heard about the Bonnard family. "He says he has heard that I have an uncle who drinks all his life, and another uncle who chases after all the women, and that my father is a crazy musician, so no wonder I am like I am and draw dirty pictures." And the principal, Mr. Frye, has ordered Bibi to report to his office every day and have his hand beaten with a strap until he confesses.

Mild, amiable Papa becomes a man aroused. The honor of the family is at stake. "We must fight!" Desmonde and Louis are with him. Bibi informs them that Mr. Frye probably still is at school, and Papa declares, "My brothers! There is a man named Frye who seeks the truth. Shall we go to help him find it?" They shall indeed, and in their Gallic fervor they are not unlike Athos, Porthos, and Aramis, three other Frenchmen who waged glorious battle for the right. On the way out Uncle Louis is thoughtful enough to grab a bottle of wine.

The curtain falls.

ACT III

At school the principal is in his office enjoying *La Vie Parisienne,* but he hides it in his lap when there is a knock on the door. The three musketeers step in, ominously, and Papa introduces himself as Bibi's father.

Mr. Frye is inclined to shrug off the trouble with offensive ease. It always happens that a boy denies he did something, but he *knows* that Bibi is guilty.

"I am the uncle who drinks," says Louis. "We will have some wine."

The principal coldly declines and as coldly asks the gentlemen to leave. "I have heard of you," he sneers, "and I understand now why the picture was unbelievably obscene." The men restrain themselves from violence, and Papa tries to reason with Mr. Frye. The principal becomes more coolly insulting, even in the face of physical menace. Louis has found the strap hanging on a wall and brandishes it; Desmonde is ready to take a punch. Threatening his callers with jail if they lay a hand on him, Mr. Frye rises and orders them out—and as he rises the magazine falls from his lap.

The Bonnards enjoy his discomfiture. Desmonde, taking the magazine, shows a picture and says, "I like this one, don't you?" The principal primly asserts he has not looked at it. Papa, picking up Desmonde's cue, has a devilish idea. "Look at this man," he says to Desmonde. "You have seen him before? In this—of obtaining the garters?"

Desmonde is not too slow. "Ah, oui." He peers closely at Frye's face. "I have seen you before."

"At the Casino Burlesque, no?" queries Papa.

Desmonde joyfully seizes the fiction and elaborates on it. This is the man who sits in the front row and pays no attention to any part of the show except the taking off of the clothes. The more frenzied the principal's denials become, the more certain the Bonnards are that he is a patron of the Burlesque. "You are mistaken. How can you say that?" says Frye, now plainly worried.

Papa says, grimly, "We can say it. And people will believe us." They could do to the principal just what the principal has done to Bibi. Madame Charbon, who keeps the grocery on Rideau Street, would be a good one to tell because this old gossip is better than a newspaper. And the doorman at the Casino Burlesque is a friend of Desmonde's. Surely *he* will remember Mr. Frye.

They now have the principal in a panic. Papa takes command. "Louis, there are paper cups in the hall. We will have some wine. And now, the class will come to order. . . ."

Lights fade; the curtain falls.

SCENE II

The musketeers are returning home—obviously joyfully, for Bibi can hear them singing the "Marseillaise" as they approach. "Bibi," Papa announces, "the truth has won a great victory today."

"My principal now understands that I did not draw the picture?"

"Understands!" chortles Desmonde. "He *insists* that you did not draw the picture." Louis pours wine and offers a toast to the Bonnard family, from Charlemagne to Bibi. "You are very great men," says the boy.

Action and triumph have so stirred Louis that he now proposes to go out and look for Alfred and bring him back and make peace. Bibi is inspired to do a little crusading of his own—to go next door and shake up the fleas of one Sally O'Hare.

It would be a happy, relieved household, but Mignonette is packing to leave, according to Maman.

DESMONDE—Why?

MAMMAN—Why? After what you've done? (*With anger and frustration.*) Desmonde, I never really thought you took them. And now I'm so ashamed! This girl is different! You could see that she is different! (*She turns to* PAPA.) You'll have to speak to him. He's admitted that he has them.

PAPA (*worried*)—Desmonde, you have them?

DESMONDE—Mignonette told you? Yes, I have them. But this is nothing to slap a man for; this is no reason to pack up and go. I thought she had a sense of humor!

MAMAN (*horrified*)—A sense of humor!

PAPA (*holding his head*)—Mon Dieu! Desmonde! How did you get them?

DESMONDE—She forgot them.

MAMAN—Forgot them? How could she forget them?

DESMONDE—How? She was wearing them, she took them off, she forgot them! Right here!"

PAPA—Here? The living room? She took off her nightgown in the living room?

DESMONDE—Oui! We came in and—nightgown? How, nightgown?

PAPA—This that we speak of! The nightgowns of Mignonette that you have taken and . . .

DESMONDE (*overlapping him*)—What nightgowns? I speak of gloves!

PAPA—. . . hidden away so that you might . . . Gloves?

DESMONDE—Gloves! (*Demonstrating.*) Gloves!

MAMAN—Desmonde! What have you done with Mignonette's nightgowns?

DESMONDE—What nightgowns? I know nothing of nightgowns! Name of a name, who is crazy here?

PAPA—Not me. I say no more. I am through. (*He goes to get a drink.*)

DESMONDE—This is like coming into the cinema in the middle of the picture! Why do I not have a synopsis?

MAMAN (*desperately*)—Desmonde, we've always laughed at the things you've done, but this . . . ! I don't think I'll ever forgive you for this. You broke that girl's heart with those pictures of the house up the Gatineau and then on top of it, to do this nasty, childish thing . . . ! She's a *nice* girl! I don't want her to go, she's all alone! Oh, I could beat you. I could really beat you.

DESMONDE (*just as desperately*)—For what?

MAMAN—What have you done with the nightgowns?

DESMONDE—Suzanne! I have taken no nightgowns! Believe me, I do not eat this kind of bread! Somebody has to believe me! (*And he runs out into the hall towards* MIGNONETTE'S *room.*) Mignonette!

PAPA—Susan, I do not believe my brother did this.

MAMAN—Of course he did it! (*She starts for the stairs.*)

PAPA—Where are you going?

MAMAN—Upstairs to look through the laundry again. (*She goes up.* PAPA *takes a large swallow of his drink, puts the glass down and starts after* MAMAN. *He trips over* BIBI'S *roller skates.*)

PAPA—Name of a cow! (*He picks up the skates and strides to the window seat, pulls open the lid, and throws the skates in. He stands looking at the clutter in there, shakes his head with a half smile and says to himself, "What junk!" and starts messing around with some of the things, then decides it's no use, closes the lid and walks away. He gets halfway across the room before he slowly begins to realize that he saw something in that window seat that shouldn't be there: the nightgowns. He stops short, his jaw drops, his eyes pop, then he turns and leaps for the window seat. He bangs open the lid, and starts pulling out nightgowns in a fury of amazement, at the same time calling:*) Maman! Maman! Maman! (*He bangs down the lid and with the nightgowns bundled in a ball against his stomach, he rushes for the dining room and is almost there before he remembers that* MAMAN *is upstairs. He turns and heads for the stairs, begins to lose a nightgown, has to renegotiate.*) Maman! Maman! (*He runs upstairs. A moment, then he comes rushing down again, with* MAMAN *right behind.*)

MAMAN—Where is he?

PAPA—He went next door, to see Sally! (*Still holding the night-gowns, he takes her hand and they run for the door.*) The back way! It is quicker the back way!

Desmonde, the gay, the debonair, the wolf, now is pleading earnestly and desperately with Mignonette to listen and to believe him. He stole no nightgowns and has no idea who stole them; all he did was keep a pair of gloves. But hard is the heart of Mignonette, and to her Desmonde is a man who steals night-gowns, garters, gloves and girls. Did he not, indeed, once say to her "From you I will steal something of greater significance?"

"I meant your heart! I love you!" Desmonde cries—and he is just as amazed at what he has said as she is. "Bibi," Desmonde continues, "did you hear? I *love* her!"

This declaration is of the utmost importance to Bibi, for he knows now what he must do—but he has to think it out aloud. Standing before Desmonde and Mignonette, he muses, "Then we have a question of truth and love both, n'est-ce pas? . . . And when the two are together, truth and love, it is very strong . . ."

It is hard for Bibi to do what he must—but he does it. "I, too, am a Bonnard. When one is hurt, all are hurt. I—" he gulps— "I stole the nightgowns."

Mignonette does not believe it, not by half. But after a moment of puzzlement Desmonde does—he believes, and understands. When Bibi repeats most solemnly that he filched the garments, Mignonette begins to believe, too. "But why?" she asks.

Desmonde interposes, "One does not need to say why. He walks in his sleep."

Bibi goes to the window seat to retrieve his troublesome loot, opens the lid and finds the garments gone. He cries, "There is a thief in the house!"

Maman and Papa have heard him. Papa commands his son, "Come here, please," and the others find it convenient to go elsewhere.

PAPA—Bibi . . . Bibi . . . this has been a bad day for you, Bibi. Let us sit down. (*They sit together on the sofa. Pause. *PAPA, *staring straight ahead, unconsciously pulls a cigar out of his pocket and starts to offer it to the boy, then realizes and hastily puts it back. Another pause.*) There is no need to ask why you took the nightgowns.

BIBI—No.

PAPA—The reason is obvious. You took them because . . . (*His face goes blank.*) Why did you take them?

BIBI—I wished to see . . . I wished to see . . . Ah, Papa! One kiss can change a man's life, n'est-ce pas?

PAPA—Mais oui.

BIBI (*dreamily, stretching out, remembering*)—Yesterday in the movies with Mignonette, holding hands, so nice and warm, watching Rudolph Valentino chase Vilma Banky, I look up at Mignonette and I think: "She is so pretty in the face—how is the rest?"

PAPA—You are curious.

BIBI—Oui. Curious.

PAPA—Nothing more.

BIBI—There is something more. But I do not know what it is.

PAPA (*nodding*)—Eh bien, it is this something more of which we will speak.

BIBI—You know what it is?

PAPA—I know. But first, the nightgowns; I still see no reason.

BIBI—If a woman has no nightgown, then, when she walks from the bedroom to the bathroom—(*He stops, and the two stare at each other.*)—I am as stupid as an owl.

PAPA—I agree. Bibi, we have a saying in French: "Le coeur a ses raisons, que la raison ne connait point." Tu comprends?

BIBI (*translating it slowly*)—"The heart has its reasons—which reason knows nothing of." No, I do not understand.

PAPA—It means that when a man is in love, he is as stupid as an owl.

BIBI—Oh, oui!

PAPA—It means also that one can trust the heart—if the heart is pure. Bibi, this desire you have is not evil, en soi-meme. It is a desire not only to see, it is something more—which you do not yet know—but since it is natural, it cannot be evil. It becomes evil only when the reason is evil. This is why the world is mixed up.

BIBI—I, too, am mixed up.

PAPA—And I. Let us try to unmix ourselves. We speak now of love, Bibi.

BIBI (*remembering*)—Love. It is almost impossible to know. (PAPA *looks at him, startled.*)

PAPA—That is correct. But when one knows it . . . ! Ah, then! And where there is love, my son, there is also desire. They go together; love must have the desire; I do not believe there can be love without it. But! It is possible to have the desire without love and this is where the world falls into evil. For example!

You do not understand why the principal of your school beat you.

BIBI—No.

PAPA—It is because he has been brought up to believe that the desire is wrong. And since he himself has the desire, he is even more mixed than we are. He has been brought up in a world where the desire has been used so badly, so badly, believe me, that now it, itself, is thought to be bad. And this is wrong. It is wrong, Bibi. And the reason for this condition? It is because so many people are without love.

BIBI—Many people?

PAPA—Many. (*Long pause.*)

BIBI—Uncle Louis? (PAPA *glances at him and nods.*)

PAPA—You love your Uncle Louis.

BIBI—I love him strongly.

PAPA—It is good. He has great need of love. Without love, one is defeated.

BIBI—But this love is different. The love I have for Uncle Louis is different from the love I have for you. And this, also, is different from the way I love Maman. And then—Mignonette!

PAPA (*he's almost talking to himself now*)—Oui! And this love we speak of now, Bibi, when it is real, when it is true, it is the greatest love of all. I know; we have it here in this house, Maman and I. It is the best, it is the most natural—the true love for the one of your life, the only one. In this way the world comes down to a house and a room and a bed, and all the world is in that bed, if there are two people in love. This is something you will not know for many years, Bibi. It is possible never to know it. I hope you will. If you are as lucky as I am, you will.

BIBI—I will look for someone like Maman.

PAPA—No, look for your heart's need—and she will come. Eh bien! I have said everything and nothing. And still you do not know what I wish to say.

BIBI (*hesitantly*)—I think so . . .

PAPA—Perhaps when you are older, and we speak of this again, I will find better words . . .

BIBI—Is it what Grandpa has said? That one must have the knowledge to use the mind and the heart and the glands together correctly?

PAPA (*positively*)—Ah, oui! C'est ca! This is it! He is no fool, your grandfather!

The entente has been established, man to man. Papa offers his son some wine and the boy accepts it with dignity. Then Papa suggests that the lad go to his father's closet and get therefrom a

certain dark blue suit and put it on. Bibi understands. This is his
growing-up. Quite formally he shakes hands with his father and,
moving toward the stair, says, "A bientôt, mon vieux."

Maman slips out of the dining room, having listened, of course,
to every word. Tenderly she kisses her husband and the kiss is as
tenderly returned. This might have gone on longer, but Uncle
Louis is back—with Alfred in tow. Alfred is not exactly in bad
shape, but is wobbly . . . and quite happy. Louis explains that,
after a search all the way down to Rideau Street, he has found
Alfred right outside in the bushes.

Alfred makes for Louis' water cooler as Louis explains that all
problems have been settled. Alfred's sons will go to the University and the daughters will go to work.

Félice appears, absorbs the situation with some pleasure and
some dismay, and takes charge. Louis and Alfred will both come
home with her—now! For once Louis is willing to go home, for now
he has a son-in-law who will defend him. All is well, too, with
Desmonde and Mignonette, and as an act of both renunciation and
gratitude Desmonde brings down as a present for his nephew The
Collection—a large, glassed picture frame containing some of the
most ornate women's garters you ever saw in your life.

Bibi, who has come down in his father's suit, which is not too
large, is enchanted, but Maman once again is scandalized. Papa,
the old diplomat, confiscates the hoard and advises his son, "If you
wish to be a man who collects garters, do not do it secondhand."

But Bibi must have something from his grateful Uncle Desmonde
—a medal! Desmonde opens his coat, unpins a decoration from
the lining, and bestows it ceremoniously upon the boy. The group
is momentarily joined by Grandpa, who descends in his "faire
l'amour" outfit. "I am late," says Grandpa.

"You should be in bed!" Maman protests.

Gently the old man says, as he leaves, "It is only a matter of
time."

And now, to complete the picture, there arrives from next door
one Sally O'Hare—a new Sally, with her tooth braces gone and her
hair beautifully curled. She almost swoons at the sight of Bibi in
long pants. "Oh, Robert!" she exclaims. Maman says how sweet
Sally looks, and observes that her braces are gone. Sally answers
with a mouthful of firm, white teeth on display. All the grown-ups
find convenient reasons for going to other parts of the house, leaving the adolescents alone.

SALLY—Gee, you look different, Robert. (BIBI *stands quietly
sure, and a little arrogant.*)

BIBI—Do I? Why did you do this today? Why did you get me into trouble?

SALLY—I don't know.

BIBI—This is an answer? Name of a name! You know I did not draw that picture! Who drew it?

SALLY (*very much smitten*)—Jimmy Bishop.

BIBI—Then why didn't you say so?

SALLY (*dreamily*)—Who cares about Jimmy Bishop? Gee, you look nice. (*And she puts her hand to her hair.*)

BIBI—Huh? (*He will never figure that one out.*) Come here. (*She comes quite close.*) We will have the truth now. I did not draw the picture.

SALLY—No, Robert.

BIBI—My Uncle Louis is a fine man.

SALLY—Yes, Robert.

BIBI—Also my Grandpa, also my Uncle Desmonde, also my Papa, also my Maman.

SALLY—Yes, Robert.

BIBI—Bien. (*The case is closed. He looks at her hair, nods, then motions to her mouth.*) The teeth, please. (*She shows them gladly.*) Bien. You wish to be my girl?

SALLY (*coyly enigmatic*)—Mmmmmmmmmmmm?

BIBI—But if you are my girl, you won't get me in any more trouble. (*No answer. That worries him, but he lets it pass.*) Bien. You are my girl. I will give you something. (*And he starts to unpin the medal.*)

SALLY—Oh! Robert! For me to wear?

BIBI (*more like* DESMONDE *every minute*)—It is a very famous medal, accepted personally from Le Général. (*The medal unpinned, he gets her into position.*) Eh, bien! (*And with exactly the same flair that* DESMONDE *showed, he pins the medal on her breast and gives its resting place a few loving pats. As* MIGNONETTE *did before her,* SALLY *jumps back, but then, being a different type, she clenches her fist and takes a lusty swing.* BIBI *ducks it easily and laughs.*) Oho! You Americans! (*PAPA enters hastily.*)

PAPA—Bibi, could I speak to you for just one moment?

BIBI—It is nothing, Papa. I merely—(*And his voice breaks disastrously. He clutches his throat.*)—I merely—(*His voice breaks again. A look of fright comes over his face.*) Papa! What happens here?

CURTAIN

THE WISTERIA TREES *

A Play in Three Acts

BY JOSHUA LOGAN

Based on Anton Chekhov's "The Cherry Orchard"

£VER since he was in Princeton, along with Henry Fonda, Myron McCormick and other since-famous contemporaries, Joshua Logan had wanted to do something about Anton Chekhov's "The Cherry Orchard." He did not want to do merely another version or adaptation—he wanted to change its locale to America, for he felt that similar social problems existed here. When, in 1949, Helen Hayes expressed lively interest in the undertaking, Mr. Logan went to work on "The Wisteria Trees." The first Boston tryout performances were worrisome, for audiences were missing points. To any showman of wisdom and experience, this would mean that he had failed to *make* his points; so Logan went to work rewriting and Miss Hayes and her company spent the ensuing weeks learning new speeches and cues and unlearning old ones. When the play made its bow in New York all were in agreement that Miss Hayes was giving a rich and splendid performance—but there was a division of opinion about the work of the dramatist. Some felt that Mr. Logan had missed the subtlety and the irony of Chekhov's comedy, or had despoiled it by jerking it out of its native soil and transplanting it. Others, including the editor of this volume, believed that Mr. Logan had done a skillful job which had done no disservice to the memory of the Russian creator; they believed, indeed, that Mr. Logan was something of a creator on his own in adding a pleasant warmth and an appreciable clarity to "The Cherry Orchard."

In "The Wisteria Trees" the chatelaine of the Russian fruit orchard has become Lucy Andrée Ransdell, a lady from an old Louisiana French family. Her estate has become an ancient Louisiana holding, Wisteria Plantation. The park outside the great mansion had been achieved by a pioneer who had planted live oak trees, and by the pioneer's wife, who went along behind him planting young wisteria vines. For a time the trees grew—long enough to be tall enough and strong enough. Then the vines, thick, sturdy and grasping, had done what a wisteria will always do if it is allowed to; they had killed the trees and continued to use their dead trunks for support. Thus Lucy Andrée Ransdell's park had become a grove of wisteria, and in Spring a place of great beauty.

It is April now, some time before the turn of the century, and Lucy is coming home after five years abroad. It is a great house, for even the room which is being made ready now, the children's nursery of the days before the Civil War, is large and elegant, although it is in disrepair. The ceiling is tall, the moldings are carved, and there is a crystal chandelier. There are reminders of the children of old—a child's piano, children's furniture, some old toys. On a shelf are two stuffed animals made of felt, now bedraggled—one a frog in a frock coat with a sword and pistol at his belt; the other a mouse in a white satin dress and a bridal veil. Facing the park and a gallery are two very tall French windows equipped with wooden blinds; above them is a fan-shaped West Indian blind. A tall archway leads to the hall and the rest of the house, and in it are more French windows. The vines have grown so thickly and so close to the house that they screen out any view of the outside; indeed, one of them has started pushing into the house and has partially wrecked the blind on the fanlight above the windows.

Not much of the room can be seen until Dolly May, a young Negro girl, brings in a lamp, for it is four o'clock in the morning and some time before dawn. Dolly May hears the whistle of a train and imitates its sound; then she calls to another part of the house, "Miss Martha, that's the train," and Martha brings in another lamp. She is 25 and pretty, but she dresses very plainly. She asks Dolly May to turn up her lamp to make the room look more cheerful—but the light reveals more than cheer. The rain has come in again and more plaster has broken off. She asks that the lamp be turned down a little bit, then changes her mind. "No—leave it up," she says. "She might as well face facts." She calls for one Henry Arthur Henry to bring more fireplace wood.

Henry Arthur Henry is carrying a bunch of flowers as well as an armful of wood. He puts the flowers on a table but they fall off—and in reaching for them he drops the wood. "Did you see that accident happen to me?" he asks in the tone of one who has long been pursued by mischance. Giggling, Dolly May explains to

Martha that this sort of thing is why Henry Arthur is called Mister Misery.

Martha hears a horse and Dolly May runs to see who it is. "Mista Yancy Loper's comin'," she announces, and Martha starts to walk away. The Negro girl inquires, "Don't you want to see your fiancé?"

Martha stiffly denies that she and Yancy Loper are engaged and Dolly May rejoins, "Everybody says you all is ideal mates! He's rich and you're poor. It's ideal!"

Loper comes in. He is about 40. His face and neck are very sunburned. He is dressed in expensive clothes but he does not wear them well; his shoes are perhaps too yellow, his vest too loud, his tie completely wrong. "I expected you all to be havin' a comin'-home party," he says, and is told the train was late. Martha goes to fetch him some coffee, which gives Dolly May a chance to get in some good work. "She could use a rich husband, Mista Yancy," she hints but Loper isn't listening. He has gone to the window and is looking out. "What are you lookin' at?" asks Dolly May.

"That poor little plantation store. Dolly May—one day before you was born Miss Lucy was over there buyin' candy from us. My daddy threw an empty corn-whiskey bottle at me and smashed me in the face—give me a nosebleed. Miss Lucy dragged me in here . . . right here . . . used to be a washstand there . . . and she bathed my face with rose water. 'Don't cry, little poor one,' she said, 'you're gonna live.'" But Mista Roper doesn't look so poor to Dolly May.

The sound of horses *and* carriage wheels means that Lucy has arrived. First to enter is Scott, an old Negro in a coachman's coat, who merely crosses to the rear quarters of the house. Next are Martha and Antoinette. Antoinette, Lucy's daughter, is 17 and very beautiful. Following is Cassie, Antoinette's Negro nurse—and over her bandanna Cassie wears a huge Paris hat. She deposits a bag and various packages.

"And Mama brought some pretty clothes for *you*, Martha," Antoinette exclaims. Then, Mama still has no idea what money means." She calls, "Mama, come see the children's parlor!"

Shortly Lucy does come, clad in a smart traveling costume. She is at once elated and deeply moved by her return to this room of her childhood. She plays the little piano a moment, looks lovingly at familiar objects, then calls eagerly for Gay to come in and Antoinette repeats the call—"Uncle Gay!" Lucy, with a "Little ol' Cousin Martha!" gives Martha a hug. Soon Gay—Gavin Leon Andrée, a well-tailored man in his early fifties—joins them, and so does Bowman Witherspoon, a florid man in his sixties.

Old Scott returns—pushing a shy little Negro girl who has a bouquet of flowers and a palmetto fan to Lucy. "What's your name?" Miss Lucy inquires. "Miss Lucy. I'se your namesake." Warmheartedly, Lucy asks Cassie for the box of chocolates they have brought with them and gives it to the Negro Lucy.

Lucy is so elated, so full of remembrance, that she does not seem to notice the disrepair of the room. She recalls a time their mother made a white satin suit for her brother Gay when he was 6, so he could go to Mardi Gras as the Young Prince, and he wouldn't wear it—burned it, in fact—because a Negro boy laughed at him. "Oh, Gay—my brother, my dreamer," she exclaims, kissing him. "You've been holding up the roof all by yourself, haven't you?" Next she greets Witherspoon, asks how his plantation is doing.

"We've had a bad year."

Her rejoinder is, "I've had five of those." And to Martha she says, "You're just as young as the day you walked into this house—" and, finishing by turning to Gavin, "—almost apologizing because her parents had died!"

Antoinette has discovered the frog and the mouse and Lucy begins an old nursery song about them—about a frog who went a-courtin' Miss Mouse. Loper, who has been standing aside and not too much at ease, steps up and greets Lucy with a hello.

"I remember who you are 'cause you're blushing," she laughs. "You're Yancy Loper! You may own half of Louisiana now, but you'll always be the same sweet little boy who used to sell us jelly beans and corn candy—and blushed with every scoopful. And Antoinette tells me that there's a lot of talk about you and our darling Cousin Martha. I do hope there's something to it." There is a strange silence in the room and she inquires, "Have I said something wrong?"

Bowman Witherspoon asks Cassie what she thinks of Paris and Cassie replies, "Oh, it got a lot of parks, but they all too laid out for me. And there's marble statues of nekkid men all over the place—most of 'em's called Apollo. Miss Lucy says 'Isn't they beautiful statues, Cassie?' And I says, 'Miss Lucy, I dressed and undressed your little son Lee before he got drowned in the river, and afore that I dressed your little boy cousins—all ages! Honey, these here Apollos ain't no recreation for me!' "

Breakfast is ready, and Lucy, Loper, Witherspoon and Dolly May start for the dining room, but Antoinette holds the others back. "I didn't tell Mama about the plantation," the girl confesses to Martha and Uncle Gay. "She doesn't know!" Martha, amazed, queries, "You mean to say you and Cassie traveled seven thousand miles

and you never told her what might happen?" Cassie confides that
Miss Lucy was in no condition to hear bad news.

"Then why'd she come home?" demands Martha.

"To get away from *him*."

Antoinette relates how she had gone to Paris with Cassie to see
her mother for the first time in five years, and how Lucy had ex-
claimed, "Oh, my little girl, thank God you've come. Take me
home—take me back to Louisiana."

Martha makes up her mind: "Then she's *not* going to hear about
this auction. Uncle Gay, what are you going to do?" Gavin evades
a reply and goes on to breakfast, while Antoinette asks Martha if he
has collected this month's rent from the tenants. "Uncle Gay? He
can't ask a Negro for money. They're *all* his friends," Martha
answers.

Loper comes back with a plate of food, then, seeing who is there,
ducks out. It is two years since people started saying Yancy and
Martha were "right" for each other, but he hasn't asked her yet.
Cassie offers some advice: Some day she should sneak up on Mister
Yancy, look him straight in the eye and give him a nice, big smile,
instead of just looking at him sideways. When Antoinette and
Cassie have gone to breakfast Martha turns to the mirror over the
mantelpiece, smiles a practice smile, drops her face into her hands
and prays: "Oh, God, take care of Antoinette and everybody and
let Cousin Lucy keep this place—and let me be able . . . to look
him in the eye."

After Martha has left the room Dolly May brings in a coffee tray
to pick up coffee things in the room, and is encountered by a debonair young Negro whose name used to be Jock, but now it is Jacques
—for he has been Lucy's servant in Paris. He has exaggerated Con-
tinental manners and he tries out his French on Dolly May. "Who,"
he inquires, "*êtes vous?*" She identifies herself—and she remembers
an encounter with him among the cotton bales years ago. Jacques
deposits a leather hatbox and umbrella, removes one of his gloves
and, bowing low, kisses the girl's hand—a performance so startling
that she drops a cup and saucer. The crash brings Martha running,
and in a moment old Scott comes too, to order Dolly May to fetch
cream for Miss Lucy, who is going to have her coffee in here.

Lucy and Gavin saunter in and Lucy is full of plans for redecorat-
ing the house from top to bottom. The sun has come up and the
window blinds are opened, to reveal the wisteria in all its beauty.
Loper appears in the doorway, asking, "Miss Lucy, can I come in?"

Lucy—Why, yes, Yancy.

Loper—I got to be on my way. Dawgonnit, I sure hate to leave.

Lucy—Well, it was a real treat to see you, Yancy.

Loper—Oh, I'm not going 'til it's all settled.

Lucy—Settled?

Loper—Miss Lucy, I've gone to a lot of trouble for your family. Even though your brother here stands in front of the post office every Sunday mornin' havin' his shoes shined and talkin'. Seems he don't approve of a turkeyneck havin' bought up land 'round here. Seems he talks about me like I wasn't even dirt. (Scott *enters with coffee tray.*)

Lucy—Where's my coffee? Thank you, Scott. Thank you, my sweet old rock of Gibraltar. I'm so glad you're still alive.

Scott—Day before yesterday.

Lucy (*to* Gavin)—What?

Gavin—He doesn't hear well.

Lucy—Oh. (*To* Scott.) Day before yesterday.

Scott—Dat's right.

Lucy (*turning to* Martha)—I wonder what we're talkin' about.

Loper—Miss Lucy, you did something for me once. Now you're in trouble and I'm going to do something for you.

Lucy—My troubles are over, Yancy. I'm back in this house. (Scott *places a taboret for* Lucy's *coffee cup. She pats his arm.*)

Scott—Day before yesterday.

Loper—Miss Lucy, I figured out a way to keep this place from going up for auction.

Lucy—What?

Gavin (*throwing his dice*)—Box cars.

Lucy—Put those dice away, Gay. What, Yancy?

Loper—Now it isn't scheduled 'til the twenty-second of September, so we got plenty of time if we work fast.

Lucy—Auction? Oh, Yancy, people have been talking about auctions and foreclosures ever since I was a little girl. I've always found that Mama had the best plan for them. Ignore them!

Loper—But, Miss Lucy, you can't ignore the facts.

Lucy—Oh, yes, you can, Yancy, if you put your mind to it. (*A more important thought occurs to her. She rises suddenly and crosses to* Gavin.) Gay! You never wrote me about our old Mary Ann's funeral. Was she in the main parlor?

With Loper's problem thus taken care of, Lucy and Gavin talk animatedly about the funeral of an old colored woman—but Loper is a stubborn man. He brings up his subject again and warns Lucy forcefully that unless something is done she will lose Wisteria Plantation. Lucy lightly assures him they *will* do something—take out another mortgage or sell some more cotton land.

Gavin is forced to tell her the cotton land is all gone, but she does not seem to mind. They'll just have to do something else. She spies Gavin's old dominoes on the table and is more interested in them. But Loper persists and tells Lucy there is only one thing to do. "You see, this old park don't have to stay the way it is. It could be cut up for strawberry patches and truck farms and leased out."

Lucy objects that there isn't enough room for the little truck farms, and Loper explains, "Naturally, we'll have to tear down some of these old buildings—the carriage house and the old slave quarters. But before that, you got to clear out the whole park—cut down all this damned wisteria!"

For the first time, Lucy is hit. She tries to tell Loper about this park—how it was part of a grant to her family from the King of France, and how her grandfather planted the live oaks and her grandmother followed behind with the gardeners and planted the little wisteria vines beside them. "This park is a masterpiece," she exclaims. "You wouldn't want us to destroy it just to make a living, would you?"

Grimly Loper counters with, "Don't you want to eat?" Gavin sides with his sister in refusing to cut down the trees, and Loper snorts, "Trees! Stop callin' 'em trees! They're just old vines that climbed up around young live oaks and choked 'em to death. . . . Stop treatin' 'em with respect! They certainly ain't treatin' you with any! Are they wrappin' themselves around your brains?" He strides off, with a warning reminder that September 22 is the date of the auction. Lucy comments, "He's very nice. He's just a little upset, that's all."

Bowman Witherspoon has been dozing in a chair. Lucy rouses him and he promptly asks her for a loan of $240 for the interest on his mortgage. When they tell him about their own troubles he says cheerfully that they shouldn't worry, and wanders off.

But Martha sees someone else coming through the park. "Here's Peety. Came in last night," she informs Lucy. Peter Whitfield is young, lean and athletic, but his hair is too long and his clothes are shabby. There is an intensity about him. Lucy looks at him blankly until he identifies himself and explains, "Rode all the way from Memphis under a freight car, especially to see you."

Now Lucy remembers, and she embraces him, weeping and crying, "Oh, Peety, you made my son into a little god. He could run like a young horse, and you taught him to swim before he was six years old. How could it happen?" And Peter, the ex-companion and tutor for Lucy's son who was drowned, says, "The current was too strong for him."

Under Lucy's questioning Peter tells of himself. He didn't make enough money tutoring to graduate. He used to make up funny jingles at the dinner table, but now he is publishing a small magazine of new verse forms. He has brought her a copy, slightly smudged with freight-car grease. Lucy is touched at the autograph in it— "To Lucy Andrée Ransdell, who gives to the old South one reason for existing." She riffles through it and is brought up short by a poem titled "The Southern Gentleman . . . May His Tribe Decrease"—a verse which asks protestingly who made up the rules about white supremacy.

"And it's in print," Lucy marvels. "Louisiana certainly has changed since I've been away." The change, however, cannot be generally noticeable, for Peter's magazine has come out only once.

Martha suddenly remembers two telegrams have come for Lucy and she brings them. But they are cablegrams, not telegrams. Lucy takes them, starts toward the table to read them, looks at Peter and suddenly tears them up, throwing the pieces on the floor. She suggests that they all go to sleep. She heads for bed, Peter goes to the river for a swim, and Martha, Antoinette and Gavin remain for a council of war.

They analyze their chances. Antoinette could marry a rich man, for example. Gay didn't collect any rent, for the Negroes have had a bad year. He did get $10 from Ephram—but he won it shooting dice. Martha explodes, "Uncle Gay, don't you see—you're easy game! They feed you corn whiskey, start singin' and dancin'—then they pull out the dice and you're gone!"

Another possibility is rich Aunt Catherine in Charleston—but Aunt Catherine disapproves of Lucy's behavior and Martha made the mistake of calling Aunt Catherine a narrow-minded old fool. Gavin, suddenly the man of decision, announces a three-barreled campaign: Lucy will talk with Yancy Loper, and no man ever refuses Lucy; Antoinette will go to Charleston to see her dear Aunt Catherine—and he will go down to the courthouse again and talk about getting a loan on a promissory note.

The council is broken up by the arrival of old Scott, who glares angrily at Gavin and orders him to bed as if he were a little boy. Gavin tells him to go away, that he'll get undressed himself—but Scott just glares at him until he weakens and says, "All right, you old heathen." And to the girls, "Nightie night." Martha and Antoinette go to bed, too. After a moment Lucy is seen slowly walking along the gallery. She enters the room through one of the French windows and looks around it. Seeing the torn cablegrams, she hesitates for a moment, then kneels and begins picking up the pieces tenderly.

The curtain falls.

ACT II

It is Summer, and with the windows all open the children's room looks as if it were outdoors. The vines are covered with leaves and the setting sun highlights the three servants who are working in the room—Henry Arthur, Dolly May and Jacques. Soon Lucy, Gavin and Loper come in from a stroll, and Loper is still trying to get the pair to think and talk business. He warns them that Texas truck farmers are just itching to get at this place, and time is getting short. And B. J. Henderson, a big Chicago business man, is coming here personally for the auction.

"Well," Lucy announces, "Mister B. J. Henderson is not going to get this plantation. Tell him about our Aunt Catherine, Gay." Smugly Gay informs Loper, "Mrs. Marius Andrée Berringer of Charleston, South Carolina, is sendin' us some money."

Loper demands why they hadn't said so before, and he is relieved until Lucy mentions the amount—$20,000. Loper almost explodes. "You two," he roars, "are the most flibberty-gibberty people I've ever seen in my life. Twenty thousand dollars!"

Lucy innocently asks if that is too much and he almost explodes again. He starts out, roaring, "Well, I'm either gonna bust out cryin' or foam up in a fit! Mister Gavin Andrée, you are a chicken-hearted old ninny!"

Lucy pleads earnestly with him to stay, saying, "I had a terrible feeling, the way you were walking out there, that you were goin' to wrap your arm around one of those Corinthian columns and pull it out and the whole house was goin' to crash down and bury us alive!" She breaks, covering her face and crying, "Oh, my God in heaven! . . . It's true! Your punishments come before you die."

LOPER—Punishments? (*He laughs.*) Why, you never committed a real sin in your life! (LUCY *looks at him in amazement.* GAVIN *senses hysteria.*)

GAVIN—Let's go, Lucy.

LUCY—I never committed a sin in my . . . Who's bein' chicken-hearted now, Yancy Loper? I'm being punished. Not Gay—me! I've been willful. When it came to gettin' married, I defied everybody. Our blood was runnin' thin so I decided to change it. I married an up-and-coming lawyer, and then found his one ambition was to be lord of a plantation and drink all the whiskey in the world. So . . . I filled his glass 'til it runnethed over. Before he died he used to bring some strange, crude men around for poker. There was an arrogant one that . . . well, after my lawyer husband died, those times I went to New Orleans to see the opera, I didn't see the opera . . .

GAVIN—Lucy, honey, that's all over.

LUCY—Gay, please! Even you'll admit I was punished then, Yancy. While my little son was showin' me how well he could swim, the river swallowed him up in front of my eyes. These trees turned yellow, the river turned black. I flew the coop! I took a boat for Europe, but not too fast for him. He was standin' in my cabin with a big, white smile. "Not so fast, Honey—you need someone to take care of you." God save me, it sounded good! So I gave him some money and he bought me a villa near a place he knew called . . . Monte Carlo. Then he got sick and I nursed him for three years.

GAVIN—Why didn't you send for me, Lucy?

LUCY—Oh, Gay, darling! The villa was sold to pay for the doctors, and he was well, so we went to Paris—a beautiful city, Yancy, with great, wide boulevards—and the most *exquisite* punishment of all. One morning while I was asleep he unlocked my dresser drawer and took Mama's diamonds—and then he went to live with a lady we'd met. A few days later he came knockin' at my door, but I had a new strength. My daughter was there. I'd almost forgotten I had one. She brought me back home where I thought I'd be safe. And you say I've never committed a sin—that I've never been punished? (*She breaks down. To cover her tears she takes her handkerchief from her purse and realizes that she has a cablegram. She holds it up.*) He's sittin' at our little café under the chestnut tree. (*Music can be heard faintly.*) He's sick again. He needs me. Do I hear music playin'?

GAVIN—Out back. Our famous plantation symphony orchestra—violin, tin horn, syrup barrel, wash tub . . .

LUCY—Is that still goin'? You know, we ought to give a soirée—with Japanese lanterns! But who is there left around here that we could . . . Would you come to our party, Yancy?

LOPER (*deeply moved*)—I don't think so.

LUCY—What do you want—a formal and written invitation?

LOPER—I wouldn't write you back. A lady once said my handwritin' looked like a chicken walked through an ink puddle and then on across the writin' paper. I was brought up just over there, where people don't write so good.

Lucy—You need somebody who could write letters for you. (*She walks over, touches his shoulder.*) A woman, Yancy . . . a wife. You could be an important man.

Loper—I'm real proud you think so.

Lucy—You wouldn't have anything against marrying a member of the Andrée family, would you?

Loper (*looking at her incredulously*)—I don't quite know what you're gettin' at, Miss Lucy.

Lucy—Her mother was a cousin of ours. Didn't you know that?

Loper—Her?

Lucy—Martha!

Loper—Oh, I think she's a wonderful young lady, Miss Lucy.

Gavin is full of surprises this afternoon. He now announces to his sister that she may have to find somebody else to run the plantation for her. "That little old Bank of Commerce over there wants me to be vice-president—three thousand dollars a year." It seems incredible, unless the bank just wants his fine old name to put on the front in gold letters; but Gavin explains that the bank has a new policy—it wants Negro depositors and Gavin has lots of Negro friends.

The budding banker is cut down to size by his old manservant, Scott, who brings in a cape and orders Gavin to put it on against the damp. Lucy asks Scott how old he is, but he is so deaf he can't understand her. Loper uses his big voice to do the questioning. Scott can't remember how old he is—but people were trying to get him mated before Gay's and Lucy's father was born. "Den I got Marse Gay when *he* was born." He turns to Gavin and scolds, "You tried to run away from me and go to war, but you didn't get far, did you?"

"Wish I had," Gavin replies. "That Proclamation emancipated everybody but me."

Loper asks Scott why he wouldn't go free and the old man answers, "Ain't sayin' I didn't want to go. Jest I was too busy with this little white nuisance here. I couldn't take time off to get 'mancipated. 'Member what a jubilation it was? Dey didn't know deirselves what dey was jubilatin' about! Them days everybody knew just where dey belonged. Now it's hard to figure out who's what."

The mosquitoes are beginning to buzz outside and Antoinette, Peter and Martha seek the shelter of the room. Loper begins to ride

Peter, taunting him about his poetry magazine, calling Peter Shakespeare and predicting the second issue will come out about a year from next Winter. Peter fights back, angrily, but trying to be analytical. Yancy, he says, is a poor man who has become surely and suddenly a rich one. He must be a part of the metabolism of nature—"just as there is a use for the beast who wolfs down everything that gets in his way, in our society there must be a use for you!"

Peter is no fool, and he is an intellectual rebel. He tries to put into words what is happening to the South:

"We're changing, like some lazy, prehistoric animal shedding its old skin. The only trouble is, there's no new one grown yet, and we don't even know what kind we need. And if anybody asks questions, that's treason. I could be tarred and feathered for just what I'm saying now. We've created nothing. Nobody paints anything but china. The Negroes do our singing. It's all right for a man to breed dogs, but he better not play the piano or he might be called a sissy, which means among other things a hermaphrodite. And you know we're lazy. We've stuffed ourselves with delicious food prepared by strong, black hands, and it's made us sleepy. And *who* wants to listen to all this? That little magazine of mine was fifty cents, and I reduced it to a quarter, but if anybody would have bought it I would have sold it for a penny. It wasn't any good because—you're right, Mister Gay—I don't know what I think. I hardly ever saw my father or my mother. We were all brought up in the kitchen, weren't we? How's this for the dinner table? (*Quoting.*)

> Lucky little Southern chillun
> Have *two* mothers, white and black.
> While Mummy's in the parlor
> They're with Mammy in the back!

I had one. Her name was Amy Lane. She weaned me at the kitchen table, picked me up when I fell down, slapped me when I was bad. I didn't even know she was black. I thought her skin was made out of purple velvet, and there was a place between her shoulder and her arm that was soft and warm and aromatic, and I could sleep there better than anywhere. Then they stopped me from eating in the kitchen. I don't know what's right or wrong—or good or bad. Do you?"

Peter's outburst has its impact. For moments they all are lost in thought. Then most of them go their various ways, with Loper departing with another warning about the twenty-second of September. Antoinette and Peter find themselves alone. The girl is surprised that Martha has left them alone, and Peter comments that Martha is afraid he will take advantage of Antoinette. The girl agrees. "She's still hoping I'll marry a fine, rich man so this place will stay in the family, but I don't care whether it stays in the family or not any more." Antoinette, too, seems to be part of the change in the South—and she confesses Peter has made her feel this way. The girl invites Peter for a stroll to the river, and it is obvious that she is deeply interested in him—but Lucy calls from the drawing room, "Peety! Come in here and be sociable!"

"Come on," says Peter, but Antoinette does not move. "Come on," he urges once again—and then he runs out. Antoinette raises her hands to her head in a gesture of frustration and anger.

The curtain falls.

Scene II

It is an Autumn night, and a party is in progress. The big chandelier is lighted and Japanese lanterns are hung along the gallery. An orchestra is playing a Lancer's Piff-Paff-Pouf for the dancers on the gallery, and Bowman Witherspoon can be heard calling the dances. Inside the room some of the furniture has been moved aside and Jacques and Dolly May are dancing to Wither-spoon's calls. Scott is carrying a tray with a bottle of whiskey; the Negro girl, Little Miss Lucy, is carrying a large cocoanut cake which she is trying to serve to two little children sitting in two of the little children's chairs; Henry Arthur Henry is moving chairs. There are punch cups on a side table.

Another dance ends and Scott pronounces indignantly, "In de old days we had General Lafayette and de Crown Prince o' Naples at our parties. Now, it's the livery-stable man an' de postmaster— and even *dey* isn't anxious to come." Cassie warns him to be quiet, for the two children sitting there are the postmaster's.

Martha comes in to ask if Mister Gay has come back from the auction and Jacques saucily volunteers the guess that the auction is over and Mister Gay is afraid to come back. He begins to laugh and says, "I was just thinkin' if Miss Lucy loses this place she'll *have* to go back to Paris." Martha stiffly informs him that Mr. Andrée has power of attorney from his aunt to buy the place, no matter how much it costs, and he even has a cash deposit.

Witherspoon comes puffing in, commenting that dancing is a problem with high blood pressure. "That postmaster's wife can wag a healthy tail, I'm tellin' you." The Negro Miss Lucy offers cake around, with no takers.

Another part of the party is about to begin—the children's part. Martha, Lucy and Antoinette enter, and Martha sits at the piano. Scott takes down the two stuffed animals. The children, black and white, are ranged in chairs. Witherspoon, noting Lucy's strained features, jollies her: "Lucy, your plantation is saved and we're celebrating the fact, aren't we? Where is your party face?"

LUCY—I'm terrified that something's gone wrong. Poor Gay—he worked so hard at the University of Virginia, and what did he learn? To conjugate Greek verbs! (SCOTT *hands her the dolls.*) All right, Martha—oompa, oompa. (MARTHA *starts playing.*) Sorry to have kept you waitin' all this time. That's the orchestra. I would like to present Froggie and Miss Mouse. I met them a long, long time ago—and now I'd like to introduce them to you. (*She sings.*)

FROGGIE WENT A-COURTIN' HE DID RIDE.   UM-HM.

SWORD AND A PISTOL BY HIS SIDE.

ASKED MISS MOUSE IF SHE'D BE HIS BRIDE.   UM-HM.

(*She puts the two dolls together and makes a kissing sound.* MARTHA *plays a bit of The Wedding March.*) Now they're walkin' down the aisle. (*She makes the two dolls bow in front of the children.*) I now pronounce you Frog and wife. (*She puts the frog down on a chair.*) He's the man, so he gets a chance to rest. (ANTOINETTE *brings the little boy to stand in front of* LUCY.) What's your name, Honey?

ANTOINETTE—Frankie!

LUCY (*looking around*)—Frankie!   Frankie . . . Frankie . . . Frankie . . .

THE FIRST GUEST TO COME WAS LITTLE FRANKIE.   UM-HM.

(*Still looking around the room.*)

THE FIRST GUEST TO COME WAS LITTLE FRANKIE.

(*She has spied a red bandanna in* WITHERSPOON'S *hip pocket and quickly takes it at the next line.*)

AND HIS WEDDIN' GIFT WAS A BIG RED HANKIE.   UM-HM.

(*She hands the bandanna to the little boy, then makes the mouse take it from him. She makes the mouse blow its nose.*) K'choo! Oh, my, just in time! (*She puts the bandanna on the chair by the frog.* ANTOINETTE *brings a little girl to stand in front of* LUCY. LUCY *looks at* ANTOINETTE *as if to ask the child's name.*)

ANTOINETTE—Gracie.

LUCY—
THE NEXT GUEST TO COME WAS LITTLE GRACIE. UM-HM.
(*She looks around for a prop.*)
THE NEXT GUEST TO COME WAS LITTLE GRACIE.
(*She looks around, still with no idea. She continues the song, stalling for time.*)
—eeeeeeee . . .
(*She sees* ANTOINETTE'S *fan.*)
AND HER GIFT WAS A FAN ALL FRILLY AND LACY. UM-HM.
(*She hands the fan to the little girl, has the mouse take it from her and fan itself.*)
It's very hot tonight. (*At this point,* DOLLY MAY *and* JACQUES *can be heard talking excitedly as they come in from the gallery.*) What is it, Dolly May?
DOLLY MAY—There was a man in the kitchen now said the plantation was sold today!
LUCY—Sold? To whom?
JACQUES—Just some old black tramp blabbin' away. He done left, Miss Lucy. Come on, Dolly May! (*They exit.* LUCY *looks around the room, confused.*)
LITTLE NEGRO GIRL—Can I be a weddin' guest?
LUCY—Of course you're a weddin' guest . . .
THE NEXT GUEST TO COME WAS LITTLE MISS LUCY. UM-HM.
THE NEXT GUEST TO COME WAS LITTLE MISS LUCY.
(*She takes the cake from the girl and hands it back to her.*)
WITH A COCOANUT CAKE ALL FLUFFY AND JUICY. UM-HM.
Now that's all, children. The weddin's over and they're startin' on their honeymoon. Come and see us again some time— (*As the children go out with* CASSIE.) —if we're still here. (*She turns to the other guests.*) Go on out on the lawn and have your supper, everybody. It's just a rumor. It's not founded yet. (*The* GUESTS *laugh and exit.* MARTHA *takes the toys and puts them on the shelf.*)

Lucy's perturbation increases and Peter tries to soothe her. Gay has never seen an auction, she worries, with all those people shouting and raising fingers. "Gay's always been taught that it's rude to point," she laughs hysterically. Trying to get a grip on herself and change the subject, she says to Peter, "You're in love with Antoinette, aren't you?"

"Miss Lucy, I assure you my relationship with Antoinette is somewhat higher than ordinary love." She asks if he is criticizing her for being ordinary, then apologizes, saying the idea of losing the place has got her talking in a nightmare and is so unreal. . . .

Peter assures her it is not unreal   "The great plantation life ?

gone—the path's grown over." She tries to make him understand her side—that the house ties with her life, and the roots of the trees are her roots. She takes out her handkerchief and a cablegram falls to the floor. "Peter," she says, "you think I'm against you, don't you? But I'd let you marry Antoinette if you could just get settled and get that little magazine of yours right so people would buy it—trim it around the edges a little." Touching his hair, she tells him to go comb it; he's too good-looking to be writing free verse and getting fuzzy-looking like that old Walt Whitman."

Suddenly she pulls away from him, looks down at the cablegram and asks Peter to pick it up. He offers to throw it away for her, but she clutches it, saying, "I get one every day now. Oh, I ought to go to Paris for a few weeks." Peter stiffens and she notices it, and asks, "Well, what do you want me to do? Who'll give him his medicine at night?" Peter is shocked, and Lucy taunts him, calling him just another Southern gentleman—a dress suit stuffed with courtesy. She waxes more frank. "I love him, Peety—that's obvious, isn't it? . . . He's a stone hanging around my neck and pulling me down to the bottom, and I am in love with this stone and cannot live without this stone."

Peter has no regard for this man, who has lived on women all his life and has picked Lucy clean, and she retorts that he must be driving her little girl crazy with his sanctified softness. Anger rising again, she taunts him. "You're shiff-less! . . . A man of your age without a mistress!"

He implores her not to say things like that—and then, suddenly, impulsively and passionately, he embraces her, but they both immediately break away. "I guess this was going to happen since I first came here," he says. "I got all tangled up in these trees and you—so tangled up I couldn't see what's happened to you. Don't go back to him, Miss Lucy." He walks away from her and she runs after him, pulling him back. She implores his forgiveness. If she had found somebody like him when she was a young girl she might not now be callous and vulgar and confused the way she was just now.

Witherspoon breaks it up by coming in and asking, "Lucy, may I have the honor of this waltz?" They go to the gallery.

Antoinette appears and she and Peter take a glass of punch from the tray Jacques is passing. She asks directly, "What is it about, Mama?" He pretends he doesn't know what she means—but she has been listening from the hallway. And she takes it lightly, reminding him that she is not really a part of the old Southern aristocracy. "I'm a half-breed. I'm the daughter of a drunken lawyer. Mama decided to change the family's blood—and look what happened. Want to dance with me? I won't put any vines around you."

But before they can dance Loper arrives and soon there is a crowd around him. Bowman comments that he smells like whiskey. Lucy's questions tumble out and Loper answers them. Gay will be along directly. The auction was held, all right, but it took them so long because they missed a train. Gay comes in, carrying a package and wiping his face with a handkerchief.

LUCY—Gay, Honey—what is it? Speak, for the love of God!

GAVIN (*turns to* SCOTT)—Here, take these—a nougat and some pralines. It's been quite a day. (*He crosses left.*) Scott, help me to get cleaned up. I'll need some help. (*He exits, followed by* SCOTT.)

LUCY—Yancy, is it sold?

LOPER—It's sold.

LUCY—Who bought it?

LOPER—I bought it. (*After a moment.*) I'm so mixed up about this thing I don't know exactly what to say. Mister Gavin Andrée had power of attorney to buy the place, but only fifteen thousand dollars in cash, and B. J. Henderson, the big millionaire, right off bids thirty. Mister Andrée starts fumblin' through his papers but he don't say nothin'. I look at Henderson and bid forty. He bids forty-five. I bid fifty-five and look at Mister Andrée. He's just standin' there starin' at me and in three minutes it's finished. I heard myself biddin' sixty-five thousand dollars and at that point Wisteria Plantation become my personal property. Good God Amighty! Tell me I'm drunk—tell me I'm crazy! Little Yancy, who had to run around nekkid over there 'til he was eight years old, owns the place where his pappy wasn't even allowed in the kitchen with the blacks! (MARTHA *crosses to* LOPER, *taking the keys from her purse, and drops them on the ottoman in front of him, walks back and stands near* LUCY. *He picks up the keys, jangles them, and puts them in his pocket.*) Thank you. What's the matter with the music? Come on, everybody, and you'll see how Yancy Loper swings the axe on them wisteria trees. They're gonna go ker-plunk. We're gonna dig up all these roots, turn up this land, and plow this plantation right off the map. Things is just gettin' started, so go on back to your music. Go on! (*He turns to* LUCY, *very emotional.*) Why didn't you pay attention to me when I talked? Oh, Miss Lucy, it's done now and can't be undone.

WITHERSPOON (*trying to take* LOPER's *arm*)—Let's go out to the gallery and listen to the singin' . Come on.

LOPER (*shaking off* WITHERSPOON)—Little poor one! (*He turns up to the window.*) What's the matter, everybody? Let's hear some music! Things is gonna be the way I want 'em from now on. Massa Tom Turkeyneck has just took over this plantation, so let's have some more music.

LUCY (*rising from her chair and calling offstage*)—Did you hear what Mister Loper said? There's a party goin' on and we'd like some music. It's the same party . . . we've just changed hosts in midstream, that's all. What music would you like, Mister Loper? (*He just looks at her. She calls offstage.*) Whatever you were playing! (*The music starts.*) Martha! Mister Loper would like to dance with you. (LUCY *leads* MARTHA *to* LOPER, *who starts to dance with her.* LUCY *looks around and sees* PETER *bow to* AN- TOINETTE *and start waltzing with her.* MARTHA *and* LOPER, PETER *and* ANTOINETTE, *dance off onto the gallery.* LUCY *is alone.* GAVIN *enters from left and comes to her.*)

GAVIN—Lucy . . . (*She turns to him. He holds out his arms and they begin to waltz.*)

LUCY—Oh, Gay, what's going to happen to us now. We can't just keep on dancin' . . . can we? (*As they waltz, the noises of the party grow in volume.* LUCY *buries her head in* GAVIN's *shoulder.*)

The curtain falls.

ACT III

Winter—Winter without and Winter within. The curtains are gone from the windows, the paintings and toy shelves are gone from the walls. The sofa still is in the room, and a few chairs are stacked together. Although suitcases, boxes, bundles, and baskets are piled in the hall and on the gallery, there is a sense of empti- ness. Jacques stands in the room holding a tray on which there are champagne glasses, and Loper is filling them. Outside, Negroes are singing, and when the song ends Gavin and Lucy can be heard calling their thanks.

"They's all come in to say good-by," says Jacques. "You know, these cotton pickers and cane cutters is nice enough. They just don't know nothin'."

Lucy is pale and even her face trembles as she comes in, followed by Gavin.

GAVIN—Why did you throw them your purse, Lucy? And your earrings!

LUCY—I just couldn't help it. (*They cross the stage, paying no attention to* LOPER, *exiting.*)

LOPER—Wait a minute. Ain't you goin' to join me in a little glass of champagne to say good-by? I brought it in from town! (*He follows them to door and calls offstage.*) Don't you want any champagne? (*There is no answer. He seems offended.*) Well, I don't want any either. (JACQUES *puts the tray down on a trunk.*) You drink it. (JACQUES *immediately picks up a glass.*)

JACQUES—Good luck to the ones who are leavin' and Lord help the ones who are stayin' behind. (*He drinks, then makes a face.*) This is not vintage champagne.

LOPER—Cost plenty. (*He looks around the room.*) It's chilly in here.

JACQUES—Nobody's built any fires today. (*He laughs, then sings.*)

> Sur le pont, d'Avignon
> Honey dances, honey dances.

(*He laughs again.*)

LOPER—What are you laughin' about?

JACQUES—About goin' to Paris.

LOPER—Miss Lucy's goin' to live in New Orleans.

JACQUES—She'll change her mind.

LOPER—I thought she was unhappy in Paris.

JACQUES—That ain't gonna keep her from goin' back. And if she goes, Frère Jacques goes, too. (*He dances off, singing.*)

> Sur le pont, d'Avignon
> Honey dances, honey dances.

LOPER (*looking at his watch*)—Folks, ought to start for the station pretty soon. Get all your things together.

PETER (*entering and looking around*)—Where the dickens are Mister Gay's overshoes? Everybody's lookin' for them but with Scott gone nobody can find them. (*Calling offstage.*) Martha, Mister Gay's rubbers aren't in here. I can't find them!

MARTHA (*offstage*)—Well, keep lookin'.

LOPER—I'll be ridin' down to the station with you.

PETER—I'm afraid there won't be room in the surrey.

LOPER—I'll ride alongside you on my horse. I'm gonna live in Baton Rouge this winter. Thinkin' of goin' into politics.

PETER—Politics! You're gettin' bigger every day!

LOPER—They held a little election down in my parish—and by golly, all the river rats come out of their holes and voted for me! Even got some of the plantation owners. There's a little turkey-neck in everybody. (*Looks at* PETER.) Glass of champagne?

PETER—I won't if you don't mind.

LOPER (*echoing*)—I won't if you don't mind.

PETER—Why did you come here today, Yancy? Do you just enjoy seeing people suffer?

LOPER—I'm here to see that the house gets closed up tight—'til spring, when it gets tore down. What are you doin' around here?

PETER—I'm goin' to New Orleans with Antoinette and Miss Lucy and help them get a place to live.

LOPER—What are they gonna live on?

PETER—They've still got the cash deposit their aunt sent them to buy the plantation. If they don't spend too much, it'll last them quite a while.

LOPER—What are you gonna live on? Them?

PETER—I'm going to get a job—diggin' ditches if necessary.

LOPER—Want me to let you have a little money?

PETER—No, thanks very much.

LOPER (*echoing*)—No, thanks very much.

PETER—Where the dickens are Mister Gay's overshoes? (AN-TOINETTE *enters through window, from gallery, very angry.*)

ANTOINETTE—Mister Loper, there are a lot of men standin' out there with axes. They say they're truck farmers and they want to get started clearing out the park. Do you hate my Mama enough to do a thing like that to her?

LOPER—Why, of course not! I'll take care of it. (*He goes out.*) Hey! Wait a minute, you turkeynecks! Those axes ain't itchin', is they? Hello, Ed!

Antoinette has been to the mail box for the last time, and has brought something for Peter. Tantalizingly she asks him what he would rather have than anything else in the whole world, and he answers, "A job . . . because then I could ask for something else." She says, "I think you'd rather have this"—and she waves a piece of paper. "It's a check for fifteen dollars from the *Times-Picayune* in New Orleans. I asked you for your jingles so I could learn them, but I really wanted to send them in to a newspaper."

Peter, the serious-minded but disappointed poet, gets paid for silly rhymes—the ones he used to make up at the dinner table, and ones like them! Exultantly, he kisses Antoinette. This check, he notes, is for only one jingle, and two more payments are coming. "Two more?" crows Antoinette. "They want as many more as you'll write—as long as they're funny." She picks up the letter from the newspaper, which she has laid on a trunk, and says, "Oh! And they'll also give you a job as night watchman!"

Peter asks Antoinette if she will marry him. She will—if Mama doesn't mind. But she doesn't want to ask her today, because Lucy has been planning to live with them and take care of her daughter.

Jacques brings in another box for the pile and Antoinette asks him if Scott has been sent to the hospital. Jacques assures her; he and Mister Gay drove him over in the surrey this morning. Henry Arthur, bringing in a heavy valise, adds, "I'm afraid old Scott is unrepairable on this occasion. He probably does not realize how fortunate he is." Henry Arthur, who frequently yearns for an end to his hapless life, sets the valise on a paper hatbox crushing it. "I might have known that was gonna happen," he mourns. Jacques extricates the box and pulls out one of Lucy's French hats, holds it up, observes that it looks better than it did before, and replaces it.

Peter and Antoinette go off to help Martha and Dolly May seizes the opportunity to be alone with Jacques. "You're leavin' me," she cries, throwing herself into his arms.

JACQUES—Now don't start that, my little cabbage. This has all been talked out before. Excuse me, I gotta help Mister Yancy get rid of this stuff. (*He picks up a glass of champagne, drinks it.*) Miss Lucy won't be able to stay in New Orleans very long, listenin' to those boat whistles in the harbor. (*He makes a noise with his voice, imitating a boat's whistle and an engine disappearing into the* distance.) Whooo-whooo—oomph-pa-cha, oomph-pa-cha, oomph-pa-cha. "Jacques, pack my bags! Allons, enfant!" Oh, man! It's not my style around here. (*He drinks another glass.*) Paris is in my bones! I got a lot of unexplored territory ahead of me over there. (*He drinks another glass.*) If I ever come back here, it'll be as a tourist! (*He is about to drink another glass when he hears someone coming. He turns to* DOLLY MAY.) Dolly May, would you like to help Mister Yancy with the rest of this champagne?

DOLLY MAY—Thank you, Jacques.

JACQUES (*handing her the glass*)—I think you better go outside to drink it. Somebody's comin'. (*She exits docilely with glass.* JACQUES *walks to the other side of the stage, eyeing the hallway. He puts his hands in his pockets and looks off, making the sound of the boat whistle.*) Whooo-whooo . . . (*Enter* LUCY.) Can I do something for you, Miss Lucy?

LUCY—Yes. Take my things out to the surrey, Jacques.

JACQUES—Yes, ma'am. (*He starts off, then turns.*) You ain't really goin' to live in New Orleans, is you, Miss Lucy?

LUCY—Of course I am. Why?

JACQUES—I was just wonderin'. I'll take care of your things. (*He exits, singing.*)

Sur le pont, d'Avignon
Honey dances, honey dances . . .

(LUCY *looks after him a moment, then goes to the piano and sits.*
Enter GAVIN, *who crosses to* LUCY.)

GAVIN—Lucy . . .

LUCY (*looks up and smiles*)—Gay, I'm sorry about Scott.

GAVIN—Yes, but he's very old, you know, Lucy, and he shouldn't
get as angry as he does, at his age. When I accepted the position
as vice-president of the bank against his wishes, he lost control of
himself. What's wrong with working in a bank? In some ways,
Scott is very old-fashioned. (*He turns and smiles at her.*) You're
lookin' mighty pretty for a homeless waif, Lucy.

LUCY—Thank you, Gay.

GAVIN—Are you going back to Paris, Lucy?

LUCY—No. I'm not going to do anything to disgrace the family
again, Gay.

GAVIN—You can't disgrace the family, Lucy. When this house
goes, the family will have no more importance.

LUCY—No. He tells me he's dying. But that might go on for
years. I've got to stay down here, Gay, and take care of Antoinette. I've neglected her so long. And when Aunt Catherine's
money runs out and I'm really poor . . . Well, I might be able to
sell my tatting like that old lady down the river—with the squinty
eyes.

Antoinette brings Cassie in for a farewell; Cassie has a new job
nursing a baby at the Brewsters' place. She warns Gavin not to
let the bank cashiers get him mixed up. She warns Antoinette that,
if she should get married and have a baby, that baby belongs to
Cassie. "And honey, don't let Miss Lucy go crazy and run away
from you."

Antoinette advises her mother not to listen to Cassie, and suggests
that Lucy take a little trip somewhere before they settle down.
It would only cost two or three hundred dollars to go to Europe
and back cabin class.

Witherspoon arrives—to say good-by and to bring exciting news.
Before he can tell it, Loper follows him in, and Witherspoon
astounds the group by slapping $400 into Loper's hand. It seems
that a Yankee has looked around his land and found some kind of
oil and the oil is worth money. Witherspoon gives Lucy another
$400, and promises the rest later.

Loper's business instinct is aroused and he demands to know what

Yankee it is, but Witherspoon ignores the question and goes on to tell that he has leased the mineral rights to his land for twenty-four years, and is rich for the time being. He starts to go. "Got plenty more stops to make. Why, I owe money all up and down the river." He gives Lucy's hand an affectionate pat and says, "And you be happy, too, 'cause God's gonna take care of you."

Loper pursues him to the gallery, calling, "I want to find out some more about that oil!" Bowman answers vaguely, "You'll have to ask that Yankee—I don't know anything about it."

Lucy and Loper are alone, and Lucy wants to clean up one more loose end—Martha. Martha's job, working for the Yarboroughs in a crowded house, will be no good. Lucy has caught her weeping in corners. She tells Yancy directly that everybody always thought he and Martha were right for each other—and she is a lovely person.

"Miss Martha's a fine young lady," he agrees. "I'd do anything for you."

Lucy is relieved and happy. She calls Martha, and Loper remembers that they have some champagne for the occasion—but they don't, for Jacques has lapped it up. Lucy hurries out, and Martha, finding herself confronting Loper alone, embarrassedly pretends she is looking for something. He asks her where she is off to, and she tells him the Yarboroughs'. Uneasily, he makes more conversation by announcing that he won't be coming back here. He is leaving Henry Arthur Henry to look around the grounds until they are all cleared out. Next, he talks about how good the weather is this time of the year—and then, explosively to himself, he says "No!" Then, pretending someone has called him, he flees.

Lucy comes in, sees Martha slumped over the baggage, and guesses what has happened. She tells the girl they must be going, and Martha starts for the surrey. Lucy turns to go, but is halted by the returning Loper. He explains he couldn't do what he promised because he got all stirred up, so he went outside—and outside he saw the wisterias covered with long, purple blossoms, and they were the most beautiful things in the world.

Lucy thinks Loper must be mad, for it is December and the vines are nude.

LOPER—Miss Lucy, I was lookin' at 'em in April, I reckon, because—they'll still be standin' there. I'm not going to cut 'em down. You can have 'em. You can have 'em forever.

LUCY—Yancy!

LOPER—And you can live in this house forever.

LUCY—But it's your house, Yancy.

LOPER—That's right. But it can be our house, Miss Lucy. Our trees. (*He looks at her pleadingly, desperate.* LUCY *looks back, seeing that he means it and that possibly it could all come true. She cannot speak.*) We'll prune 'em back like they was when you was a little girl and we'll spread white oyster shells thick along that driveway—all the way down to the river. We'll paint these old Corinthian columns white—'til they're gleamin'. This'll be one of the greatest places that ever was. I'll even make it better than it was before. (LUCY *still looks at him.*) I'll make the money to do it, Miss Lucy. That's easy for me, makin' money. And with you here still, as the lady of this house, as my . . . (*He is overcome by the picture of what might happen.*) Good God Amighty, Miss Lucy, I'll own this state! Everybody will fight to get asked to dinner with us, and to meet you . . . and me. We'll have 'em all workin' for us, Miss Lucy. That's what I saw when I looked at them trees. That's why they was covered with purple flowers in December. Do you want 'em, Miss Lucy? Do you want them . . . and me? 'Cause I go with 'em, you see.

LUCY—Yancy, oh, Yancy . . . if I'm hearin' what I hear, thank you. But aren't you bein' sentimental? I'm not right for you, Yancy.

LOPER—You're the only one that's ever been right for me. That's been the trouble. I didn't know it. I didn't even know why I bought this place—but I knew just now. I bought it for you. You're what I need. And this old place needs you, too. The only chance it's got is with you in it.

LUCY—But it wouldn't be me. I'm not strong enough to do it. God knows I wish I were. I can't rise to the occasion. Believe me, Yancy, I'm not good enough for you. I can't be your lady, Yancy, much as I'd like to. I've missed *all* the right people. You were hidden across the road behind those chinaberry trees. I can't even understand where you sprung up from or how you got to be so smart —so strong! You frighten me!

Loper, once aroused, will not be halted. He promises Lucy anything—if she tells him to hop, he'll hop, and if she tells him to lay down and roll over he will do that, too. She can have those trees forever. "Don't you want them?" he asks.

"Yes, I do."

"Well, there's one way you can have them." It is an ultimatum. Lucy, with a strange inner strength, looks at him coolly and agrees. "That's right, Yancy. Just one way I can have them forever. . . .

Cut 'em down—cut 'em down now!"

Loper stiffens as though he had been struck, and his face hardens as he says, "I won't be ridin' to the station with you. I'll be too busy here." And then emotion recaptures him for a moment as he exclaims, "I wish you hadn't washed away that nosebleed. It would have been easier for me if you'd let it go on bleedin'." Then his hardness returns as he calls through the French windows, "Come on, everybody, let's cut 'em down . . . Give me one of them axes."

Lucy runs to the gallery as the ax blows begin to fall, watching the beginning of the ruin and holding a column for support. Antoinette and Peter come into the room looking for her, and not realizing that she is on the gallery where she can see them, they kiss. But Lucy has seen, and all she asks is, do they love each other. When they say they do she says, wearily, "I'm glad something good is happening."

Lucy is broken—and puzzled. The men down there are laughing as they chop down the trees, and up here must be the ridiculous people—the jokes. She wishes the house had been torn down before she was born—before she learned to love it so much.

"Do somethin' for us, Peety! Write something we can understand and ask people to have mercy on us, will you? And, Antoinette, you work out a way to live, do you hear me? Figure out what I did, and then, for the love of God, do something else!"

Henry Arthur, now Yancy's major domo, comes in and begins to close up the shutters. The sound of the axes grows louder as the group begins to depart—Antoinette and Peter and Jacques. Gavin has come to take Lucy, and when they are alone Gavin, with affection and understanding, says quietly, "I know. Go back to Paris, Lucy. That's all right." She accepts the inevitable. "When I'm gone," she instructs, "send half the money to me, will you, and give the rest to Antoinette?" Gavin will—and he ought to be able to send a little bit himself, off and on. "I hope you know what you are doing, Lucy," he says.

"I know," she admits. "I'm going to tie that stone around my neck and go down for the last time." She throws herself into her brother's arms. Outside at the surrey Antoinette is calling.

"Come on, Lucy Andrée," Gavin urges. "Let's see how many pretty teeth you got." She forces a smile and he calls that they are coming. The axes are very loud now. Gavin holds out his arm and Lucy takes it. At the door she turns and whispers to the room, "Good-by . . . good-by."

CURTAIN

I KNOW MY LOVE *

Comedy in Three Acts

BY S. N. BEHRMAN

WHEN Alfred Lunt and Lynn Fontanne came to New York in
S. N. Behrman's "I Know My Love," they celebrated the twenty-
fifth anniversary of their first appearance as an acting team. In
the preceding quarter century they had indisputably established
themselves as the First Team of the American stage. As befitted
their eminence, they celebrated their silver anniversary by appearing in a hand-made comedy—a play fashioned to fit their brittle
humor, their byplay and their interplay. "I Know My Love" was
tailor-made by an expert in parlor comedy—yet it was far from a
perfect fit at the first try-on, or tryout. The brilliant Lunts could
be excused for wanting, on this anniversary occasion, to run the
gamut—if not of emotions, at least of time; they wanted to play a
little of everything, from youth to very old age. Mr. Behrman was
happy to oblige.

The Lunts are wise, sensible and loyal. They are among the few
front-rank players who are profoundly conscious that their public
is not limited to Broadway, but is nation-wide. They enjoy their
long runs in New York—and they take to the road with equal
enthusiasm. As long as a play of theirs has a public, they will
play in it, and because of this loyalty they are among the very
few stars who can tour successfully without the benefit of a Broadway run. In the case of "I Know My Love" they put the cart
before the horse and had an extended tour before opening at the
Shubert Theatre in West 44th Street. This was a financial insurance which, happily, they did not need. It also was an artistic
insurance which, apparently, they did need—for the comedy, which
juggled the stars around from period to period, required re-routin-
ing and reconstruction by Mr. Behrman. This work was accomplished during the tour.

The setting is the living room of an old family mansion on

Boston's Commonwealth Avenue, in which dwell Thomas and Emily Chanler. The room is very Boston and very old-family, and ancestral portraits are prominent on the walls. Most prominent is a formidable, full-length Sargent of Emily Chanler's father, Jerome Talbot. The time is January, 1939, and the well-organized, well-staffed house is now abuzz with preparations for a notable event—the fiftieth wedding anniversary of Emily and Thomas.

The servants are busy and the clan is gathering. Lucy, the house-keeper, is calling for William, another veteran servant, to come into the room and interview a man named Reilly. William does so. Reilly has come in response to an ad in the *Herald,* and is applying for the chauffeur's job. His references are good; he was with Mrs. Brubaker four years, until she died, and in that post got to know who Mr. Chanler is. William's efficient questions elicit all that needs be known about Reilly, and Reilly's questions reveal something of the household habits. For example, the Chanlers used to go to Europe every Summer, but now they go only to Bar Harbor. And Mr. Chanler likes to drive out on Sundays, so Reilly will have to choose another day off. Reilly is accepted by William, and Reilly accepts the job—with one regret. "I always get jobs with old people," he grumbles. "They die on me." William spirit-edly retorts that Mr. Chanler is in the best of health. Having observed the extraordinary bustle in the house, the new chauffeur asks what is going on and is told about the golden wedding. He is impressed, saying, "That's a long time for people as rich as the Chanlers to stay married." William dismisses him with a final instruction: Reilly is to speak very distinctly to Mrs. Chanler because she is rather deaf.

William himself is about to leave the room when he is encountered by Frederic. Frederic is Mr. Chanler's son; he is 47, authoritative, arrogant—and, at the moment, much preoccupied. He asks if William has delivered that letter to Mr. Seymour and the servant explains that he has not done so yet, because he wanted very much to be present for the celebration. He intends to go directly after, and he already has telephoned and learned that Mr. Seymour will be at his home by six-thirty.

Frederic snaps, " I don't wish to argue. Go at once."

William's disappointment is obvious as he accepts the order with a "Yes, sir." Lucy hurries in to tell William there is someone at the door, and to say to Frederic that she expects it's the Ballards. "Oh, Mr. Frederic," says Lucy, "we are all so excited, and to think the doctor is allowing Mrs. Chanler downstairs this evening!"

Frederic dismisses her by announcing that the presents will be opened after dinner.

The arrivals are the Ballards. There is Claire Ballard, who is Frederic's sister. There is Nicholas Ballard, who is Claire's husband—an in-law. And there is Nicola Ballard, their spirited and handsome young daughter. Apparently they have been summoned early, for Nicola queries, "What's the great rush, Uncle Frederic? I hardly had a chance to finish dressing." He replies rather ominously that she will find out. Nicola's mother also asks, "Frederic! Why the imperial summons?" She observes that her brother is here unusually early and he explains that his wife, Blanche, and their son, Eugene, are spending the night here on account of Eugene.

Frederic has summoned the Ballards because he wants to talk to them before Mr. and Mrs. Chanler come down for the party. But before he can begin on what he has in mind, his wife and son come down the stairs into the living room. Blanche is pretty, but so effaced by her husband that it may be said of her that she survives rather than that she exists. Eugene is 10; he has beautiful manners, but is rather old for his age, being pedantic and over-cultivated. Frederic shows his annoyance at his wife's intrusion by saying, "Blanche—I asked Claire and Nicholas to come early because I wanted to speak to them." Blanche, understanding that he means it is something private, starts to withdraw, but Nicola speaks up, saying, "Oh, come now, Uncle Frederic, it can't be as private as all that." He grudgingly gives in—but orders his son back to his room to memorize his speech.

Eugene has memorized the speech already and is not a bit nervous. Why should the fact that Grandpa and Grandma have been married fifty years make him nervous? But he does go back to his room. Blanche asks, "Are you perfectly sure, Frederic, that I won't be in the way?" He says gruffly, "I said you might stay if you liked," and Claire comments, "Blanche, if I were married to Frederic I'd shoot him and any jury would acquit me!" Nicholas also offers to withdraw, but is commanded to sit down with the others. Frederic stands over them like a schoolmaster and ominously asks Nicola what she did last night. The girl replies that she went to Symphony Hall, the Copley-Plaza for a drink with the Seymours, and then home.

"You did none of these things," he remarks coldly. Nicola's mother says, "But you must have gone to the Symphony. Mrs. Seymour asked me, too. She told me you were coming." Nicola frankly replies, "Mrs. Seymour was mistaken, Mother."

Uncle Frederic knows what happened, and his niece asks him how much he paid the head waiter to keep him informed. Nicola did have dinner with Bill Seymour at the Ritz, all right, her uncle concedes; but she did not go with Bill to the Symphony. "Why not?" asks Claire.

"Because during dinner I broke my engagement to Bill." She repeats this information to her astounded listeners, adding, "I told him, for the fourth time, I should say, that I wouldn't marry him. This time I convinced him, I think."

This is even worse than Uncle Frederic thought. Claire protests that the engagement has been announced in the *Transcript* and Nicola jauntily declares that it will be broken in the *Herald*. In fact, she has already phoned the *Herald*. The family are worried about how Grandmother might take this news if she heard about it. Blanche murmurs a sympathetic "Poor Bill!" and Nicola retorts with an unsympathetic "Poor Bill, my foot!" Frederic splutters about this being what comes of progressive education, giving little tots their own way about everything.

Nicola, the ex-tot, declares that the engagement with Bill never was any good and she should have known from the start that it wouldn't be—because Uncle Frederic was so anxious for it to happen. Her mother reminds the girl that she, too, was anxious and Nicola says, "Yes, Mother, for Uncle Frederic's reasons. Not very good reasons. It would suit your book very well, Uncle Frederic, to have me in the Seymour family. I know that perfectly well— and moreover, I know why, too. Unfortunately for you and Mother, it does not suit me."

Blanche expostulates that Nicola is being insolent and the girl turns on her with, "Poor Aunt Blanche. Uncle Frederic's rubbed you out like an eraser. You'll forgive me if I don't permit him to do it to me."

They all pause in their cheerful discussions while Lucy goes through the room and on upstairs to help Emily Chanler dress for the party. When the servant is gone they resume. Frederic has more news: No sooner had Nicola dispatched Bill Seymour to face his parents alone at the Symphony, than she sauntered out of the dining room of the Ritz to the bar, where she spent the evening billing and cooing with a nondescript young man. Nicola admits it, and says in reply to her mother's obvious question that the young man is nobody she'd know—not remotely.

FREDERIC—What other virtues has he—besides the great one, of course, of being anonymous?

NICOLA—If you must know, my dear Uncle, with him it clicks physically . . .

BLANCHE—Well, really . . .

NICOLA—. . . which was not true at all with Bill Seymour.

FREDERIC—Uninhibited, you see. My congratulations, Claire.

NICOLA—Besides which he's brilliant and he's gay and he makes me laugh and I make him laugh and we're wonderful together and as soon as he gets a job, we're going to be married.

NICHOLAS—Oh, Nicola!

FREDERIC—As soon as he gets a job?

NICOLA—As soon as he gets a job.

FREDERIC—He is, then, I gather, unemployed?

NICOLA—He's doing postgraduate work at Harvard. And he has to support his mother.

FREDERIC—But why need you wait for him to get a job? You will, as he must be aware, have enough for two.

NICOLA—You mean you will cut us off. We have anticipated that too.

CLAIRE—I will cut you off, Nicola. I will.

NICOLA—I told him you probably would and it amuses us.

CLAIRE—You'll make me hate you, Nicola.

NICOLA—I'm sorry, Mother. I have only to tell Grandpa and Grandma what you've planned for me. . . .

FREDERIC—Nicola, I suggest you don't do that.

NICOLA—I'm not afraid of you, Uncle Frederic. I used to be. I'm not now.

FREDERIC—I still advise you not to do it.

NICOLA—Why don't you leave me alone? (*Long pause.*) Is it because Grandpa won't let you do anything at the factory that you take out your dictator complex in his house? I will tell Grandpa and Grandma about this. I will. (*Runs up the stairs. Stops halfway up.*) And what do you think they'll say?

CLAIRE—I forbid you to mention this to Father. Do you hear?

NICOLA—To spare them or to spare Uncle Frederic?

CLAIRE—To spare all of us.

NICOLA (*at her grandparents' door*)—Shall I tell them now?

FREDERIC—Come down, Nicola.

NICOLA—Eugene is working on his speech to Grandpa. Well, I'll work on mine.

CLAIRE—Drop these heroics, Nicola. You're enjoying them far too much. They don't suit you.

NICOLA—I know, Mother. I've always been a nice child, haven't I? Well, I'm not any more. (*She goes on upstairs.*)

FREDERIC—Charming, isn't it?

Blanche tries a cheerful note, saying this young man may not be so bad. "After all, he is a Harvard man." But her husband points out that he's only post-graduate, and God knows where he got his A.B. He is worried, saying, "Nicola has only to suggest that I'm against her to have Father's sympathy." Nicholas contributes, "I've heard your father say repeatedly that as long as he lived there'd be no Chanler-Seymour merger—nor any merger."

"And afterwards?" Frederic's question is pointed. His wife sympathizes with his unspoken ambitions, saying, "After all, Frederic, you have waited so long to run things at the factory, can't you wait just a little longer?" He bursts out, "How long—forever? I'm going on fifty. In all my life I've never been allowed to be myself— to act on my own!"

Lucy comes out of the Chanler's room onto the landing and announces, "She's dressed! They're coming down!" The servant is told to warn Eugene and Nicola, and presently Eugene descends, reciting, "Dear Grandfather, dear Grandmother, you have been married fifty years today. . . ." Lucy corrects him: "This blessed day." The manful Eugene assures his tremulous mother that everything will be all right and he will not forget his speech—and if he should it would merely indicate he was overcome with emotion. Blanche asks if her son has his handkerchief, speaking of emotion, and Eugene has forgotten it. Nicola, who is just coming down the stairs, volunteers to run back and fetch one. Lucy, Louise and Katy, the female servants, crowd in, politely greeting the family and admiring the looks of the room. The moment has come for Emily and Thomas to appear—and they do.

The Chanlers are old—but handsome. Emily appears somewhat frail, but her husband is erect and vigorous. There is a chorus of greeting, of admiration for Emily's dress, and a cry of "Bravo!" from son-in-law Nicholas. Thomas holds up a hand for silence and says, "One second, children." When they have negotiated the stair Thomas escorts his wife to the sofa, eases her gently into it and asks her if it is too cold or too warm, and if she is all right.

"I feel twenty," Emily replies—and, with a smile at the group in the room, "but when I look at my children, they seem to me to be dismally middle-aged!" They all laugh. Thomas, with a careless, rather grand gesture, turns to the others and says, "Well, do your worst. We're at your mercy!"

The speech comes first, and Blanche, asking once more if her son is nervous, leads Eugene forward. The boy begins, "Dear Grandfather. Dear Grandmother . . ." Thomas interrupts by asking his wife, very loudly, "Can you hear him all right?" She says she hears him perfectly, and Thomas advises his grandson to take his time after that superb introduction.

Eugene continues, ". . . On this day—on this blessed day we desired that our whole family should unite here to celebrate with you this glorious occasion." Thomas applauds, "That's splendid!" Eugene goes on, "It is our common sentiment today—" and Thomas, affecting surprise, asks, "Oh, is there more of it?"

"Quite a lot," admits Eugene.

"In that case, won't you just kiss us? All orators, you know, stop in the middle for a drink." The boy dutifully kisses his grandparents, and throws his arms about Thomas's neck. The old man, pleased, says, "Well, you like your grandfather and grandmother, I see. Don't you?"

"Very much. I find you both very amusing." Thomas exclaims, "Why, Emily, he's got a sense of humor, this boy."

"Yes, Tom," the old lady agrees. "Jumped a generation, didn't it? He's charming, our Eugene. And so good-looking. Oh, my, he's the image of his father, isn't he?" Thomas agrees, and at this comparison Eugene abruptly begins to cry. His father roars, "What's the matter with you, you little imbecile?" Eugene's parents lead him across to the stair and are about to send him upstairs when Emily tries to make amends by saying, "Why, Eugene, your father was very good-looking at your age." At this the lad breaks into a loud wail and runs up the stairs.

Nicholas approaches his parents-in-law, evidently with more ceremony in mind, but Thomas halts him and indicates the servants with a nod. "I don't want to keep these good people waiting. They don't have all the time in the world—as we have." Lucy steps forth with a speech on her lips, but also is stopped when Thomas notices that William is missing. Shrewdly guessing, he asks his son if he knows where William is and Frederic admits he sent the man on an important errand. "Aha! Aha!" says Thomas, and then, "Forgive me, Lucy."

Lucy's speech comes out as flustered as she is, and is confused with "on behalf of the kitchen behalfs, on behalf of all our behalfs . . . long life, happiness and prosperity." Weeping, Lucy cries to the other servants, "Oh, I've made a mess of it!" The servants start out but Thomas stops them and makes a little speech of gratitude, which sends all three of the servants out weeping.

Nicholas won't be held back any longer. He kisses Emily, embraces Thomas. Claire and Blanche follow, and there are expressions of sentiment and affection. When the kissing is over, Thomas leans back beside his wife as one who has completed an exhausting chore. Frederic shakes his father's hand and suggests that he might try to say something suitable—but Thomas bids him desist; the father can tell what the son is thinking, so why should it have to be said?

Only Nicola's felicitations remain, and now she asks, "What about me?" Her grandfather charmingly answers, "Since you are the youngest—and the freshest—and the most hopeful, we keep you to the last." The girl wastes no words on congratulatory phrases; instead, she announces that she must talk with Thomas, golden wedding or no golden wedding—and stricken sounds are heard from Blanche and Claire. Nicola continues, "I have to get this out before the others do. Uncle Frederic wants me to marry someone I don't like."

"Poor Frederic," sighs Grandfather. "He never changes."

"And he's got Mother on his side."

"That's bad. Oh, how bad it is! Now, Nicola"—and a mock note of sternness comes into Thomas' voice—"you listen to me. You honor your parents. You respect them and you obey them in everything—except precisely this." He posts the inquiring Emily on the conversation, explaining loudly, "They want her to make a reasonable marriage."

Apparently Emily also is on the liberal side, for she remarks, "But *our* marriage was so unreasonable. My father hated the idea of my marrying you. It would be a pity if we in our family suddenly started to make reasonable marriages." Emily would like to know who the unreasonable prospect is, and is informed it is Bill Seymour. The news doesn't upset Emily one jot. Nor does her husband want her to be upset; therefore, he announces that he has something he wants to say to his wife alone, and shoos the others out of the room.

It is a charming and not too sentimental tête-à-tête for the old couple. They assure themselves that they still love each other and that in spite of everything they are still happy. Indeed, Emily would be willing to begin it all over again, although she is a bit tired now. But she asks, "Do you resent it that you've been happy?

THOMAS—Oh, my dear, how shrewd you are.

EMILY—I know you resented our happiness. It confined you. You had some mad impulse for experience that would carry you beyond happiness, some pang of living that would cut through you like pain . . .

THOMAS—Well, that's true.   When I was young—even when I was fifty—

EMILY—Oh, especially when you were fifty.

THOMAS—Well, if you don't mind, we won't go into that.   As I remember it, I was young for a long time and it was you who gave me that youth, you know.   I swam in the migraine of my imagination.   I used to think: is this all there is to life, to wake in the morning, to go to the factory, to return in the evening, to be happy. . . ?

EMILY—I know.   You yearned for the luxury of despair.   You must forgive me that I denied you that.

THOMAS—Yes, my darling.   You denied me that, and I'm very grateful.   All those vague cravings, impossible to satisfy. . . . You know it's this damned Puritan mysticism.   You know, that's a New England disease!   (*She laughs.   They sit there holding hands.   A silence.   She puts her head on his shoulder.*)   Fifty years!   Emily, aren't you bored with me?

EMILY—Now, Tom, don't be coquettish.

THOMAS—My consciousness is very active today.   Just now, just at this moment—I feel a razor-edge of awareness . . . and it is so powerful, so insistent—you know, it is like a sound that I can hear, a humming that I can hear. . . .

EMILY—I hear it, too.

THOMAS—You hear it, too?

EMILY—I, too.

THOMAS—Even when I do not speak?

EMILY—Especially when you do not speak.

THOMAS—You know, Emily, you are tactless!

EMILY—Am I?

THOMAS—Yes, you are even rude!

EMILY—Oh!   On this one day I didn't wish to hurt your feelings.   It is only that . . .

THOMAS—Well?

EMILY—When you are silent the sound I hear is everything you have ever said to me—all the words, said and unsaid, all the thoughts, all the hopes—those that we won—and those that we lost.   It is . . .

THOMAS—Yes, Emily?

EMILY—It's all our memories—made audible.   (*A pause.*)

THOMAS—Yes. . . . And yet . . . and yet . . .

EMILY—What now?

THOMAS—I'm angry.

EMILY—Angry?   With me?

THOMAS—No, no, not with you. It is only that all this that we hear now, all this that we feel now . . . will melt into the anaesthesia of death. All the hours between us—all our days—all our nights—which are now alive because we remember them—will vanish, and they will be as if they had never been. You know, Emily, they are too good to lose, and I am angry!

Emily is protesting that what they have known and what they feel now cannot be lost and will endure beyond them—will be a sound that others sitting on this sofa will hear, too—when William brings in a letter for Frederic. He thought Mr. Frederic was here and tries to bow out—but Thomas calmly demands and takes the missive. William offers his belated congratulations, and then is told to go to the library and tell Mr. Frederic to come in. Emily would like to have her husband open the letter, but he says he already knows what is in it and awaits his son.

Frederic sees the letter as soon as he enters the room, and coldly demands it, saying it is private. His father assures him that it is unopened and hands it over. "But I know what it says," he adds. Mr. Seymour consents to what you suggest. Well, the difficulty is— I do not consent. You tell Seymour to take this up with me again . . . ten years from now. I know you've been buying Seymour stock. With what have you been buying it?" Claire comes into the room and sits by Emily and the two women chat while the men continue their battle.

Thomas worms out of the reluctant Frederic the admission that he has been selling his shares of the family stock—the Chanler factory's stock which had been given to Frederic by his father—to the Seymours. "Then comes the merger. That's your plan, isn't it?" the old man declares. Frederic utters a defiant "Yes!"

Thomas points out that the scheme will not work, for Frederic controls only thirty per cent of the family stock. Whereupon Claire drops her chitchat with Emily and interposes, "Frederic wasn't alone in it, Dad. I have sold my stock also." Emily is dozing intermittently and hearing nothing of this business crisis. Once she awakens and senses something is wrong, but her husband puts her off by saying it is a surprise the children have been arranging for him. And to the children he states:

"I am so curious to know why you did this. Outside of the enormous stimulus of my being against it, it is such a bad deal. This joint betrayal—this betrayal on the installment plan—will get you nowhere because, even against you two, I still control the stock. And

I'll never permit this merger."

Claire is genuinely surprised at her father's grim attitude and seems sorry she has gone along with her brother. She tries to explain to her father that they thought the merger would make it easier for him to retire and give him leisure for the things he loves—his books and the writing he has wanted to do. Thomas declares, "I still have time for all the things I love and I shall continue to run my business as well."

"What do you mean?" The question is Claire's.

"I mean that I never want to see you again. Neither you nor Frederic. On my death-bed, perhaps, if I'm not too busy, but not before. . . . As for you, Frederic, you may continue at the office if you wish. I am seldom conscious of your being there."

This is indeed a bombshell—but Emily hasn't heard the explosion. She wonders what is doing at the Symphony these days and talks of dear Dr. Koussevitzky. William announces the arrival of two photographers who are to record for the press the golden anniversary of the Chanlers. Frederic warns them, "No interview," and the cameramen begin to arrange their venerable subjects. Emily protests that she should not be photographed—but all the same she is busy primping. One of the press men ignores Frederic's admonition and says, "Mr. and Mrs. Chanler, I won't ask for an interview, but I know that our readers would like to learn your formula for a happy marriage."

Emily asks "What?" and her husband says loudly, "He wants to know our formula for a happy marriage." Then, to the photographer, "Marriage is a war and the victory goes to the one who wins the last battle." "I," Emily adds, "was lucky enough to win the last battle." She will not smile for the picture; she says she is too happy to smile. The cameramen suggest that they just talk, then, and Thomas begins:

"First, I ask your pardon for all the pain I've caused you—for all the pain I've caused you not meaning it—and for all the pain I've caused you meaning it. . . . And now I ask your forgiveness for keeping you to myself so much, like a great egotist, and for longing for things outside our love when your love was infinite. I simply tell you I adore you."

Emily asks another "What?"

"I adore you."

Suddenly Claire breaks into loud sobbing.

The curtain falls.

ACT II

The room is the same, except for a gas chandelier, for the time is Christmas Day, 1888. The wall panels are a deep red cut velvet. After surviving many changes, the room found itself in 1939 about the way it was in 1888. The wall space for the large Sargent is empty, but Fuller, the butler, is holding up the portrait for Agnes and Jerome Talbot to admire. Jerome Talbot, the ancestor of Frederic and Daniel, is an impressive, strong, hard, domineering, extremely vain man, richly and severely dressed. He is a churchgoer and a dyspeptic. Agnes, his wife, is as demolished and extinguished as Blanche will become. At the moment she is raptly admiring the portrait of her husband. Jerome does not admire it; it cost so much. The eyes are good, he thinks, but he is dissatisfied with the mouth.

"It's Daniel's mouth," says his wife.

"I don't want Daniel's mouth. It's weak like Daniel. . . . Where is Emily?"

"Out paying Christmas calls, I expect."

"On whom? The Chanlers?"

"She went to take little Richard Chanler a Christmas present. I'm sure he doesn't get many."

Jerome Talbot grumbles violently about several things, including the newfangled notion that fresh air is not poisonous. The Chanlers are a degenerate family, he also observes. Tom Chanler's father is not only divorced—he is bankrupt—and Irish. "To think that my daughter should be carrying on with a cheap newspaper scribbler!"

Agnes rather favors Tom Chanler, who has ambitions toward serious writing, but in Jerome's eyes he is dangerous; just recently the young man wrote an article demanding a thirteen-hour day in Lawrence and Lowell. And how did his daughter happen to meet this man, any way?

"She met him at an auction. She went to the sale of Tom's father's effects. The poor man had to sell all his lovely things to pay his debts. Tom was there. Emily came home with a charming what-not."

"Evidently," snorts Jerome, "she came home with two what-nots." And another thing, he admonishes his wife. "You've been sending money against my wishes to that scapegrace, Daniel, in Paris." Daniel should be here with his father, learning the textile business, and not dabbling in art. Who will run the business after Jerome is gone? Agnes suggests that Emily may, or the man she marries. Agnes begins to weep.

The subject of the conversation comes home—a radiant, young

Emily, who sees her mother's tears and says, "Oh, I see, it's Father. Really, Father, not on Christmas Day. . . . What's happened? I remember all our Christmases when I was a child. You were so dear and tender. What's gone wrong?"

Jerome's only answer is that as children grow older one loses them. Emily tells of her visit. Tom was not there, but Mr. Chanler was, trying so gallantly to be cheerful, and the little boy, Richard, and she gave Richard some toy soldiers. . . . When Jerome leaves the room Emily talks with her mother about him. The girl wants particularly to love him, but he won't let her.

Agnes explains, "He disapproves very much of your friendship with Tom Chanler."

"He needn't worry about that any more. It's over." No, there has been no quarrel; Emily has just decided to be rational. Besides, Tom is too attractive to girls—and he likes girls. One particular girl, Sally McCombe, has set her cap for him.

Emily's mother suggests that Warren Caldecott is a nice boy and Emily agrees; she wouldn't have any trouble with Warren, would she? . . . But an odd thing happened today at the Chanlers'. When Emily gave the soldiers to Richard he began to play with them, and then suddenly began to cry and ran from the room. His father went after him, and when he returned he told Emily that the boy detests her. "He said that he hated himself for enjoying the soldiers because they came from me," Emily reveals. "He's jealous of me. He says that since I came into Tom's life, Tom thinks of nothing but me. . . . He says Tom talks about me in his sleep."

The mother shrewdly observes that Emily is quite pleased about young Richard's hatred and guesses that her daughter, in spite of being rational, is quite in love with Tom. Emily nods agreement and the two embrace. "But," continues Agnes, "is he right for you? After all, we do live in Boston . . ."

"But, Mother, you made what is known as a good match. Are *you* happy?" Agnes equivocates, saying she has Emily and Daniel. Emily asks pointblank if it would make her mother unhappy if she married Tom, and Agnes replies, "It's not me. It's your father. He's done something, you know. I'm sure he has. He's very angry with Tom."

Emily stoutly declares. "I'm not afraid of Father. Neither is Tom."

The butler announces the presence of Mr. Thomas Chanler to see Miss Talbot. The young man is shown in and there are Christmas greetings around. Emily tells Tom she has just come from his house. Agnes accommodatingly retires to the library, leaving the young people alone.

Tom is obviously preoccupied. "I love you," he declares to Emily, "but it's impossible. I mean anything serious between us. It's impossible."

"Why should we be put off by the impossible?" asks the stout-hearted girl.

But Tom is firm. They mustn't see each other again, and he has come to say good-by. It's her family, he explains.

"My family?"

"Yes. They're not good enough." The mother is nice enough, he admits, but extinguished, and he does not want to be like that. He has set himself a crusade—a crusade to use all his strength and energy to fight the terrible influence exercised by people like Emily's father. Emily's father is a sanctimonious hypocrite with God on one shoulder and Mammon on the other.

Tom is a youth of fire and purpose. He denies that his decision concerns another girl—say Sally McCombe. Sally isn't fit to touch the hem of Emily's garment. But women are not for him; he needs his energy to help the condition of the human race.

Emily begins to laugh at him, and Tom, remembering his dignity with great effort, bids her a formal farewell, saying, "There are other things in life beyond personal happiness. Good-by, Emily." They shake hands—and suddenly he pulls her to him and repeatedly kisses her, murmuring, "Oh, Emily, I do love you so."

Jerome Talbot interrupts the embrace at last and pronounces, "Mr. Chanler!" His wife follows him in. Tom takes the opportunity to thank Mr. Talbot for his Christmas present. Emily doesn't know there was one, and Tom explains what it was—thanks to Mr. Talbot, Tom has lost his newspaper job. Mr. Talbot wrote the editor, threatening to withdraw his advertising if he continued to employ a dangerous radical like Tom Chanler.

THOMAS—If you only had the wit to see it, it's I and my kind who are trying to save you from the dangerous radicals. . . .

EMILY—Louder. He's deaf.

THOMAS—. . . and if you don't do something to improve the conditions in your mills, Mr. Talbot . . .

JEROME—I shall conduct my business in my own way, without interference from outsiders like you.

THOMAS—Outsider! I know! Anyone who isn't a Talbot is an outsider and that includes just about the rest of the human race. Oh, I know what you think of yourself and I know what you think of me . . . an outsider trying to get into your charmed circle but you're wrong. I want to be an outsider, I'd be ashamed to be anything else. I don't acknowledge your superiority, not in any way. I love Emily . . .

EMILY—Louder! Louder!

THOMAS—I love her . . . but I had to tell her that her family isn't good enough. So you see, Mr. Talbot, from my point of view, it is you who are the outsider.

JEROME—This interview is at an end.

THOMAS—Oh, well, that'll be all right with me.

EMILY—No, Tom Chanler. . . .

THOMAS—I know when I'm not wanted.

EMILY—You stay right there. No, Father, it's not at an end.

JEROME—Emily.

EMILY—I love Tom and he loves me. We're going to be married.

JEROME—On what? Love and clear water?

EMILY—Love and clear water.

JEROME—You don't know me. If you persist in this, I shall never see you again.

EMILY—That will be a great grief to me, Father, but you don't know me. I'm your daughter, I have your character. Nothing can separate us now. You approve of us, don't you, Mother?

AGNES—Yes, I do. The nightfall will come soon enough, now, when you're young, follow the sun.

JEROME—What did you say, Agnes?

AGNES—I do approve of them. I do.

JEROME—Agnes, you're a fool. I've always thought so. It won't last, this kind of fly-by-night marriage can't last. You'll come crawling to me on your hands and knees for assistance.

EMILY—We want nothing of you, Father, but your blessing. Won't you give us your blessing?

JEROME (*from landing*)—No. Emily, this is my last word to you. The sorrow you bring on my head now, your children will, one day, bring on yours. (*Exit* JEROME.)

EMILY—If they do, I know it will be my fault, not theirs. Oh, Mother, you'll give us your blessing, won't you?

AGNES—Yes, dear, I will. (*They embrace.*)

Tom is speechless with admiration for Emily—but when they are both alone they admit they are a little scared. Tom has no job, no money and a young brother to support. Emily can get out of it if she wants to. Certainly he could never afford anything like this Talbot house.

"Well," says Emily, "perhaps you can afford some fresh air and take me for a walk." She twits him about his ambition, saying, "You'll want everything and I'll want only you." She reminds him of Sally McCombe, and he protests that she is raking up his past before he's got one. There will be other Sallys, she predicts. He replies in protest, "I want you to understand that I'm not entering on this lightly."

As they start for their walk she pats him cheerfully and says, "Don't worry, darling, I'll take you seriously when the time comes."

The curtain falls.

SCENE II

The room is now of the 1902 period. Richard Chanler, Tom's younger brother, is on the sofa reading the tragic ending of "The Sorrows of the Young Werther." He is about 20, intense, precocious to the point of genius. He is famed already as a mathematical prodigy and is one of Harvard's youngest law students. His frame is almost perpetually shaken by emotion that seems too violent for his body and spirit to contain.

Lucy, the maid, encounters him, remarking that she hasn't seen him all day. Where was he at breakfast? Richard informs her that he had to get up early and go to the steamship line, for he is taking a trip—a long trip—and alone. "I've lived with them ever since they were married. It's about time I got out," he announces. Lucy says they all will miss him—particularly Mr. Chanler, who is very fond of his little brother. Richard hates being called "Mr. Chanler's little brother." He wishes Lucy would go away, but she doesn't; she is fixing tea things and asking silly questions—doing this while, right here in Richard's book, Young Werther is gasping out his life. There is only a page and a half to go, and Richard bids the maid to listen.

"How old is this Mr. Werther?" asks Lucy.

"He's nineteen. He's younger than I am."

"Why must he die?"

"Because he wants to."

"Poor little fellow."

"He's *not* a little fellow. He's a giant, a giant who sees clearly in a world of pygmies." As Richard expounds upon Werther, living in an environment that doesn't comprehend him, Lucy thinks it is quite sad—but it is tea time. The young man shouts that Lucy is nothing but a Philistine, and the girl breaks into tears. Emily, coming downstairs and stopping on the landing, asks what the tears are for and the maid says Richard has called her a dirty name. "He called me a Philippine. I'm from Malden."

Emily laughingly sends Lucy on her way and chides her brother-in-law for baiting the girl, and he explains that he was only reading Goethe. He is upset because Emily sees humor in the situation and complains that she is always making fun of him. "If I laugh," she soothes, "it is with deep affection." She protests that she is fond of Richard—and proud; he is something of a genius and has already made them famous. But fame is nothing to the boy—"the babblings of the obtuse about the obtuse." He is not at Cambridge today, he goes on to announce, because he is through with it; never wants to see Harvard again—a childish place and a waste of time.

Suddenly the boy queries, "Do you think I'm arrogant?" She replies that she does not, since she knows him so well, and he continues, with passion, "If you knew how humble I am, Emily, before you. If you knew how I abase myself." She seeks to cheer him by saying he is enchanting and clever—a boy whom everybody would love if he would let them. Richard makes violent protest against being loved by everybody, and brings himself to crying, "I'm in love with you. Terribly in love with you. . . . I even steal your handkerchiefs to have part of you with me always!"

So that is where those handkerchiefs have been going—and this is the boy who used to hate Emily! She speaks to him sharply, telling him he is acting like a child.

Lucy reappears to tell Emily that her brother is here and wants to know if he may come in.

"My brother wants to know if he may come in? . . . Oh, Lucy, you mean he's . . ."

The maid answers the unfinished question: "Rather much so, I'm afraid, ma'am."

Daniel is asked in, and Daniel is drunk. When his sister offers him tea he says tea is for the child prodigy. "All day," he relates, "I struggled in my studio against a mounting sense of inadequacy, so I went to the bar of the Touraine where I got happily drunk." Most tenderly Emily says, "Oh, Dan, my poor old boy."

Daniel seems to taunt Richard, calling him a precious embryo, and, oddly, Richard does not resent it. He goes into agonies of anger if he thinks others are laughing at him, but he explains quite simply, "I love Daniel because he suffers."

Daniel denies Richard's statement, saying he is happy, but the boy continues his cruel analysis. Daniel suffers and is a drunkard, he declares, because Daniel wants to be a great artist and knows he never will be. But, at least, he doesn't live on sweated labor the way Tom does. Emily swiftly defends her husband, but Richard goes on with his attack, talking of the Lawrence and Lowell workers who look like tired prisoners with green skins after a ten-hour day in an airless factory. Then, not trusting his temper further, the boy runs upstairs.

"He needs a girl," Daniel observes. "Even a Utopian girl. Isn't he sweet on Lucy?"

Emily commands him not to be silly. "What's silly about that?" he says. "*I'm* sweet on Lucy. . . . Do I offend you?" He does indeed offend Emily, and her brother observes, "From behind the moat of your happiness with my brother-in-law, it is easy for you to be offended by the vulgarity of outsiders." Seriously, gravely, Emily tells Daniel he is wrong; being happy in marriage is not easy. She assures him, "It's a job, I can tell you." He argues that she is more tolerant of Tom's lapses than of his, or other people's, and she replies that this is because Tom is her job. Daniel wants another drink, and protestingly Emily pulls the bell cord for Lucy. When the maid appears Daniel addresses her in mock romantic terms, and the girl goes giggling to fetch the whiskey.

Thomas comes home, greeting his wife with a "darling" and Daniel with an ironic *cher maître,* and asking how the children are. They are all right, the day's only event being Frederic throwing Claire out of bed. Tom says he will see the children later, but now he has something serious to talk about. No, it isn't the factory; it is running better than ever, and Emily's father would turn over in his grave if he knew how well Tom is doing with it. And Daniel's studio? he inquires. Humming, he supposes. Daniel says it is in a temporary lull and Thomas says, "Never mind. I saw George Pemberton and I may get you his wife. Daniel, whose thoughts have been on Richard's needs, protests that the last thing on earth he wants is Mrs. Pemberton and her buck teeth. " I mean to paint," says Thomas shortly.

Daniel retires to the kitchen with his drink and Thomas reveals to his wife what is bothering him. It is Richard. The boy has been expelled from Harvard for writing a scurrilous examination paper in Professor Joyce's course on moral philosophy. Richard's paper reviewed a Joyce book in a feverishly insulting fashion. He also denounced President Eliot, the Mayor of Cambridge and even the plumbing in the dormitories, and Harvard is quite definitely through with its brilliant student. Thomas grimly declares he is going to find out the reason why Richard deliberately sought expulsion, and Emily begs him to remember that Richard is a child. Her husband angrily ticks his brother off as being a conceited freak who needs discipline.

EMILY—You're wrong, Tom. You couldn't be more wrong.

THOMAS—Forgive me if I disagree. And forgive me if I handle this in my own way.

EMILY—He breaks my heart, that boy. You say he's conceited. Do you know that when I'm with him, I'm holding my breath always because I feel he's perpetually on the verge of some violence. That's my terror . . . that he'll commit some violence.

THOMAS—That's pathetic blackmail. Why doesn't he grow up? He's over twenty, he's had every advantage. If he wants to quit, why doesn't he quit? Why does he have to go sniveling about? Why does he have to insult his betters? I tell you suddenly, I'm sick to death of humoring a freak every day of my life. And that's what he's been since he was a child, if you must know. . . . (RICHARD *enters in archway right.* EMILY *sees him and stops* THOMAS *with a gesture. He turns to* RICHARD.) If you heard what I said, I'm very sorry.

RICHARD—I don't mind a bit.

THOMAS—I've had a letter from the Dean.

RICHARD—I thought you would.

THOMAS—I feel very badly that you are giving up your college career.

RICHARD—It can't be helped.

THOMAS—Well, I don't see why not. Perhaps if I saw the Dean, maybe if you apologized.

RICHARD—I don't wish to.

THOMAS—Did you want to be expelled?

RICHARD—Had my object been to ingratiate myself, I should have written otherwise.

THOMAS—Will you stop patronizing me and explain yourself?

RICHARD—I'm afraid I can't stop patronizing you. I can't be a hypocrite.

THOMAS—Please, Richard, will you . . .

RICHARD—I'll explain if you insist but I scarcely think you will relish the explanation.

THOMAS—All right, then, tell me why did you want to be expelled?

RICHARD—Because I am going abroad. I am going to Italy.

THOMAS—At whose expense?

RICHARD—At my own. I shall work my way. I am going on a cattleboat.

THOMAS—Have you made any arrangements yet?

RICHARD—No. I mean to.

THOMAS—Well, you may encounter difficulties. They'll want tougher fellows than you on cattleboats. You're pretty soft for that sort of thing.

RICHARD—I know. I haven't your rampant virility. You are so proud of it, aren't you? And you exercise it so constantly, don't you?

THOMAS (*to* EMILY; *this has nettled him deeply because he knows that* EMILY *knows what* RICHARD *means by it*)—You ask me to be careful. Now you must admit that makes it very difficult.

RICHARD—Why be careful?

THOMAS (*tries again*)—Why do you want to leave? Aren't you happy here?

RICHARD—No, I am not happy here.

THOMAS—Why not? We've tried in every way. . . . I don't know what more I can do. . . .

EMILY (*senses what is coming, determined to head it off at all costs*)—Go upstairs to the children. Claire's crying for you. . . . Leave Richard to me.

THOMAS (*with a sigh*)—Gladly. I will leave Richard to you forever.

RICHARD (*in an odd voice*)—Will you?

THOMAS—Gladly.

RICHARD—She hasn't told you then.

EMILY—Richard!

RICHARD—She hasn't told you then?

Emily's pleas go unheard as the boy launches upon an outburst of passion and denunciation. He declares he is going away because the spectacle of Tom's and Emily's life together has become unendurable. Thomas pauses on the stair to listen, then comes angrily back down the stairs, shouting, "I ought to kick you out of my house bodily!" Richard reminds him that it isn't his house, but his wife's. And, he informs his astonished brother, he loves Emily and she knows it. He openly berates his brother for crudeness, acquisitiveness and vulgar flirtations with other women which Emily pretends not to see. "Some day," he says, "she'll meet someone who'll love her the way she deserves to be loved. . . ."

Thomas's fury becomes uncontrollable. Grabbing Richard by the collar, he slaps his face hard and pushes him out of the room. Then, instantly sorry, he calls, "Richard! Come back here and put on your overcoat, you damn fool!" But Richard does not return.

Thomas knows he has behaved badly and knows also that his anger is not really at Richard, but at himself. Emily also is very angry with him. "Quite an alliance against me," he grumbles. "You and Richard. Your father despised me, too. So does Daniel." He brings up the vulgar flirtations Richard spoke of; if they get on her nerves, it might be a little more human of her to show it once in a while. Why does she pretend not to see?

"Because," says the wise woman, "I knew from the first I'd have that to contend with. My blindness is a bargain I made with myself."

Thomas is defenseless. "You're so possessive," he rails.

She doesn't think so. Didn't she let him go alone to a party the other night when she had a cold?

"That's not what I mean when I say you're possessive," he declares urgently. "It isn't when you're present that you're possessive—it's when you're not present. When you're not present, you're present just the same, only more so—you're always tiptoeing around in my mind."

"I am?"

"So critical—so mocking—I can never talk to a woman without thinking how silly this would sound to Emily."

She agrees, "It does. It does."

"It's that silent unheard mockery that I can't endure. I have no privacy—I can never be alone by myself for a minute! That's what I mean when I say you're possessive."

Emily has begun to laugh and Thomas, who has been so earnest, is hurt. She analyzes him—and herself. She can understand his resenting living in her house, and managing a business built up by her father, and not having some other career. Moreover, she adds, she doesn't think he was meant to be a husband. He laughs melodramatically and shouts, "You want to get rid of me!" She doesn't, she says. She asks why they can't be candid with each other. They have been married twelve years and now they have reached the critical point.

He asks, "Why can't we be at peace like other people?"

"Peace is the last thing you want. You want adventure; so do I. . . . But I want my adventure—with you." Thomas contritely confesses that he hit Richard because he saw a threat to themselves—saw Emily transferring her adoration to some unknown man. Emily breaks in, saying, "Do you realize something? We have had our first major quarrel. . . . And we've survived. Oh, darling, we should be so grateful to Richard." She is worried about the boy and asks her husband to find him and bring him home. Thomas would—

but suddenly they hear shouting outside—or think they do. He says he will go look for his brother—but first he will go upstairs to see the children. From above he calls, "Oh, Emily, there's such a load off my mind!"

Emily summons Lucy and asks her to make tea for Mr. Chanler—and to bring some of the special Sunday cake for Richard. The doorbell rings, and there is also the sound of loud knocking and muffled voices. Daniel calls from outside that he can't open the door, and Lucy goes to open it. The voices increase in volume, and one can hear somebody saying, "They couldn't stop the horses." In the entrance Daniel calls a warning to his sister not to come out, and in a moment the door is closed and Daniel, obviously shocked into sobriety, enters the room.

"Richard?" Emily asks.

Her brother answers, "He threw himself in front of the horses. It's all over. . . . He's dead. What made him do it? I heard Tom shouting at him."

Emily cries, "I did it! I ridiculed him. Oh, my poor Tom!" She calls up the stair, "Tom, Tom, dear."

The curtain falls.

ACT III

It is 1918. Emily has been playing solitaire at a card table, but now her head is bowed in her hands. Lucy, bringing a pitcher of water to the liquor table, offers her some and Emily declines. "Wasn't that the mailman?" she asks. "No, ma'am. Now don't you go worrying about Mr. Chanler. You'll be hearing from him soon."

But Emily does worry. She hasn't heard from her husband in forty-eight days. Lucy sensibly argues that, since Mr. Chanler is on a destroyer in the North Atlantic, he can't very well mail any letters. Lucy comfortingly points out that it is lucky Mr. Chanler isn't fighting in dirty trenches but on a nice clean ship. . . . And about dinner: Will Mr. Nicholas be staying? Emily says she'd thought of telling them both to go out—"them" being her daughter Claire and Nicholas.

Claire, Nicholas and a girl named Sissy arrive. Sissy has a taxi waiting outside, but she has stopped to tell Mrs. Chanler that she has had a letter from Frederic. Frederic has become an ace, she reports, and has had a leave in Paris. "And what do you hear from Mr. Chanler?" Sissy inquires. Claire informs the girl they have not heard lately, but will any minute. "Mother sent him your poems, Sissy—the ones you gave me . . . and if Dad likes them, he'll give them to one of his publisher friends. . . ." Sissy returns to her taxicab and a Red Cross meeting, and Emily goes to the door with her.

Nicholas urges Claire to change her mind about not going to dinner with him and his friend Felix, who is being shipped to France day after tomorrow. Claire replies that she isn't up to meeting a stranger tonight.

He asks, "Won't you go to the station with me?"

"Won't your mother be going?"

"No. I asked her not to. I told her I wanted to spend my last evening with my sweetheart. Do you mind?"

"Of course I don't," says Claire. "It's little enough to do for a hero." But Nicholas doesn't feel like a hero. He has been overseas, but now he is assigned to training troops here.

Emily, returning, asks Nicholas why he doesn't take Claire out to dinner and the young man says, "I've been trying to persuade her but she won't come. She doesn't want to leave you alone." Emily says she won't be alone—Daniel is coming. "Don't take no for an answer," she advises Nicholas. Again, suddenly, Emily asks if that wasn't the doorbell ,and her daughter assures her the bell hasn't rung. "Please, Mother," she urges, "stop imagining things. Father's all right. I know he's all right."

Emily is certain he isn't. She has a feeling. Like the feeling she had one day when it suddenly seemed cold and she just knew that something had happened to Tom. She'd been out walking, and when she came home there was a message to call the factory. Tom had been demonstrating a machine to an apprentice and something went wrong and his hand was crushed.

Claire points out that the hand wasn't permanently injured, and Emily apologizes for her fears and starts for her room. She will have her dinner on a tray up there, she says; but Claire informs her that she and Nicholas are staying for dinner. "Oh, poor Nicholas," Emily sympathizes, and speaks vaguely of ordering dinner on the house phone in her room. Nicholas still is begging Claire to dine out with him, but she says her uncle Daniel is undependable and might not appear. He is expected, but whether he arrives depends on how many bars he passes between the Back Bay station and here.

Lucy is heard giggling at the door, and to Nicholas' relief Daniel makes his appearance and immediately says, "Lucy, I haven't had a drink since I left the train ten minutes ago." The maid fixes him one. Claire exclaims how well her uncle looks; the war must be

agreeing with him. He asks how Emily is and is told she is not well
—she's sure something has happened to Thomas.

"Could be," Daniel says matter-of-factly. His niece begs him to
say nothing like that in front of Emily, and he promises. "What
on earth did Tom want to enlist for anyway—at his age?" he asks.
Claire replies that her father wanted to do his bit, but Daniel maintains it was bravado, romanticism, pure heroics. His speech is cut
short by Emily's appearance. She greets her brother affectionately,
and he jollies her, saying, "You don't think that Tom, with his infal-
lible gift for success, is going to succumb to a German submarine at
his time of life, do you? Besides, Emily, you appear to forget that
I am stationed in Norfolk, Virginia, personally camouflaging our
ships. The Germans are wasting their torpedoes."

Daniel accepts his sister's invitation to dinner, and Claire agrees
to go out with Nicholas. The girl runs upstairs to change her dress,
and Nicholas goes to the library to telephone his friend Felix. Emily
and Daniel are alone, and Emily comments on her brother's cheerful
mien.

DANIEL—At least, down there in Norfolk I'm needed.

EMILY—Why not? It's very useful work.

DANIEL—Yes, I suppose so. But here in Boston—I'm not useful.
Oh, I don't deceive myself, Emily, I know that the commissions I
get here I get solely because I'm Tom Chanler's brother-in-law.

EMILY—Is that why you resent Tom?

DANIEL—Possibly. It must burn Tom up that he's an ensign and
his son is a captain in the Air Force.

EMILY—Isn't it ridiculous?

DANIEL—Why? War is the special privilege of the young, at
least they ought to get the honors, such as they are.

EMILY—Oh, you think that life on a destroyer is less dangerous
than flying a plane?

DANIEL—I'm afraid you're more of a wife than a mother, Emily.
You were rather a bore with your happiness, you and Tom. You
shut out the rest of the world.

EMILY—Could we help it that we were happy? Really, Daniel.

DANIEL—It's sometimes expensive for others—such happiness.

EMILY—Now what do you mean by that?

DANIEL—It was expensive for his own brother, wasn't it? Richard might have been alive today if Tom . . .

EMILY—You blame Tom for that, you always have.

DANIEL—Yes, I do blame him.

EMILY—I know you do. It's always been in the back of your

mind. Well, now you've said it.

DANIEL—Yes, now I've said it.

EMILY—Don't forget that I was present and you weren't. I know what happened and you don't, and yet you've passed on your version to Frederic . . . and such a distorted one. You've turned him against his father.

DANIEL—I know. For you Tom can do no wrong.

EMILY—And for you he can do no right. And I know why.

DANIEL—Emily. . . .

EMILY—It's because he did your job for you. You failed in art and he succeeded at your job.

DANIEL—Let's drop this, Emily.

EMILY—No, it's out now—let it come out. When Father died it was your place to come home and carry on the business. Tom was doing very well in journalism—he wanted to be a writer and he would have been. But no, you had to stay on in Paris—you allowed him to take over and because he succeeded at your job, your job, Daniel, you never forgave him. You won't even forgive him now . . . now that . . .

DANIEL—Emily, you and I had always been so close, I admit it. I couldn't help it. I hated it when you married Tom.

EMILY—Well, there's nothing left now to resent.

DANIEL—No, nothing left to resent. Nothing left for me at all. What you say is true. . . . I know I'm not much of an artist, I know I'm not much of a man.

EMILY—Daniel, why are we doing this? I think I'm saying these things to you because you're alive and I know you're alive. Oh, Dan, forgive me. (LUCY *enters with a letter.*)

LUCY—Mrs. Chanler, it's come, a letter—a real one—a heavy one —I'll tell Miss Claire.

Claire hurries down, relieved; a letter from her father means he is all right. But her mother, still taking the dark view, points out that the letter was written ten days ago. Nicholas, having finished his phone call, joins them, and they all are eager to hear what Thomas says. Emily begins to read: "My wife: We have had several minor inconveniences . . ." Emily breaks off and says, "You see, something terrible happened to his ship. I knew it." They urge her to keep on reading and she begins again: "My wife: We have had several minor inconveniences which have probably been distracting to the younger and less experienced members of our crew, but which, to an old salt like me with the sea in his blood, were scarcely noticeable. . . ."

Thomas continues with comments on receiving news that his son is working up in the comparatively unimportant branch in which he is serving. And, as for himself, he reports that he is in exultant spirits. Emily, the reader, interprets this statement as meaning that Thomas has been close to death and is exultant because he has escaped. Claire cuts her mother's speculations short and urges her to go on with the letter. Thomas wants to know how Claire is behaving, and advises that she have as good a time as she can because, when he returns, he will reinstate the Spartan regime. Thomas has received the poem by Claire's friend, Sissy, and he thinks it is brilliant. Emily concludes her reading: "For the rest, my dear, the war from the standpoint of adventure has been rather disappointing. It's necessary work, I suppose, and has to be done; but it's routine, humdrum, prosaic. I never recommend war to anyone seeking adventure. There is more adventure in my office on State Street and far more in my house. My darling, I miss you terribly. . . ."

Emily breaks off reading and Claire urges her to go on. "I can't," says Emily with emotion. "It's too personal."

The curtain falls.

Scene II

It is December, 1920. The room is about the same, the only recent improvement being a mahjong set laid out on a table and ready for play. William brings in a tray laden with decanters, glasses, an ice bowl and other fittings for drink. William is a young man and it is the first day of his new job in this house. Lucy is at hand to instruct him on where things go, and making sure the lint is off his coat. The telephone and the doorbell ring almost simultaneously; Lucy goes to the phone in the library and William to the door. It is Eleanor Peabody—the young poetess, Sissy—at the door. Sissy has become a very attractive young woman of the world.

Eleanor is asking for Mr. Chanler, but Mr. Chanler has not yet come home, she is informed by William. Mrs. Chanler is here, and so is Mr. Frederic. Eleanor asks William for a scotch and water, and while he is preparing it Lucy appears with a message for Eleanor. Mr. Chanler has telephoned to say he has been delayed, but he hopes Miss Peabody will wait until he gets home.

Frederic comes downstairs. He has been dressing for dinner, but his tie is not yet tied. Eleanor knots it for him. "Well," he says, "I hear that Boston's become too small for you and you're off to Paris. Your poems must be selling very well. . . . I'm going, you know." Lucy appears with a telephone message for Mr. Frederic: Miss Blanche Griswold was on the wire and she wondered if Mr.

Frederic has seen "Broken Blossoms." Mr. Frederic has seen it four times, and he tells the maid to remind him to call Blanche later. Right now he would rather be with Eleanor.

Eleanor declares that Blanche Griswold would be very good for Frederic. Blanche cares for him madly, Eleanor observes; she's good-looking and she is related by blood to the oldest trust funds in Boston. Eleanor predicts, "She'll get you. She'll get you eventually by attrition."

"No," contradicts Frederic. "No, perhaps that's how, eventually, I shall get you. . . . Sissy, why don't you come to Paris with me?" He declares he is going to Paris to become an artist, because he believes there are only two things in life—art and love. He has decided to quit those loathsome mills of his father's. He also has decided that Eleanor is the only person on earth who could ever make him happy.

"It's too late," says the amused Eleanor. "I'm interested in someone else."

Frederic is a practical young man, and he begins adding things up. Eleanor's poems are not selling, so somebody must be paying for her trip to Europe. His father paid for publishing her poems. . . . Perhaps his father is paying for Eleanor's trip, too. The facts dawn upon him and he exclaims, "You and Father! It's incredible!"

Nicholas arrives, asking for Claire. He confesses to Frederic that he can't get Claire off his mind for a moment, and lately she has been acting quite strangely. "I know what it is," volunteers Eleanor. "It's that war buddy of yours, Felix. Until Claire gets over him all you can do is mark time. Why don't you go away for a bit?" "I am going away," says Nicholas, "but she won't even notice it."

Thomas gets back from the office with a greeting for everyone. Lucy tells Nicholas that Mrs. Chanler would like him to come upstairs to her sitting room. Says Thomas: "You know, Nicholas, it's not Claire you're worried about. It's Felix. Well, you recommended him too highly for your own good. You overdid it." Nicholas goes upstairs.

Frederic announces to his father that he is through with the office and that he is going to Paris to study painting. Thomas takes this news ironically; he has seen his son's sketches and admits they are clever and show talent. But art, he says, requires character and passionate devotion—two qualities he has never felt in his son.

FREDERIC—But I tell you, even if I knew I were going to fail, I'm still going to try it. At least it will be my own failure. My uncle, Daniel, was an artist.

THOMAS—Yes, and a very poor one.

FREDERIC—And I'm sure you made him aware of his inadequacy.

THOMAS—Oh, no, he was aware of it, all his life, and so he drank himself to death. God rest his unhappy soul. Well, do you blame me for wishing to save you from that?

FREDERIC—Why didn't you save Uncle Richard?

THOMAS—Please, Frederic!

FREDERIC—He died, too, didn't he? . . . and it wasn't of drink.

THOMAS—Please, Frederic. . . . I want to apologize, Sissy. . . .

FREDERIC—No, I'm sure you needn't do that. She's been most impressed, haven't you?

ELEANOR—I should not have been present.

FREDERIC—Oh, yes, you had to be present. It's precisely because you are present that he's been so eloquent. Aren't you impressed by his clairvoyance? He knows everything. He knows whether people will succeed or fail. He sets the boundaries to their talents, their ambitions, their desires. I'm sure you're deeply impressed but on me his effect is different, quite different. (FREDERIC *exits upstairs*.)

THOMAS—So, he's still in love with you. You said he wasn't. Is he or isn't he?

ELEANOR—He's not in love with anybody. He's merely vain.

THOMAS—He's so ingrown he's the price we pay here in Boston for three centuries of introspection. I came in feeling wonderful. He depresses me.

ELEANOR—Why should you let him depress you?

THOMAS—Not for long. Well, Sissy? How do you do? (*He lights her cigarette*.)

ELEANOR—Well, Thomas?

THOMAS—Today I spent in a mirage.

ELEANOR—Was it pleasant?

THOMAS—In a fantasy.

ELEANOR—Was that pleasant?

THOMAS—I came home wrapped up in it.

ELEANOR—And did Frederic disturb it?

THOMAS—Partly. But you restore it.

ELEANOR—If it was pleasant, I'm glad that I restore it.

THOMAS—Isn't it extraordinary? I put in a hard day. I saw quite a few people. I did all the right things and I had two visions.

ELEANOR—Two? Simultaneously?

THOMAS—Simultaneously. In one I saw all my past days—which I have spent in almost the same way as I did this one, and then I saw all my future days, which I will spend in almost the same way

as I did this one. I saw them all flash by—like white columns in a
subway . . . all the same, all immaculate. Then I didn't see anything any more. But I heard Time whistling at me derisively, saying: "Is this all the use you are going to put me to? Get up. Walk
out of here!"

ELEANOR—And yet you're even later than usual?

THOMAS—I put in an extra hour. I punished myself. It's my
Puritan conscience.

ELEANOR—Do you feel better?

THOMAS—Sissy, I shall follow you to Paris.

ELEANOR—Really?

THOMAS—Really.

ELEANOR—Are you going to tell Emily?

THOMAS—Yes.

ELEANOR—She will hate me.

THOMAS—Yes.

ELEANOR—How much do you think she guesses now?

THOMAS—It's hard to say. Sometimes I think—nothing. Sometimes—

Emily appears on the landing and comes down, saying, "Sissy, I've
been reading your new poems. They're wonderful. So agonized."
And to her husband, quizzically, "Tom, dear, what do you think of
our little Sissy?" Thomas feels more than a little uneasy. His wife
pointedly asks what time it is, and both Thomas and Eleanor react
to her question; but Emily indicates that she is only worried because
Claire has not come home yet.

Eleanor is a forthright young woman and she thinks it is time for
a clear statement. She begins to Emily, "You've known me ever
since I was a little girl. But that doesn't mean that I've remained—"

Emily cuts her off with a murmur about how fond she has been
of Eleanor. Eleanor persists, "But I must tell you something, Emily,
and I want Thomas to hear it, too."

"Please don't confess to me, Sissy," says Emily. "I hate confes-
sions."

"But I must tell you. . . ."

Emily turns aside whatever it is Eleanor wants to tell. She says
she is more concerned about Nicholas, who has just told her he is
going away to San Francisco. He has been weeping on her shoulder
and mourning about Claire. Says Thomas, "The trouble with Claire
and Nicholas is, they don't quarrel. He just bores her. He bores
her to death. You know, that's the one form of homicide you can

indulge in without paying the penalty for it. It's the one great gap in our jurisprudence."

Claire comes home and is told Nicholas is upstairs. She goes up. Eleanor takes her leave, and Thomas goes with her to get a taxi. When Claire comes down in a moment she asks her mother if Felix has called, and is told that he hasn't. Claire is full of news about Felix; she tells her mother that he has been offered a contract in Hollywood. She seems unhappy, and Emily asks what is wrong. Claire explains that Felix doesn't really want to go to Hollywood and has been trying to make up his mind—and by now, quarter after six, he should have called.

William announces that Mr. Felix Burrill is on the telephone for Miss Claire—and Claire surprisingly asks her mother to listen in on the extension, saying, "You'll be able to tell me . . . you'll know . . . please, Mother." Mother and daughter leave for the telephones, and soon William reappears with a box of flowers—just as Nicholas comes downstairs. They are Nicholas' flowers, and he tells the butler he will give them to Miss Claire himself.

Thomas, returning from his parting with Eleanor, asks humorously if the flowers are for him and Nicholas laughingly apologizes and says no, they are for his daughter. 'I really like you very much, Nicholas," says Thomas. "I prefer you to Felix. Now, your problem is to make Claire share this preference—and in that enterprise I wish you luck."

Claire has finished her telephone conversation and returns, radiant. She accepts the flowers and embraces Nicholas. The young man is so astonished that he asks, "Is it for the flowers that you are hugging me?" "Oh," says Claire, "are these flowers? Thank you, Nicholas."

"Is it Felix?" Nicholas persists.

"Yes. It's Felix I love. It's Felix I'll always love. . . . Nick, I have to tell you—I want somebody to know. I'm going to marry Felix in a month and in August I'm going to have our first child."

The dazed Nicholas can almost be heard counting. Claire continues, "No matter how you count it, Nicholas, it's August. You shall be its godfather. . . . We shall name him after you—and if it's a girl we'll name her after you, too—Nicola!"

Nicholas asks, "Does Felix know?"

"Not about the baby. I only found out myself today. I shan't tell him about it till after we're married. . . . I don't want him to feel he has to."

Nicholas takes this blow with surprising good grace, and says he is happy for Claire since it makes her happy. "I just want you to know, Claire, if something should happen, you can always count on me."

Emily enters and Nicholas departs. "Did you listen?" Claire asks her mother, and Emily nods.

"Well, what do you think?"

"Put Felix out of your mind, dear. He's no good to you."

Claire does not believe her mother. Felix has just told her he will not go to Hollywood. "He will," says her mother. Furthermore, Emily predicts that Felix will not take Claire with him; he was lying on the telephone. He said he was going to New York to turn down the contract only to evade Claire because he hadn't the courage to tell her he didn't want her.

The girl's faith is unshaken. "When he calls me tonight," she says, "if he wants me to I'll go to New York with him tonight—and I won't come back here." She is angry with her mother and accuses her of being unfair to Felix. She runs upstairs and Frederic passes her on the way down.

Frederic knows about his sister's romance, and chuckles to his mother that he wants to be on hand when his father is told that Claire wants to marry an actor. Emily protests, "You're so considerate of me, dear. And yet about your father—you're so ungenerous."

Frederic bluntly informs his mother that she is about to lose this husband of hers. Would she like to know why Thomas doesn't want Frederic to go to Paris? "I'd rather he told me himself," says Emily, and her son retorts, "He hasn't the courage to tell you."

Thomas comes back, and Frederic, the bit between his teeth, tells both his parents what he had been trying to tell to his reluctant mother. "He doesn't want me to go to Paris because he wants to send Sissy there, and, who knows, perhaps he wants to go there himself." Thomas dismisses his son with a brusque "That will be all. That will be all." The father is furious—and he also is surprised to discover that, for the first time, he is resenting his wife. Somehow, just now with Sissy, Emily made it seem trivial, inconsequential. He is frank in his confession to Emily and she is calmly amused. "It didn't last long, did it?" she comments.

THOMAS—Emily, there's something I want to tell you.

EMILY—Everyone wants to confess to me today.

THOMAS—Emily, things are not what they were . . . the war . . .

EMILY—How convenient the war . . .

THOMAS—Nevertheless . . .

EMILY—And when it isn't the war, we say it's post-war. After all, every period is either pre-war or post-war, isn't it?

THOMAS—Nevertheless, you can't ignore it. I didn't learn about the war from a book, you know. And I swore that if ever I returned . . .

EMILY—That you would live. It's easy to make a scapegoat of the war, Tom, but you were exactly the same before it.

THOMAS—No, no . . . do you remember what your mother said in this very room the day we decided to be married?

EMILY—What?

THOMAS—While you are young, follow the sun. . . .

EMILY—Oh, yes . . . the nightfall will come soon enough.

THOMAS—I don't feel the nightfall—I feel young. Oh, I know what other people will say, "Middle-aged madness," but I don't expect you to say it. And I've even felt—I couldn't possibly tell you this unless I wanted to conceal nothing—I've even felt a certain triumph that to Sissy I seemed even younger than Frederic.

EMILY—To me you even seem younger than Sissy.

THOMAS—You are hard. . . . Do you think it was easy for me to say those things to you?

EMILY—Oh, Tom, do you think it was easy for me to listen?

THOMAS—It's no use.

EMILY—No, Tom, you're right, it's no use. You belong to Sissy now. She'll be waiting for you in Paris. Go to her, my dear, you're perfectly free to go.

THOMAS—You want me to go?

EMILY—Yes.

THOMAS—No, you can't leave, not until . . .

EMILY—Not until what? We have nothing left to say to each other—no plans to make—no need for any. The future is only too clear to me. This dream you have with Sissy, it will elude you—it will vanish. Go, Tom. You will return.

THOMAS—And you'll not be here?

EMILY—Oh, yes, I shall always be here. But you will return to a house emptied of everything you knew—everything you used to love so well.

William interrupts. He has a telephone message for Miss Claire. Mr. Felix Burrill has called to say he has been called away from the city suddenly and will be unable to meet Miss Claire this evening. "He doesn't love her. He doesn't want her," says Emily.

Thomas asks, "Is she very unhappy about this?"

"She's desperate." Emily starts upstairs to break the news to her daughter, but Thomas holds her back. His wife tells him she has known about Sissy for some time, but, oddly, it didn't hurt her much. Ten years ago it would have hurt, but now it is too late. The contrite Thomas berates himself for having an evil spirit that he yields to, that he cherishes—"and it has destroyed me."

EMILY—No, Tom, it has not destroyed you. It is a dream of pleasure which I understand. But, oh, my darling, perhaps it is too late for that. I do not speak to you of pleasure, I speak to you of love.

THOMAS—Still?

EMILY—Still.

THOMAS—You can't. You can't love a man like me.

EMILY—Tom, you're part of my life, like my hands or my eyes. I don't say to myself, do I love my hands or my eyes, they're part of me, that's all.

THOMAS—Oh, Emily, would you consider . . . I don't know why for the first time in my life I should suddenly become shy . . . but would you consider going away with me . . . just you and I together . . . alone?

EMILY—Where to, Tom? Paris?

THOMAS—No, no, not Paris, you fiend, in the opposite direction . . . the east . . . the east. . . .

EMILY—Where? Where east? India? China?

THOMAS—Java! Bali! The fiery portals of the east.

EMILY—It seems to me that all you want is to travel with a lady friend.

THOMAS—Emily. . . . No. . . . Please don't joke.

EMILY—But, Tom, a moment ago you were on your way to Paris.

THOMAS—That's quite true. A moment ago I was leaving you . . . and then I don't know . . . You told me that I could go . . . and then I don't know, something happened. What was it that happened?

EMILY—Were you touched by my generosity?

THOMAS—No, I was not touched by your generosity. I was leaving you, in fact, I was deserting you. And then suddenly you made me feel that you were deserting me. You know, Emily, that was a very dangerous thing for you to do. I might have gone, you know.

EMILY—Yes, Tom, I knew that when I said it.

THOMAS—What?

EMILY—I say I knew that when I said it.

THOMAS—You're so enigmatic I don't even know what you mean by that. It's been a lifetime of manipulation, hasn't it, Emily? Chasms opening between us—lifelines flung across—and you walking that lifeline with me on your shoulders—and I worrying about your equilibrium? Was I going somewhere else to find adventure?

EMILY—Oh, Tom, you were going somewhere else.

THOMAS—Why? Will you tell me why? No, you won't tell me. Oh, Emily, you're so diabolically right and always at the wrong moment. And you're so inhumanly strong. Oh, the violence of your gentle understanding. Where could I find excitement so concentrated as in the smallest things you do or say? Why, you can make a crisis by just smiling and a climax with a tiny intonation of your voice. And I find it all very invigorating. I always have and I always will. You are coming with me.

Emily protests that she cannot go with him. The offer is attractive—but she cannot leave Claire. Thomas grudgingly says he will take his daughter as far as San Francisco. . . .

Simultaneously they get an idea. Nicholas has gone to San Francisco. He can take Claire from there. It seems an ideal solution, and the parents relax. "Shall we start tomorrow?" Emily asks.

"Oh, Emily," says Thomas. "I adore you."

Says she, lightly but fondly, "Oh, Tom, I know you do."

CURTAIN

THE ENCHANTED *

A Comedy in Three Acts

BY JEAN GIRAUDOUX

Adapted by Maurice Valency

IN his lifetime, Jean Giraudoux was most noted in the American theatre for his saucy version of the Amphitryon legend, which was played by Alfred Lunt and Lynn Fontanne. Some years after his death he gained a new and greater prominence with "The Madwoman of Chaillot," which was a success of the 1948-1949 season and which toured for twenty-two weeks in 1949-1950. The adaptation of "The Madwoman" had been made by Maurice Valency, of Columbia University. Mr. Valency next turned to another of Giraudoux' philosophical fantasies, "The Enchanted," which considered life, death and political bureaucracy. As was its predecessor, "The Enchanted" was a comedy of wit and pith, but it was not so happily in accord with the taste of New York playgoers. Its critical reviews were respectful, not enthusiastic, and its local stage career was brief.

The scene is a clearing in the woods just outside a provincial town in France. It is late afternoon in the Spring of almost any year. The field is very open, but in one spot weeds have overgrown the ruins of what might once have been a Summer house. For the rest, the scene is innocence itself. A shout from the Mayor announces the approach of the Mayor. He has been calling "Hello!" and is disturbed because there is no echo. In the clearing he tries once again—and this time he turns in fear as the echo answers, "Hello!"

From the opposite side the Doctor enters the clearing and he chuckles at the Mayor's reaction to the echo, asking, "Did you think it was he?" This is no joking matter to the Mayor. "We all know he doesn't exist—most likely," he pronounces. "All the same, there's something queer about this place. . . . This is where he is supposed

---

to appear. It's nothing but an hallucination, of course."

The Doctor shrugs that if it's nothing but an hallucination, they could have met just as well in Town Hall; but it was the Inspector himself who chose this place. The Mayor asks the Doctor if he feels a little nervous here, and the Doctor replies no, that the spot looks as green and innocent as a golf course. They seldom haunt a golf course, he explains. "A golf course is the epitome of all that is purely transitory in the universe, a space not to dwell in, but to get over as quickly as possible. In a golf course everything is calculated, limited and foreseen, and every blade of grass is registered."

MAYOR—This place is full of weeds.

DOCTOR—You're right. Well! This place is by no means as innocent as it looks. There are all sorts of malignant things quietly growing here—hellebore—and henbane—and even—yes, by God!—mandrake!

MAYOR—You think it's true what they say about the mandrake?

DOCTOR—With regard to constipation?

MAYOR—With regard to demonology. They say, when a mandrake is impregnated with the seed of a hanged man, the child grows up to be a fiend. Can you believe that?

DOCTOR—It's entirely possible.

MAYOR—You don't suppose that this—apparition—is a thing of that sort?

DOCTOR—What does this ghost look like? Dwarfish? Crooked? Black?

MAYOR—Tall. Young. Handsome.

DOCTOR—Have there been any hangings in the district?

MAYOR—During my term of office, only one. The grocer's wife. You may remember the case. In the time of the ration cards. But she hanged herself by the feet, and only sprained her ankle.

DOCTOR (*shaking his head*)—It has to be a man, and with his feet down. . . . I'm beginning to think our colleagues are lost.

MAYOR—No fear of that. I've asked the Supervisor of Weights and Measures to meet the Inspector at the station. The Supervisor knows exactly where we are.

DOCTOR—In my opinion, a committee of three would have been ample.

MAYOR—But the Supervisor is such a marvelous chap! Did you hear what he did last night at the dinner? With a single phrase, imagine, he completely rehabilitated Catherine the Great. And, mind you, in the very teeth of the Fire Captain!

DOCTOR—I wasn't talking about the Supervisor.

MAYOR—The Supervisor considers himself the local champion of the weaker sex, you know. And if anyone so much as opens his mouth . . .

DOCTOR—I meant the Inspector. Couldn't we have done without him?

MAYOR—The Inspector? Oh, impossible! The Inspector insists on investigating in person all cases of subversive activity in the jurisdiction.

DOCTOR—And what gave him the idea that this ghost is subversive?

MAYOR—The Inspector considers everyone guilty until he's proved innocent. You've heard of his latest inquiry, no doubt?

DOCTOR—You mean that silly business of the water nymphs of Limoges?

MAYOR—After three weeks of fact-finding, he decided to pave over the brook where they lived. The army engineers did the job. Nobody's seen any water nymphs since. . . . Then there was the case of the pretty mare that was accused of making eyes at the young men—

DOCTOR—He considered *her* subversive?

MAYOR—He had special blinders made; the poor beast has to wear them even in her stall at night.

DOCTOR—And this is the man who is coming to investigate our ghost!

It is time the others should have arrived and the Doctor suggests giving a shout—but his companion is fearful: you can't tell who might answer. The Doctor shouts anyway and is answered by a veritable chorus of shrill hellos. A little throng of excited girls about ten years old appears. After them comes Isabel. The children, clad in bright pinafores, are hunting botanical specimens and Isabel is their teacher. Isabel, radiant, wholesome, very much the outdoor type, in her early twenties, is only a substitute teacher; the regular one is off having a baby. The Mayor is disturbed that the children are not in their classroom and dubiously accepts Isabel's statement that Spring is their classroom today. "We are collecting all sorts of fascinating things—monkshood and hellebore and henbane and foxglove. . . . And now we're after the most interesting of all. I know exactly where it grows," says the teacher. The little girls chorus, "The mandrake!" They troop off on their hunt.

A rustling in the bushes presages the arrival of the Inspector and his guide, the Supervisor. The Inspector is, as one might suppose, a pompous authoritarian. The Supervisor is a young chap of pleas-

ant appearance and rather serious mien. The Inspector is going to
waste no time over ghost stories; since the spirit world does not
exist, he intends to prove its nonexistence in the shortest possible
time and be done with it. The gentlemen now with him *do* agree
that if there are spirits, they can hear what the Inspector is about
to say; they can hear him defy them. The Inspector patronizingly
offers the spirits a simple way of proving their existence—no blowing
of invisible trumpets or anything like that; just that, at the count
of three, they should cause an ordinary sparrow to fly into the air.

The Inspector counts "One, two, three"—and at three his hat flies
into the air. "Phew! What a wind!" he exclaims. The Doctor
drily observes that the leaves are hardly stirring. The Mayor points
out that the Inspector's address was too general—that he should have
addressed one particular spirit, like Aspharloth. So the visiting dignitary obliges by daring Aspharloth to make him snap his fingers
when he stretches out his arm. He stretches out his arm—and
sneezes; clear proof that Aspharloth does not exist. The Inspector is
wroth with the Mayor for the report he has written about the town
being haunted; but the Mayor sticks to his story and is backed up by
the Supervisor.

Says the Supervisor, "We are haunted by an occult presence which
is clearly bent on sapping the foundations of civilized society." For
example, dogs which are beaten no longer cringe; they bite the
beaters. And children who are mistreated simply leave home. And
women! "The women," the Supervisor reveals, "have quietly left
their husbands and gone off with more attractive men." The Doctor
further shocks the Inspector by declaring, "In this community, it is
no longer respectable to be unhappy." The Mayor cites some ex-
amples: In the civic lottery a deserving couple won the prize, instead
of the town millionaire. And when a motor truck ran over two
people, the two weren't the youngest and healthiest, but the oldest
and most decrepit. Obviously, fortune for the first time is display-
ing some intelligence.

The Inspector demands how long these scandals have been going
on and is told, ever since the Ghost first appeared.

Into the clearing come two spinster ladies, the sisters Mangebois.
Léonide is hard of hearing and carries an ear trumpet. The other,
Armande, keeps Léonide abreast of events by means of the trumpet.
They, being co-chairmen of the Ladies Aid, know everything that
goes on in the community, and they have come to make a statement
to the Inspector. To begin with, they believe the Ghost exists; they
haven't seen it, but they know people who have, and they describe it

as a pale young man dressed in black, hatless, who is to be seen here, near the edge of the lake, just at nightfall.

INSPECTOR—Have there been any other phantoms prowling about the neighborhood?

ARMANDE—Never. Never before the crime.

INSPECTOR—Aha! Now we come to the crime!

MAYOR—Please don't say anything against the crime, Inspector. It was a superb example of a crime of passion, the only one ever to take place in this jurisdiction. I shall always look back upon it with emotion and pride. It was the crowning point of my career.

INSPECTOR—It was a routine shooting, of which the only interesting aspect was the extraordinary stupidity of the police.

SUPERVISOR—It was a beautiful crime. A crime of taste and distinction.

INSPECTOR—Did anyone here personally know the assassin? Did you?

MAYOR—No. All we know about him is that he arrived from Paris on the night train, and came directly to the château where his wife and his friend were spending the weekend together.

INSPECTOR—Did anyone see his face?

MAYOR—No, but the station master positively identified his hat.

INSPECTOR—So that, after shooting his wife and his friend, he simply vanished? Except for his hat?

SUPERVISOR—He didn't vanish at all. He's right here. In the lake.

INSPECTOR—What makes you so certain that he drowned himself?

MAYOR—What possible doubt can there be? His hat was found at the water's edge. As he stepped into the lake, he took off his hat . . .

INSPECTOR—. . . and said "how do you do" to the hereafter. Very touching. But the body was not found.

DOCTOR—The lake is deep.

INSPECTOR—So is the young man.

MAYOR—No, no, no, Inspector. The young man is above suspicion. All the roads were watched. The countryside was combed for weeks. The coroner's inquest established the suicide beyond a reasonable doubt.

INSPECTOR (*to* ARMANDE)—Is that what you think?

ARMANDE—It is our opinion that the drowned man has come back in the form of a ghost.

INSPECTOR—He might have come back without being a ghost. A

murderer returns to the scene of the crime like a boomerang to the hand of the thrower.

LÉONIDE—What's he saying?

ARMANDE (*into trumpet, loudly*)—That a boomerang returns to the hand of the thrower.

LÉONIDE—Amazing!

INSPECTOR—So you believe that the scandalous behavior reported in this community is all due to this ghost?

ARMANDE—Oh, no, Inspector. Not at all. We know who's at the bottom of that.

INSPECTOR—You do?

ARMANDE—Of course. That's an entirely different line of activity. But we do think that these lines are converging. It won't be long before they meet. That's why we thought you should take action at once. Inspector, I don't know how much of the scandal has been reported to you . . .

INSPECTOR—I've heard all about it.

ARMANDE—You are aware of everything?

INSPECTOR (*impatiently*)—I am aware, Madame, that at the moment, this district is completely arse over tip.

LÉONIDE—What does the Inspector say?

ARMANDE—Nothing in particular.

LÉONIDE—Armande, I insist that you repeat the end of each important sentence, as always.

ARMANDE—Arse over tip.

LÉONIDE—Ah! You are discussing Madame Lambert.

ARMANDE—We are not discussing Madame Lambert.

LÉONIDE—No? Then who else can it be?

INSPECTOR—Ladies! I was not aware that Madame Lambert was in any way embraced in this discussion.

ARMANDE—You may not be aware of it, but Madame Lambert is embraced in every way, and by everybody. Except her husband.

SUPERVISOR—I beg your pardon. I consider this an utterly false and malicious piece of slander. Madame Lambert is not embraced by everybody!

INSPECTOR—Mr. Supervisor, don't you think our task is sufficiently difficult without your dragging in Madame Lambert?

SUPERVISOR—I have no intention of dragging her in. But so long as she has been wantonly attacked, it is my obvious duty to defend her. Madame Lambert is one of the glories of France!

ARMANDE—He's mad!

MAYOR—Mr. Supervisor, please. This is neither the time nor the place . . .

SUPERVISOR—Whoever is so fortunate as to catch a glimpse of Madame Lambert bending over the counter of her shop as she buckles a watch on a young man's wrist or opens a locket with the tip of a rosy nail, will willingly concede that the chief glory of France is neither its cathedrals nor its châteaux, but this young woman who, with her delicate figure and her charming smile, reminds us from day to day that life is worth living.

LÉONIDE—What is the Supervisor talking about?

ARMANDE—Absolutely nothing.

SUPERVISOR—I am saying, Madame, that wherever she is—and in our country I am glad to say she is everywhere—Madame Lambert is a living proof of the imperishable beauty of France. I gladly pay her this homage, and I will defend her honor to the last drop of my blood!

INSPECTOR—Bravo! The inquest is adjourned.

ARMANDE—And I suppose you would say as much for Miss Isabel!

SUPERVISOR—Miss Isabel is the soul of purity. Whoever dares breathe a word against Miss Isabel will have to reckon with me.

Whereupon Armande and her sister go to work on the character of Isabel, for it is concerning her that they have come to make a statement. Armande suggests that the Mayor call his little niece from the botany class and determine what she is being taught by this "soul of purity." Léonide and Armande know all about Isabel —for they have her diary. The young teacher had dropped it in the street and the spinsters picked it up and, of course, read it. They offer it in evidence—evidence that it is Isabel who is breaking up households and turning dogs and children against authority. They hand it to the Mayor and suggest that he sample the entry for March twenty-first.

It is quite scandalous. It records that Isabel organized a little Spring festival for her children and compared the beauty of nature with the beauty of the human form. As a practical class exercise they held an election and unanimously elected the Supervisor of Weights and Measures as the most beautiful man in town. The Inspector orders that the teacher and her class be summoned immediately, and the Supervisor goes to fetch her. Armande suggests that the Mayor sample the entry for the fourteenth of May—which was yesterday.

This entry is another gem. "Today," wrote Isabel, "I feel sure the ghost knows what I am doing, and that he wants to help me. But, poor thing, he is terribly shy. The moment I come near him, he vanishes in embarrassment. All the same, he's certain to take the

final step within a day or two. And when he does, what wonderful
things he will have to tell me! Together we shall make the town
perfect—and after the town, the district—and after that—who
knows? I have a feeling it will be tomorrow!"

Isabel and her class are approaching, so the spinster sisters make
an immediate escape. The Inspector announces that he wants to
examine Isabel's class and demands, "Who is at the head of the
class?" Isabel replies, "Nobody, Inspector. They're *all* at the head
of the class."

The Inspector chooses a little girl named Gilberte and asks if she
knows what a tree is. The child replies that a tree is a tall person
who is rooted to the ground, and in tree language a murderer is called
a woodcutter, a corpse is lumber and woodpeckers are fleas. The
Inspector, outraged, gives Gilberte the mark of zero and Isabel informs him that in her class zero is the highest mark, being closest
to infinity. She invites Daisy to explain the flower. Says Daisy:
"The flower is one of the most beautiful aspects of nature. It is a
practical demonstration of the beauty of the sexual process." Daisy
would go on with her little lecture, including the part about the bee,
but the Inspector has had enough botany.

The Mayor tries geography and asks little Viola what causes earth-
quakes. "It's the Harmonizer," says Viola, and Isabel explains that
she doesn't believe children should be taught that Nature is violent
and destructive. "The power that destroys things in the interests
of the ultimate harmony, we call the Harmonizer."

The Inspector's wits are tried even further as he probes the children's curriculum. France is bounded by the love of its neighbors;
a right angle is what one imagines when one is weary of curves. He
notices that each child has a red mark on its neck. A vaccination?
"No, sir," says Lucy. "It's the mark for the spirits. Isabel puts it
on us every morning with her lipstick. When the Inspector orders
the children to rub it off they chorus a protest: "The Spirit wouldn't
like it!"

The angry dignitary addresses himself to Isabel, whom he accuses
of having undertaken to teach her pupils the way to happiness.

Isabel replies modestly that she teaches them what God has in
store for them.

"Nonsense. It says nowhere in the Bible that when God created
the world, He created happiness. Day and night, yes. But not
happiness. What He created was certain compensations for the
habitual misery of humanity—such as fishing, bridge and love. You
have deliberately misled these children as to the nature of life.
And that is conduct unbecoming a teacher. . . . You are relieved

of your post, effective immediately." The Inspector transfers the Supervisor of Weights and Measures to the Education Department, temporarily, until Paris can send along a proper substitute for Isabel.

The class is dismissed, in charge of its new teacher. The Inspector adjourns the meeting to the Mayor's office, and he and the Mayor depart.

The Doctor remains—and now he seems a very odd doctor as he smiles upon Isabel and explains that he is remaining only for a moment in order to be the transition. "I am a sort of usher. Between, for example, a foolish moment and a moment of solemnity— obviously, by itself the one could never become the other. To fuse the precise with the vague, the ridiculous with the sublime—that is my function. . . . Then also, there is the transition to manage between the Isabel we know and another Isabel—an ethereal, transparent and ineffably lovely Isabel, of whom as yet we can only surmise the quality. . . ."

The Doctor demonstrates how simple it is—a gesture; a silence— this silence; his assistants—the owl, the frogs, the crickets. All that remains is for Isabel to pronounce the name of this moment, and she replies "The twilight."

"Yes. And when it is twilight, what sound is it that echoes away from a little French town?"

"The trumpets of the garrison"—and as Isabel speaks trumpets are heard in the distance.

"And when the trumpets are quiet, what is it that rises among the weeds and the willows, moving through the shadows of cypress and pine, itself hardly more than a shadow?"

Isabel smiles, "The Ghost." The transition is done and the Doctor vanishes. He doesn't walk off the way the Inspector and the Mayor did; he vanishes. Behind Isabel appears a very pale and hatless young man. She speaks to him without turning—and this time he answers. So much—oh, so much!—is there that Isabel wants to know from this gentle young man. She tells him her name does not matter when he asks what it is. What matters is, "How can the dead believe in death? With us, of course, it's different. Since it's good to think that fatness and falsehood will have an end one day, we are forced to concede that kindness and beauty, which are so much more fragile, will also die. But the spirits—refined and free of flesh—how can they be so silly as to believe in death?"

Quite sensibly, seemingly, the Ghost counters, "You expect the dead to believe in life?"

Isabel does, indeed—at least in the life of the spirit. To be frank about it, it seems to her that the dead are a little relaxed. If they had a little more initiative it would be so much better for us all. "If they would only give us—those of us who are trying, I mean—their attention, their support, what marvelous lives we could lead—in both our worlds! All we need, really, is some energetic soul to stir them up a bit."

The Ghost suggests that perhaps the dead are waiting for her. Isabel has thought about it and is not sure she would be particularly useful once she is dead. She believes she must do what she is able to do while she is alive—and her dream has always been to make life as sensible and happy as a fairy tale. She has tried to help the living, but it isn't easy because they are so steeped in flesh that they are afraid to move. But the dead, who are so light, so wise and so gentle—oh, if she could only get *them* to help her!

The Ghost rather incredulously asks the girl if she wants the dead to come back to the world, and she replies that she wants it so much. "We are afraid to live because we are afraid to die. But the dead have died; they know the magnitude and meaning of life. How easily they could teach us to live not like clods, but like spirits! And really, what could be simpler? There is only the wall of silence between us. And there are loopholes in the wall."

The Ghost can't see any loopholes until she points out that he has just come through one in talking thus with her. If only there could be found a young spirit with energy and imagination—perhaps he and she together could rouse the other dead to a sense of adventure. The Ghost is dubious; the dead are not adventurous—they are dead.

Isabel pooh-poohs this attitude. "Do you think you are dead?" she demands, and the Ghost falters, "Why . . ."

"You see! Death is nothing but a state of mind. And not a very reasonable one, really. Now tell me all about it. Tell me—what happens when you die? The very first thing?"

The Ghost asks that she tell her name first, and she says it is of no interest. She does admit that she lives in the town. "Now tell me," she urges, and the Ghost begins, "Well, the moment one dies . . ."

There is silence. Isabel urges him to continue, but there is no answer. She looks around—and he has vanished. Desperately she cries, "Isabel! My name is Isabel! It's Isabel!"

The curtain falls.

ACT II

The setting is the same clearing in the woods, but from another point of view. The Spring is more advanced and the hedges have burst into flower. It is some time before sunset, and the Supervisor is conducting a class in elementary astronomy. He is sitting on a log, and about him are the little girls, each carrying a flashlight. He commands, "The Triangle!"—and, joyously twinkling their flashlights, the children form a sort of triangle and sing:

> *Magellan stared with open mouth,*
> *He didn't know that in the south*
> *The starry Triangle is where*
> *We normally expect the Bear.*

The Supervisor orders the Compass, and, forming a new pattern, the girls sing:

> *There is a Compass in the sky*
> *But our advice is, never mind it,*
> *It's just as well to pass it by;*
> *You need two compasses to find it.*

They have begun to form the Clock when the Doctor strolls in and asks if they are playing in the woods again. "No, they're playing in the sky," the Supervisor explains. The girls mystifyingly chorus a "Good night" to the Doctor, although it is afternoon. However, the Supervisor makes things a little clearer. Since the Inspector has ordered all the students in bed by sunset, they never see any stars overhead. They look down at their feet to see them. Moreover, they study only the southern stars, because the ancients never saw the southern sky and did not have the opportunity to people it with monsters. Southerners have a sensible sky full of laboratory equipment—the Clock, the Furnace, the Compass, the Microscope, even the Air Pump. The Supervisor asks little Viola to jump from the Triangle to the Telescope and she asks, "By way of the Furnace?"

"No, the Doctor is on the Furnace. Over the Table."

Viola hesitates. "It's quite a jump, you know. It's thirty million billion miles."

The Supervisor concedes, "Take two jumps. . . . Now, children, the Southern Cross." They sing, as they form the Cross:

> *Lapérouse was quite excited*
> *When first the Southern Cross he sighted;*

There really isn't any use
For steeples now, said Lapérouse.

The Supervisor confides that the girls, in addition to liking their astronomy lessons, are all in love with the Ghost. "And so is Isabel!" add the children. So that the two men may have a private conversation, the class is ordered to disperse in the woods. The Supervisor is worried about this Ghost; he is more in evidence all the time, and wherever he is, Isabel is with him. The Inspector is getting daily reports on her activities.

DOCTOR—What if he is? There's no law against being friendly with ghosts.

SUPERVISOR—To be friendly with ghosts is to be ghostly. It's irregular. People are gossiping. Besides, you don't really think that this Ghost of hers is a ghost?

DOCTOR—I think he soon will be.

SUPERVISOR—I don't follow.

DOCTOR—I have a distinct impression that before long we are going to witness the birth of a phantom. A real phantom.

SUPERVISOR—How? Why?

DOCTOR—I don't know. But everything we have seen in the past weeks points toward some monstrous birth. Depend on it, Supervisor, Nature is hatching a surprise for us. It was after some such series of events as these that, one day, before the eyes of the astonished animals, the first man took shape.

SUPERVISOR—There is certainly something queer going on.

DOCTOR—Yes, our town is enchanted. It is in that strange condition when every dream comes true and every wish is granted. In an individual that would be called a state of ecstasy. That's it. Our town is in a state of ecstasy.

SUPERVISOR—It's strange. This morning, for no good reason, I dreamt of a chimpanzee. And as I opened the front door to take in the milk, what do you suppose was the first thing my eyes lit on? A chimpanzee. True, it was a tame chimpanzee on the end of a leash held by a gypsy. Nevertheless, there was my dream sitting on my doorstep.

DOCTOR—It's just as well you didn't dream of a crocodile. I tell you, my boy, we're in an uncanny state, all of us—we're in the vein, like a gambler who can't lose. Nature is pampering us. We shall soon know why.

SUPERVISOR—Doctor, while this lasts, we mustn't let Isabel out of our sight for a moment. This is no joke.

Doctor—You're right.   When the mountains give birth, it is
never mice that issue forth from their wombs, but thunder and lightning.   Everything here is collaborating to produce a phantom—the
light, the darkness, our fears, our imagination, the other world perhaps, and certainly the Inspector.   (*Enter the* INSPECTOR.)   You
see?   The Inspector!   (*The* MAYOR *follows.*)

The Inspector has called this meeting because he has had a letter
from the Government by special courier which particularly concerns
them.   He hands a letter to the Mayor and asks him to read it.   This
dignitary glances over it, then asks, "You think it really concerns
me?"   It most certainly does, the Inspector insists—particularly the
last paragraph.   "Read it aloud," he commands, and the Mayor
begins, "It kisses you on your adorable mouth, asks you for a hundred francs and signs itself, yours ever, Adele."   The Inspector embarrassedly snatches the missive and gives another one to the Mayor.
This one is indeed from the Government—from the Superior Council.
It begins nicely enough, felicitating the Government's constituents
on having chosen a happy middle course between primitive druidism
and contemporary radical thought, and on their triumph over clerical
superstition in this flowering of the native folklore which is one of
the glories of the national heritage.

Then the communication gets to business: "Nevertheless, the character of the perturbations brought about by the alleged phantom on
the communal life of your district is judged to be not sufficiently in
accord with the ideals of the Socialist party to warrant the tacit
collaboration of the Government.   Consequently, the Council re-
quests you to take all necessary steps for the prompt liquidation of
this apparition, and for this purpose places at your disposal all available military and civil powers with full authority in the premises."

So now, the Inspector vows, the case is going to be wound up.
People must resume normal dreams.   What, for instance, was the
Mayor's dream last night?   The official confesses that he dreamt he
was chasing two enormous ducks and, after many transformations,
the ducks became his two feet.   "It is no joke to chase your own feet
all night, especially when they cackle."   Toward morning the Mayor
had become further bewildered by becoming a centipede.

At the Inspector's insistence the Supervisor hesitantly details his
own dream.   He was madly in love with a woman who eluded his
advances by springing back and forth over an open grave.   She wore
only a short cloak and her right breast was bare—and the woman was
the Inspector.

The Inspector has made his point.   He demands of the Mayor,

"Are you going to tell me that a dream like that, however flattering for me, can be for a moment considered a normal French dream? Is this, multiplied by forty-two million, a product worthy of the nightly endeavors of the most rational and practical nation in the world?"

The Supervisor interposes. "I doubt if sixty-four million Germans could do any better." The Doctor, amused, says, "Don't tell us, Inspector, that you are beginning to notice some supernatural influence?"

The official would rather call it a conspiracy against constitutional authority—not only by a young girl and a ghost, but by the whole town. How does it happen the clock strikes thirteen at midnight? How is it that when a high Government official sits on a public bench, the bench becomes sticky with green paint? And why is it that, at the café, the sugar in other people's coffee dissolves, but in the Inspector's coffee it doesn't? He is primed for a showdown this evening—a showdown between the gentlemen here, Isabel, the Ghost and himself.

The Mayor protests that Isabel has nothing to do with recent phenomena, but the Inspector believes otherwise. This movement must be stopped before it spreads; everywhere he looks people are smiling and neglecting their duties. And he has noted that Isabel drifts out of town every evening at six with an air of false innocence. As her hands are always empty, the Inspector believes that the food she brings her invisible friend is only her youth, tenderness and vitality. Yet, the Inspector has observed that, for a girl with a figure like hers, Isabel eats enormous meals. "It's perfectly obvious," he now persuades himself, "that this girl is eating for two. The only question is—who is the other?" Somehow, she must be passing on her excess calories to someone who does not eat. The Inspector soon will know, for their meeting place is right here and he is planning an ambush.

The Supervisor begs for a chance to talk with Isabel first. Perhaps he can persuade her of the dangers of her position.

The Inspector cuts him off. Tonight he is going to end Isabel's influence in this community once and for all, by employing force. He admits he agrees with the theory that Isabel's ghostly friend is the young man whose hat was found on the edge of the lake—but he believes that this young man is still very much of the flesh—and he is to be killed by the armed agents of the state. He asks the Mayor what armed agents are available—and there aren't any. The trout season opened yesterday, so the game wardens are out; and the police force is quarantined with the measles. The Inspector, having foreseen such difficulties, has enlisted the services of the one official in France who has no fear whatever of ghosts—a man who happens to be a resident of this town. He is the Public Executioner. He has been offered 5,000 francs, and this is sure to fetch him. He will come armed.

The agitated Supervisor begs once more for a chance to talk with Isabel, who is due any moment, and is given five minutes. The Inspector, Mayor and Doctor withdraw.

When the young woman arrives the Supervisor exclaims, "How lightly your foot falls, Miss Isabel. You walk on the seams of the forest like a skillful burglar who keeps the stairs from creaking by stepping just where the treads are nailed." He is more than a little overcome by his own speech.

ISABEL—You have a gift for expression, Mr. Supervisor.

SUPERVISOR—I speak well when I have something to say. Not that I ever say what I mean. It's always something else by the time it comes out.

ISABEL—I have been meaning to compliment you on the stand you have taken on the question of Madame Lambert.

SUPERVISOR—When I speak of Madame Lambert, you know, I am not speaking of Madame Lambert.

ISABEL—I know. You are defending our sex in general. It is very gallant and brave of you. Especially since you know how the Inspector hates us. Have you heard what that man is doing? He is employing spies. I am being watched day and night.

SUPERVISOR—I know.

ISABEL—But why?

SUPERVISOR—The administration thinks your interests are abnormal.

ISABEL—Are the interests of the administration entirely normal? Are yours?

SUPERVISOR—Oh, yes, Miss Isabel. It may not be normal for anyone to be as lovely as you, but my interest is very normal.

ISABEL—Very prettily put. And surely not at all what you meant to say.

SUPERVISOR—Oh, Miss Isabel—this time—yes.

ISABEL—And in what way are my interests abnormal? Is it because I believe in spirits? That doesn't seem abnormal to me. What seems abnormal is the dull indifference of the living to everything that goes on outside their lives. Or else we are all hypocrites—and the millions who say they believe in the afterlife don't believe in anything of the sort.

Supervisor—To believe in the afterlife is one thing. To see ghosts is another. Do you see ghosts, Miss Isabel?

Isabel—So far only one.

Supervisor—He's very handsome?

Isabel—He's quite nice-looking.

Supervisor—Young?

Isabel—About thirty. I'd rather become ageless at thirty, wouldn't you, than with a long white beard?

Supervisor—Does he come near you? Do you let him touch you?

Isabel—He never comes near me. He is too fragile. And he knows how clumsy we can be.

Supervisor—But you look at him. You talk to him?

Isabel—Of course.

Supervisor—Do you really think that's wise, Miss Isabel?

Isabel—I have spent the greater part of my life, Mr. Supervisor, staring at teachers. And I have come to the conclusion that, if they represent wisdom, I have a horror of being wise.

Supervisor—But, after all, there is such a thing as science. . . .

Isabel—As far as I can see, science is nothing but another form of ignorance. In the name of science, we are taught to forget everything that a child knows, everything that a savage knows. Education makes us more stupid than the brutes. A thousand voices call to us on every hand, but our ears are stopped with wisdom. There are unimaginable wonders everywhere, but we wear the blinders of science. Well—I have taken off my blinders. I have unstopped my ears. . . .

The young man tries to get Isabel to consider reality. Suppose a living man asks her to be his wife. Will she continue her relations with this Ghost? One knows how devoted ghosts are, and he warns her of their dishonorable intentions—which are to cut one off from the rest of humanity and its healthy interest in such things as neckties and petticoats and bread and cheese. "Take care!" he admonishes.

Isabel seeks to calm him. After all, of all the multitude of the dead, her Ghost is the only one who has established communication on our sphere. But she can feel, in the vast sea of the dead, powerful currents flowing toward her—the pressure of their longing as it merges with hers. She declares, "I know that through me at last they will find a way to flow back into the world of the living." This sounds like madness to the Supervisor. He implores her to stay away from the outer bounds of life; if she should open the gate to the beyond she would destroy us all, for who knows what horror might surge through?

More particularly, the Supervisor implores Isabel not to meet the Ghost tonight. He tells of the trap the Inspector has set. She sniffs disdainfully that her Ghost doesn't fear the Inspector's traps—and now will the Supervisor please go? He does not budge; he is going to see this Ghost, and unmask him.

"*There* he is," she points behind him. "You seem to amuse him. He is smiling." The Supervisor can see nothing. Suddenly she points skyward and invites him to look at the moon. "Genuine silver. See? The hallmark?" And while he is looking she slips away, laughing, and the Inspector, the Mayor and the Doctor return. The Inspector orders the young man to gather his class and take them home, as it is getting dark. When the Supervisor has gone the Inspector beckons forward two men and asks, "Which of you is the Executioner?"

"I am," says the first man.

"Then who are *you?*" the Inspector inquires of the second.

"The Executioner."

One or the other must be lying, although both deny it, and the Inspector demands their papers. The first man's papers identify him as a cornetist by profession. He explains that the police never register an Executioner's real profession; they always put him down as a musician. The second man is officially identified as a contra-bassoonist.

The Mayor is ordered to take inventory of the men's pockets, and the contents look normal—a corkscrew, cigarettes, a little money, a toothpick, a pen, two cough drops, a rubber band, a broken comb and a key. No clue yet as to which is the Executioner. The Mayor tries an oral examination, and each gives the proper answers a student of their trade would know, such as the construction of a guillotine and what Mme. du Barry said when she mounted the scaffold. When they are asked to sing the Executioner's Song they ask the Mayor which one, and he names "The Headsman with the Golden Hair." The First Executioner sings:

> *When I set up my guillotine*
> *Upon the village square*
> *The dawn pours rosy brilliantine*
> *Upon my golden hair.*

The Second Executioner takes it up promptly:

No trace of Houbigant for Men
No fragrance of Chanel
Clings to my golden ringlets when
I greet my clientèle.

Together they finish:

My shirt is starched, my cuffs are white,
My blade gleams in the morning light;
Can I be blamed if people stare
And say, what lovely golden hair?

The Inspector has had enough of the examination. If the Executioner insists on being twins he can divide the fee with himself—which is fair enough to the Executioners. They are told what they must do. First, they will see a young girl, then a young man. The two will be permitted to talk together for a moment. At a given signal, they are to aim their pistols at the man and shoot to kill. After some discussion it is agreed that the signal to fire will be when the man says the word "alive"—which he is sure to do in a moment or so.

The paid assassins go to their ambush and the Inspector asks his companions to withdraw with him. The Doctor pauses for a moment and takes some objects out of his pocket.

"What's that you've got?" the Inspector asks.

"My pitch-pipes. My tuning fork."

"What are they for?"

"We are about to pass from the minor into the major." Again the Doctor begins to look a little odd. The Inspector, tapping his forehead as though he believes the physician to be a bit touched, walks off. The Doctor seems absorbed in his toys and pays little heed to the Mayor's agitation, even when the Mayor reminds him that a life is at stake. Is the Doctor counting on this whistle to protect Isabel?

The Doctor is not worried about Isabel. At this moment the entire universe is protecting her, he reassures his companion. The only question is, are they in tune with Nature? If they are, they're all right. And if not, he has his pitch-pipes.

The Mayor demands, "Do you think you can tune Nature like a piano?"

"Oh, no," is the reply. "Like a choir." The Mayor, now of the same mind as the Inspector, goes to join that gentleman. The Doctor, alone, holds up his hand and calls, "Attention, please!"   He blows into his pipes.   Nature takes his pitch and all of it resounds in a chord of complete harmony.   He nods, satisfied, and tiptoes out. As he does so, Isabel and the Ghost are revealed sitting on a rock.

Isabel is disappointed that he has come alone again.   "Couldn't you have got someone to come with you just this once?"

"No."

"We thought yesterday that the kind of sound that might wake them would be a sort of wailing scream—like the screech of a locomotive in the middle of the night.   Did you try that?"

"Yes."

"And didn't you find then that, one by one, innumerable voices rose up to echo yours?"

"No."

"They must sleep very deeply, the dead," observes the disappointed girl.

"Compared with the sleep of the dead, the sleep of the living is moonlight sparkling on the water."   The Ghost is afraid it will always be thus, but Isabel will not give up hope.   What about himself?   He is here—but will he be content to spend the rest of eternity just haunting a lake?

The Ghost admits this isn't much of a prospect.   Perhaps he should just vanish.

"You can't," the girl informs him.   "I've caught you in my trap. I have a ghost trap in my room."

"Are you a sorceress?"

"My sorcery is very simple.   For a long time, I wondered what would be most likely to attract the dead.   I decided it wouldn't be their friends or their books or anything of that sort—it would be something quite modest and homely.   Perhaps a little pattern of light and shade—the glitter of a doorknob, the flash of a white petal, the pink nose of a cat—a little mosaic of living things . . ."   And so she arranged her room very cleverly.   It looks like just a room for a living girl—but it is calculated to the last detail—the curve of a pot, the surface of a table.   By day they catch the sun and by night the lamplight or the moon.   And she wasn't at all surprised the night she saw his face peering in at her window as she brushed her hair.

He admits he has been caught—but by another of her patterns: her voice, her face, and most of all her spirit—a spirit so generous and innocent it could harbor not the faintest suspicion that all this while he might be deceiving her cruelly—that he might be, in fact, no Ghost at all, but very much—

"Very much what?" she asks, and he replies, "Alive!"

Two shots ring out and the Ghost falls. Those in the ambush rush in. The Inspector is triumphant, for he has bagged a genuine corpse and not a ghost. The Doctor, after an examination, confirms the fact that the young man is dead. The Mayor takes Isabel comfortingly in his arms and berates the Executioners—but the Inspector compliments them on having, with two shots, rid society of a criminal, the girl of an obsession and the town of a Ghost.

The Doctor, still kneeling beside the corpse, says, "Forgive us, Isabel. And you, poor Ghost—we beg your pardon!"

The Inspector asks what he is apologizing for and the Doctor explains, "I apologize because in this world the truth is always vulgar. I apologize because life has no spirit, and death no dignity. Because the illusions of youth are illusions, and age is generous only in destruction. I apologize because in this world the Inspector is always right, and the specter is false."

And now something extraordinary takes place before them all—all but the Doctor, who sees nothing. From the corpse rises a phantom which is exactly like the Ghost, point for point—but this one has authenticity. All who see it realize that it is indeed a ghost, and they babble incredulously. Except the Inspector, who urges calm and says the apparition is a well-known phenomenon, a mirage—marsh gas—static electricity in the evening mist. To dispel it he blows upon it—and the Ghost grows brighter as it calls, "Until tomorrow, Isabel!"

The Inspector can scarcely believe his ears. The Ghost calls again, "Tomorrow at six, Isabel! I will come to your home, Isabel! And this time, I will come with the others, Isabel! With all the others!" And he vanishes.

Most of them go to the town—the Inspector a little ill. The Doctor helps the executioners lift the body and is about to follow them when he hears the voices of the little girls. Their lights flicker in the foliage as the Supervisor shepherds them home. Lucy seems to be missing, but she runs into the clearing when the Supervisor calls. He chides her for always lagging behind, and she explains she was looking for glowworms with her flashlight. That sounds improbable to the Supervisor, so Lucy switches her story to a search for her garter. The Supervisor sees it in her hand, and remembers she was using it for a sling. Then he notices the Doctor and says he heard shots. "Has something happened?"

"Yes. Something has happened. Your moment has come. . . . The moment when you must fight your rival for the one you love."

"I love someone?" asks the Supervisor.

"Isabel! Isabel!"

"I have a rival?"

It is the girls, not the Doctor, who answer, "The Ghost! The Ghost!" The Ghost suddenly appears behind them.

The Doctor urges the girls to go on ahead, and, taking the Supervisor by the arm, begins to tell him of the evening's extraordinary events as they walk toward the town. Lucy has hung back again and is alone. From a distance the Supervisor calls, "Lucy!"

The little girl answers, "I've lost my beret"—and she flings her beret high in the air. As she looks up to catch it she catches sight of the Ghost, and for a moment she mimics the movements of his floating figure. Then, as the Supervisor is heard calling again, she answers, "I have it!" And, thumbing her nose at the Ghost, she scampers off.

The curtain falls.

ACT III

Isabel's room has a balcony with French windows through which the town square is visible. Distant sounds of the military band tuning up can be heard—faint flourishes, soft ruffles on the drums. It is late afternoon. Isabel's room is unoccupied and locked, but the Inspector gains entrance with a key and is followed on tiptoe by the worried Mayor and the little girls.

MAYOR—I hope you realize that this constitutes breaking and entering.

INSPECTOR—How else do you expect us, at our age, to enter a young girl's room? What time is it?

MAYOR—By the sun, I'd say five-thirty.

INSPECTOR—I doubt if ghosts go by the sun.

MAYOR—If they go by my watch, it's five-thirty-eight.

INSPECTOR—That gives us exactly twenty-two minutes. The Ghost said he'd come at six. There's just time to man our defenses.

MAYOR—What defenses?

INSPECTOR—Mr. Mayor, at this historic moment when humanity is faced with the most terrible invasion it has ever known, the honor of manning the outposts falls on us. I hope you are fully aware of the responsibility.

MAYOR—Inspector . . .

INSPECTOR—The enemy is in its trenches, massed for attack.

MAYOR—Where? In the cemetery?

INSPECTOR—No. In the beyond.

MAYOR—So at last you have come to believe in spirits!

INSPECTOR—Mr. Mayor, I always believe in the enemies of France.

MAYOR—What if Isabel finds us here?

INSPECTOR—She won't. I have had the town clock set back an hour. Furthermore, I am posting Gilberte at the window. Gilberte! If you see anything come this way, you will report immediately.

GILBERTE (*at the window*)—I see the Mangebois sisters coming. Shall I report them?

INSPECTOR—Report everything.

GILBERTE—They've stopped.

INSPECTOR—Good. And now . . .

GILBERTE—The druggist's poodle is coming.

MAYOR—Inspector, do you mind telling me what we have come to do here?

INSPECTOR—We have come to exorcize a ghost.

MAYOR—You mean with bell, book and candle? Do you have a priest?

INSPECTOR—Do you expect me to appeal from one superstition to another? I am going to exorcize this ghost in my official capacity as administrative head of the sub-prefecture.

MAYOR—You think the Ghost will be impressed?

INSPECTOR—Ghosts are impressed by any sort of rubbish. For hundreds of years the Church has scared them off simply by telling them to go away in Latin. I have no doubt that the official adjuration which I composed this morning will be much more effective. At least, they will know what I am saying.

GILBERTE—You want me to report trees too?

INSPECTOR—Trees don't move, silly.

GILBERTE (*retreating from the window step by step in awe*)—And yet—I think . . . And yet—I think . . .

INSPECTOR—You may relieve Gilberte, Viola. She's getting nervous.

MAYOR—I don't know that I exactly blame her.

INSPECTOR—Are you nervous too?

MAYOR—To tell the truth, I'm in a perfect sweat. The more so as with this hocus-pocus you're keeping me from the drawing of the civic lottery, at which I invariably preside.

INSPECTOR—Is this a time to worry about lotteries?

MAYOR—Well, it's a very important civic function.

INSPECTOR—And what we are doing is not an important civic function, I suppose! Has it not yet dawned upon you, Mr. Mayor, that what we are involved in is not merely of local, or national, or

even international importance, but absolutely universal in its conse-
quences?

MAYOR—Are you serious?

INSPECTOR—Do you realize what it would mean to France if the
inhabitants of the other world were permitted to colonize this district? I say nothing of their influence on the local community, which
is already mad. But take notice that these ghosts would not be
aliens. They would be natives of France, and therefore entitled to
all the rights and privileges of citizens, including the right to vote.
And when you stop to think that the dead of this district outnumber
the living in astronomical proportion—you can see what the conse-
quences might be. Within five years, with perfect legality, they
could capture any electoral post in the nation. The President of the
Republic would be a ghost, the Prime Minister would be a ghost,
the members of the high court, all ghosts. . . .

MAYOR—You think we would notice any difference?

INSPECTOR—As ghosts don't eat, and require neither clothing nor
shelter, they would hardly understand our interest in the material
things of life. In a short time the human race, vastly outnumbered
everywhere, would be reduced to the level of slaves, the death cer-
tificate would replace the passport, and wherever one turned one
would be confronted with phantoms, hordes of phantoms, clouds of
phantoms—we should have to plow our way through phantoms like
ships in a fog!

The horrors of the prospect dawn upon the Mayor. There would
be no privacy; he could no longer pretend to be studying official
papers while playing with his stamp collection. The only safeguards
of human dignity, the door and the door latch, would vanish. And
the window shade, too.

The Inspector prepares for his ceremony of exorcism by decorating
himself with a collection of medals from his pocket, and the Mayor
dons his official sash. The little girls pay close attention and echo
the last words of the Inspector's formal sentences. This worthy, ad-
dressing spirits and powers of darkness, charts the rise of humanity
from primitive superstition to the beneficences of steam, gas, electricity, radio commentators and the atom. With great earnestness
and the weight of his office behind him, the Inspector declares the
Spirits of Darkness to be obsolete, useless and undesirable, and for-
bids them to enter this jurisdiction.

At the end of this very impressive performance another little girl
lookout, Daisy, reports the approach of Miss Isabel and the Doctor.
Quickly the Inspector, the Mayor and the girls hide in another room.

As Isabel enters she is thanking the Doctor for reminding her of the time, and is tremulously wondering if the Ghost really will come. The Doctor believes he will—for he needs Isabel and probably will want her to join him.

The girl asks, "Couldn't I be just as useful—even more useful— alive?"

"To us, yes. But to him . . . ?" She agitatedly asks the Doctor to stay with her and he agrees. As they look out the window the clock strikes five and there is a knock at the door. They do not move. The door swings open and the Doctor turns to look. "Has he come?" whispers Isabel.

"Yes," smiles the Doctor. "And I think I'll leave you alone with him after all, my dear." As the Doctor leaves Isabel discovers that the visitor is the Supervisor, looking pale and very formal. He is dressed in his Sunday best—black jacket, striped trousers, chamois gloves; he has a gold-headed stick in one hand, a bowler hat in the other. Quite imperiously for him he bids the girl be silent and listen. She cannot help saying that he looks so grand, and he replies that all that sustains him at the moment is his finery and the thought of those who should be wearing it, who would be here with him if they were alive.

The Supervisor has brought his own ghosts and he presents them with grave formality: his grandfather, the stick; his great-uncle, his watch and chain; his father, his hat; his uncle Albert, his gloves. "The rest," he admits, "is myself." He stows his relatives in a chair. Bowing ceremoniously, he announces that he and his relatives have come to ask Isabel's hand in marriage. They do not require an answer now; she needs only listen to this proposal, and now they will all depart. The Supervisor takes up his things and moves to go, but the girl urges him to stay—even if he did come at such a moment!

"I chose the moment deliberately," says the astonishingly confident young man. It being the Ghost's moment, it is the logical time to offer her another road to the other world. His is a road which leads slowly, easily, but very surely, to death. It is Life.

"Life with you?" she asks.

This is not important, he says. What he offers is not so much life with *him* as life with a Government employee, and he describes the pleasures and delicious uncertainties of this life. A Government employee moves from post to post, from year to year, with the smoothness of time, moving from youth to death without break and without transition. Yet . . . it is exciting—sheer poetry, in fact. Isabel cannot believe there is sheer poetry in the Bureau of

Weights and Measures, but he argues that there is. Suppose he is checking barrels in a distillery and gets bored with liters: all he needs do is transform liters to gallons, and in a twinkling he is in America; or into versts and he is in Russia, and so on.

She begins to be impressed, and he continues with his measurements. If he tires of kilograms of grain he can measure them in hins, and becomes an ancient Hebrew. If he takes a height in cubits, he is with Cleopatra.

"You *are* a poet, aren't you?" she exclaims.

And then, he entices her, there are the most delightful surprises. He must change posts every three years, and he knows his new post will be one of two—in this case, Nice or Tours. But not until he is ready to move is he told which one—so he has the delicious torment of this continual uncertainty. And then, at last, he will come to Paris! "Do you like it, Miss Isabel?"

"I think—I like it very much."

Masterfully, the Supervisor bolts the entrance door, locks the windows, shuts the dampers and serves formal notice on all intruders to keep out. All the two of them need do is wait quietly a few minutes, and they will be safe.

But the young man is wrong. The bolted door flies open and in comes the Ghost—asking politely if he may come in after he is in. "Ask this man to leave us," he says to Isabel—but the Supervisor stoutly remains, saying he is here to protect the girl. "And suppose I am not alone," suggests the Ghost. "Suppose that Death is here with me. Suppose that Isabel sees something that you do not see."

"A girl sees all sorts of things that her husband doesn't see. It makes no difference—so long as he's there." The Supervisor suggests that the Ghost go, but Isabel cries that he has come to give her the answer to the riddle that has troubled her all her life—the riddle of death—the death of a man who is now the Ghost. The Supervisor taunts the Ghost, saying that when his own time comes he can, as a dependable man, be relied upon as a ghost, too. People will know that he lived his life fully to the extent of his capacity, never flagging in duty or in devotion to those he loved. People will know that in the years he spent in Isabel's town, he never let a day pass without assuring himself that Isabel was well and happy.

The girl, overcome, murmurs, "Dear Robert!"

This appellation shows the Ghost where he stands and he thanks Isabel, saying, "You have saved me from committing a great folly, the greatest possible folly. I was about to betray an inviolable secret for the sake of a girl. Luckily, she betrayed me first."

The Ghost discourses upon young girls; how, between the world of a young girl and the world of the spirit, the wall seems no more than a gossamer—and then the man appears! She watches him intently; he has found some trick with which to enhance his worth in her eyes. "He stands on his hind legs in order to shed rain better and to hang medals on his chest. He swells his biceps. They quail before him with hypocritical admiration. . . . And as they gaze at him, the windows of the soul, through which once they saw the myriad colors of the outer world, cloud over, grow opaque—and in that moment the story is over."

"And life begins," says the triumphant Supervisor. But it is not life to the Ghost; it is merely the pleasure of the bed, the pleasure of the table; the habit of pleasure, and the pleasures of jealousy and cruelty, and suffering, and indifference. "So," he argues, "little by little the pearl loses its luster and long before it dies, it is dead."

It has been an impressive argument, and Isabel is wildly swayed. "Oh, Ghost—Ghost," she cries, "if this is what life is, save me from it!"

The Ghost answers a firm "No." She does not belong with his kind, for she is false and shallow. What she loves is not truth, but the pleasure of vibrating endlessly between two falsehoods, Nice and Tours. It is not through her that the riddle will be solved and the miracle accomplished.

Desperately Isabel begs the Ghost to tell her, and then she throws herself into his arms. He kisses her tenderly and pushes her away, bidding her "Farewell, Isabel." He goes; for a moment the girl stands still—then she falls. The Supervisor runs to her, crying for help, crying for the Doctor.

But it is the Inspector who is the first to arrive, asking if the Ghost has been here. The young man answers, "He tried to take her with him. But she's still breathing. . . ." Isabel opens her eyes and asks, weakly, "Where am I?" and the Supervisor murmurs, "In my arms, darling." She faints again.

The Inspector shows a flash of intelligence and tells the Supervisor, "She is trying to come back from very far away. She requires precise directions. Your answer was insufficient."

Again Isabel stirs and asks where she is. This time it is the Inspector who answers precisely: she is on the planet Earth. Her name is Isabel and she is one of the higher mammals. A first-rate specimen of the human female.

There is a sound in the room and the girl asks what it is. She is told it is the military band rehearsing. The Inspector explains about sound—a wave of motion of the air vibrating on her eardrums. To the Supervisor he nods, "You see? Nothing like a dose of science to restore one to one's senses."

But now the Supervisor cries for the Doctor in earnest—for Isabel's heart has stopped. The Doctor appears immediately and soothes the young man with quiet authority. "It's all right. I've brought the remedy," he says. The others flock into the room, including two townsmen and the spinsters.

The Doctor's preparations are quite odd for a medical man. He pays no attention to the corpse, and when somebody advises that the windows be opened he points out that Isabel doesn't need air because she is not breathing. His first order is for the townsmen to sit at the table and play cards—any game. Casino. When the children crowd round the Inspector would send them out, but the Doctor bids them stay, saying, "When I give the word, you will start reciting your lessons—any lessons. The spinsters, Armande and Léonide, are commanded to start chattering at the same signal.

"What is all this nonsense?" the Inspector demands, and the Doctor answers, "Don't you understand? Isabel is neither drowned nor run over. Her body is in perfect condition. But her spirit has left it. To induce it to return, we must batter at the gate of death with the sounds of life."

Isabel had thought she had fashioned a ghost-trap; the Doctor is now making a life-trap. It is only the little girls who understand at once. The Mayor is bidden to go forth and take charge of the street noises—the blacksmith, the carpenter, the carts, the trucks. . . . The Inspector is bidden to contribute at intervals the resounding phrases of his profession.

And the Supervisor . . . He knows what to do without being told. He exclaims, "I love you, Isabel!" They all practice a bit, tuning up. Somehow, the Doctor has produced a baton, and he taps it, admonishing, "Please remember this is a very difficult transition to manage. We must keep in time. Ready?"

The Doctor gives the down beat, and the symphony begins—loud, soft, legato or staccato, according to his direction. There is a measured cacophony of card bids, arithmetic lessons, Inspectorial phrases like "imperishable honor," recipes, gossip and "I love you, Isabel!"

Armande says, "She wore black lace petticoats!" Her sister marvels, "Black lace? Really?" And Isabel, shuddering, repeats, "Black lace! Really!"

The Doctor chuckles, "If black lace petticoats won't do the trick, nothing will." He urges his orchestra to redoubled efforts, and from outside come the many sounds of the town. Suddenly the girl sits up and cries, "Robert!" He answers, "I love you!" . . . and she is in his arms.

"She's saved!" cry the members of the orchestra.

"She's lost," comments the Doctor.

The Mayor runs in breathlessly with great news. "The lottery! Guess who won the motorcycle? The Mother Superior!"

"Aha!" says the Inspector. "And the grand cash prize?"

The little girls have guessed, and they chorus, "Monsieur Dumas." The Mayor confirms them, "Monsieur Dumas! The millionaire!"

Isabel is heard to state, "I love you, Robert."

The Doctor has done his work, and now he pronounces, "The interlude is over." Outside, the military band crashes into a fanfare.

CURTAIN

CLUTTERBUCK *

A Comedy in Three Acts

By Benn W. Levy

ENGLAND'S Benn W. Levy, a specialist in humor, is the author of fifteen plays. American audiences have known best "Mrs. Moonlight," "Art and Mrs. Bottle," his adaptation of "Topaze" and the perennial "Springtime for Henry," in the last-named of which Edward Everett Horton toured the Summer theatre circuits for many years. "Clutterbuck," the fifteenth play, is frankly about as light and unimportant as a comedy can get. Like his compatriot in the novel field, P. G. Wodehouse, Mr. Levy can make the slightest supply of plot and incident go the greatest possible distance, and "Clutterbuck" is a *tour de force* in the manufacture and maintenance of a light and shiny soap bubble. It was first produced in London in 1946.

The five persons principally involved in the amours of a gentleman named Clutterbuck, who is frequently seen but never heard, find themselves cruising to the tropics aboard a luxury liner, and their favorite rendezvous is the deck. A full moon is flooding the deck with lovely light when Julian Pugh appears in a doorway. He is lean, shaggy-haired, about 35, and he manages to look unkempt even though he is in a dinner jacket. He is carrying a crossword puzzle book and a glass of brandy, and he is quite furtive about making certain he is alone before settling in a steamer chair. Julian's repose is of only an instant's duration, for at the sound of male voices nearby he hoists himself from the chair and, with a wary backward glance, strolls off down the deck and out of sight.

The next visitor is Arthur Pomfret, solidly handsome, solidly well-dressed and solidly self-assured; he is about 45. He is carrying a novel, a copy of *The Times,* and some brandy, and he engages in much the same maneuvers Julian Pugh did, settling down in a chair,

arranging a rug—and suddenly taking flight through the door leading to staterooms. Something he has seen farther along the deck
has put him in motion. With Pomfret gone, Pugh comes back, looking wistfully at his chair but deciding not to pause; but he is not
quite out of sight when Pomfret returns to retrieve the book he had
left by his chair with the brandy. Pomfret sees Pugh and Pugh sees
Pomfret, so there is no use hiding any more and they may as well
talk.

POMFRET (*casually*)—Hallo, Pugh.

PUGH—Hallo, Pomfret.

POMFRET—Taking a walk round?

PUGH—Yes. Then going—er—up on the sun-deck to have a bit
of a blow.

POMFRET—A blow?

PUGH—Yes. Unless of course—

POMFRET—No, no. Certainly not. I—I just came back to get
my book.

PUGH—Oh, where are you off to?

POMFRET—Who? Me?

PUGH—Yes.

POMFRET—Oh, just going in to—to have a game of Housie-housie.

PUGH—Housie-housie?

POMFRET—Yes.

PUGH—With your book?

POMFRET—What? Yes. One doesn't want to lose the place.

PUGH—You're very kind.

POMFRET—Not at all, my dear fellow. It's not merely because
you wrote the thing. One never does want to lose one's place. I
mean one always wants to know where one is.

PUGH—It's asking a good deal.

POMFRET—Yes. What? Yes. Well—um— (*Pause.*)

PUGH *and* POMFRET (*together*)—Where's Deborah? Where's
Jane?

POMFRET—I'm sorry. What were you saying?

PUGH—Oh, nothing. I just said where's Deborah?

POMFRET—Oh, Deborah. I expect she's in her stateroom. She
went back after dinner to powder her nose.

PUGH—Oh.

POMFRET—Where did you say—er—Jane was?

PUGH—I—I think she's in her stateroom. Powdering her nose.
(*A formal laugh from both is followed by another pause.*) Now, I
suppose, we commit a pungent little aphorism on women.

POMFRET—What's that?
PUGH—Nothing.
POMFRET—Oh. Thought you said something.
PUGH—No. Not a thing. (*Another pause.*) Well, see you later.
POMFRET (*cheered*)—Yes. Cheerio, Pugh.
PUGH—So long, Pomfret.

Shortly after the men have gone off in two directions a very
lovely woman in a superb evening dress pauses in the doorway,
breathes deeply of the night air, sighs at the moon and quotes a bit
of rapturous literature concerning the moon. Then, noticing that
nobody is present to catch her performance, she reclines in the chair
recently vacated by Pomfret. She is Deborah Pomfret, Arthur's
wife. Presently another very lovely woman in a delicious evening
dress pauses in the doorway, sighs at the moon and exclaims, "Crikey,
what a night!" She is Jane Pugh, the novelist's wife. Jane sits
beside Deborah. These two are old, old friends, but they haven't
seen each other for five years, as Deborah points out.

JANE—True, you get married and spend five years planting rubber
in Mah Jongg or whatever it calls itself. But can planting rubber
turn a girl inside out?
DEBORAH—I didn't plant it: Arthur did.
JANE—Very well, Arthur did and you, presumably, like a good
wife stood and watched him plant it.
DEBORAH—It isn't like that a bit. A man doesn't suddenly say,
"I'm going to plant a bit of rubber today; come and watch."
JANE—What does he say?
DEBORAH—Nothing.
JANE—You just have to guess?
DEBORAH—Certainly not. One of the many nice things about
Arthur is that there's never any guessing. You know exactly what
he's going to do or say or think a full minute before he does. It's
surprisingly restful.
JANE—And in return he never knows what *you're* thinking.
DEBORAH (*appalled*)—My dear, of course not! Don't let's be
sordid. He'd hate to know what I was thinking. That's only nat-
ural. After all, nobody ever does think the things he likes to think
I'm thinking. It all comes down to a question of honesty.
JANE—You took the word out of my mouth.
DEBORAH—I meant to. I repeat, common honesty. Arthur
wanted to marry a certain kind of woman and I undertook to provide what he wanted. There is a moral contract. He wanted a

CLUTTERBUCK

woman of sensibility. I said, here you are. He wanted the kind of woman who sighed and quoted poetry in moonlight. I quoted. He wanted a woman who choked with emotion at chamber music that he'd have liked to have liked himself. I duly choked. He wanted a woman who gurgled with delight when bestial little children dragged their jammy fingers over her fresh make-up. I gurgled. The result was he married me. And now you come back with your immoral Machiavellian exhortation to be myself. No, my girl, I'm an honest woman and a contract's a contract. I still gurgle, I still choke, I still quote. Be myself indeed! Is that what Julian has to put up with? Are you yourself?

JANE—I'm afraid I am. You make me feel rather badly but I don't really think Julian minds. At least he's awfully nice about it. Perhaps he just pretends not to notice.

DEBORAH—He's a very nice man.

JANE—You see, in a way it's different. You're cleverer than Arthur but Julian's cleverer than I.

DEBORAH—My darling, you don't mean it! How dreadful for you!

JANE—No. It's surprisingly restful. It means I don't have to choke or gurgle or quote. If I started doing any of those things, he'd probably fetch a doctor. As it is, if any small child brings its jammy fingers within striking distance, I'm at complete liberty to knock it into the middle of next week. It's lovely: children are terrified of me.

DEBORAH—And Julian doesn't mind?

JANE—He doesn't seem to. He likes people to be natural. You know, we met on a cross-channel steamer in a ghastly storm, and I was being so violently natural all over the deck that he fell in love with me there and then.

DEBORAH—How very odd.

JANE—Well, with that kind of start there was not much point in trying to pretend anything. I suppose, being a novelist he's always a little suspicious of people in real life trying to write themselves a juicy part.

DEBORAH—And the soul should be greater than the part.

JANE—Oh, darling, promise you won't talk like that in front of Julian! He hates epigrams.

DEBORAH—Mm! I suppose Julian won't insist on *my* being myself?

JANE—Heavens, no, darling. He adores you as you are—or as you aren't, perhaps I should say. He says you're a piece of minor art.

DEBORAH—That's lucky because I really don't know how I should even begin to be myself. I very much doubt if I've even got a self to be.

JANE—I know. That is the difficulty at first. But you'd find something, if you dug around long enough.

DEBORAH—Terrifying. Heaven knows *what* I should find. Anyhow that's what you really do?

JANE—That's what I really do.

DEBORAH (*reflectively*)—Really. Really. And you carry that out consistently?

JANE—I think so.

DEBORAH—Supposing, for example, you want to belch, what do you do about that?

JANE (*exhaling her cigarette*)—I belch.

DEBORAH—Do you really? Doesn't Julian mind?

JANE—Mind? Unless I belch explosively after dinner—at least twice—he thinks I'm being affected.

DEBORAH (*dreamily*)—It's funny, isn't it, the different things that enchant different men.

JANE—I don't say that it enchants Julian any more than it disenchants him. I don't mean he goes off to his club and says proudly, "Do you know, old man, my little woman can out-belch any cab driver in London." He just takes it for granted. Which reminds me.

Jane has felt a belch coming on, but the inspiration passes, and she asks for a sip of the brandy Arthur has left under his chair. Then Deborah has a sip, and finally Jane polishes it off. It is exceptionally fine, rare and expensive stuff. The two old friends fall to talking about their husbands. Says Jane, "We've only been aboard three days and it's perfectly apparent that before another three days are up they'll have driven each other crazy"—but Deborah thinks they will hit it off in time.

Jane asks petulantly, "Why did you have to marry a rubber planter?"

"Well, really, that's a bit thick. I've been married nearly five years; you've only been married five months. Why didn't *you* pick someone who'd fit in with Arthur?" Deborah thinks the men will get along, for Arthur was thrilled when he heard that his wife's friend had married a novelist. "He's got a morbid hankering to do what he calls 'interesting' things and meet interesting people."

Jane agrees that the men should get on—but for the opposite reason. Her Julian thinks interesting people are dull and he was looking forward to meeting Arthur because he knew Arthur *wasn't* interesting. But the two haven't hit it off, because Arthur wanted to talk to Julian about his newest book and Julian hates to talk about his books—particularly with people like Arthur, who haven't the foggiest idea what Julian is writing about. "Arthur's whole charm is that he is fat-headed," says Jane, and Deborah agrees romantically: "I know; he's the most fat-headed man in all the world. But he's got a passion for broadening his mind."

The fat-headed subject of this discussion appears and is pleased to find the two women but no Julian. He has just settled beside Jane when Julian hurries around the corner of the deck, looking backward like a hunted thief. When he sees Arthur he tries to make a bolt for it, but his wife orders him to sit down and talk. Soon everybody subsides into silence, with Arthur grumpy at finding his brandy has been drunk and with Julian concentrating on his cross-word puzzle.

Soon the peace and beauty of the night eases the tension. Deborah cheers Arthur up with a compliment on how handsome he is in a dinner jacket. Then she urges, "Look at that little boat out there, miles away. Isn't it pretty! Lonely little cockleshell tossing on the breast of eternity. Heigh ho!" Arthur beams at her fondly but Jane looks astonished. Presently Jane belches. "Enjoy yourself, darling," urges Julian. From the belch Jane proceeds to the hiccoughs.

Arthur comes up from his book with an "I say, Pugh. There's a point here I don't quite follow. What exactly does Greenways mean on page a hundred and forty when he says to Sheila, 'And the same to you'?"

"I don't know. He just means 'And the same to you.'"

Deborah, getting bored and fidgety, urges her husband to make some conversation by telling Julian about the plot for a novel that he has thought up—a suggestion that would make any novelist sick with apprehension. Julian weakly declares he'd love to hear it—some time. Jane staves off the ordeal by warning that the recital must wait until Julian has finished his puzzle, because if he doesn't finish a puzzle before he goes to bed he can't sleep a wink. Julian, thus rescued, agrees brightly, "That's right. I have nightmares, don't I?"

"As a matter of fact," says Arthur, game but miffed, "I'd quite like to read this chapter again. One hasn't quite got the hang of it."

Deborah wails, "And what am *I* going to do?" Her dear friend counsels, "You look at the bloody cockleshell."

Arthur, frowning over his book, inquires, "Why is the book called

'Cicero's Bicycle'? I mean the story's got nothing to do with Cicero and so far there isn't a bicycle."

JULIAN—There isn't a bicycle anywhere.

ARTHUR—Then why exactly—if one isn't being slow—?

JULIAN (*a little irritably*)—I don't know why. I haven't a cut and dried reason for every word I write.

ARTHUR—I see. One *is* being slow.

JANE—No, you aren't, Arthur. I've never seen the point of the title either. And Julian's so inarticulate.

JULIAN—Inarticulate! There are two hundred thousand words in that book! Quite possibly *none* of them means anything! I thought they did, that's all.

ARTHUR—One didn't say they didn't. One merely ventured to inquire about the title.

JULIAN—Well, isn't it obvious? The book is a study in antinomies. And if "Cicero's Bicycle" isn't an antinomy I don't know what is!

DEBORAH—I don't know what is either.

JANE—I don't know either.

ARTHUR—Well, one has a vague idea. It was meant to be a perfectly innocent question: not a criticism. Naturally one wouldn't presume.

DEBORAH—Now, Arthur, be good.

ARTHUR—Well, I mean one would think it was a favor to be allowed to buy the book. (JULIAN *delves in his pocket.*)

JULIAN—Here's your money back.

JANE—Now, Julian.

ARTHUR (*handing him the book*)—Thanks very much. (*He pockets the proffered ten-shilling note.*)

JANE—Well, bust my boiler!

DEBORAH—Darling, we should never have married them.

JULIAN—I'm waiting for my change. Eighteen pence, please.

ARTHUR—Is that all? Excuse me. (*He finds the coins and hands them over.*)

DEBORAH—How can you both be so childish?

ARTHUR—I'm not being childish, but if Pugh chooses to pay me not to read his books, then all right.

JULIAN—I'd pay you a large retaining fee not to read them. I don't pretend I can plant rubber; why do you pretend you can read?

ARTHUR (*angrily*)—One *can* read! You know perfectly well.

JULIAN—Congratulations.

ARTHUR—Listen, Pugh, if you want to start a row—

DEBORAH—Start it! Hasn't it even started?

JULIAN—By no means! Give me a minute to crank up and I'll show you what articulacy really is!

ARTHUR—Are you threatening me?

JULIAN—Oh, nuts!

ARTHUR—Did you say nuts to me, Pugh?

JULIAN (*fed up*)—Yes, I did.

ARTHUR—Then—then, by Jiminy—then, nuts to you too!

JANE—Good. Now that's all settled.

DEBORAH—Yes, now you can be friends again.

THE MEN (*together*)—Friends!

DEBORAH—Oh, stop it. Arthur, be a good boy and say you're sorry.

ARTHUR—Sorry? What for?

DEBORAH—Never mind what for. Just say it.

ARTHUR—Well, if that's all, certainly. I'm sorry. Hm!

DEBORAH—That's right. Now, Julian; your turn.

JULIAN—With pleasure, my dear. (*He is back to his puzzle.*) I apologize. Good old Pomfret!

Everybody subsides once more, until a man wearing a dinner jacket, a scarf and a cap strolls by. Deborah has seen him and is puzzled and arrested. Jane hadn't noticed him, but Deborah thinks she knows who he is. She muses, "I wonder if his wife's on board. . . . They say she's awful . . . an actress or something. They say she looks like a streetwalker. . . . We were invited to a party with them. We didn't go."

Deborah chatters on, but Jane is only half listening—until Deborah says she met this man in Venice. To Jane this is a piece of really interesting information and she wants more—but in confidence. It takes some doing, but the wives finally manage to make their husbands understand that they have something private to talk over and the men reluctantly leave.

"What shall I tell you?" asks Deborah—and Deborah knows very well what she is going to tell her friend. "We met. No, we didn't even meet. He picked me up. It was in a lift. I was in shorts and a tennis vest; and he just looked at me; every conceivable inch of me. It was the most blatant thing you ever saw in your life. I went scarlet from head to foot. And prayed the lift would never stop! Then he grinned at me shamelessly and I grinned back shamefully and he whispered 'Cocktails?' And I whispered 'Yes.' I still don't know why he whispered; there was no one in the lift but us! . . . Oh, dear! . . . And then, ten days of heaven!"

It was a confused paradise, this heaven of Deborah's, and all she remembers is gondolas and the mosquito netting over the bed.

"Ah, that mosquito netting!" sighs Jane, surprisingly. Jane, too, has been to Venice. Did the man mention marrying Deborah? No, but Deborah had mentioned it, and he had said, "We mortals shouldn't be too greedy of joy."

Jane pricks up her ears and demands, "What else did he say?"

"He said there were islands in time as well as in space and we had been lucky enough to discover one together."

By now Jane is fairly certain, and her foot begins tapping ominously. Why did the man have to return to London and what was his job there?

"He was a curator at the British Museum."

"The *British* Museum? You're sure you don't mean the Victoria and Albert?"

"Yes, that's right."

"I knew it!" Jane explodes. "Clutterbuck!"

Deborah is amazed that Jane also knew the man, and wants to know where and when and how. It was in Venice, and in a lift—and there had been fourteen days of "something rather precious, not just a genteel bout of catch-as-catch-can."

The two dear friends are friends no longer, for Clutterbuck has come between them. To Jane, her own adventure is something sacred and it makes her feel slightly sick to hear it parodied by Deborah's squalid little story. On the other hand, Deborah thinks that Jane, being "natural" all over Venice with Clutterbuck, should have been locked up or deported. The women are both on the edge of furious tears when their husbands come back and resume their chairs, inquiring, "Have you finished your gay girlish confidences?"

Jane volunteers to Arthur, "Deborah's not quite herself. She's been seeing ghosts. She thought she saw an old friend on board. . . . I wonder if you knew him."

"No," snaps Deborah. "Arthur doesn't know him." And then, to Julian, "But Jane does, Julian." Julian, however, is drowsy and not interested.

Arthur asks, "What's his name?"

"Clutterbuck."

Arthur remembers a Clutterbuck, vaguely, and asks, "Was he the chap who married a girl called—"

"Yes, he was!" snaps Arthur's wife.

The women have had enough. Deborah pleads a headache and Jane discovers she is going to be sick soon, but Arthur goes cheerfully on, "I happened to know a girl once who married a man called Clutterbuck."

The wives make their escape and Arthur continues to muse on the name Clutterbuck and the girl he happened to know—before he was married, of course. "This girl was living with an artist when I met her . . . and she left him for me!" Julian, bored, offers his congratulations.

"And I can't say I wonder that she left him, living knee-deep in filth in a top attic in Charlotte Street."

As had Jane a few minutes before, Julian suddenly becomes interested. "Where?" he demands.

"I said Charlotte Street."

"What number?"

"Thirteen. Why?"

"Good God! Are you sure he was a painter?"

"Painter or sculptor or writer or something. Why?"

"What was her name? Melissa?"

"Yes!"

"Good God!"

Arthur wants to know how Julian happened to know the name. "How?" Julian retorts. "I was the writer!"

Arthur is full of apologies but Julian is just as full of forgiveness. An exchange of confidences reveals that Arthur and Melissa had been together for six months, but Julian and Melissa had lasted two years. Arthur's adventure ended when Melissa, wanting to get married and settle down, met Clutterbuck, and Arthur met Deborah. There had been no hard feeling.

Julian confides that there had been no hard feeling with him, either. He remembers how Melissa used to talk about Arthur in glowing terms. "Did you ever meet her husband?" he asks.

ARTHUR—Yes, I did once; only for a few minutes. About a year ago.

JULIAN—What was he like?

ARTHUR—Nothing; nothing at all. Wouldn't know him again if I saw him. Complete nonentity. Don't suppose any woman had ever looked at him before in his life!

JULIAN—Funny, isn't it! I wonder why *she* did!

ARTHUR—Women are odd creatures.

JULIAN—True indeed. I say, do let me get you another brandy.

ARTHUR—No, no, no. I'm quite happy without it.

JULIAN—Well, look, I'll tell you what. Give us your glass. (*He takes the glass and pours half his own brandy into it.*)

ARTHUR—I say, that's awfully good of you.

JULIAN—Not a bit. Cheers!

ARTHUR—Cheers! (*They drink!*)

JULIAN—Do you remember—

ARTHUR—What?

JULIAN—She was a queer domesticated little animal in a way. She always loved the winter because there was a fire in the grate.

ARTHUR—Yes, I know. Do you remember how she used to like taking her shoes and stockings off in front of the fire?

JULIAN—Funny, that's just what I was thinking of! She had lovely feet.

ARTHUR—They were the one thing she was vain of.

JULIAN—Yes, like Trilby.

ARTHUR—Is it? (*They finish their brandy slowly and then sigh a little.*) Have another brandy, old chap; do.

JULIAN—No thanks, my friend. That was *just* enough.

ARTHUR—Yes, it was really. (*They settle back in their chairs. For a moment or two they stare contentedly into the night.*)

JULIAN—What a lovely night!

ARTHUR—Yes, isn't it gorgeous!

The curtain falls.

ACT II

The luxury liner has stopped at a tropical port and the passengers have been put up at the Hotel Palais Nacionale, which is a very luxurious place. There is a broad terrace overlooking the sea, with steps leading from it to the beach, and the nearest doorway to the hotel has a neon sign over it proclaiming "American Bar." On the terrace are bright chairs and tables and parasols. Right now it is noon and very hot. The terrace is raised about four feet above ground level, and on the ground level, in rather widely separated chairs placed in the shade of the terrace wall, are Jane and Deborah, not talking.

Clutterbuck leans on the railing above them, but he does not see them. He is admiring the seascape through binoculars. He sneezes, and, as the ladies look up at him, he strolls back into the hotel. Presently Julian and Arthur stroll into sight, arm in arm—Julian in old, stained clothes, Arthur in the smartest of linen suits, a panama hat and his old school tie. They are deep in discussion of Shakespeare's "Othello" and they merely tip their hats to their wives as they pass. Deborah has to ask twice where they are going before she gets an answer from Arthur. "We're going upstairs to the lounge for a moment. I want to show old Pugh the view. After you, Pugh."

Deborah and Jane continue to sit it out, grimly. A Filipino waiter appears, grinning, and asks if he can get the ladies something. He cannot—but Jane tries a little conversation with him. "Where *is* everyone? It's very empty." The waiter replies, "They have a siesta. Nobody goes out at this hour except—" He grins and breaks off, and Jane finishes for him: "Except mad dogs and Englishmen." The waiter assures Jane that everybody will be on hand for the Santa Luiza procession in the afternoon and the fireworks at night. Deborah, tired and quarrelsome, has been inordinately bored by this chatter and is about to wind up for a good scrap with Jane when she sees a young woman coming out of the hotel. This vision puts an end to her combativeness, for the young woman is wearing only two diminutive scraps of bathing dress and is very fair and soft and silken and small—like an appealing kitten. She is Melissa Clutterbuck—and as she comes down the terrace steps, passes the silently embattled Jane and Deborah and continues through the trellis gate toward the beach, she is pursued by Arthur Pomfret. "Hi! Melissa!" he hails.

When Arthur beholds his wife and Jane his pursuit subsides to a nonchalant saunter and, reluctantly abandoning the chase, he takes a seat between them and makes obvious and strained small talk. Soon his wife wearies of it and heads for the beach, leaving Jane and Arthur alone. Their intimate and friendly conversation is at last interrupted by the waiter, who brings on a tray and presents at her elbow a crème de menthe frappé.

"I didn't order that," says Jane. The waiter agrees, but points significantly at a note which also is on the tray. Jane takes the note and becomes flushed and smiling as she reads it; the waiter puts the frappé on the table and accepts from Arthur an order for two gin slings—one for Arthur and one for Jane. The waiter asks Jane if there is any answer to the note. "Just say," she just says, "I'm glad time and tide wait for women and that they'll only have to wait two more minutes now."

Jane spends these two minutes being nice to Arthur, then, after taking the crème de menthe and straightening her dress, she makes for the hotel. Arthur dreams pleasantly about how nice Jane has been to him and how attractive Melissa still is, and he waxes cheerful as he heads for the beach in search of Melissa. His departure has been witnessed by Deborah and Julian, who have come to the terrace, but not together.

"What's the matter with Arthur?" Deborah wonders.

Julian doesn't know. "Do you think he's looking for me?" He offers Deborah a drink and they both decide on a gin sling. Just then the waiter appears, as if by magic, with two gin slings, which they capture. The drinks are Arthur's. Julian thinks it would be nice if Deborah and Jane would stay ashore tonight, have a nice family foursome, and watch the fireworks. But Deborah wants to go back to the boat; fireworks always give her neuralgia. "That's exactly what Jane said," says Julian. "I'd just as soon go back with her, but Pomfret insists on my seeing the fireworks. What a remarkable chap he is, you know. So sensitive and discerning and responsive and perceptive, with that depth of understanding and quick interest that's positively fascinating."

DEBORAH (stunned)—Who are you talking about?

JULIAN—Pomfret. It just shows how superficial a snap judgment can be. When I first met him, I misunderstood him completely and I'm not usually far wrong. After all, understanding people is my trade. But Pomfret—I simply never guessed the intellectual warmth of the man, the eager enquiring darting intelligence behind that conventional handsome stolid rocklike façade. It's a lesson to me, I promise you.

DEBORAH—It's something or other to me!

JULIAN—For instance, he was talking to me about my book on deck last night after you two went to bed. I assure you it was an education. He'd seen things in it that I hadn't seen myself.

DEBORAH—I'm sure.

JULIAN—You know, it's not an easy book. There's a great deal in it I've never really understood, I don't mind confessing. But not Pomfret. Take the chapter when Sheila gets out of bed after her first night with Greenways. He fastened on that.

DEBORAH—He would.

JULIAN—What is the first thing she does when she gets up? Mind you, she hadn't wanted that night; she'd fought against it, fought like a spiritual tiger-cat. It isn't stated of course in so many words but she fought all right between the lines.

DEBORAH—That's where we do a lot of that kind of fighting.

JULIAN—Of course Greenways didn't know it.

DEBORAH—Wasn't she lucky?

JULIAN—He went right on.

DEBORAH—Good old Greenways.

JULIAN—He wouldn't have cared anyway.

DEBORAH—The beast.

JULIAN—But, in spite of all this, what is the first thing she does next morning?

DEBORAH—I don't remember. Tell me.

JULIAN—She makes a wreath of daffodils, and puts them on her head. There she was in a London back street with four penn'orth of daffodils on her head.

DEBORAH—The daring of it!

JULIAN—I tell you it was a complete surprise to *me*.

DEBORAH—You must have been amazed.

JULIAN—I was.

DEBORAH—What did Greenways say?

JULIAN—Not a word. He never noticed.

DEBORAH—He wouldn't.

JULIAN—Do you think so? I thought he would. But you were right; he didn't. Anyway as soon as I'd written it, the whole incident began to puzzle me. But not Pomfret. He understood it at once. He'd seen right inside the girl.

DEBORAH—He had.

JULIAN—The night, he explained, had released her from the long torment of doubts. She'd stopped asking questions, thrown self-examination into the dustbin. And now at last she knew relief. So naturally she does the only thing she could do. She takes the daffodils from their dirty little vase on the filthy broken-down little wash-handstand, and makes herself a wreath. It was inevitable. But *I* didn't see it; not until Pomfret explained it to me.

DEBORAH—Do you mean he said all that?

JULIAN—Oh, no, not in those words. All he said was: "I suppose the little twirp found she was in love." But I knew what he meant. He meant she unconsciously reached out for a symbol of joy. (*A little pause.*)

DEBORAH—Do you think she did?

JULIAN—Yes. Don't you? (*She shakes her head.*)

DEBORAH—No. Symbols are dramatic devices, not human expedients.

JULIAN (*surprised*)—That's a very profound remark.

DEBORAH—Is it? That's what comes of living with a man like Arthur.

JULIAN—I suppose it is. Still I wonder if you're right.

DEBORAH—About the daffodils?

JULIAN—Yes.

DEBORAH—You mean, would she have done it?

JULIAN—Yes.

DEBORAH—I'm afraid she wouldn't. She'd carry the symbol in

her brighter eyes, her readier heart, her springier step. She might sing, she might even dance. She might want to tell the inattentive world about her new-found glory but she wouldn't, for she's not a novelist and so—she wouldn't know how.

Arthur comes back through the gate, still on the hunt, and not noticing his wife and Julian until the latter hails him. Arthur lamely explains that he has been looking for his cigarette case, and they all are busy peeping under the tables and chairs when Melissa, carrying a small bottle, floats by. Spying Julian, she utters an ecstatic cry and enfolds him in her arms. They kiss fondly. "Oh, my little Julie-Pughlie!" Melissa coos. Arthur knows his turn is coming, and it does. Upon seeing him Melissa cries, "Oh, my little Artie-Pomegranate! Darling!" and embraces him. A slightly chilled Deborah is introduced.

Melissa, firmly seating the men on each side of her, explains why nobody has seen her aboard ship. "I've been ick, ea-ick." Deborah doesn't get it, so Arthur translates. "Now," the young siren continues, "I'm as fiddle as a fiddle-de-dee. Are you fiddle, Artie?"

"Quite fiddle, thank you. Hm."

"But haven't you got a little fattle round the rum-tum-tummy-i-do?" Deborah is beginning to enjoy this.

Melissa, who has seen the names on the passenger list, inquires how long her old friends have been married. "Five months," says Julian, and "Five years," says Arthur. She wants to know if Julian's wife is smartle. "Very smartle," he informs her. Melissa bubbles with reminiscence—how Julian used to take her to the Purple Crow and Artie would take her to the Berkeley Grill. Julian always wanted her to look like a romantic slut, but Artie wanted her to resemble an American debutante. Despite Deborah's presence, the men warm themselves in the glow of happy recollection. "They were pleasant days," Julian avers, and Arthur agrees, "They were indeed!" Melissa unscrews her bottle, which contains sunburn oil, and orders Julian to do her back. She invites all to come bathe with her and they accept—even Deborah seems to like this happy creature and does not mind it when Melissa throws a shapely leg over Artie's knees and demands that he oil it.

Melissa catches a tune the orchestra has been playing, hums a bit of it and exclaims, "That's my signature tune! They played this all the time the day we got married."

Julian says, "I didn't know you were married, darling."

"Yes, you did, old chap," Arthur reminds him. "I told you last night. Didn't you marry a chap called Clutterbuck?"

Deborah utters a "What!" that sounds like an explosion. Instantly she becomes outraged. "And what," she inquires icily, "does your husband like you to represent, Mrs. Clutterbuck—an artistic slut or an American debutante?"

"Clutterbuck?" Melissa replies cheerfully. "Oh, I'm afraid he really likes me to look like a Riviera tartle. Darling Clutterbuck! It's funny but he's never attracted to a woman unless she looks like a tartle. I suppose it's the museum; a kind of reaction."

Deborah, rising in a fury, announces, "I shall *not* bathe with you," and sails off for a walk to the village.

Melissa would like to stay ashore for the fireworks and so would the men. But Deborah and Jane don't want to, and neither, it develops, does Clutterbuck—but Clutterbuck has said Melissa can stay if she finds a party to join up with. Arthur and Julian quickly volunteer to be the party; they have already booked a room for themselves, and they will get another for Melissa. "Go off and book it," she orders, "and then get yourselves some bathing suitles and come right back. I'll finish the oiling myself." They comply.

Melissa is alone, finishing the oiling, when Jane shoots ecstatically through the hotel door with a Nijinsky leap and follows with a few classical ballet steps. Then, stopping, she inhales deeply and beats her breast as Tarzan might. She is on top of the world, and when she sees Melissa she gives her a friendly greeting. Jane burbles, "I feel like a goddess made of cold champagne and beaten white of egg!" The secret of this good feeling? Jane confides it: "Simply look round one sunny day and find your past smiling and winking at you."

MELISSA—Oh.

JANE—For preference, pick a day when you feel disgruntled and frowsty. When you're sick of the monotonous sight of yourself in the mirror, when your best friend seems a hundred times as pretty and smart and lively as yourself, all the things you know you'll never be, when you look forward with sick foreboding to endless happy peaceful years spent with a husband you adore till the grave makes garbage of you both, with never another quickened heart-beat, with never another silly heart-beat, with never another folly or stupid delirious joy to break the awful tedium of unmitigated happiness ahead. Then, suddenly out of a clear sky, you turn and what do you find?

MELISSA—I don't know.

JANE—A crème de menthe frappé at your elbow! Winking and

smiling at you! How did it get there? How? How on earth? Who sent it?

MELISSA—A man.

JANE—Correct. A man who'd whispered to you in Venice! And in many a dim dream since. What happens? In a flash your thick reluctant blood is cold champagne, your weary flesh the gossamer white of egg and, incorporeal, you ache no more!

MELISSA—Sounds a bit of all rightle.

JANE—Sounds what? It sounds Paradise! It is Paradise! Deborah! (*For at that moment* DEBORAH, *glum-faced, comes out of the hotel.*) Deborah darling! My sweet, my pet, where have you been? (DEBORAH *halts a moment, looks at her in astonishment, then continues on her way.* JANE *trots beside her.*) Have you been having a little siesta? I say, stop a minute. Darling, that's one of the prettiest dresses I've ever seen. You look divine in it.

DEBORAH—Have you gone raving mad?

JANE—No, darling. Why should you think I'm mad because I say something nice?

DEBORAH—It seems to me sufficient reason.

JANE—Oh, darling. I wish I could say witty things like you. Oh, you two don't know each other, do you?

DEBORAH (*grimmer still*)—Yes, we do, thank you.

JANE—Do you? *We* don't! (*She laughs from sheer exuberance.*) Deborah's my best friend, you know. (*She takes her arm.*) The one I was telling you about. (DEBORAH *disengages herself, more than a little bewildered.*) We've known each other for years but we're still devoted to each other, aren't we, darling?

DEBORAH—You *are* mad! (*She crosses to the gate, turns there and after one more puzzled glance goes through it.*)

MELISSA—Not very politel.

JANE—Oh, take no notice of that. She's like you are this morning; she's not feeling well.

MELISSA—But I'm—

JANE—Oh, no, you're not; neither of you. Listen, where had I got to? (*She seats herself on the table next to* MELISSA.)

MELISSA—You'd got to the man and the crème de menthe. Was it an "old" man?

JANE—No, a young man—or young enough! A sublime man! A man with the gift of language!

MELISSA—I didn't mean that kind of old man. I meant old as distinct from new.

JANE—Ah, a "former" man? That's right. A former man. My only former man.

MELISSA—And you met him in Venice?

JANE—That's right.

MELISSA—What happened?

JANE—A little rapture.

MELISSA—And how does the crème de menthe come into it?

JANE—He liked crème de menthe. And he insisted on my liking it. I drank it till I was almost ill, jugsful of the sticky stuff simply because he said it made my eyes a deeper green than ever.

MELISSA—How sweet!

JANE—So you see.

MELISSA—So I see!

JANE—And then suddenly, a half an hour ago, that little yellow archangel with the smiling tombstone teeth and a white jacket brings me a cooling, healing drink all the way from Venice!

With the drink was a little note about time and tide and the initial C. And Jane saw him, and he began where they had left off. He didn't care if she was married—he just wanted to make the fourteen days they had had together into fifteen. She drags Melissa toward the hotel and points, "There! Can you see him?" She guides Melissa's gaze.

"I can see only one man," says Melissa.

"There *is* only one." With her eyes fixed on the man, Jane does not observe Melissa's face as it assumes the surprised expression of one who has unexpectedly somersaulted on a slippery pavement. Melissa's knees buckle and she finds a chair. Jane burbles on: "He said he'd planned it all for tonight. I was to come to his cabin late. And sometime during the day he was going to try and find a party who'd chaperone his wife, if she stayed ashore after the fireworks, and I'd got to do the same for my husband! . . . Of course, I refused. God forgive me, I refused; but it was lovely to be asked!"

Melissa begins to howl aloud, and then to stamp wildly on the ground. Julian and Arthur, dressed for bathing, emerge from the hotel, happily, and stride purposefully to the beach without noticing Jane and her hysterical companion. "There!" Jane comforts. "You'll be better soon. . . ."

The curtain falls.

ACT III

It is the next morning, on shipboard. Julian, Arthur and Melissa cross the deck, a little subdued after their night ashore. Melissa is wearing a Quakerish little frock. She heads straight for her cabin and the men pause on deck. Arthur observes that Melissa seems subdued. "I wonder why," says Julian. "Yes," Arthur agrees, giving his friend a sidelong glance, "I was wondering the same thing." Arthur goes in to see if Deborah is awake yet, and neither man has confirmed his suspicion of the other.

Jane emerges, still feeling splendid, and fondly kisses her husband. Too bad about the storm last night, she observes; it must have spoiled his fun.

"What do you mean?"

"Spoiled the fireworks."

"Oh, that."

Julian asks where Deborah is and Jane shows surprise. She thought Deborah must have been ashore. "She's not in her cabin. I knocked and there was no answer and the door was locked." Arthur returns, and he, too, is puzzled. He can't find his wife and the cabin is locked. Jane takes Arthur off on a search for Deborah, and a moment later Melissa comes back through the hatch, looking cheerful. Julian notes the cheerfulness and concentrates on Melissa's feet, musing, "I wonder if that might fairly be described as a springier step. And is that perhaps a readier smile?"

MELISSA—Readier than what?

JULIAN—Readier than before. That's the trouble with Life as compared with Fiction. It's so hard to follow just what's happening. If Life were a novelist and knew its job, it would be perfectly clear why you're prancing about and grinning like a rising sun. But Life, as Deborah pointed out, doesn't understand the convenience of using symbols. And she's right. Life underwrites most abominably; just roughs in a springier step, a brighter eye and a readier heart and leaves us to make the best we can of it. That's bad writing. It won't do, you know. It's amateurish. Do you think I'd be satisfied to do a job like that? The reviewers would soon be after me if I did!

MELISSA—What would you do?

JULIAN—What *would* I do? What *do* I do? What *have* I done? What did I do with Sheila?

MELISSA (*sitting beside him*)—What *did* you do with her?

JULIAN—I slapped a wreath of daffodils on her head.

MELISSA—You didn't! Where did you get them from?

JULIAN—There were some in her room. There's nothing so odd about that, is there?

MELISSA—No, of course. I've got some in my room right now. Then what happened?

JULIAN—What happened? Why once I'd put that wreath on her, immediately everything was crystal clear. The whole world knew at once what had happened between her and Greenways the night before. Everyone could tell instantly how she felt about it—even Pomfret. And it saved me about four chapters of explanation.

MELISSA—Oh, you mean the girl in your book?

JULIAN—Exactly. Symbols. But does life do that? Oh, no! It just bungles along clumsily, boring the pants off everyone through sheer lack of elementary technique! Take yourself.

MELISSA—All rightle.

JULIAN—Now I don't say I'm curious exactly. After all I realize that what you do is your affair. I no longer have the right to be curious. It is your affair; and Mr. Clutterbuck's. But suppose I *were* interested: for purely academic psychological reasons. What clues are there, what symbols? Deborah says one must look for such manifestations of self-satisfaction as a springier step. But that's extremely hard to gauge. Or a readier smile. And who in the world can spot a quickened heartbeat?

MELISSA—Yes, it *is* tiresome.

JULIAN—Tiresome. It's infuriating. I loathe incompetence.

MELISSA—But there's one thing, you know, that real life lets you do.

JULIAN—What's that?

MELISSA—Well, you can ask questions. I'm only a silly but I often think if a novelist let his people ask each other a few plain questions he wouldn't have any novel left. It would be wonderful.

JULIAN (*thoughtfully*)—Questions. Plain questions. *That's* a very ingenious idea. All right. Why not? Very well, then. Did you or did you not last night—I mean Pomfret's a very decent fellow. I like him.

MELISSA (*slightly surprised*)—Artie-Partie? What has he to do with it?

JULIAN—Let me put it another way. Why are you so bloody cheerful this morning?

MELISSA (*confidentially*)—I'll tell you. Yesterday on the island I had rather a nasty shockle.

JULIAN (*indignant*)—There! I knew it!

MELISSA—You knew? How did you know?

JULIAN—How? I don't know *how* I knew. I suppose because I must have *some* discernment. I couldn't do my job if I didn't sense a *bit* of what was going on all round me. And it's a damned shame!

MELISSA—No, it isn't; it's all right now. That's why I'm so cheerful. Yesterday I thought for a moment because of something

he did—you know, Clutterbuckle—I thought I was slipping. And
I don't want to slip. But this morning it's all right. I just met the
stewardoodle downstairs and he said Clutterbuck was frightfully worried about me this morning in case the storm had upset me last
night because storms always scare the knicker-knackles off me, so he
persuaded the captain to let him go ashore for me first thing in the
pilot's cutter, so of course we just missed each other and if that isn't
love, I'll take ginger wine.

Arthur reappears, no longer worried. He has found Deborah.
He fetched the steward to unlock the cabin door, but the door wasn't
locked at all—and Deborah was in the bath. Jane returns, too, and
is told Deborah has been found. The business of the door being
unlocked is puzzling, for she had tried it herself. "Hello, stranger,"
she greets Melissa.

"Do you two know each other?" Arthur inquires.

Jane replies that they've met but don't know each other. "I'm
Jane Pugh," she offers.

"I'm Melissa Clutterbuck. How do you do?"

Jane mutters the usual "Delighted to meet you," and then, belat-
edly, the significance of the name penetrates. She turns a horrified
countenance toward Melissa and then pitches onto her back in a
dead faint, leaving Julian and Arthur looking helpless. At Melissa's
urging they get Jane upended, but she is still out. Julian picks her
up and starts for their cabin, muttering, "Extraordinary thing! I
wonder what *that's* a symbol of?"

Having deposited his wife in bed, Julian returns to ask Melissa
if she has any cologne; she has, and she goes to fetch it to Jane.
The two men debate the cause of Jane's faint, but arrive at no answer, except that women are unpredictable. Even Melissa. "Funny
girl," observes Arthur, and Julian agrees. Each tries to draw the
other out, with elaborate feints, concerning what might have happened last night. Julian confesses that he lay awake quite late,
"conscious of nothing except that Melissa was in the room next to
mine and that you were in the room next to that."

Arthur adds, "With a communicating door between!"

Julian asks, "It was locked, wasn't it?" Oh, yes, it was locked.
And Julian assures Arthur that his communicating door was locked,
too. The men confess that each had been suspicious of the other,
and they are glad everything has been all right. Melissa comes back
from her errand of mercy and commands Julian and Arthur to sit
beside her. "Now I'm going to lecture you. Some very peculiar
things happened. After I'd been in bed about half an hour and was

just going off to sleep, I heard a tiny gentle tapping at the door on my left."

ARTHUR—Really! I say!

JULIAN—You—you were probably dreaming.

MELISSA—That's what I thought at first. But it went on. So I got out of bed, just to make sure the door was locked, and then got back again.

ARTHUR—Well, I'll be—if that isn't—

MELISSA—Then I was just drowsing off again when I'm sorry to say I heard a tiny gentle tapping at the door on my right.

JULIAN (*indignantly*)—What? Do you mean to tell me that—

MELISSA—Yes, I'm afraid so.

ARTHUR—It—it was probably from the other door again. You must have made a mistake.

MELISSA—No. You see, I got out of bed to listen and make sure.

JULIAN—Well, of all the damned insolence!

ARTHUR (*hotly*)—Insolence! What about yourself?

JULIAN—That's completely different. I—

ARTHUR—What's different about it, pray?

MELISSA—I don't want to interrupt this but this is my lecture.

JULIAN—Please, Melissa, keep out of this. It has nothing to do with you.

ARTHUR—No, this is between Pugh and me.

MELISSA—You can say what you have to say afterwards. You must let me say my say first.

JULIAN (*with no good grace*)—Very well. Get on with it.

ARTHUR—Well, if you'll excuse me, I think I'll be off.

MELISSA—Artie, you stay where you are.

ARTHUR—I don't see why we should discuss these things in public: it's not respectable.

MELISSA—Sit down; please.

JULIAN—Sit down! (*At this* ARTHUR, *who was about to sit, changes his mind.*)

MELISSA (*a hand on his arm*)—Artie. (*And so he sits.*) Now I don't want you to think I'm cross with you both. I could never be that. It's not exactly that I was insulted. I know you didn't mean any harm. After all it's silly to blame tom-cats for being tom-cats.

ARTHUR—I say, really!

MELISSA—Please, Artie. It's more that I was sort of disappointed in you.

JULIAN—You're right. It was rude of us.

MELISSA—Not rude, exactly. But foolish. I thought you knew me better.

ARTHUR—Well, really! I mean to say, one doesn't want to be a cad but aren't you forgetting something?

MELISSA—No, Artie. I'm forgetting nothing and I hope I never shall. Six lovely months with you and two lovely years with Julie-Pughlie.

ARTHUR (*embarrassed*)—Well, really!

MELISSA—But I was never your mistress.

ARTHUR—What? What—what *was* all that then?

MELISSA—No, I was never your casual mistress: at least I didn't think so. In everything but name you were both husbands to me.

JULIAN—That's true.

MELISSA—So were all the men before you. I was never promiscuous.

Julian and Arthur are penitent toward Melissa—but are becoming very angry with each other and begin trading insults. When they rise menacingly and physical violence looms, Melissa takes charge, saying, "Now, now, now, now, now! Peace upon earthle and good willikins among millikens. That's not a nice way to talk, Artie. I think you ought to apologize." So Arthur grudgingly apologizes to Julian, and Julian offers his hand in peace.

Deborah's appearance is a surprise to all. She is radiant, full of great cheer—and she is wearing a wreath of daffodils. She gives her husband a great hug and burbles poetry: "Banish dull thought and let the pulses leap, for morning dews are winking from the earth. . . ."

Melissa's eyes have suddenly fastened upon the wreath of daffodils, and Deborah's effusions are halted by a loud series of boo-hoo's from Melissa. All seem vastly puzzled as the weeping wife trots away down to her cabin. But Deborah's concern doesn't last long, for her thoughts now are for her husband. She has brought him his paper and his book, and asks if he has had a nice evening ashore.

Which reminds Arthur of a funny thing that happened. "When I came aboard just now I couldn't find you."

Alarmed, Deborah asks what time he arrived. "About half an hour ago."

Involuntarily she exclaims, "Whew! I knew my watch was slow." Then she offers the lame excuse that she meant she overslept. "What happened?"

Her husband relates how he banged at the door and thought it was locked. "But it wasn't. You were in the bath all the time. I made a mistake."

"That's it," his relieved wife agrees. She hugs him again, exclaiming, "Oh, you sweetie! I couldn't have a husband who suited me better!"

Jane, having recovered from her faint and having recovered her good spirits as well, joins the trio and is given a fulsome greeting by Deborah, who gushes about Jane's beauty and the beauty of her dress. The two women set off for a once-around-the-deck before the ship sails, and they vanish, caroling, "Sailing, sailing, over the bounding main. . . ."

Good will gets into Julian and Arthur, too—for a moment, at least, and they are profuse with apologies and expressions of friendship and understanding. They shouldn't have let their tempers get the better of them. The only one of the little party who still is in a temper is Melissa, who appears in the doorway, faces the men angrily, then bursts into tears again. Julian and Arthur rise in concern and inquire what is the matter.

"What's the matter?" she howls. "Did you see what she'd got on her head?" Arthur hadn't noticed and Julian doesn't think Deborah was wearing a hat at all. "Now really, darling," he asks Melissa, "you didn't come up here specially to tell us you didn't like Deborah's hat?"

She is barely intelligible through her tears as she exclaims, "I came up here to tell you that I hate everyone, including you two, and if ever you come tapping at my door again, next time you won't find it locked, I promise you!" With a fresh burst of sobbing and stamping of feet she is off again to her cabin, and the two astonished men thoughtfully resume their seats. Presently the significance of Melissa's last words overtakes them and on their faces dawns a gentle, complacent beam. Then, as they become conscious of each other, the smug smiles fade and they make small talk about its being time for the boat to move.

Julian's irritability returns as he asks Arthur, "Why don't you read your book?"

"You mean why don't I read *your* book?"

"No, I don't. Get yourself something simple from the library." Arthur rises angrily, but any plan he may have had for assault is sidetracked by the reappearance of Jane and Deborah, still singing gaily. The girls take chairs, and Deborah commands Arthur to sit down. Julian snarls, "You sit where you're told!" Arthur subsides, tosses Julian's novel contemptuously into an empty chair and opens *The Times.* The ship's whistle sounds.

Deborah carols, "We're off again."

"On we roll," choruses Jane.

"How beauteous the sight from here, how beauteous the morn," Deborah sighs. Jane, sighing too, says, "Crikey! What a view!" Presently Clutterbuck strolls past them along the deck.

"Heigho!" says Deborah. And Jane agrees, "Heigho!"

THE CURTAIN FALLS

THE PLAYS AND THEIR AUTHORS

THE COCKTAIL PARTY, by T. S. Eliot

T. S. Eliot, widely held to be the greatest living English poet, is described by one biographer as believing that a poet should write as little as possible. His collected verse fills only a thin volume—yet in 1948 he won the Nobel Prize for Literature. Aware that even prolific poets often starve, Eliot is a business man on the side, being a partner in the publishing firm of Faber and Faber, Ltd., in London. He has written two other dramas in verse, "Family Reunion" and "Murder in the Cathedral," but "The Cocktail Party" is his first commercial success.

Eliot is generally regarded as an austere and forbidding man in his early sixties, but to his London intimates he is known as Tom or Old Possum, and is known for his addiction to whimsical verse and practical jokes. Thomas Stearns Eliot was born in 1888 in St. Louis, of New England stock. He was the youngest of seven children. His father was a wholesale grocer and brick manufacturer —and the Eliots were a literary family. The father read Dickens to his children; the mother once wrote a dramatic poem about Savonarola. Eliot got his A.B. from Harvard in three years, his M.A. in the fourth. Next he spent a year in Paris and wrote his first serious poem, "The Love Song of J. Alfred Prufrock." Then he returned to Harvard for three years of graduate work. In 1914 he won a traveling fellowship and went to Germany—and to Britain when World War I exploded. He stayed in Britain, went to work for Lloyds Bank, married Vivienne Haigh, a ballet dancer. (He had volunteered for the U. S. Navy, but his ensign's commission did not come through until after the Armistice.) Ultimately Eliot gave up his American citizenship and became a British subject. In 1927 he was confirmed in the Church of England, and his Anglican philosophy is discoverable in "The Cocktail Party."

THE MEMBER OF THE WEDDING, by Carson McCullers

"The Member of the Wedding" is Carson McCullers' first play. It was Tennessee Williams who urged her to adapt her novel of the same name. She had seen only six plays in her life, two Broadway and four school productions, and her only instruction in playwriting was, "go ahead and write." A person of great sensitivity and deep feeling, there is an aura of genius and success around Carson Mc-Cullers. As long as five years has elapsed between her novels (she has written three) and each has been considered to rank high in contemporary literature. She was born in Columbus, Georgia, in 1917. She came to New York to study music with the intention of becoming a concert pianist. Losing her tuition money in the subway she turned to a variety of jobs, studied at Columbia and N.Y.U. at night, had some success in selling short stories with the result of receiving an award from the American Academy of Arts and Letters and twice a Guggenheim fellowship. In 1937 she married Reeves McCullers, also a Southerner.

THE INNOCENTS, by William Archibald, based on Henry James' short novel, "The Turn of the Screw"

Among the new talents the season of 1949-1950 brought to attention, William Archibald's appears to be the most varied. He has been a dancer in Broadway musicals like "One for the Money" and "Two for the Show," and in night clubs and on television. He has been a singer with the Humphrey-Weidman dance group, in night clubs and on television. He has written short stories, and for the theatre has written the book and lyrics of Katherine Dunham's "Carib Song" and the libretto of a ballet opera, "Far Harbor." Many playwrights and scenarists have been tempted by "The Turn of the Screw," but Mr. Archibald's is the first adaptation to reach the New York stage. And, when his playscript was published by Coward-McCann, Inc., Mr. Archibald did the full-page illustrations for the volume. He was born in Trinidad, B. W. I., in 1919 and came to the United States in 1937.

LOST IN THE STARS, by Maxwell Anderson, music by Kurt Weill, based on Alan Paton's novel, "Cry, the Beloved Country"

Maxwell Anderson and Kurt Weill were partners in 1938 when they wrote the memorable "Knickerbocker Holiday." Their sympathetic understanding of human values and problems reached a high pitch in "Lost in the Stars." A third collaboration was cut short during the Winter by the death of Mr. Weill, a great loss to the theatre and music world.

Maxwell Anderson, champion of major playwrights, "Lost in the Stars" being his seventeenth work included in the Best Plays, came from a background that was in no sense theatrical. His father was a Baptist minister in Atlantic, Pa., in 1888, the time of his birth. He went to the University of North Dakota, received his M.A. degree at Stanford where he became a member of the faculty. He wrote editorials for the San Francisco Bulletin before coming to New York where he did newspaper work. His first success was "What Price Glory" written in 1924 with Laurence Stallings.

Kurt Weill, a thorough musician who was equally at home writing atonal symphonic or chamber music and hit tunes for Broadway musicals and a rarity in that he wrote the complete scores and orchestrations for his musicals, was born in 1900 in Dessau, Germany. His father was a cantor. Among his teachers were the famous Humperdinck and Busoni. He achieved early success, his first opera being produced in 1926. The most sensational, "The Three Penny Opera," ran three years in Berlin and long seasons in 150 theatres. He came to this country in 1935 and received his citizenship in 1943. His American successes include "Johnny Johnson," "Lady in the Dark," "One Touch of Venus" and "Street Scene." At the time of his death he had completed five songs for "Twain on the River," a musical version of Mark Twain's Mississippi River stories, in collaboration with Maxwell Anderson.

Alan Paton for the last twelve years has been principal of the Diepkloos Reformatory for delinquent children in Johannesburg. He was born in South Africa and has lectured and written extensively on African race problems. "Cry, the Beloved Country" was his first piece of fiction.

COME BACK, LITTLE SHEBA, by William Inge

Each season's end, *Variety* polls the New York drama critics on various "bests" of the theatrical term. In the category of "most promising" playwright for the 1949-1950 season was William Inge, author of "Come Back, Little Sheba." This was his second play; the first, "Farther Off from Heaven," was produced by Margo Jones in Dallas in 1947.

Inge credits Tennessee Williams' "The Glass Menagerie" for his playwriting impetus. At the time a resident of St. Louis, he saw the Williams drama on a visit to Chicago. "It was the first real experience I had felt in the theatre for years," he said later. "Six months afterward I had completed my first play." "Sheba" is a drama stemming from Inge's own experience, the characters in it being people he has known. He says it is simply an endorsement of Henry Thoreau's conviction that "we all live lives of quiet desperation."

The idea for "Sheba" occurred to Inge several years ago when he was reading a great deal about dream analysis. He first wrote a short story about the reformed alcoholic and the wife who mourns the loss of her dog. In 1948 he wrote it as a one-act play. Shortly thereafter, on the advice of his agents, William Liebling and Audrey Wood, he expanded his one-acter into its present form.

Inge was born in Independence, Kansas, in 1913. He received a B.A. from the University of Kansas, an M.A. from Peabody College, Nashville, Tennessee. For some time he taught with Maude Adams at Stephens College, Columbia, Missouri, and once conducted a small night class in playwriting at Washington University, St. Louis. He was drama, film and music editor for the St. Louis *Star-Times*—a post which led him to see "The Glass Menagerie" in Chicago. He now lives in Connecticut.

THE HAPPY TIME, by Samuel Taylor; adapted from the stories by Robert Fontaine

Of "The Happy Time" Samuel Taylor writes: "This play is not a revision, or a new version, nor did it ever make the rounds of producers in New York. There was a play that Bob Fontaine wrote that went through five or six versions and floated around town for several years, but there is nothing of that play in mine. When I came into the picture I went at my job without reference to anything that had been done before. I took the book (Fontaine's stories) to Maine, wrote the play in three months, sold it to the first person who read it."

Samuel Taylor was born in Chicago in 1912. He grew up in San Francisco, attended the University of California—where he edited the campus humor magazine, *The Pelican*. Coming to New York, he managed his first toe-hold through the help of the late Sidney Howard, who got him a job as a play reader. The job as play reader brought Taylor the opportunity to rewrite "What a Life." George Abbott produced this comedy, and its success led to Taylor's spending nine years in the lucrative radio field, writing more stories about Henry Aldrich and his family. In the Spring of 1950 Taylor went to Europe, with plans to write another play.

Robert Fontaine was born in Marlboro, Mass., and moved to Ottawa with his family when he was 3. His father played the violin and conducted the orchestra at the Dominion Theatre, a vaudeville house. In "The Happy Time" the father is Papa and Robert is Bibi. Robert attended the Ottawa Collegiate Institute. When he was 18 the family moved back to the States. Some ten years after that,

Fontaine was a police reporter on the Washington *Daily News,* and subsequently became a feature writer and radio editor. When he was fired from his radio job he went home to his parents in Springfield, Mass., and began free-lance writing. He has contributed to the humor departments of many magazines and has published 400 short stories. He still lives in Springfield, with his wife and two daughters, and is at work on a new play, "Happiness Is a Woman." Papa— Louis A. Fontaine, 75—has written two songs for the play, and also contributes songs to various radio shows his son writes.

THE WISTERIA TREES, by Joshua Logan, based on Anton Chekhov's "The Cherry Orchard"

Joshua Logan has been steadily branching out in the theatre since he first became an enthusiast of the Princeton Triangle Club and later helped found the University Players on Cape Cod with such members as James Stewart, Henry Fonda, Margaret Sullavan, Myron McCormick and Kent Smith. Mr. Logan first attained distinction on Broadway as a director of "On Borrowed Time," "I Married an Angel," "Knickerbocker Holiday" and other successes. With Gladys Hurlbut he collaborated on writing a musical, "Higher and Higher," but his first great success as an author came when he collaborated with the late Thomas Heggen on the play version of "Mister Roberts." Next Logan collaborated with Oscar Hammerstein II on the libretto of "South Pacific"—which he also staged. Ever since his Princeton days, when he visited Russia one Summer and saw the Moscow Art Theatre, he had been wanting to write a version of "The Cherry Orchard." At one time he contemplated using it as a musical libretto. Then he decided on transplanting the cherry orchard to Louisiana and making it into a wisteria-covered old plantation— with Helen Hayes as the impoverished Chatelaine. Mr. Logan is a Texan.

I KNOW MY LOVE, by S. N. Behrman, adapted from the play *"Auprès de Ma Blonde"* by Marcel Achard

S. N. Behrman is no stranger in these volumes, this being his sixth play in the lists of the Best Ten. The others were: "Brief Moment," 1931; "Biography," 1932; "End of Summer," 1936; "No Time for Comedy," 1939; "Jacobowsky and the Colonel," 1944. His score in Broadway productions starring the Lunts is almost as high, having reached the total of five. It is the second time they have made the Best Ten together. The first was with "The Second Man" produced by The Theatre Guild in 1927. Samuel Nathaniel Behrman was born in Worcester, Mass., in 1893, attended Clark College, then Harvard where he studied under the late George Pierce Baker in the 47 Workshop. He earned his M.A. degree at Columbia University. He wrote his first play, "Bedside Manners," with Kenyon Nicholson in 1923. As a boy he had experimented with vaudeville sketches, even acting in them. He has been a play reader, done theatrical press-agentry, contributed many stories and articles to magazines, written many films for Hollywood and was one of the founders of The Playwrights' Producing Company.

THE ENCHANTED, by Jean Giraudoux; English play by Maurice Valency

Maurice Valency has converted another play by the late French playwright, Jean Giraudoux, into a successful Broadway production. Last season the combination was represented by "The Madwoman of Chaillot." Mr. Valency, who is an associate professor of Comparative Literature at Columbia University, has the ability of keeping the spirit of the original while translating into American idiom. He has written several original plays and one is scheduled for production next season. In addition to "The Enchanted" he wrote the lyrics for a song in the revue, "'Dance Me a Song," last winter.

Giraudoux was born in 1882 and died in 1944, before the production of "The Madwoman" because he refused to have it put on while his country was in the grip of the enemy. One of the most popular novelists and dramatists in France, he had enjoyed success in this country, too. His "Amphitryon 38" was produced by The Theatre Guild in 1937 and Eva Le Gallienne gave a showing to "Siegfried" in 1930. He wrote "Intermezzo," "Judith," "La Machine Infernale" and "Supplement au Voyage de Cook."

CLUTTERBUCK, by Benn W. Levy

It might be enough to say that Benn Levy wrote "Springtime for Henry," that perennial bit of fluff which has been performed so often and in so many places that it has had a large share in keeping Summer theatres, stock companies and certain actors alive. Benn Levy's facility in writing light dialogue was given ample production on Broadway in the 20's and 30's. Clutterbuck is his first play in the U. S. since "If I Were You" in 1938. Mr. Levy was born in London in 1900. He was educated at Repton and University College, Oxford, and wrote his first play while there. It was not produced for five years when he dug out the manuscript while he was managing director of a publishing business.   In contrast, while in this country later, it is in the records that he wrote a play in two weeks, had three running one season, two of them hits, and two the next.   Other plays of his are: "Mrs. Moonlight," "Topaze," "Art and Mrs. Bottle" and "The Devil Passes."   He is said to be shy and hate parties.   His wife is Constance Cummings.   He once said, "A manuscript is something which is more blessed to give than to receive."

PLAYS PRODUCED IN NEW YORK

June 1, 1949—June 3, 1950

(Plays marked "continued" were still playing on June 3, 1950)

CABALGATA

(76 performances)

Spanish musical cavalcade, produced by S. Hurok at the Broadway Theatre, July 7, 1949.

List of performers—

Carmen Vasquez
Pepita Marco
Floriana Alba
Pilar Calvo
Aurea Reyes
Jose Toledano
Paco Fernandez
Julio Toledo
Sebastian Castro
Fernando Vargas
Miguel Herrero
Rosa de Avila
Enrique Barbera
Victor Torres
Rafael Hernan
Jose Cortes

Manuel Medina
Paco Millet
Violeta Carrillo
Maria Castan
Pepita Durango
Conchita Escobar
Carmen Gamez
Luisa Garcia
Paloma Larios
Zenia Lopez
Teresa Martinez
Catalina Maytorena
Elba Ocaiza
Pepita Ramirez
Gracia Rios
Rocio Santisteban

Malena Telmo
Armonia Villa
Andres Aguirre
Carlos Castro
Gustavo Delgado
Raul Izquierdo
Gustavo Garzon

Guillermo Marin
Fernando Marti
Rene Ochoa
Luis Riestra
Ricardo Solano
Jose Valois
Juan Villarias

Staged by Daniel Cordoba; musical director, Ramon Bastida; settings by Luis Marquez; costumes by Daniel Cordoba; orchestrations by Ramon Bastida; stage manager, Miguel del Castillo.

"Cabalgata"—cavalcade—came to New York after seven years of performances in Spain, Latin America and Western U. S. A. It was an interpretation of Iberian folklore in song, dance and spoken word, organized by Daniel Cordoba in Madrid in 1942.

(Closed September 10, 1949)

MISS LIBERTY

(308 performances)

Musical comedy with book by Robert E. Sherwood and music and lyrics by Irving Berlin, produced by Irving Berlin, Robert E. Sherwood and Moss Hart at the Imperial Theatre, July 15, 1949.

Cast of characters—

Maisie Dell.............Mary McCarty
The Herald Reader.......Rowan Tudor
James Gordon Bennett....Charles Dingle
Horace Miller.............Eddie Albert
Police Captain.........Evans Thornton
The Mayor...........Donald McClelland
French Ambassador.......Emile Renan
Carthwright.............Sid Lawson
Joseph Pulitzer.........Philip Bourneuf
The Sharks...........Forrest Bonshire,
    Allen Knowles, Leonard Claret,
        Robert Pagent
Bartholdi.............Herbert Berghof

The Models........Stephanie Augustine,
        Trudy Deluz, Marilyn Frechette
Monique DuPont..........Allyn McLerie
The Boy....................Tommy Rall
The Girl................Maria Karnilova
The Acrobats.........Virginia Conwell,
        Joseph Milan, Eddie Phillips
Strong Man..............Leonard Claret
The Countess..............Ethel Griffies
A Lover...................Ed Chappel
His Girl................Helene Whitney
A Gendarme................Robert Penn
A Lamplighter....Johnny V. R. Thompson
Another Lamplighter........Tommy Rall
A Socialite...........Marilyn Frechette
An Actress..............Helene Whitney
A Minister.................Ed Chappel
An Admiral...........Robert Patterson
The Boys........Bob Kryl, Ernest Laird
The Mother............Elizabeth Watts
The Policeman..........Evans Thornton

The Brothers............Lewis Bolyard,
David Collyer
The Train....Eddie Phillips, Erik Kristen,
Joseph Milan
Reception Delegation....Dolores Goodman,
Virginia Conwell, Fred Hearn,
Bob Tucker, Allen Knowles
A Maid..................Gloria Patrice
The Dandy................Tommy Rall
Ruby..................Maria Karnilova
A Sailor..................Eddie Phillips
His Girl ....Dolores Goodman
Richard K. Fox......Donald McClelland
The Judge................Erik Kristen
A Policeman............Robert Patterson
Immigration Officer......Evans Thornton
A Boy....................Ernest Laird

Act I.—Scene 1—Printing House
Square. Scene 2—Bartholdi's studio,
Paris. Scene 3—Bennett's office. Scene
4—Under a Paris bridge. Act II.—Scene
1—Cabin on the RMS *Aurania*. Scene 2—
The waterfront. Scene 3—North River
dock. Scene 4—On tour. Scene 5—Salon
in the Fifth Avenue Hotel. Scene 6—
Walhalla Hall (the Policemen's Ball).
Scene 7—Castle Garden. Scene 8—Finale.

Book staged by Moss Hart; dances and
musical numbers staged by Jerome Robbins; settings by Oliver Smith; costumes
by Motley; orchestrations by Don Walker;
musical director, Jay Blackton; stage
managers, Terence J. Little and Francis
Spencer.

Principal items of the plot include: a
New York newspaper circulation war
between James Gordon Bennett and Joseph
Pulitzer; the impending dedication of the
Statue of Liberty; a young photographer
who discovers in Paris a girl whom he
believes to have been Bartholdi's model
for the statue, and the girl's raffish old
mother. The finale is Mr. Berlin's musical
setting for the Emma Lazarus poem, "Give
Me your Tired, Your Poor," which is
carved on the base of the Statue of
Liberty.

Principal musical numbers: Act I.—"A
Little Fish in a Big Pond"; "Let's Take
an Old-Fashioned Walk"; "Homework";
"Just One Way to Say I Love You."
Act II.—"The Train"; "You Can Have
Him"; "Me and My Bundle"; "Give Me
Your Tired, Your Poor."

(Closed April 8, 1950)

KEN MURRAY'S BLACKOUTS OF 1949

(51 performances)

A vaudeville revue, produced by Ken
Murray and David W. Siegel at the
Ziegfeld Theatre, September 6, 1949.
Music and lyrics by Charles Henderson
and Ray Foster; settings by Ben Tipton.

List of players—

Nick Lucas
Pat Williams
George Burton
Owen McGiveney
D'Vaughn Pershing
Jack Mulhall
Harris & Shore
Les Zoris
Peg Leg Bates
Shelton Brooks
Charles Nelson
Alphonse Berge

Dot Remy
Elizabeth Walters
Irene Kaye
Crystal White
Hightower & Ross
Al Mardo
Danny Duncan
Danny Alexander
Joe Wong
Mabel Butterworth
Milton Charleston

Mr. Murray's vaudeville show ran for
more than seven years in Hollywood.
With a New York television contract in
the offing, Mr. Murray and Mr. Siegel
brought their show to the Ziegfeld to open
the Fall theatrical season in New York.
The entertainment consisted of variety
turns—among them such old favorites as
Nick Lucas' singing and Owen Mc-
Giveney's protean performance of "Oliver
Twist"—plus the decorative qualities of
several pretty girls. The run at the
Ziegfeld was a disappointment to Mr.
Murray, who acted as master of ceremonies.

(Closed October 15, 1949)

TWELFTH NIGHT

(46 performances)

Comedy by William Shakespeare, in
two parts, produced by Roger Stevens at
the Empire Theatre, October 3, 1949.

Cast of characters—

Orsino, Duke of Illyria....Henry Branden
Curio..................Robert Hartung
Valentine................Michael Wyler
Viola....................Frances Reid

Sea Captain........Tom Emlyn Williams
First Sailor..............Winston Ross
Second Sailor..............Paul Menard
Sir Toby Belch........Carl Benton Reid
Maria....................Ruth Enders
Sir Andrew Aguecheek....Philip Tonge
Feste....................Harry Townes
Olivia......................Nina Foch
Malvolio..................Arnold Moss

First Lady in Waiting..Sally Chamberlain
Second Lady in Waiting....Helen Marcy
Sebastian.............William Bromfield
Antonio.................Walter Klavun
Fabian...................Truman Smith
First Officer.............Winston Ross
Second Officer.............Paul Menard
A Priest...........Tom Emlyn Williams

Staged by Valentine Windt; setting and
costumes by Louis Kennel; stage manager,
John Paul.

Being one of the Bard's lesser pranks,
"Twelfth Night" is not often seen on
Broadway, although the role of Viola is
a tempting one for reasonably stream-
lined stars. Beginning October 15, 1930,

Jane Cowl gave it for 65 performances at
Maxine Elliott's Theatre. It was a scenic
novelty in which Feste, the clown, changed
the scenes by turning the pages of an
immense book. Beginning November 19,
1940, Helen Hayes played Viola 129 times
at the St. James Theatre, with Maurice
Evans as her co-star in the role of
Malvolio.

This most recent production of "Twelfth
Night" originated in May, 1949, at the
Ann Arbor, Mich., Drama Festival. Roger
Stevens, a wealthy theatre patron, saw
it there and deemed it worthy of trans-
porting to New York.

(Closed November 12, 1949)

YES, M' LORD

(87 performances)

Comedy in three acts by W. Douglas
Home, produced by Lee and J. J. Shubert
and Linnit & Dunfee, Ltd. at the Booth
Theatre, October 4, 1949.

Cast of characters—
The Earl of Lister (Lord Lieutenant)
                        A. E. Matthews
The Countess of Lister.....Mary Hinton
June Farrell..............Elaine Stritch
Bessie.....................Diane Hart
Beecham.................George Curzon
Lord Pym..................Hugh Kelly
Lady Caroline Smith.......Gladys Boot
Mr. Cleghorn...........Tom Macaulay

The scene is a sitting-room at the Earl
of Lister's ancestral castle in England.
Act I.—Scene 1—The day after the general elections, Summer, 1945. Scene 2—
The following morning. Act II.—Scene
1—Saturday evening of the following week

end. Scene 2—The by-election. Morning
of nomination day. Act III.—Scene 1—
Lunch time, two weeks later. The by-
election result day. Scene 2—After dinner
that evening.

Staged by Colin Chandler; costumes and
setting by Edward Gilbert; stage manager, Philipa Hastings.

The Earl of Lister is an old gentleman
who has retired from politics and is concerned with the problem of keeping up
a huge castle with only two servants. But
there is plenty of politics around. The
Earl's son, Lord Pym, runs for election
on the Labour ticket and is defeated by
the Earl's butler, Beecham, a Conservative.

(During the run of the comedy, on Nov.
22, 1949, A. E. Matthews was given a
reception at the Hotel Astor by the producers in celebration of his eightieth birthday.)

(Closed December 18, 1949)

GILBERT AND SULLIVAN REPERTORY

(24 performances)

"The Mikado," "The Pirates of Penzance" and the double bill of "Trial by
Jury" and "H.M.S. Pinafore" were presented for one week each by S. M. Chartock at the Mark Hellinger Theatre, beginning October 4, 1949.

Cast of "The Mikado"—
Nanki-Poo................Morton Bowe
Pish-Tush.............Earle MacVeigh
Pooh-Bah.................Robert Eckles
Ko-Ko.....................Ralph Riggs
Yum-Yum.............Kathleen Roche
Pitti-Sing...............Beverly Janis
Peep-Bo.................Elaine Malbin
The Mikado of Japan....Joseph Macaulay
Katisha..................Jean Handzlik

Go-To.................Craig Timberlake

Cast of "The Pirates"—
Samuel.................Earle MacVeigh
Frederic..................Morton Bowe
Ruth ....Jean Handzlik
Richard.................Joseph Macaulay
Kate.....................Beverly Janis
Edith....................Elaine Malbin
Isabel.....................Marie Petek
Mabel.................Kathleen Roche
Major-General Stanley.......Ralph Riggs
Edward..................Robert Eckles

Cast of "Trial by Jury"—
Usher....................Robert Eckles
Defendant................Morton Bowe

Judge......................Ralph Riggs
Counsel.................Earle MacVeigh
Barrister..............Howard Andriola
1st Bridesmaid............Joyce Carroll
2nd Bridesmaid............Marie Petek
3rd Bridesmaid...........Natalye Green
Foreman of the Jury....Craig Timberlake
Plaintiff.................Elaine Malbin

Cast of "Pinafore"—

Little Buttercup..........Jean Handzlik
Tommie Tucker.............Marie Petek
Bill Bobstay..............Robert Eckles

Dick Deadeye.........Joseph Macaulay
Ralph Rackstraw..........Morton Bowe
Capt. Corcoran.........Earle MacVeigh
Josephine................Kathleen Roche
Sir Joseph Porter..........Ralph Riggs
Cousin Hebe..............Beverly Janis
Bob Beckett...........Craig Timberlake

Staged by S. M. Chartock; settings by Ralph Alswang, costumes by Peggy Morrison; production manager, Lewis Pierce.

(Closed October 22, 1949)

THE BROWNING VERSION and HARLEQUINADE

(69 performances)

Two one-act plays by Terence Rattigan. Produced by Maurice Evans at the Coronet Theatre, October 12, 1949.

Cast of characters in "The Browning Version"—

John Taplow.........Peter Scott-Smith
Frank Hunter..............Ron Randell
Millie Crocker-Harris..........Edna Best
Andrew Crocker-Harris....Maurice Evans
Dr. Frobisher.............Louis Hector
Peter Gilbert.........Frederick Bradlee
Mrs. Gilbert..............Patrica Wheel

The scene is the sitting-room of Crocker-Harris in a private school in the south of England.

Cast of characters in "Harlequinade"—

Arthur Gosport..........Maurice Evans
Edna Selby..................Edna Best
Johnny................Bertram Tanswell
Dame Maud Gosport......Bertha Belmore
Jack Wakefield.............Ron Randell
George Chudleigh.......Harry Sothern
First Halberdier........Peter Scott-Smith
Second Halberdier....Tom Hughes Sand
Miss Fishlock............Olive Blakeney

Fred Ingram.........Frederick Bradlee
Muriel Palmer.............Eileen Page
Tom Palmer..............Peter Martyn
Mr. Burton................Louis Hector
Joyce Langland.........Patricia Wheel

The scene is a theatre stage in a Midlands town.

Staged by Peter Glenville; settings by Frederick Stover; costumes by David Ffolkes; stage manager, Ralph Edington.

The first playlet concerns Andrew Crocker-Harris, a teacher of Greek. He is ailing and embittered. He has been discharged, he knows that his wife, Millie, is unfaithful, and he has lost the respect of his students. When one boy, John Taplow, gives him a copy of a Browning version of a Greek drama as an act of esteem and affection, Crocker-Harris is deeply moved and finds renewed faith in himself.

In "Harlequinade" Arthur Gosport and Edna Selby are a middle-aged acting team who are rehearsing "Romeo and Juliet." It is a very light comedy about backstage life.

(Closed December 10, 1949)

TOUCH AND GO

(176 performances)

Revue in two acts, with sketches and lyrics by Jean and Walter Kerr and music by Jay Gorney. Produced by George Abbott at the Broadhurst Theatre, October 13, 1949.

The list of players—

Kyle MacDonnell
Dick Sykes
Jonathan Lucas
Daniel Nagrin
Mary Anthony
Eleanor Boleyn
Art Carroll

Lydia Fredericks
Arlyne Frank
Nat Frey
Pearl Hacker
Nancy Andrews
Muriel O'Malley
Helen Gallagher

David Lober
Greb Lober
Ilona Murrai
Carl Nicholas
Ray Page
Beverly Purvin
Merritt Thompson
Dorothy Scott
George Hall
Peggy Cass

Pearl Lang
Lewis Nye
Richard Reed
George Reich
Larry Robbins
William Sumner
Beverly Tassoni
Bobby Trelease
Parker Wilson
Mara Lynn

Staged by Walter Kerr; sets by John Robert Lloyd; dances by Helen Tamiris; musical director, Antonio Morelli; lighting by Peggy Clark; stage manager, Robert E. Griffith.

Principal sketches: Act I.—"Gorilla Girl," "Disenchantment," "Easy Does It," "Great Dane a-Comin'." Act II.—"What It was Really Like," "Cinderella."

Principal song numbers: Act I.—"This Had Better Be Love," "Be a Mess." Act II.—"Wish Me Luck," "Miss Platt Selects Mate."

This revue originated at Catholic University, Washington, D. C., where Mr. and Mrs. Kerr are members of the faculty. It was done there by a student company. On Broadway, with a Broadway company, it was greeted warmly by many reviewers, who found it fresh and intelligent, and a good successor to such recent revues as "Lend an Ear," "Make Mine Manhattan" and "Call Me Mister."

(Closed March 18, 1950)

MONTSERRAT

(65 performances)

Play in two acts by Lillian Hellman, adapted from the French play of the same title by Emmanuel Roblès. Produced by Kermit Bloomgarden and Gilbert Miller at the Fulton Theatre, October 29, 1949.

Cast of characters—

Zavala	Richard Malek
Antonanzas	Nehemiah Persoff
Soldier	Stefan Gierasch
Montserrat	William Redfield
Morales	Gregory Morton
Izquierdo	Emlyn Williams
Father Coronil	Francis Compton
Salas Ina	Reinhold Schunzel
Luhan	William Hansen
Matilde	Vivian Nathan
Juan Salcedo Alvarez	John Abbott
Felisa	Julie Harris
Ricardo	George Bartinieff
Monk	Edward Groag
Monk	Kurt Kasznar
Soldier	Robert Crawley
Lieutenant	Stephen Lawrence

The scene is the outer room of the General's palace during the Spanish occupation of Valencia, Venezuela, in 1812. The action is continuous.

Staged by Lillian Hellman; setting by Howard Bay; costumes by Irene Sharaff; stage manager, Del Hughes.

Izquierdo, commanding officer of the Spanish troops at the General's headquarters, is in pursuit of Simon Bolivar, the South American rebel and patriot. Bolivar has barely eluded a trap, having been warned by a disloyal Spanish officer. Izquierdo discovers that this officer is a young aristocrat, Montserrat, and determines to torture Montserrat into revealing Bolivar's hiding place. The torture is mental and spiritual, not physical—for Izquierdo rounds up at random six innocent Valencians—two women and four men—and announces that they will be shot if they cannot make Montserrat give up his secret. Montserrat will not talk, and they are shot, one by one.

(Closed December 24, 1949)

LOST IN THE STARS

(250 performances)
(Continued)

Musical tragedy in two acts, based on Alan Paton's novel, "Cry, the Beloved Country," produced by the Playwrights' Company at the Music Box, October 30, 1949. Words by Maxwell Anderson; music by Kurt Weill.

Cast of characters—

Leader	Frank Roane
Answerer	Joseph James
Nita	Elayne Richards
Grace Kumalo	Gertrude Jeannette
Stephen Kumalo	Todd Duncan
The Young Man	Lavern French
The Young Woman	Mabel Hart
James Jarvis	Leslie Banks
Edward Jarvis	Judson Rees
Arthur Jarvis	John Morley
John Kumalo	Warren Coleman
Paulus	Charles McRae
William	Roy Allen
Jared	William C. Smith
Alex	Herbert Coleman
Foreman	Jerome Shaw
Mrs. M'kize	Georgette Harvey
Hlabeni	William Marshall
Eland	Charles Grunwell
Linda	Sheila Guyse
Johannes Pafuri	Van Prince
Matthew Kumalo	William Greaves
Absalom Kumalo	Julian Mayfield
Rose	Gloria Smith
Irina	Inez Matthews
Policeman	Robert Byrn
White Woman	Biruta Ramoska
White Man	Mark Kramer

The Guard...............Jerome Shaw
Burton.................John W. Stanley
The Judge...............Guy Spaull
Villager...............Robert McFerrin

Singers: Sibol Cain, Alma Hubbard, Elen Longone, June McMechen, Biruta Ramoska, Christine Spencer, Constance Stokes, Lucretia West, LaCoste Brown, Robert Byrn, Joseph Crawford, Russell George, Joseph James, Mark Kramer, Moses LaMar, Paul Mario, Robert McFerrin, William C. Smith and Joseph Theard.

The time is the present. Act I depicts, in twelve scenes, various locations in Ndotsheni, a small village in South Africa,

and in the city of Johannesburg, including Stephen Kumalo's home, the railroad station, a tobacco shop, Mrs. M'Kize's house, Hlabeni's house, a Shantytown lodging, a dive in Shantytown, Irina's hut in Shantytown, Arthur Jarvis' home, and the prison. Act II includes the tobacco shop, Arthur Jarvis' doorway, Irina's hut, a courtroom, a prison cell, Stephen's chapel and Stephen's home.

Staged by Rouben Mamoulian; settings by George Jenkins; Johannesburg backdrop by Horace Armistead; orchestrations by Kurt Weill; costumes by Anna Hill Johnstone.

REGINA

(56 performances)

Musical drama produced by Cheryl Crawford in association with Clinton Wilder at the 46th Street Theatre, October 31, 1949. Libretto and music by Marc Blitzstein; libretto based on Lillian Hellman's play, "The Little Foxes."

Cast of characters—

Addie....................Lillyn Brown
Cal....................William Warfield
Alexandra Giddens......Priscilla Gillette
Chinkypin...............Philip Hepburn
Jazz.........William Dillard (trumpet)
Angel Band.....Bernard Addison (banjo)
                Buster Bailey (clarinet)
                Rudy Nichols (traps)
                Benny Morton (trombone)
Regina Giddens............Jane Pickens
Birdie Hubbard...........Brenda Lewis
Oscar Hubbard...........David Thomas
Leo Hubbard.............Russell Nype
Marshall................Donald Clarke
Ben Hubbard.............George Lipton
Belle.................Clarisse Crawford
Pianist..................Marion Carley
Violinist...............Alfred Bruning
Horace Giddens......William Wilderman
Manders.................Lee Sweetland
Ethelinda................Peggy Turnley

Townspeople: Ellen Carleen, Earl McDonald, Robert Anderson, Kay Borron, Kayton Nesbitt, Sara Carter, Keith Davis, Barbara Moser, Karl Brock, Isabelle Felder, Derek MacDermot.
Dancers: Misses Wana Allison, Joan

Engel, Barbara Ferguson, Kate Friedlich, Gisella Weidner, Onna White. Messrs. Leo Guerard, Robert Hanlin, Regis Powers, Boris Runanin, Walter Stane, John Ward.

Prologue.—Late morning in Spring, 1900. The Veranda of the Giddens home in Bowden, Alabama. Act I.—Scene 1— Living room of the Giddens home, same evening. Scene 2—The same, a week later. Scene 3—The ballroom and the veranda, later the same night. Act II.— The living room, the next afternoon.

Staged by Robert Lewis; sets by Horace Armistead; costumes by Aline Bernstein; dances by Anna Sokolow; orchestrations by Marc Blitzstein; musical conductor Maurice Abravanel; stage manager, Jules Racine.

Mr. Blitzstein's work was, in effect, an opera, and there were no set musical numbers as in a musical comedy. It was reviewed by both drama and music critics and got "mixed" notices—but the music critics seemed to regard it more highly than did the playgoers. When "Regina" closed, a commercial failure, Producer Cheryl Crawford said that it was ahead of its time, and would be reviewed some day and become a success. Much interest was attached to the work of Jane Pickens, a radio and night club singer, in the role made famous on the stage by Tallulah Bankhead.

(Closed December 16, 1949)

I KNOW MY LOVE

(246 performances)

A comedy in three acts by S. N. Behrman, adapted from the French "Auprès de Ma Blonde," by Marcel Achard. Produced by the Theatre Guild and John C. Wilson at the Shubert Theatre, November 2, 1949

Cast of characters—

Lucy.....................Esther Mitchell
William............William Le Massena
Reilly...................Charles Bowden
Frederic Chanler.........Geoffrey Kerr
Nicola Ballard.........Betty Caulfield
Claire Ballard...........Katharine Bard
Nicholas Ballard.........Thomas Palmer
Blanche Chanler............Doreen Lang
Eugene Chanler............Allen Martin
Katie....................Mary Fickett
Louise....................Renee Orsell
Thomas Chanler...........Alfred Lunt
Emily Chanler............Lynn Fontanne
First Photographer..........Roy Johnson
Second Photographer.....Sandy Campbell
Jerome Talbot...............Noel Leslie
Agnes..............Lily Kemble-Cooper
Fuller....................J. P. Wilson
Richard Chanler..........Henry Barnard
Daniel Talbot............Hugh Franklin
Eleanor Peabody (Sissy)...Anne Sargent

The setting is the Chanler drawing room in an old Boston mansion. Act I.—January, 1939. Act II.—Scene 1—Christmas, 1888 (before Tom Chanler marries Emily Talbot). Scene 2—May, 1902. Act III.—Scene 1—July, 1918. Scene 2—December, 1920.

Staged by Alfred Lunt; settings, lighting and costumes by Stewart Chaney; stage manager, Charva Chester.

Thomas and Emily Chanler are discovered celebrating their fiftieth wedding anniversary, among their children and other relatives. Then the story cuts back to the days of their courtship, and follows them through the domestic, business and family crises of the ensuing years. When, in 1920, Tom has a middle-aged man's urge to stray, Emily recaptures him with wisdom and understanding.

(Closed June 3, 1950)

LOVE ME LONG

(16 performances)

A comedy in three acts by Doris Frankel. Produced by Brock Pemberton at the 48th Street Theatre, November 7, 1949.

Cast of characters—

Abby Quinn...............Shirley Booth
Mr. Sharp..............Harry Bannister
Jim Kennedy............Russell Hardie
Moving Man..................Carl Low
Ike Skinner...............George Keane
Louise Ulmer..........Jennifer Howard
Margaret Anderson........Anne Jackson
Phone Man........Heywood Hale Broun
Cleotus P. Anderson........Daniel Reed

The scene is the fourth-floor apartment of a remodeled house overlooking the East River. Act I.—Scene 1—A Saturday afternoon in the Fall. Scene 2—A few hours later. Act II.—Saturday night. Act III.—Sunday morning.

Staged by Margaret Perry and Brock Pemberton; setting by John Root; costumes supervised by Margaret Pemberton; stage manager, Paul A. Foley.

Abby Quinn and Jim Kennedy, who are to be married, move into an apartment. Ike Skinner and Margaret Anderson, who also are to be married, move into the same place. Abby and Ike used to be married to each other and find they are still in love. Also, Jim finds he liked Margaret better than he does Abby. This one took a beating from the critics as an unfunny rehash of Noel Coward's "Private Lives."

(Closed November 19, 1949)

THE FATHER

(69 performances)

Drama in three acts by August Strindberg, in an English version by Robert L. Joseph, produced by Richard W. Krakeur and Robert L. Joseph at the Cort Theatre, November 16, 1949.

Cast of characters—

A Captain of Cavalry....Raymond Massey
A Soldier................Charles Snyder
The Pastor.............Philip Huston
Another Soldier...........Paul Larson
The Captain's Wife......Mady Christians
The Doctor...........John D. Seymour
The Nurse..................Mary Morris
The Captain's Daughter......Grace Kelly

The scene is the Captain's house at an army post in the north of Sweden. Time, 1887. Act I.—Evening. Act II.—Late that night. Act III.—Next afternoon.

Staged by Raymond Massey; setting by Donald Oenslager; costumes by Eleanor Goldsmith; stage manager, Elmer Brown.

Strindberg's violent anti-woman drama had not been done locally for twenty years. In October, 1949, it was given a rather successful off-Broadway performance by Studio 7 at the Provincetown Playhouse, with Ward Costello and Anne Shropshire as the husband and wife. Mr. Massey had been contemplating his own performance since early in the Summer of 1949.

(Closed January 14, 1950)

THAT LADY

(78 performances)

Romantic drama in three acts by Kate O'Brien, produced by Katharine Cornell at the Martin Beck Theatre, November 22, 1949. Adapted from Miss O'Brien's Novel, "For One Sweet Grape."

Cast of characters—

Rodrigo, Duke of Pastrana
                              Douglas Watson
Anichu....................Jada Rowland
Bernardina Cavero......Esther Minciotti
Pablo.....................Peter Barno
Juan de Escovedo.....Joseph Wiseman
Another Footman........Anthony Radecki
Philip II, King of Spain....Henry Daniell
Ana de Mendoza y De Gomez,
    Princess of Eboli....Katharine Cornell
Antonio Perez............Torin Thatcher
Cardinal Gaspar de Quiroga
                              Henry Stephenson
Esteban.................Richard Sterling
Paca.....................Lita Dal Porto
Don Mateo Vasquez........Will Kuluva
King's Footman........Wallace Chadwell
Manuel Ortega.........David J. Stewart
Anichu, at 18, Countess of Pastrana
                              Marian Seldes
A Doctor...................Oliver Cliff

Act I.—Scene 1—A drawing room in the Eboli Palace, Madrid, September, 1577. Scene 2—The King's workroom, in the Alcazar, Madrid. Midnight, four months later. Scene 3—Ana de Mendoza's bedroom, Eboli Palace. A few nights later. Act II.—Scene 1—The drawing room, eight months later. October, 1578. Scene 2—The King's workroom, nine months later. Scene 3—The drawing room, two weeks later. Act III.—Scene 1—The King's workroom, eighteen months later. January, 1581. Scene 2—The bedroom, two weeks later. Scene 3—The drawing room, nine years later. April, 1590. Scene 4—The same, a week later.

Staged by Guthrie McClintic; settings and costumes by Rolf Gérard; stage manager, James Nielson.

In the reign of King Philip II of Spain, the widowed Princess of Eboli finds that a casual assignation with Antonio Perez, the Secretary of State, has resulted in true love on both sides. This love endures in spite of the King's jealousy and in spite of imprisonment and torture. When Perez escapes from Spain, with his paramour's help, she is content to allow the King to wall her up in her own castle, in total darkness. This fate is only half as bad as it sounds, because the Princess lost one eye at the age of fourteen in a dueling accident, and ever since then has worn a black patch.

(Closed January 28, 1950)

TEXAS, LI'L DARLIN'

(221 performances)
(Continued)

Musical comedy in two acts, produced by Studio Productions, Inc., and Anthony Brady Farrell Productions at the Mark Hellinger Theatre, November 25, 1949. Book by John Whedon and Sam Moore; music by Robert Emmett Dolan; lyrics by Johnny Mercer.

Cast of characters—

Harvey Small..............Loring Smith
John Baxter Trumbull......Charles Bang
Parker Stuart Eliot........Alden Aldrich
William Dean Benson, Jr...Edward Platt
Frothingham Fry.........Ned Wertimer
Brewster Ames II........Fredd Wayne
The Three Coyotes:
                   The Texas Rhythm Boys
Bunkhouse...............Eddy Smith
Muleshoes................Bill Horan
Fred...................Joel McConkey
Hominy Smith..........Kenny Delmar
Dogie Smith...........Betty Lou Keim
Amos Hall.............Dante Di Paolo
Sherm................Cameron Andrews
Duane Fawcett.........William Ambler
Branch Pedley................Ray Long
Delia Pratt............Ronnie Hartmann
Red......................Merrill Hilton
Jo Ann Woods...........Elyse Weber
Calico Munson...........Dorothy Love
Rebecca Bass..................Carol Lee
Sally Tucket............Ruth Ostrander
Sue Crocket..............Doris Schmitt
Sarah Boone..............Arleen Ethane
Belle Cooper.............Yvonne Tibor
Dallas Smith.............Mary Hatcher
Easy Jones................Danny Scholl
Sam.......................Jared Reed
Melissa Tatum............Kate Murtah
Three Little Maids........Elyse Weber,
                    Carol Lee, Dorothy Love
Three Prospectors.......Elliott Martin,
                    Edmund Hall, Carl Conway
Stan.....................Edmund Hall
Herb...................Ralph Patterson
Jack Prow.................Bob Bernard

Harry Stern..............Joey Thomas
Cowboys.....................Ray Long,
        Dante Di Paolo, Merrill Hilton
Oil Workers..............Jack Purcell,
            Carol Lee, Tommy Maier
Drum Majorette.......Jacqueline James
Cheer Leader..............Elyse Weber
Football Player...........Edmund Hall
Texas Rangers...........Charles Bang,
        Ralph Patterson, Edward Platt,
                    William Ambler
Voice of "Trend".........Edward Platt
"Trend" Secretaries....Jacqueline James,
        Ronnie Hartmann, Elyse Weber,
            Dorothy Mary Richards,
            Marion Lauer, B. J. Keating
Guard.......................Ray Long
Radio Announcer.........Charles Bang
Engineer.................Alden Aldrich
Joe Raker..............Cameron Andrews
Neighbors................Elliott Martin,
        Patricia Jennings, Carl Conway,
    Lloyd Knight, Jo Gibson, Muriel Bullis

Staged by Paul Crabtree; dances by Al White, Jr.; sets by Theodore Cooper; costumes by Eleanor Goldsmith; musical director, Will Irwin; orchestrations by Robert Russell Bennett; production manager, Herbert Brodkin.

Hominy Smith is a grassroots politician who keeps getting elected in Texas by employing a singing daughter, singing cowboys and a homespun if not actually unwashed personal appearance. He is opposed by Easy Jones, a young war veteran. Harvey Small, a New York picture magazine publisher, becomes interested in Hominy as possible Presidential timber.

Principal musical numbers: "Whoopin' and a-Hollerin' "; "Texas, Li'l Darlin' "; "They Talk a Different Language"; "A Month of Sundays"; "Down in the Valley"; "Hootin' Owl Trail"; "The Big Movie Show in the Sky"; "Take a Crank Letter"; "Politics"; Affable, Balding Me."

THE CLOSING DOOR

(22 performances)

Melodrama in two acts by Alexander Knox, produced by Cheryl Crawford at the Empire Theatre, December 1, 1949.

Cast of characters—

Norma Trahern............Doris Nolan
David Trahern...........Jack Dimond
Connie...................Jo Van Fleet
Vail Trahern..........Alexander Knox
Ollie Stevenson...........John Shellie
Grandma..................Eva Condon
Doctor Ed Harriman.....Richard Derr
Basil Johnson.........Ronald Alexander
Don...................Randolph Echols
Hector Trahern..........Alan Norman
Guard.................Lonny Chapman

The setting is the living room of Vail Trahern's apartment. Act I.—Scene 1—Noon. Scene 2—Four-thirty P.M. Scene 3—Fifteen minutes later. Act II.—No lapse of time.

Staged by Lee Strasberg; set by Paul Morison; costumes by Robert Stevenson; stage manager, Henry Martin.

Vail Trahern is going insane, and his wife knows it. But Vail is a foxy maniac and he avoids being taken to a hospital until the play is over. Many of the New York reviewers seemed to think that both Vail and the state of the drama would have been better had he been a good boy and gone to the hospital right away.

(Closed December 17, 1949)

CLUTTERBUCK

(210 performances)
(Continued)

Comedy in three acts by Benn W. Levy, produced by Irving L. Jacobs in association with David Merrick at the Biltmore Theatre, December 3, 1949.

Cast of characters—

Julian Pugh..............Tom Helmore
Arthur Pomfret.......Arthur Margetson
Deborah Pomfret............Ruth Ford
Jane Pugh................Ruth Matteson
Clutterbuck............Charles Campbell

Waiter................Tom Chung Yun
Melissa.................Claire Carleton

Act I.—The deck of a luxury liner. Act II.—Ashore: outside the Hotel Palais Nacionale. Act III.—Back on deck, early next morning.

Staged by Norris Houghton; settings by Samuel Leve; costumes supervised by Alvin Colt; stage manager, Peter Xantho.

See page 322.

METROPOLE

(2 performances)

Comedy in three acts by William Walden, produced by Max Gordon at the Lyceum Theatre, December 6, 1949.

Cast of characters—

Fanner	John Glendinning
Miss Merriam	Frances Waller
Stumm	Henry Jones
Frederick M. Hill	Lee Tracy
Mrs. Killian	Jane Seymour
Curtis	Reed Brown, Jr.
Miss Harrington	Edith Atwater
Lois Dantine	Jean Carson
Carpenter	Burton Lewis
Mr. Young	Malcolm Lee Beggs
Crowell	Reynolds Evans
Ellington	Royal Dano
Carolyn Hopewell	Arlene Francis
Furniture Movers	George Cotton, Lee Parry

The scene is the office of Frederick M. Hill, editor-in-chief of *Metropole.* Act I.—An afternoon in Spring. Act II.—A month later. Act III.—The following day.

Staged by George S. Kaufman; setting by Edward Gilbert; costumes by Bianca Stroock; stage manager, Randell Henderson.

The character of editor Frederick M. Hill was based, according to gossip, on the personality of Harold Ross, editor of *The New Yorker.* Mr. Hill, tempestuous and temperamental, surmounts many troubles, including ex-wives, weird staff members, the threat of a competing magazine and being frozen out of his own job.

(Closed December 7, 1949)

GENTLEMEN PREFER BLONDES

(204 performances)

(Continued)

Musical comedy in two acts, produced by Herman Levin and Oliver Smith at the Ziegfeld Theatre, December 8, 1949. Book by Joseph Fields and Anita Loos, based on Miss Loos' collection of stories under the same title; music by Jule Styne; lyrics by Leo Robin.

Cast of characters—

Dorothy Shaw	Yvonne Adair
A Steward	Jerry Craig
Lorelei Lee	Carol Channing
Gus Esmond	Jack McCauley
Frank	Robert Cooper
George	Eddie Weston
Sun Bathers	Pat Donohue, Marjorie Winters
Lady Phyllis Beekman	Reta Shaw
Sir Francis Beekman	Rex Evans
Mrs. Ella Spofford	Alice Pearce
Deck Stewards	Bob Burkhardt, Shelton Lewis
Henry Spofford	Eric Brotherson
An Olympic	Curt Stafford
Josephus Gage	George S. Irving
Deck Walkers	Fran Keegan, Junior Standish
Bill	Peter Birch
Gloria Stark	Anita Alvarez
Pierre	Bob Neukum
Taxi Driver	Kazimir Kokic
Leon	Peter Holmes
Robert Lemanteur	Mort Marshall
Louis Lemanteur	Howard Morris
A Flower Girl	Nicole France

Maitre d'Hotel	Crandall Diehl
Zizi	Judy Sinclair
Fifi	Hope Zee
Coles and Atkins	Themselves
The Tenor	William Krach
Policeman	William Diehl
Headwaiter	Kazimir Kokic
Mr. Esmond, Sr.	Irving Mitchell

Show girls: Pat Donahue, Anna Rita Duffy, Fran Keegan, Annette Kohl, Junior Standish, Marjorie Winters.

Singers: Angela Castle, Joan Coburn, Ellen McCown, Candy Montgomery, Judy Sinclair, Lucille Udovick, Beverly Jane Weston, Hope Zee, Bob Burkhardt, Jerry Craig, William Diehl, William Krach, Shelton Lewis, Bob Neukum, Curt Stafford, David Vogel.

Dancers: Suzanne Ames, Florence Baum, Nicole France, Pauline Goddard, Patty Ann Jackson, Alicia Krug, Mary Martinet, Caren Preiss, Evelyn Taylor, Norma Thornton, Polly Ward, Prue Ward, Helen Wood, Charles Basile, Bill Bradley, Rex Cooper, Robert Cooper, Crandall Diehl, Aristide, J. Ginoulias, Peter Holmes, John Laverty, Eddie Weston.

The time is 1924. Scenes in Act I include the French Line pier, New York; the sun deck and boat deck on the *Ile de France;* Lorelei's boat suite; the Place Vendôme, Paris, under the Eiffel Tower, and the Ritz Hotel, Paris. Scenes in

Act II include the Pré-Catelan Cafe, a Paris street, the Ritz again, and the Central Park Casino, New York.

Staged by John C. Wilson; sets by Oliver Smith; costumes by Miles White; musical director, Milton Rosenstock; musical arrangements by Don Walker; vocal direction and arrangements by Hugh Martin; general stage manager, Frank Coletti; music for dances arranged by Trude Rittman.

Principal musical numbers: Act I.—"It's High Time"; "Bye, Bye Baby"; "A Little Girl from Little Rock"; "I Love What I'm Doing"; "Just a Kiss Apart"; "It's Delightful Down in Chile"; "Sunshine"; "I'm A'Tingle, I'm A'Glow"; "House on Rittenhouse Square"; "You Say You Care." Act II.—"Mamie Is Mimi"; "Diamonds Are a Girl's Best Friend"; "Gentlemen Prefer Blondes"; "Homesick Blues"; "Keeping Cool with Coolidge"; "Button Up with Esmond."

CAESAR AND CLEOPATRA

(149 performances)

Comedy by Bernard Shaw, revived by Richard Aldrich and Richard Myers in association with Julius Fleischmann at the National Theatre, December 21, 1949.

Cast of characters—

Caesar................Cedric Hardwicke
Cleopatra..................Lilli Palmer
Nubian Slave..........Robert Earl Jones
Ftatateeta...............Bertha Belmore
Centurion.................Ronald Telfer
Pothinus..................Nicholas Joy
Theodotus................Ivan Simpson
Ptolemy..................Donny Harris
Achillas.................Michael Harvey
Belzanor................Norman Roland
A Persian..................Jules Getlin
Rufio......................Ralph Forbes
Britannus.............Arthur Treacher
Lucius Septimus.............Si Oakland

Roman Sentinel........Clifford Carpenter
Apollodorus...........John Buckmaster
Porter...............Robert Earl Jones
First Auxiliary Sentinel...Andrew George
Second Auxiliary Sentinel....Jules Getlin
Boatman.................Norman Roland
Harpmaster...............Harry Irvine
Iras.....................Julann Caffrey
Charmian..................Mary Scott
First Palace Official........Ronald Telfer
Second Palace Official.......John Ware
Major-Domo...........Anthony Randall
Priest....................Harry Irvine

Staged by Cedric Hardwicke; settings and costumes by Rolf Gérard; lighting by Jean Rosenthal; incidental music by Irma Jurist; stage manager, John Effrat.

(Closed April 29, 1950)

THE RAT RACE

(84 performances)

Play in two acts by Garson Kanin, produced by Leland Hayward at the Ethel Barrymore Theatre, December 22, 1949.

Cast of characters—

Mac....................Joseph Sweeney
Helen Brown..............Betty Field
Soda....................Doro Merande
Artie Bray..............Rex Williams
The Telephone Man.......Ray Walston
Gus Hammer.............Barry Nelson
Bo Kerry................Pat Harrington
Edie Kerry.............Dennie Moore
Frankie Jay.............Joe Bushkin
Tip.....................Sherman Kane
Carl....................Georgie Auld
Carl's Girl...............Toni Tucci
Ralph....................Hal Green
Artie's Man................Lou Oles
Police Department.......David Edelman
Policeman................Paul Shiers
The Waiter.........Joseph E Bernard
The Neighbors............Johnny Dale,
                          Belle Flower

The time is Summer. The place is a rooming house in "a piece of Manhattan." The action is continuous, with one intermission.

Staged by Garson Kanin; setting by Donald Oenslager; clothes by Lucinda Ballard and Joseph Fretwell III; stage manager, Paul Shiers.

Helen Brown, who once won a beauty contest in her home town, came to New York to conquer Broadway—but that was a long time ago; now she is a disillusioned, but not embittered, dance hall hostess. Into her room comes a young man from the Middle West, bent upon conquering Broadway with his saxophone. Crooks steal his musical instruments and he has a hard time generally—but Helen comforts him and sticks by him. Greek-chorus comments on the young people and on New York life in general are made by "Soda," the rooming-house proprietress, and Mac, another tenant.

(Closed March 4, 1950)

THE VELVET GLOVE

(152 performances)

Comedy in three acts by Rosemary Casey, produced by Guthrie McClintic at the Booth Theatre, December 26, 1949.

Cast of characters—

Mary Renshaw	Barbara Brady
Mother Hildebrand	Grace George
Sister Athanasius	Muriel Starr
Sister Lucy	Naomi Riordan
Mr. Barton	Ben Lackland
Prof. Pearson	James Noble
Sister Monica	Jean Dixon
Bishop Gregor	John Williams
Father Benton	Will Davis
Monsignor Burke	Walter Hampden

The scene is Mother-General Hildebrand's office in the Convent of St. Paul in a city in northern New York. Act I.—A Wednesday morning in February of the present year. Act II.—Friday afternoon. Act III.—Late Monday afternoon.

Staged by Guthrie McClintic; setting by Donald Oenslager; stage manager, Windsor Lewis.

Mother-General Hildebrand is about to be honored for her fiftieth year in the Convent, but the happiness of the occasion is dimmed because Professor Pearson, a lay teacher of history, has been hired by Bishop Gregor for supposed too-liberal utterances. Mother Hildebrand and others in the convent are on young Pearson's side, and so is Monsignor Burke. Mother Hildebrand quietly and humorously circumvents the Bishop.

(On January 6, 1950, Grace George's husband, William A. Brady, died. It was a Friday. In the theatrical tradition that the show must go on, Miss George and another Brady in the cast, Barbara, continued in their roles without interruption, playing both Saturday performances and all succeeding ones. Barbara Brady is the daughter of Katherine Alexander and the late William A. Brady, Jr. This was her Broadway debut.)

(Closed May 13, 1950)

HOW LONG TILL SUMMER

(7 performances)

Play in two acts by Sarett and Herbert Rudley, produced by Leon J. Bronsky and Edward M. Gilbert at the Playhouse, December 27, 1949.

Cast of characters—

Johnny Burns	Charles Taylor
Josh Jeffers	Josh White, Jr.
Mr. Burns	Sam Gilman
Kate Jeffers	Ida James
Mary	Evelyn Davis
Harold Carver	Milton Williams
Al Gaige	Leigh Whipper
Mathew Jeffers	Josh White
Dr. Dan Benson	Frank Wilson
Mrs. Dexter	Fredi Washington
Fred Johnson	Arthur O'Connell
Harlan	Maxwell Glanville
A Man	Peter Capell

The action occurs in an alley, the Jeffers' apartment and several places real only in Josh Jeffers' imagination. Act I.—Late afternoon, Spring, 1948. Act II.—Two hours later.

Staged by Herbert Rudley; settings by Ralph Alswang; costumes by Enid Smiley; production stage manager, Ben Ross Berenberg.

Josh Jeffers, small Negro boy, has a fine playmate in Johnny Burns, who is white, until Johnny's drunken father draws the color line and threatens the terrified Josh with several dire fates. Josh's father, Mathew, a respected Negro lawyer, is campaigning for Congress with the support of a gangster. First-nighters found more confusion than conclusion in the drama.

(Closed December 31, 1949)

SHE STOOPS TO CONQUER

(16 performances)

Farce by Oliver Goldsmith, revived by the New York City Theatre Company at the City Center of Drama and Music, December 28, 1949.

Cast of characters—

Lamplighter	Paul Anderson
Diggory	Jack Fletcher
Pimple	Olive Dunbar

Tony Lumpkin...............Ezra Stone
Squire Hardcastle.............Burl Ives
Mrs. Hardcastle.........Evelyn Varden
Miss Neville............Carmen Mathews
Tom Twist..............Richard Vintour
Jimmy.....................Tom Moore
Slang..................Robinson Stone
Muggins.................David Perkins
Stingo.....................Pat Malone
Young Marlow............Brian Aherne
Hastings................Staats Cotsworth
Dick...................Maurice Shrog
Roger.....................Royal Dano
Thomas......................Al Thaler
Jeremy...................Bethell Long
Hastings' Servant.......Robert Hartung

Sir Charles Marlow......Richard Temple

Staged by Morton Da Costa; sets by
Peter Wolf; costumes directed by Emeline
Roche; music by William Brooks; new
prologue by W. W. Watt, a professor at
Lafayette College; George Schaefer, pro-
duction executive; stage manager, Ralph
Edington.

This was the first of four plays to be
given at the City Center for two weeks
each under the artistic direction of Maurice
Evans. Mr. Evans himself spoke the
prologue.

(Closed January 8, 1950)

THE MEMBER OF THE WEDDING

(174 performances)

(Continued)

Drama in three acts by Carson Mc-
Cullers, adapted from Mrs. McCullers'
novel of the same title; produced by Robert
Whitehead, Oliver Rea and Stanley
Martineau at the Empire Theatre, Janu-
ary 5, 1950.

Cast of characters—

Jarvis....................James Holden
Frankie Addams.......... Julie Harris
Janice....................Janet De Gore
Berenice...................Ethel Waters
Royal Addams..........William Hansen
John Henry West......Brandon De Wilde
Mrs. West..............Margaret Barker
Helen Fletcher............Mitzie Blake
Doris....................Joan Shepard
Muriel....................Phyllis Love

Sis Laura................Phyllis Walker
T. T. Williams...........Harry Bolden
Honey......................Henry Scott
Barney McKean..........Jimmy Dutton

Act I.—A kitchen and back yard in a
small town in Georgia in August, 1945.
Friday, late afternoon. Act II.—Afternoon the following day. Act III.—Scene
1—Sunday afternoon. Scene 2—Just
before dawn next morning. Scene 3—Late
Fall.

Staged by Harold Clurman; sets and
costumes by Lester Polakov; stage manager, Jus Addis.

See page 91.

HAPPY AS LARRY

(3 performances)

Musical fantasy in two acts, produced
by Leonard Sillman at the Coronet Theatre,
January 6, 1950. Libretto by Donagh
MacDonagh; music by Mischa and Wesley
Portnoff.

Cast of characters—

1st Tailor..............Maurice Edwards
3rd Tailor.................Frank Milton
4th Tailor.................Harry Allen
5th Tailor................Henry Calvin
6th Tailor...............William Hogue
7th Tailor.................Jack Warner
8th Tailor....................Fin Olsen
2nd Tailor.....................Himself
Larry.................Burgess Meredith
The Widow..........Marguerite Piazza
The Gravedigger...........Ralph Hertz
Mrs. Larry..............Barbara Perry
The Doctor.................Gene Barry

Seamus....................Irwin Corey
Clotho.......................Mara Kim
Lachesis.................Diane Sinclair
Atropos..................Royce Wallace

Staged by Burgess Meredith; dances by
Anna Sokolow; settings and costumes by
Motley; orchestrations by Rudolph Goehr
and Charles Cook; musical director, Franz
Allers; vocal arrangements by Herbert
Greene; mobiles by Alexander Calder;
stage manager, Monroe B. Hack.

The action of the play takes place anywhere, any time. Act I.—Scene 1—A
casual tailor shop. Scene 2—A restless
graveyard. Scene 3—Interior of Larry's
house. Scene 4—Space. Act II.—Scene
1—Exterior of Larry's house. Scene 2—
Interior of Larry's house. Scene 3—The
tailor shop.

An Irish tailor, Larry, reminisces to his fellow workers about his grandfather, also named Larry. Grandpa had two wives, one good and one bad—but Grandpa could never figure out which had been which. With the help of Irish witchcraft, the tailors are transported backward in time to Grandpa's day for an eyewitness appraisal of the two wives.

Principal musical numbers: Act I.—

"Without a Stitch"; "Now and Then"; "October"; "Mrs. Larry, Tell Me This"; "A Cup of Tea"; "He's with My Johnny"; "And So He Died"; "Three Old Ladies from Hades." Act II.—"It's Pleasant and Delightful"; "The Dirty Dog"; "The Flatulent Ballad"; "The Loyalist Wife"; "Oh, Mrs. Larry"; "He's a Bold Rogue"; "I Remember Her"; "The Tobacco Blues."

(Closed January 7, 1950)

THE CORN IS GREEN

(16 performances)

Drama in three acts by Emlyn Williams, revived by the New York City Theatre Company at the City Center of Music and Drama, January 11, 1950.

Cast of characters—

John Goronwy Jones	Gwilym Williams
Miss Ronberry	Carmen Mathews
Idwal Morris	Billy James
Sarah Pugh	Gwyneth Hughes
A Groom	George Bleasdale
The Squire	Robin Craven
Mrs. Watty	Eva Leonard-Boyne
Bessie Watty	Darthy Hinkley
Miss Moffat	Eva Le Gallienne
Robbart Robbatch	Paul Anderson
Morgan Evans	Richard Waring
Glyn Thomas	Sherman Lloyd
John Owen	Richard Deane
Will Hughes	Louis Hollister
Old Tom	Ernest Rowan

Boys, girls and parents: O. Talbert-Hewitt, Jeanne Beauvais, Betty Conibear, Olive Dunbar, Arlouine Goodjohn, James Goodwin, Sally Hester, Cavada Humphrey, Kayton Nesbitt, Louise Severn, Robinson Stone, Dafydd Thomas, Peggy Turnley and Gloria Valborg.

George Schaefer, production executive; Herman Shumlin, volunteer consultant on direction; set by Peter Wolfe; costume director, Emeline Roche; Welsh singing and dialect directed by Gwilym Williams; stage manager, Edward McHugh.

This was the second play of a four-play series given under the artistic direction of Maurice Evans. "The Corn Is Green" was first produced and directed by Herman Shumlin at the National Theatre, November 26, 1940, with Ethel Barrymore and Richard Waring as the principals. It had 477 performances.

(Closed January 22, 1950)

ALIVE AND KICKING

(46 performances)

Musical revue, produced by William R. Katzell and Ray Golden at the Winter Garden, January 17, 1950. Lyrics by Paul Francis Webster and Ray Golden; music by Hal Borne, Irma Jurist and Sammy Fain; additional music and lyrics by Sonny Burke, Leonard Gershe, Billy Kyle, Sid Kuller; special music and lyrics by Harold Rome; sketches by Ray Golden, I. A. Diamond, Henry Morgan, Jerome Chodorov, Joseph Stein, Will Glickman, Mike Stuart and others.

Principal players are named in the list of musical and sketch numbers.

Staged by Robert H. Gordon; choreography by Jack Cole; settings and costumes by Raoul Pène Du Bois; lighting by Mason Arvold; musical direction and vocal arrangements by Lehman Engel; orchestral arrangements by George Bassman; stage manager, Michael Ellis.

Principal musical and sketch numbers: Act I.—"Alive and Kicking," sung by

Bobby Van and Dolores Starr, with chorus and dancers. "Pals of the Pentagon," sung and acted by Jack Russell, David Burns, Carl Reiner, Mickey Deems and Eve Lynn. "I Didn't Want Him," sung by June Brady, danced by Jack Cole and Gwen Verdon. "Meet the Authors," acted by Louise Kirtland, Carl Reiner, Lenore Lonergan, David Burns and Sam Kirham. "A World of Strangers," sung by Arthur Maxwell and Patricia Bybell. "Cry, Baby, Cry," sung by Lenore Lonergan, Rae Abruzzo and Laurel Shelby. "One Word Led to Another," sung and danced by Bobby Van. "Calypso Celebration," sung by the company and danced by Jack Cole and his dancers. Act II.—"Hippocrates Hits the Jackpot," acted by Earl William, Carl Reiner, Laurel Shelby, Louise Kirtland, Mickey Deems, David Burns, June Brady, Fay de Witt and Ray Stephens. "I'm All Yours," sung by Jessie Elliott and Bobby Van. "Once Upon a Time," acted by Carl Reiner, Jack Gilford, Lenore Lonergan and Mickey Deems. "French With Tears," sung by Lenore Lonergan.

"Cole Scuttle Blues," danced by Jack Cole, Gwen Verdon and Marie Groscup.

(Closed February 25, 1950)

THE ENCHANTED

(45 performances)

A comedy in three acts by Jean Giraudoux. Adapted by Maurice Valency. Produced by David Lowe and Richard Davidson at the Lyceum Theatre, January 18, 1950.

Cast of characters—

The Mayor........ ...Charles Halton
The Doctor..............Russell Collins
Isabel.................Leueen MacGrath
The Little Girls	
Gilberte.................Carolyn Grier
Daisy....................Judith Licata
Lucy..................Mimi Strongin
Viola..................Leah Chernin
Denise................Patricia Wright
Irene................Betty Richardson
Marie-Louise.........Henrietta Catal
The Inspector............Malcolm Keen
The Supervisor...........Wesley Addy
Armande Mangebois....Frances Williams

Leonide Mangebois........Una O'Connor
The Ghost................John Baragrey
First Executioner.........Joe E. Marks
Second Executioner.......James O'Neill
Monsieur Adrian...........John O'Hare
Papa Tellier..............Roland Wood

Act I.—A clearing in the woods just outside a provincial town in France. Late afternoon. Act II.—The same. A few weeks later. Act III.—Isabel's room in the town.

Staged by George S. Kaufman; production designed by Robert Edmond Jones; music by Francis Poulenc; dances by Jean Erdman; musical supervision by Albert Hague; production associate, Sue Davidson; stage manager, Al Boylen.

See page 294.

(Closed February 25, 1950)

THE MAN

(92 performances)

A melodrama in two acts by Mel Dinelli. Produced by Kermit Bloomgarden at the Fulton Theatre, January 19, 1950.

Cast of characters—

Mrs. Gillis................Dorothy Gish
Ruth................Peggy Ann Garner
Mr. Armstrong.........Robert Emhardt
Howard Wilton............Don Hanmer
Mr. Franks.............Frank McNellis
Doug...................Josh White, Jr.
Mr. Stephens............Richard Boone

The time is the present and the entire action takes place in the living room and kitchen of an old Victorian-style home situated in the unfashionable outskirts of a large American city. Act I.—Scene 1—A morning in early winter. Scene 2—An hour later. Scene 3—Several hours later. Act II.—A few minutes later.

Staged by Martin Ritt; setting and lighting by Jo Mielziner; costumes by Julia Sze; stage manager, Robert Caldwell.

Howard Wilton is given work as a handy man by Mrs. Gillis, a widow who has converted her home into a rooming house. Howard desperately wants to be loved and admired—but he is a psychopathic criminal. Mrs. Gillis has a terrified time of it right to the end of the play.

(Closed April 8, 1950)

DANCE ME A SONG

(35 performances)

Revue in two acts, produced by Dwight Deere Wiman at the Royale Theatre, January 20, 1950. Songs by James Shelton, Herman Hupfeld, Albert Hague, Maurice Valency and Bud Gregg; sketches by Jimmy Kirkwood and Lee Goodman, George Oppenheimer and Vincente Minnelli, Marya Mannes, Robert Anderson, James Shelton and Wally Cox.

Principal players—

Erik Rhodes	Tina Prescott
Marion Lorne	Wally Cox
Ann Thomas	Alan Ross

Jimmy Kirkwood
Bob Scheerer
Biff McGuire
Heidi Krall
Fracine Bond
Cynthia Rogers
June Graham
Scott Merrill
Joan McCracken
Lee Goodman
Hope Foye

Bob Fosse
Marilyn Gennaro
Dusty McCaffrey
Don Saddler
Cliff Ferre
Robert B. Sola
Marian Horosko
Douglas Moppert
Babe Hines
Silver

Staged by James Shelton; sets by Jo Mielziner; dances by Robert Sidney; costumes by Irene Sharaff; orchestrations by Robert Russell Bennett; musical direction by Tony Cabot; stage manager, Tony Albert.

Principal musical and sketch numbers: Act I.—"Average Family"; "She's No Lady"; "Glee Club"; "Strange New Look"; "Buck and Bobbie"; I'm the Girl"; "The Lunts Are the Lunts Are the Lunts"; "Documentary." Act II.—"One Is a Lonely Number"; "Texas"; "The Folks at Home"; "Hello from Hollywood"; "It's His Money."

(Closed February 18, 1950)

THE COCKTAIL PARTY

(153 performances)

(Continued)

Drama in two acts by T. S. Eliot, produced by Gilbert Miller by arrangement with Sherek Players Ltd. at Henry Miller's Theatre, January 21, 1950.

Cast of characters—

Edward Chamberlayne.... Robert Flemyng
Julia (Mrs. Shuttlethwaite)
                          Cathleen Nesbitt
Celia Coplestone............Irene Worth
Alexander MacCoigie Gibbs
                          Ernest Clark

An Unidentified Guest......Alec Guinness
Lavinia Chamberlayne.......Eileen Peel
A Nurse-Secretary........Avril Conquest
A Caterer's Man...........Donald Bain

Staged by E. Martin Browne; lighting and settings supervised by Raymond Sovey; stage manager, Donald Bain.

See page 45.

DESIGN FOR A STAINED GLASS WINDOW

(8 performances)

Drama in three acts by William Berney and Howard Richardson, produced by Jack Segasture in association with OBS Productions at the Mansfield Theatre, January 23, 1950.

Cast of characters—

Henry Maye.............Neil Fitzgerald
William Clitherow..........Charles Nolte
Tom Prior................James Dobson
Anne Tesh............Carroll McComas
Robin Flemming..........Ralph Clanton
Margaret Clitherow........Martha Scott
John Clitherow..........Charlton Heston
Judge Clinch..........A. Winfield Hoeny
Father Marsh...............John McKee
First Guard..............Donald Barton
Second Guard............Winston Ross
Third Guard..............Thomas Walsh
Little William.............Joseph Fallon
Sally...................Kathleen Roland
Henry Clitherow............David Rosen
Peter Van Lynch...........Donald Rose
Robert Hurleston........Harry Mehaffey
Azore........................A Dog

The setting is the living room of the Shambles, an Elizabethan house in York. Act I.—An evening in Spring, 1571. Act II.—Scene 1—Sunday morning in early Autumn, two years later. Scene 2—A winter evening, ten years later. Act III.—Scene 1—The following morning. Scene 2—Later that afternoon.

Staged by Ella Gerber; scenery, costumes and lighting by Stewart Chaney; stage manager, David Jordan.

John Clitherow brings his bride, Margaret, to their new home in York. Queen Elizabeth has just been excommunicated, and England is torn by the persecution of Catholics. In York, John and his friends find it easiest to renounce Catholicism and attend Protestant services, but Margaret stands firm in her faith. She hides priests, has clandestine services at home, sends a young son to France and religious freedom. She is condemned to death by torture.

Margaret Clitherow was canonized for her martyrdom, and the drama is based on historical research.

(Closed January 28, 1950)

THE HAPPY TIME

(151 performances)

(Continued)

Comedy in three acts by Samuel Taylor, based on the book of the same name by Robert Fontaine; produced by Richard Rodgers and Oscar Hammerstein II at the Plymouth Theatre, January 24, 1950.

Cast of characters—

Bibi	Johnny Stewart
Papa	Claude Dauphin
Maman	Leora Dana
Grandpere	Edgar Stehli
Uncle Desmonde	Richard Hart
Uncle Louis	Kurt Kasznar
Aunt Felice	Mary Aurelius
Mignonette	Eva Gabor
Sally	Marlene Cameron
Doctor Gagnon	Gage Clarke
Alfred	James O'Rear
Mr. Frye	Oliver Cliff

The action of the play takes place in Ottawa in the early Twenties. Act I.—Scene 1—The living room of the Bonnard home. Early Fall. Scene 2—The same. Six months later. Act II.—Scene 1—The living room of the Bonnard home, one month later. Scene 2—The same. Next day. Act III.—Scene 1—The Principal's office. Immediately following. Scene 2—The living room. Immediately following.

Staged by Robert Lewis; scenery and costumes by Aline Bernstein; stage manager, Tom Turner.

See page 197.

THE DEVIL'S DISCIPLE

(127 performances)

Comedy in two acts by Bernard Shaw, revived by the New York City Theatre Company at the New York City Center of Music and Drama, January 25, 1950.

Cast of characters—

Mrs. Dudgeon	Hilda Vaughn
Essie	Betty Lou Holland
Christie	Logan Ramsey
Anthony Anderson	Victor Jory
Judith Anderson	Marsha Hunt
Lawyer Hawkins	Somer Alberg
William Dudgeon	Louis Lytton
Mrs. William	Cavada Humphrey
Titus Dudgeon	Robinson Stone
Mrs. Titus	Janet Maria Burtis
Dick Dudgeon	Maurice Evans
Sergeant	Ian Martin
Major Swindon	Gavin Gordon
General Burgoyne	Dennis King
Brudenell	Somer Alberg

Staged by Margaret Webster; sets by Peter Wolf; costumes by Emeline Roche; George Schaefer, production executive; stage manager, Ralph Edington.

This jaunty revival of Shaw's comedy about the American Revolution was scheduled for the usual sixteen performances at the City Center, and it closed there on February 5, 1950. Critical and public reception were so enthusiastic, however, that Richard Aldrich, Richard Myers and Julius Fleischmann assumed commercial sponsorship of the production and moved it to the Royale Theatre on February 21. Since City Center productions are made possible by concessions from the theatrical unions, the new sponsors faced the paradox of having to give new financing and new scenery to an already-established hit.

(Closed May 27, 1950)

AS YOU LIKE IT

(145 performances)

Comedy by William Shakespeare, revived by the Theatre Guild at the Cort Theatre, January 26, 1950.

Cast of characters—

Orlando	William Prince
Adam	Burton Mallory
Oliver	Ernest Graves
Dennis	Robert Foster
Charles	Michael Everett
Celia	Cloris Leachman
Rosalind	Katharine Hepburn
Touchstone	Bill Owen
Le Beau	Jay Robinson
Frederick	Dayton Lummis
Lady in Waiting	Jan Sherwood
Duke	Aubrey Mather

Amiens................Frank Rogier
Lord.................Everett Gamnon
Corin.................Whitford Kane
Silvius...............Robert Quarry
Phebe.................Judy Parrish
Jaques..............Ernest Thesiger
Audrey.............Patricia Englund
Sir Oliver Martext.......Jay Robinson
William...............Robert Foster
Rowland.............Craig Timberlake
Ladies in Waiting and Shepherdesses—
    Jan Sherwood, Marylin Nowell,
        Margaret Wright
Lords, Attendants and Shepherds—
    Kenneth Cantril, Charles Herndon,
    William Sutherland, Richard Hepburn,
        Robert Wark, John Weaver,
        Craig Timberlake

Production conceived and directed by
Michael Benthall; scenery and costumes
by James Bailey; incidental music written
and traditional songs arranged by Robert
Irving; technical assistant, Emeline Roche;
production supervised by Lawrence Langner and Theresa Helburn; stage manager,
Karl Nielsen.

This production was notable for the
interest displayed by newspaper photo sec-
tions and picture magazines in the legs
worn by Katharine Hepburn in the role
of Rosalind.

(Closed June 3, 1950)

MR. BARRY'S ETCHINGS

(31 performances)

Comedy in three acts by Walter Bullock
and Daniel Archer, produced by Brock
Pemberton at the Forty-Eighth Street
Theatre, January 31, 1950.

Cast of characters—

Evelyn Taylor............Gaye Jordan
Bud Wijenski............Michael Foley
Mrs. Taylor.............Ruth Hammond
Judson Barry...............Lee Tracy
Carrie Stanwich.........Amy Douglass
Marvin Pritchard........Gene Blakely
Adolph Griswold.......Frank Tweddell
Sam Jordan..........William Gibberson
Sawbuck Sam...........Richard Carlyle
Matt...................William Sharon
The Duke................George Ives
Gabby................Howard Whitfield
Miss Ferris.......Vicki Cummings
Tom Crosby...............Scott McKay
Grover Dayton.............Dort Clark
Kenneth Plunkett.......Thomas Reynolds

Act I.—Mr. Barry's studio. An afternoon in July. Act II.—Scene 1—A hotel
room. Late October. Scene 2—The
studio. An afternoon in November.
Staged by Brock Pemberton and Margaret Perry; sets by John Root; costumes
supervised by Margaret Pemberton; production assistant, Archer King.

Mr. Barry is a genial man of many
accomplishments, including copper-plate
engraving. Just to exercise his skill he
has fabricated a very passable $50 bill.
A gang of counterfeiters headed by Miss
Ferris wants his services, and a T-man,
Tom Crosby, wants the counterfeiters.
Mr. Barry generously gives his home-made
money to needy causes, such as hospitals.
He gets into trouble—but gets out of it,
of course.

(Closed February 25, 1950)

THE INNOCENTS

(141 performances)

Drama in two acts by William Archibald,
based on Henry James' story, "The Turn
of the Screw," produced by Peter Cookson at the Playhouse, February 1, 1950.

Cast of characters—

Flora........................Iris Mann
Mrs. Grose..............Isobel Elsom
Miss Giddens.........Beatrice Straight
Miles......................David Cole

The drawing room of a country house in
England in 1880. Act I.—Scene 1—An
early Autumn afternoon. Scene 2—Three

hours later. Scene 3—The following
morning. Scene 4—Twilight, the same
day. Scene 5—The following morning.
Act II.—Scene 1—Evening of the same
day. Scene 2—The next morning. Scene
3—The same day, twilight.
Staged by Peter Glenville; setting by Jo
Mielziner; costumes by Motley; music by
Alex North; stage manager, Stanley
Gould.

See page 118.

(Closed June 3, 1950)

ARMS AND THE GIRL
(134 performances)

Musical comedy in two acts produced by the Theatre Guild in association with Anthony Brady Farrell at the Forty-Sixth Street Theatre, February 2, 1950. Based on the play, "The Pursuit of Happiness," by Lawrence Langner and Armina Marshall. Book by Herbert and Dorothy Fields and Rouben Mamoulian; music by Morton Gould, lyrics by Dorothy Fields.

Cast of characters—

Connecticut	Pearl Bailey
Franz	Georges Guetary
Jo Kirkland	Nanette Fabray
Thad Jennings	Seth Arnold
Two Sons of Liberty	Andrew Aprea and Victor Young
Town Crier	William J. McCarthy
Capt. Aaron Kirkland	Florenz Ames
Drummer	Jerry Miller
Sergeant	Norman Weise
Prudence Kirkland	Eda Heinemann
Comfort Kirkland	Lulu Belle Clarke
Ben	Sterling Hall
Matthew	Joseph Caruso
A Militiaman	Peter Miceli
Abigail	Mimi Cabanne
Betsy	Joan Keenan
Col. Mortimer Sherwood	John Conte
Aides to General Curtis	Daniel O'Brien and Robert Rippy
General Lucius Curtis	Cliff Dunstan
John	Paul Fitzpatrick
David	Philip Rodd
General George Washington	Arthur Vinton

Dancers: Barbara Ferguson, Annabelle Gold, Maria Harriton, Barbara McCutcheon, Patricia Muller, Onna White, Fern Whitney. Edmund Balin. Peter Gennaro, William Inglis, Robert Josias, Arthur Partington, Marc West, Lou Yetter.

Singers: Mimi Cabanne, Katherine Hennig, Joan Keenan, Mary O'Fallon, Shirley Robbins, Patricia Rogers, Helen Stanton, Bettina Thayer. Howard Andreola, Andrew Aprea Joseph Caruso, Sterling Hall, Peter Miceli, Daniel O'Brien, Frederick Olsson, Robert Rippy, Donald Thrall, William Thunhurst, Norman Weise, Victor Young.

The time is 1776; the locale, Ridgefield, Conn. Scenes in Act I include the hayloft of Thad Jennings' barn, the village green, the meeting house and the parlor of the Kirkland home. Scenes in Act II include the parlor, the Boston Post Road, the exterior of the Kirkland barn and the village green.

Staged by Rouben Mamoulian; settings by Horace Armistead; costumes by Audre; musical conductor, Frederick Dvonch; orchestrations by Morton Gould and Philip J. Lang; production supervised by Lawrence Langner and Theresa Helburn; stage managers, John Cornell and Herman Magidson.

Principal musical numbers: Act I.—"A Girl with a Flame"; "That's What I Told Him Last Night"; "I Like It Here"; "That's My Fella"; "A Cow and a Plough and a Frau"; "Nothin' for Nothin' "; "He Will Tonight"; "Plantation in Philadelphia"; "You Kissed Me." Act II.—"I'll Never Learn"; "There Must Be Something Better Than Love"; "She's Exciting."

(Closed May 27, 1950)

THE HEIRESS
(16 performances)

Drama by Ruth and Augustus Goetz, revived by the New York City Theatre Company at the New York City Center of Drama and Music, February 8, 1950.

Cast of characters—

Maria	Mary McNamee
Dr. Austin Sloper	Basil Rathbone
Lavinia Penniman	Edna Best
Catherine Sloper	Margaret Phillips
Elizabeth Almond	Katharine Raht
Arthur Townsend	Paul Anderson
Marian Almond	Olive Dunbar
Morris Townsend	John Dall
Mrs. Montgomery	Betty Linley

Staged by George Schaefer; set by Peter Wolf; costume director, Emeline Roche.

This was the fourth and last of the play series organized at the City Center by Maurice Evans. Several critics were of the opinion that Margaret Phillips was the best of the Catherine Slopers to play in New York—the others, during the original run, having been Wendy Hiller and Beatrice Straight.

(Closed February 19, 1950)

ALL YOU NEED IS ONE GOOD BREAK

(36 performances)

Play in two acts by Arnold Manoff, produced by Monte Proser and Joseph Kipness in association with Jack Small at the Mansfield Theatre, February 9, 1950.

Cast of characters—

Cop	Charles Cooper
Clerk	Harry Davis
Lawyer	John Sylvester
Martin Rothman	John Berry
Meyer Rothman	Reuben Wendorff
Fanny Rothman	Ellie Pine
Mrs. Rothman	Anna Appel
Charlie	Shimen Ruskin
Gordon	J. Edward Bromberg
Hockfleish	Phil Carter
Sleepy Duke	Lee Krieger
Willie the Hack	John Sylvester
Benny Numbers	Edwin Max
Sam	Phillip Pine
Helen	Marianne Loris
Diane	Lee Grant
Headwaiter	Anthony Mannino
Harry	Salem Ludwig
Ruth	Louise Craig
Esther	Ronnie Paris
The Girl	Marianne Loris
The Boy	Lee Krieger
First Discusser	Anthony Mannino
Second Discusser	Gene Saks
The Waiter	Andy Ball
Stella	Lucille Patton
Nurse	Gertrude Corey
Attendant	Anthony Mannino
Marty's Double	Gene Saks

Dice Players, Reporters, People in the Bagel, Movie Goers—Andy Ball, Phil Carter, Roy Hammerman, Charles Cooper, John Sylvester, Harry Davis, Lee Krieger, Louise Craig, Marianne Loris.

The action of the play takes place on a street in New York City.

Staged by John Berry and J. Edward Bromberg; sets by Samuel Leve; lighting by Peggy Clark; costumes by Paul duPont; production stage manager, Bernard Gersten.

Martin Rothman's small salary is not enough to support his own flashy self, an indigent father, an invalid mother and a teen-age sister. He fancies he will strike it rich playing the numbers game, but doesn't. He makes other attempts to get easy money, manages to win a small amount at craps. He winds up in jail, almost a nervous wreck.

This play got discouraging notices, closed February 11, 1950, after four performances—and was reopened by a hopeful management February 20.

(Closed March 18, 1950)

COME BACK, LITTLE SHEBA

(123 performances)
(Continued)

Drama in two acts by William Inge, produced by the Theatre Guild at the Booth Theatre, February 15, 1950.

Cast of characters—

Doc	Sidney Blackmer
Marie	Joan Lorring
Lola	Shirley Booth
Turk	Lonny Chapman
Postman	Daniel Reed
Mrs. Coffman	Olga Fabian
Milkman	John Randolph
Messenger	Arnold Schulman
Bruce	Robert Cunningham
Ed Anderson	Wilson Brooks
Elmo Huston	Paul Krauss

The action takes place in the living room and kitchen of an old house in a run-down neighborhood in a midwestern city. Act I.—Scene 1—Morning in late Spring. Scene 2—The same evening, after supper. Act II.—Scene 1—The following morning. Scene 2—Late afternoon, the same day. Scene 3—Five-thirty the next morning. Scene 4—Morning, a week later.

Staged by Daniel Mann; setting by Howard Bay; costumes by Lucille Little; production supervised by Lawrence Langner and Theresa Helburn; Phyllis Anderson, associate producer; stage manager, Philip S. Barry.

See page 173.

THE BIRD CAGE

(21 performances)

Play in two acts by Arthur Laurents, produced by Water Fried and Lars Nordenson at the Coronet Theatre, February 22, 1950.

Cast of characters—

Frank......................Mike Kellin
Cork......................John Sheilie
Eloise.....................Kate Harkin
India Grey................Eleanor Lynn
Ferdy..................Sanford Meisner
Mr. Ripley.......Heywood Hale Broun
Pearl......................Jean Carson
Wally Williams..........Melvyn Douglas
Vic.....................Laurence Hugo
Emily Williams........Maureen Stapleton
Renie Renay................Rita Duncan
Joe Williams.............Wright King

Mr. Mack..................Rudy Bond

The action of the play occurs in a metropolitan night club.

Staged by Harold Clurman; settings by Boris Aronson; music by Alec Wilder; costumes by Ben Edwards; stage manager, James Gelb.

Wally Williams is the impresario and chief owner of a night club, the Bird Cage. He double-crosses one partner, Ferdy, and maims another, Vic. He is cool toward his socialite wife, warm toward India Grey, an entertainer who proves to be a good girl. When friends, relatives and associates all turn against the cocky Wally, he sets fire to his club and, presumably, himself.

(Closed March 11, 1950)

NOW I LAY ME DOWN TO SLEEP

(44 performances)

Comedy in three acts by Elaine Ryan, based on the novel by Ludwig Bemelmans; produced by Nancy Stern and George Nichols, 3d, at the Broadhurst Theatre, March 2, 1950.

Cast of characters—

Mlle. Borotra.............Lili Valenty
Jean.....................Roy Poole
Henri..............Charles Chaplin, Jr.
Aristide..................Henry Guettel
Robert..................Charles Mayer
M. Hufnagel...........Stefan Schnabel
Vitasse...................Henry Lascoe
Miss Leonora Graves....Florence Eldridge
Poppet.....................Herself
His Excellency, General Leonidas Erosa
                        Fredric March
The Cure................Norman Barrs
The Doctor..............Richard Abbott
Clothilde.................Helen Seamon
Anselmo....................Rick Jason
Colonel Laboucher...........Rene Paul
Marsan..................Booth Colman
Alfonso Lopez............Philip Gordon
First Gendarme.........Gregory Morton
Second Gendarme.....Thomas E. Noyes
First Seaman...........Gregory Morton
Second Seaman......Thomas E. Noyes
First Workman........Robert McCahon
Second Workman......Harold E. Gordon
French Child.........Sally Anne Parsons
The Dona Bebecita.....Jacqueline Dalya
Young Mother..............Hope Miller
Ship's Officer.................Rene Paul
Young Woman............Helen Seamon

Child Passenger......Sally Anne Parsons
Ship's Steward............Norman Barrs
The Acrobat..............Charles Mayer
Albert Plaschke..........Milton Parsons
Nurse................Marguerite Lewis
Indian Dancer............Philip Gordon
Indian Drummer.......Harold E. Gordon
Chimene...................Irene Moore
Indian Child........Sally Anne Parsons
First Indian..................Roy Poole
Don Modesto...........Stefan Schnabel
Second Indian........Charles Chaplin, Jr.
Third Indian............Henry Guettel
Fourth Indian............Richard Abbott
Fifth Indian............Robert McCahon
Maria.....................Hope Miller
First Indian Woman.......Lili Valenty
Second Indian Woman....Helen Seamon
Priest....................Booth Colman

Act I.—His Excellency General Leonidas Erosa's Villa Amelita in Biarritz, 1940. Scene 1—The General's tower room. Scene 2—Miss Graves' bedroom. Scene 3—The tower room. Scene 4—The General's private dock, Biarritz. Act II.—A few days later, aboard the S. S. Xenaide Ybirricos, en route to Ecuador. Scene 1—Deck space reserved for the General. Scene 2—Cabin 14. Scene 3—The deck space. Scene 4—On deck, later the same day. Scene 5—A river landing, Ecuador. Act III.—General Erosa's Villa Miraflores, Ecuador. Scene I—The terrace. Scene 2—The terrace, some weeks later. Scene 3—The subterranean pool. Scene 4—The terrace.

Staged by Hume Cronyn; settings by Wolfgang Roth; costumes by John Derro; production assistant, Marjorie Winfield.

Forced by the war to leave the luxury of Biarritz, General Erosa engages a Greek freighter and takes his retinue to his native Ecuador. The followers include Vitasse, his chef; Miss Graves, his spinster English "governess"; a mistress, Dona Bebecita,

and a stowaway, Albert Plaschke, who becomes a valet. An earthquake buries the General, the chef and the valet beside a subterranean swimming pool. Just as rescuers dig through, twenty-six days later, the General has another of his epileptic fits and disappears into the pool.

(Closed April 8, 1950)

TOBACCO ROAD

(7 performances)

Play in three acts by Jack Kirkland, adapted from Erskine Caldwell's novel, revived by Jack Kirkland as a Negro Drama Group production at the Forty-Eighth Street Theatre, March 6, 1950.

Cast of characters—

Dude Lester.............Jimmy Wright
Ada Lester..............Evelyn Ellis
Jeeter Lester...........Powell Lindsay
Ellie May..................Baby Joyce
Grandma Lester.........Estelle Hemsley
Lov Bensey....................John Tate
Henry Peabody.......Cherokee Thornton
Sister Bessie Rice......Mercedes Gilbert
Pearl......................Delores Mack
Captain Tim...............John Mark
George Payne...............John Bouie

The action takes place at the farm of Jeeter Lester, on a tobacco road in the back country of Georgia. Act I.—Late afternoon. Act II.—Next morning. Act III.—Dawn, the following day.

Staged by Evelyn Ellis; stage manager, Vinnie Phillips.

"Tobacco Road" returned, this time with Negro players in all but one of the roles, to the theatre where it made its unpromising debut on December 4, 1933. At this theatre and later at the Mansfield the play set a new record for long Broadway runs—3,182 performances. Then "Life with Father" became the champion with 3,224 performances.

(Closed March 11, 1950)

THE CONSUL

(93 performances)
(Continued)

Opera in three acts, with libretto and music by Gian-Carlo Menotti, produced by Chandler Cowles and Efrem Zimbalist, Jr. at the Ethel Barrymore Theatre, March 15, 1950.

Cast of characters—

John Sorel..............Cornell MacNeil
Magda Sorel............Patricia Neway
The Mother..............Marie Powers
Chief Police Agent.........Leon Lishner
First Police Agent......Chester Watson
Second Police Agent.....Donald Blackey
The Secretary..............Gloria Lane
Mr. Kofner............George Jongeyans
The Foreign Woman........Maria Marlo
Anna Gomez...........Maria Andreassi
Vera Boronell...........Lydia Summers
Nika Magadoff........Andrew McKinley
Assan..............Francis Monachino
Voice on the Record......Mabel Mercer

The role of Magda Sorel played by Vera Bryner on Monday evenings and Wednesday matinees.

Somewhere in Europe. Act I.—Scene 1—The home, early morning. Scene 2—The Consulate, later the same day. Act II.—Scene 1—The home, evening, a month later. Scene 2—The Consulate, a few days later. Act III.—Scene 1—The Consulate, late afternoon, several days later. Scene 2—The home, that night.

Staged by Gian-Carlo Menotti; orchestra directed by Lehman Engel; settings by Horace Armistead; musical coordination by Thomas Schippers; costumes by Grace Houston; dream choreography by John Butler; stage manager, Charles Pratt, Jr.

Magda Sorel's husband, John, comes home, wounded by and fleeing from secret police. He plans to slip out of the country and instructs his wife to go to the Consulate and get exit permits for herself, their baby and his mother. Magda is completely frustrated by the red tape of the Consulate, and she finally goes home and commits suicide by gas.

"The Consul" was voted the best musical of the 1949-1950 season by the New York Drama Critics Circle.

GREAT TO BE ALIVE!

(52 performances)

Musical comedy in two acts, produced by Vinton Freedley in association with Anderson Lawler and Russell Markert at the Winter Garden, March 23, 1950. Book by Walter Bullock and Sylvia Regan; lyrics by Walter Bullock; music by Abraham Ellstein.

Cast of characters—

Bonnie	Bambi Linn
Prudence	Betty Low
Albert	Rod Alexander
Jake	J. C. McCord
Maybelle	Aleen Buchanan
Kitty	Valerie Bettis
Crumleigh	Jay Marshall
Butch	Earl Oxford
Leslie Butterfield	Vivienne Segal
Carol	Martha Wright
Vince	Mark Dawson
Woodrow Twigg	Stuart Erwin
Mimsey	Marjorie Peterson
Sandra	Virginia Curtis
Freddie	Russell Nype
Blodgett	Lulu Bates
Jonathan	David Nillo
The Minister	Ken Carroll
O'Brien	Don Kennedy
Rafferty	Paul Reed

Dancers: Eleanor Fairchild, Eleanore Gregory, Barbara Heath, Ann Hutchinson, Norma Kaiser, Janice Rule, Chuck Brunner, Ted Cappy, Roscoe French, David Nillo, Harry Rogers, Swen Swenson.

Singers: Leigh Allen, Jeanne Bal, Virginia Curtis, Ruth McVayne, Joyce Mitchell, Julia Williams, Fred Bryan, Ken Carroll, Ed Gombos, John Juliano, Russell Nype, Robert Wallace.

Act I.—The six scenes are played between the reception hall of an old Pennsylvania mansion and the exterior of the mansion. Act II.—Eight scenes are played between the reception hall, the exterior and the garden.

Staged by Mary Hunter; dances by Helen Tamiris; sets and costumes by Stewart Chaney; orchestrations by Robert Russell Bennett and Don Walker; musical director, Max Meth; special arrangements by Genevieve Pitot; stage manager, Larry Baker.

Mrs. Leslie Butterfield buys an old mansion from Woodrow Twigg. The place is haunted by the ghosts of all former residents—ghosts who can be seen and heard by Virgins, but by nobody else. The ghosts finally succeed in driving the living characters out of the house.

Principal musical numbers: Act I.— "When the Sheets Come Back from the Laundry"; "It's a Long Time Till Tomorrow"; "Headin' for a Weddin'"; "Redecorate"; "Call It Love"; "There's Nothing Like It"; "Dreams Ago." Act II.—"Who Done It?"; "Blue Day"; "That's a Man Everytime"; "You Appeal to Me."

(Closed May 13, 1950)

THE WISTERIA TREES

(78 performances)
(Continued)

Play in three acts by Joshua Logan, based on Anton Chekhov's "The Cherry Orchard," produced by Leland Hayward and Joshua Logan at the Martin Beck Theatre, March 29, 1950.

Cast of characters—

Dolly May	Vinie Burrows
Martha	Peggy Conklin
Henry Arthur Henry	Maurice Ellis
Yancy Loper	Kent Smith
Scott	Alonzo Bosan
Lucy Andree Ransdell	Helen Hayes
Antoinette	Bethel Leslie
Cassie	Georgia Burke
Gavin Leon Andree	Walter Abel
Bowman Witherspoon	G. Albert Smith
Jacques	Ossie Davis
Peter Whitfield	Douglas Watson
Solo Singer	Maude Simmons

Children: Irene Treadwill, Ralph Robertson, Jr. and Patsy Carol.
Guest at Party: Mary Vallee, Ellen Cobb Hill, Kitty Snapper, Patricia deCoursey, Elisa Toca and Bentley Wallace.
Other Servants: Emory S. Richardson, Reri Grist and Duke Williams.

The children's parlor and part of the outside gallery of Wisteria Plantation, Louisiana. Act I.—Spring. Act II.—Scene 1—Summer. Scene 2—Autumn. Act III.—Winter. Time, the end of the last century.

Staged by Joshua Logan; setting by Jo Mielziner; costumes by Lucinda Ballard; musical arrangements by Lehman

Engel; stage manager, Robert Linden.

See page 235.

CRY OF THE PEACOCK

(2 performances)

Comedy in four scenes by Jean Anouilh, adapted from the French by Cecil Robson, produced by James Colligan and Donald Medford at the Mansfield Theatre, April 11, 1950.

Cast of characters—

The General	Raymond Lovell
Ada	Kathleen Maguire
Nathalie	Patricia Wheel
Toto	Clifford Sales
Count	Oscar Karlweis
Countess	Marta Linden
Hector De Villardieu	Philip Tonge

Nicolas	Peter Brandon
Marie Christine	Mimi Strongin
Tutor	Richard A. Martin
General's Wife	Lili Darvas

The hall of a French château in 1912. Scene 1—Morning. Scene 2—Afternoon. Scene 3—Afternoon. Scene 4—Midnight.

Staged by Martin Ritt; sets and costumes by Cecil Beaton; stage manager, Murray Queen.

A smart group of Parisians are obsessed by sex and conversationally confined to it.

(Closed April 12, 1950)

WITH A SILK THREAD

(13 performances)

Play in two acts by Elsa Shelley, produced by Irving Kaye Davis at the Lyceum Theatre, April 12, 1950.

Cast of characters—

Anna	Lilia Skala
Dr. Walter Lucas	Philip Huston
Barry Winters	Henry Hart
Rose Raymond	Claire Luce
George Lucas	William Duff
Tony Fern	Phil Arthur
Karen Jackson	Carole Mathews
Bucky	Mary MacLeod

The beachfront home of the Lucas family. Act I.—Scene 1—Early morning, June. Scene 2—The same evening. Scene 3—Ten days later, late afternoon. Act II.—Scene 1—That night. Scene 2—Sunday, two weeks later. Scene 3—The next night, midnight. Scene 4—A month later, evening.

Dr. Walter Lucas, a surgeon, and Rose Raymond Lucas, his wife, are incompatible after twenty years of marriage. He is jealous of her. She, a former actress, wants to return to the stage in a Summer theatre production of "Candida." Dr. Lucas finally conquers his unseemingly jealousy and is nice to his wife for a change—even forgiving her for having an affair with Tony Fern, her young leading man.

(Closed April 22, 1950)

KATHERINE DUNHAM

(37 performances)

Dance revue produced by S. Hurok at the Broadway Theatre, April 19, 1950.

Members of the company—

Katherine Dunham	Eloise Hill
Vanoye Aikens	Rosalie King
Wilbert Bradley	Jen Lei
Miriam Burton	Julio Mendez
Eddy Clay	Lenwood Morris
Lucille Ellis	Julie Robinson
La Rosa Estrada	Gordon Simpson
Edward Hawkins	Anna Smith

Frances Taylor	Dolores Harper
Jacqueline Walcott	Claude Marchant

Staged by Katherine Dunham; costumes by John Pratt; Vadico Gogliano, conductor.

Miss Dunham's numbers included "Afrique," "Brazilian Suite," "Veracruzana," "Nostalgia," "Flaming Youth," "Barrelhouse," "Jazz in Five Movements" and "L'ag'ya."

(Closed May 20, 1950)

PETER PAN

(56 performances)

(Continued)

Play in three acts and an epilogue by J. M. Barrie, with new music by Leonard Bernstein, revived by Peter Lawrence and R. L. Stevens at the Imperial Theatre, April 24. 1950.

Cast of characters—

Nana....................Norman Shelly
Michael..................Charles Taylor
Mrs. Darling................Peg Hillias
John.....................Jack Dimond
Wendy...............Marcia Henderson
Mr. Darling................Boris Karloff
Peter Pan..................Jean Arthur
Liza.......................Gloria Patrice
Tootles....................Lee Barnett
Slightly..................Richard Knox
Curly....................Philip Hepburn
The Twins...............Charles Brill,
                         Edward Benjamin
Nibs......................Buzzy Martin
Captain Hook..............Boris Karloff
Starkey...................David Kurlan
Smee.......................Joe E. Marks
Jukes.......................Will Scholz
Cecco.................Nehemiah Persoff
Mullins....................Harry Allen
Noodler....................John Dennis
Cookson...............William Marshall
Whibbles..................Vincent Beck
The Crocodile.............Norman Shelly
Tiger Lily.................Gloria Patrice
Indians......Ronnie Aul, Kenneth Davis,
    Norman DeJoie, Loren Hightower,
         Jay Riley, William Sumner
Mermaids..........Stephanie Augustine,
                         Eleanor Winter
Pirates......Ronnie Aul, Kenneth Davis,
         Jay Riley, William Sumner

Act I.—The nursery of the Darlings' home.   Act II.—Scene 1—The Never Land.   Scene 2—The mermaids' lagoon. Scene 3—The home under the ground. Act III.—Scene 1—The pirate ship.   Scene 2—Under the sea.   Scene 3—The nursery. Epilogue—The treetops.

Staged by John Burrell; settings by Ralph Alswang; costumes by Motley; dances by Wendy Toye; musical arrangements by Hershy Kay and Trude Rittman; stage manager, Phil Stein.

"Peter Pan" had its New York premiere November 6, 1905, at the Empire Theatre, with Maude Adams in the title role and Ernest Lawford in the dual parts of Mr. Darling and Captain James Hook. The play ran at the Empire for 223 performances, and had another 40 performances there beginning in December, 1906. Miss Adams toured in "Peter Pan" through 1907, and toured in it again during the seasons of 1912 and 1913, starting with 24 performances at the Empire in December, 1912, and January, 1913.

Charles Dillingham revived "Peter Pan" at the Knickerbocker Theatre on November 6, 1924—the birthday of the first New York production.   Marilyn Miller was Peter Pan, Leslie Banks was Captain Hook and Wilfred Seagram was Mr. Darling. There were 96 performances.

On November 26, 1928, Eva Le Gallienne revived the Barrie fantasy at her Civic Repertory Theatre, and it had 48 performances.   Miss Le Gallienne included Peter Pan in her repertory roles until 1932.

A PHOENIX TOO FREQUENT and FREIGHT

(5 performances)

Two one-act plays produced by Steven H. Scheuer and Bernard Carson at the Fulton Theatre, April 26, 1950.   "A Phoenix Too Frequent" is by Christopher Fry; "Freight" is by Kenneth White.

Cast of characters for "Freight"—

Roty.................Maxwell Glanville
Fast Boy.................Lance Taylor
Pug...................Ernest Truesdale
Mish...................Raymond Hill
Oz....................Lloyd Richards
Bucket.............Kenneth Manigault
Lottie...................Curtis Harry
Peg Leg.............Maurice Thompson

Samp.....................Dots Johnson
Jake......................Glen Gordon

Cast of characters for "A Phoenix Too Frequent"—

Dynamene...................Nina Foch
Doto..................Vicki Cummings
Tegeus-Chromis............Richard Derr

Staged by John O'Shaughnessy; sets and costumes by Jack Landau; Lee Perry, stage manager.

In "Freight" a Southern white man hops a freight car occupied by nine Negroes.   For a while he intimidates and insults them, for he is armed with a knife. Then they disarm him and give him a lesson in race prejudice—in reverse. This play was first produced in Harlem by the American Negro Theatre.

In "A Phoenix Too Frequent," Dynamene, a widow, is practicing self-immolation in the tomb of her husband, and is accompanied in this enterprise by her handmaid, Doto. A handsome Greek soldier enters the tomb and both women decide they won't die after all. This play, stemming from Petronius, was in verse. Another Christopher Fry verse-play, "The Lady's Not for Burning," was expected to be brought from London during the season of 1950-1951.

(Closed April 29, 1950)

TICKETS, PLEASE!

(44 performances)

(Continued)

Revue in two acts, produced by Arthur Klein at the Coronet Theatre, April 27, 1950. Sketches by Harry Herrmann, Edmund Rice, Jack Roche and Ted Luce. Lyrics and music by Lyn Duddy, Joan Edwards, Mel Tolkin, Lucille Kallen and Clay Warnick.

The company—

Grace Hartman	Stuart Wade
Paul Hartman	Dee Arlen
Jack Albertson	Larry Kert
Dorothy Jarnac	Ronnie Edwards
Patricia Bright	Phyllis Cameron
Tommy Wonder	Midge Parker
Roger Price	Mildred Hughes
Bill Norvas	

Staged by Mervyn Nelson; sets by Ralph Alswang; costumes by Peggy Morrison; dances by Joan Mann; incidental music by Phil Ingalls and Hal Hastings.

Principal numbers: Act I.—"Prologue"; "Tickets, Please!"; "Roller Derby"; "Washington Square"; "Darn It, Baby, That's Love"; "The Ballet Isn't Ballet Any More;" "Les Ballets"; "Restless"; "A Senate Investigation"; "You Can't Take It with You"; "The Plot is Always the Same." Act II.—"Back at the Palace"; "Symbol of Fire"; "Tough on Love"; "Mister Proggle"; "The Moment I Looked in Your Eyes"; "Spring Has Come"; "Maha Roger"; "Maha the Great."

BRIGADOON

(24 performances)

Musical comedy in two acts, revived by Cheryl Crawford at the New York City Center of Music and Drama, May 2, 1950. Book and lyrics by Alan Jay Lerner; music by Frederick Loewe.

Cast of characters—

Tommy Albright	Phil Hanna
Jeff Douglas	Peter Turgeon
Sandy Dean	Douglas Rideout
Archie Beaton	Thaddeus Clancy
Fishmonger	Elizabeth Logue
Harry Beaton	James Jamieson
Angus MacGuffie	Angus Cairns
Andrew MacLaren	Donald McKee
Fiona MacLaren	Virginia Oswald
Jean MacLaren	Ann Deasy
Meg Brockie	Susan Johnson
Charlie Dalrymple	Jeff Warren
Maggie Anderson	Virginia Richardson
Mr. Lundie	Fred Stewart
Stuart Dalrymple	James Schlader
Sword Dancers	Wayne Sheridan, James White
Bagpiper	James McFadden

Frank	Angus Cairns
Jane Ashton	Winifred Ainslee

Singers: Misses Sylvia Chaney, Elizabeth Early, Margaret Hunter, Grayce Spence, Bobra Suiter, Eileen Turner, Lorraine Waldman, Dorothy Zurn. Messrs. Robert Busch, Arthur Carroll, Walter Kelvin, Louis Polacek, Earl Redding, Douglas Rideout, James Schlader, Stanley Simonds.

Dancers: Misses Meredith Baylis, Janice Boyd, Betty Buday, Barbara Davenport, Julie Hiller, Elizabeth Logue, Barbara McClarin, Yolanda Novak. Messrs. William Harris, Lloyd Malefonte, William Narcy, Glenn Olson, Robert Scoble, Wayne Sheridan, James White, Joseph Wiley.

Staged by Robert Lewis; dances by Agnes de Mille; settings by Oliver Smith; costumes by David Ffolkes; production stage manager, Harry Howell.

"Brigadoon" had its premiere March 13, 1947, at the Ziegfeld Theatre, where it had 581 performances.

(Closed May 21, 1950)

THE LIAR

(12 performances)

Musical comedy in two acts, based on the Carlo Goldoni play, produced by Dorothy Willard and Thomas Hammond at the Broadhurst Theatre, May 18, 1950. Book by Edward Eager and Alfred Drake; music by John Mundy; lyrics by Edward Eager.

Cast of characters—

Innkeeper	Walter F. Appler
Innkeeper's Wife	Jean Handzlik
Servingwench	Lee Wilcox
Servingmen	Leonardo Cimino, Martin Balsam
Woman at Window	May Muth
Fiori	Margery Oldroyd
Vino	David Collyer
Vegetabili	Marybelle Norton
Letter Carrier	Leslie Litomy
Urchin	William Myers
Captain of the Venetian Guards	Robert Penn
Guards	Edward Bryce, William Hogue, Laurence Weber, Walter Matthau
Lelio Bisognosi	William Eythe
Arlecchino	Joshua Shelley
Brighella	Russell Collins
Florindo Pallido	Glenn Burris
Rosaura Balanzoni	Barbara Moser
Beatrice Balanzoni	Karen Lindgren
Ottavio Ossimorsi	Stanley Carlson
Colombina	Paula Laurence
Pantalone Bisognosi	Melville Cooper
Doctor Balanzoni	Philip Coolidge
Cleonice Anselmi	Barbara Ashley

The scenes include a square, an inn and the Doctor's house in Venice, in the Spring in the Sixteenth Century. The action takes place within twenty-four hours.

Staged by Alfred Drake; musical sequences staged by Hanya Holm; musical director, Lehman Engel; setting by Donald Oenslager; Costumes by Motley; general stage manager, John E. Sola.

Principal musical numbers: Act I.— "March of the Guards"; "The Ladies' Opinion"; "You've Stolen My Heart"; "The Liar's Song"; "Supper Trio"; "Truth"; "Lackaday"; "Stop Holding Me Back"; "What's in a Name." Act II.— "Women's Work"; "Spring"; "Stomachs and Stomachs"; "A Jewel of a Duel"; "Out of Sight, Out of Mind"; "A Plot to Catch a Man In"; "Funeral March"; " 'Twill Never Be the Same."

(Closed May 27, 1950)

A STREETCAR NAMED DESIRE

(16 performances)
(Continued)

Play in three acts by Tennessee Williams, revived by Irene M. Selznick at the New York City Center of Music and Drama, May 23, 1950.

Cast of characters—

Negro woman	Eulabelle Moore
Eunice Hubbel	Peggy Rea
Stanley Kowalski	Anthony Quinn
Harold Mitchell	George Mathews
Stella Kowalski	Jorja Curtright
Blanche Du Bois	Uta Hagen
Steve Hubbel	Harry Kersey
Pablo Gonzales	Arny Freeman
A young collector	Wright King
Mexican Woman	Edna Thomas

Staged by Elia Kazan; setting by Jo Mielziner; costumes by Lucinda Ballard; production stage manager, Robert Downing.

"A Streetcar Named Desire" had its premiere December 3, 1947, at the Ethel Barrymore Theatre. It won both the Critics Circle and Pulitzer awards that season, and had 855 New York performances. The company listed above ended a long national tour with its engagement at the City Center.

THE SHOW-OFF

(6 performances)
(Continued)

Comedy in three acts by George Kelly, revived by David Heilweil and Derrick Lynn-Thomas at the Arena, 234 West 47th Street, May 31, 1950.

Cast of characters—

Clara	Carmen Mathews
Mrs. Fisher	Jane Seymour
Amy	Frances Waller
Frank Hyland	Joseph Holland
Aubrey Piper	Lee Tracy
Mr. Fisher	Walter Cartwright
Joe	Archie Smith
Mr. Gill	Howard Wendell
Mr. Rogers	Dudley Sadler

Staged by Martin Manulis; costumes and lighting by Beulah Frankel; stage manager, Clem Egolf.

George Kelly's comedy about Aubrey Piper, the blowhard, had its first performance February 5, 1924, at the Playhouse, where it had 571 performances. It was revived for the first time on December 12, 1932, at the Hudson. Many felt that this play should have won the Pulitzer Prize, but Kelly did not win this honor until the following season, with "Craig's Wife." Lee Tracy, who played the title role in the 1950 revival, had the part of Joe, the youthful inventor, in the 1924 original. The 1950 production was New York's first sample of theatre-in-the-round, being played in the converted ballroom of the Hotel Edison.

OFF BROADWAY

The urge to act is immeasurably stronger than the urge to make money by acting—which is why the theatre will never die. While the number of commercial theatre productions reached a new seasonal low, the number of off-Broadway offerings reached a new high.

According to Harold Stern, who pursues such matters for *Actors Cues* and *Show Business,* which are valuable publications for the profession, there were 264 play-producing groups which registered with him during the 1949-1950 season. He believes that at least fifty more organizations were active but neglected to submit data for his directory. Since most of these bands offered several productions apiece, it is obvious that the number of off-Broadway plays verged on the appalling.

This time there was no Cinderella success story about a new play which started in an obscure hall and moved up to Broadway and fame and fortune, as was the case of Sartre's "The Respectful Prostitute." No off-Broadway production ever did get to the Times Square area. A revival of Strindberg's "The Father" was instituted in Greenwich Village, and some time afterward a rival production starring Raymond Massey and Mady Christians was presented uptown. The downtown "Father" ran much longer than its professional competitor, and some qualified observers claimed it was better.

Since the urge to act is stronger than the urge to make money by acting, the players' union, Equity, relaxed and permitted members to act off Broadway for as little as $5 a week, under rigidly supervised circumstances. The majority of off-Broadway players got very little, or nothing, or the promise of something if they had a hit; and those taking acting courses from teachers and schools actually paid for the privilege of appearing on a stage.

The Equity Library Theatre, which has been in operation for a number of seasons on a basis of free admission and practically no pay for the actors, launched a new project which had encouraging results. It was the Equity Community Theatre, which made four productions at the Clinton Community Center in the Bronx. Here, for 50 cents, patrons saw "Lucky Sam McCarver," "Saint Joan," "The Great Big Doorstep" and "My Heart's in the Highlands." There were four performances of each play. Paid employment at union scale was given to seventy-five actors, sixteen technicians and four directors. Paid admissions totaled 12,300, and Equity began considering expanding its professional community theatre to other neighborhoods. The Bronx project, however, lost almost $2,000.

Generally speaking, Off Broadway means Public Domain. Occasionally new plays are presented and the authors are paid standard royalties; more often, old plays still copyrighted are obtained by payment of modest fees to such brokers as Dramatists Play Service and Samuel French; most often, off-Broadway fare is a revival of a play by an author who is dead and whose heirs and rights are dead, too. In the musical field during the season, Gilbert and Sullivan was the standby and Strindberg seemed to be the most promising author.

The season opened on June 6, 1949, with a presentation of Gertrude Stein's last dramatic work, "Yes Is for a Very Young Man," at the Cherry Lane Theatre. The sponsor was a new group, Off Broadway, Inc. Other June events included:

"The Fifth Horseman," fantasy by Abraham L. Goldfein, by the Experimental Theatre of the American National Theatre and Academy. "The Shoemaker's Prodigious Wife," by Garcia-Lorca, by Studio 7, a Yale Drama School group.

There was no notable activity in July, but in August Studio 7, operating at the famed old Provincetown Playhouse, distinguished itself by presenting "The Father." This production ran until October 15. At the end of August, Off Broadway, Inc., presented Molière's "The Bourgeois Gentleman" at the Cherry Lane Theatre and it ran until October 31.

On September 2 the Masque and Lyre Light Opera Company began a Gilbert and Sullivan season at the Jan Hus House in East 74th Street with "The Pirates of Penzance." Masque and Lyre operated throughout the season. The Interplayers, housed in Carnegie Hall's small theatre, offered Sean O'Casey's "The Silver Tassie." The Hudson Guild Playhouse did "The Ascent of F-6," by W. H. Auden and Christopher Isherwood. People's Drama presented John Wexley's "They Shall Not Die."

Highlights in October were: "Shake Hands with the Devil," new play by Robert C. Healey, at the Blackfriars'; "Dream House," new play by Tom Hill, sponsored by a new group called Originals Only; "Come Back on Tuesday," a musical based on Ruth Hunter's novel, played by the drama group at Fordham University, and the Equity Library Theatre's production of "Merrily We Roll Along" at the Walton Community Center in the Bronx.

In November ELT offered Emlyn Williams' "A Murder Has Been Arranged." The Players from Abroad presented Goethe's "Torquato

Tasso" in German at the Barbizon-Plaza Theatre. The Abbe Practical Workshop, one of the most energetic of the modern groups, presented a new play about postwar Germany, "The Edge of the Sword," by George Bellak. Katherine Sergava, the dancer, played the leading feminine role. On Stage offered Strindberg's "The Creditors" at the Cherry Lane. ELT began its paid-admission season with William Saroyan's "My Heart's in the Highlands." The Light Opera Theatre, in its fourteenth season, did "Ruddigore" at the Provincetown Playhouse.

In December Erwin Piscator's Dramatic Workshop began a repertoire which was to include "All My Sons," "Machinal," Noel Langley's new adaptation of "The Burning Bush," McElroy Wilkes' new "The Vintage," and "Bloomer Girl." Smith and Dale and other old-time vaudevillians were unsuccessful with a revue, "Holiday in Paris," on Second Avenue. A new group, the Laughing Stock Company, gave the first performances of Thornton Wilder's "Queens of France" at the Master Institute. "The Respectful Prostitute" had a curious revival when it was presented for five performances a day in connection with a movie at the Selwyn Theatre. Synge's "Deirdre of the Sorrows" was given at the Master Institute by the Abbe Practical Workshop. The Columbia University Theatre Associates offered Massinger's Elizabethan comedy, "The City Madam."

January of 1950 brought such items as: "A Midsummer Night's Dream" at the Provincetown Playhouse; the Columbia Opera Workshop's production of a new opera by Jan Meyrowitz and Langston Hughes, "The Barrier"; Irwin Shaw's "Bury the Dead," by the ELT, and "The Plough and the Stars" at the Hudson Guild.

In February the Abbe Workshop brought forth "Building 222," by Edward Gilmore. Elt revived "Idiot's Delight." Piscator's Dramatic Workshop submitted a new war play, "There Is No End," by Anthony Palma. The Selwyn Theatre put on a condensed version of "Ladies' Night in a Turkish Bath" as a companion to a movie.

In March the paid Equity group presented "The Great Big Doorstep," by Albert Hackett and Frances Goodrich, and followed with Shaw's "Saint Joan." On Stage Productions had another Shaw play, "Heartbreak House." Another new group, Theatre Classics, made its debut with Molière's "The Miser." The Dramatic Workshop did E. P. Conkle's "Prologue to Glory." Paul and Virginia Gilmore did "The Mollusc" and "Aren't We All?" at the Cherry Lane. The Abbe Workshop tried out "When the Bough Breaks," by John Gerstad and Robert Scott. Andre Obey's "Noah" was presented at the YMHA on 92d Street. ELT revived "Peg o' My Heart." And, most importantly, the American National Theatre and Academy acquired the former Guild Theatre on 52d Street, and planned a June production of Shaw's "Getting Married" with Sir Cedric Hardwicke and an all-star cast.

The big news of April was the merger of fifty-three off-Broadway groups, which began hunting a suitable theatre for year-round operation. The Abbe Workshop essayed Paul Green's "Tread the Green Grass." The Gilmores did "A Successful Calamity" at the Cherry Lane. A new group, the Footlight Players, put on a new play by Stacey Hull, "And So They Perish," at the Hudson Guild. The Weidman Studio offered a revue, "Come What May." On Stage revived James Bridie's "Tobias and the Angel." The Blackfriars produced "Armor of Light," by their Father Nagle. Outstanding was Piscator's presentation of "The Scapegoat," based by John F. Matthews on a Franz Kafka novel.

Chief news in May was the announcement of New York's first theatre-in-the-round or arena theatre—a form of presentation which has become popular in Texas and the West. (Of course, Billy Rose had a theatre-in-the-round production when he presented "Jumbo" at the old Hippodrome.) The new playhouse was to be installed in the ballroom of the Hotel Edison, and Lee Tracy opened there on May 31 in George Kelly's "The Show-Off." Fordham University put on Saroyan's "Sam Ego's House." Another hopeful new group, Theatre Society, made its bow with Ben Travers' "Thark." The Fifty, another new outfit, offered "Once in a Lifetime" in the Carnegie Recital Hall.

BALLET

There were two sensations in the ballet world, which is used to sensations but has not had many in recent seasons. In October Lee and J. J. Shubert imported Roland Petit's *Les Ballets de Paris,* a company of dancers numbering fifteen, and installed them at the Winter Garden. Petit, a young choreographer, is modern. He offered four numbers on his first and only bill—"Le Rendezvous," "L'Oeuf à la Coque," "Le Combat" and "Carmen." His two principal women dancers were Renée Jeanmaire and Colette Marchand. The featured number of the evening was a highly sexed ballet version of Bizet's opera, "Carmen," with settings by Antoine Clavé. "Ballets de Paris" were bold and original, and they achieved the unprecedented run, for a straight dance program, of 118 performances.

On October 9 S. Hurok brought to the Metropolitan Opera House the Sadler's Wells Ballet, Government-subsidized company from the Royal Opera House, Covent Garden, London. This company received an acclaim such as had not been accorded since the Ballet Russe de Monte Carlo made its first visit in the 1930s. The Sadler's Wells specialties were full-length, evening-long ballets—"The Sleeping Beauty," "Cinderella," "Swan Lake" among them. There also were representations of "Hamlet," "The Rake's Progress," "Wedding Bouquet," "Façade" and "Symphonic Variations." The size and perfection of the company and the splendor of their settings were eye-openers to New York audiences, and the dancers, including Margot Fonteyn, Moira Shearer and Robert Helpmann, became toasts of the town. The engagement was forced to end November 6, after which the company toured the U. S. to unprecedented business.

The Ballet Russe de Monte Carlo played the Metropolitan for two weeks beginning September 16. A new alliance, the New York City Dance Theatre, made its bow at the City Center with ten successful performances beginning December 14. The principals included Charles Weidman, Jose Limon, Doris Humphrey, Valerie Bettis and Pauline Koner. The New York City Ballet played the City Center for three weeks beginning November 23. Ballet Theatre celebrated its tenth anniversary with a three-week season at the Center Theatre, with Igor Youskevitch, Nana Gollner, Nora Kaye, Lucia Chase and Antony Tudor among its principals. Ballet Theatre also scored a coup by being appointed the official ballet of the Metropolitan Opera during the 1950-1951 season.

In April the Ballet Russe de Monte Carlo returned to the Metropolitan for a three-week season which featured Yvette Chauvire of the Paris Opera. The regular Monte Carloans included Frederic Franklin, Ruthanna Boris, Mary Ellen Moylan, Oleg Tupine and Roman Jasinsky.

STATISTICAL SUMMARY

(Last Season Plays Which Ended Runs After June 1, 1949)

Plays	Number Performances	
A Streetcar Named Desire	855	(Closed December 17, 1949)
Along Fifth Avenue	180	(Closed June 18, 1949)
Anne of the Thousand Days	286	(Closed October 8, 1949)
As the Girls Go	420	(Closed January 14, 1950)
At War with the Army	151	(Closed July 16, 1949)
Born Yesterday	1,642	(Closed December 31, 1949)
Diamond Lil	181	(Closed January 14, 1950)
Goodbye, My Fancy	446	(Closed December 24, 1949)
High Button Shoes	727	(Closed July 2, 1949)
Howdy, Mr. Ice of 1950!	430	(Closed April 15, 1950)
Lend an Ear	460	(Closed January 21, 1950)
The Madwoman of Chaillot	368	(Closed January 7, 1950)
Two Blind Mice	157	(Closed July 16, 1949)

LONG RUNS ON BROADWAY

To June 3, 1950

(Plays marked with asterisk were still playing June 3, 1950)

Plays	Number Performances	Plays	Number Performances
Life with Father	3,224	Sons o' Fun	742
Tobacco Road	3,182	The Man Who Came to Dinner	739
Abie's Irish Rose	2,327	Call Me Mister	734
Oklahoma!	2,248	High Button Shoes	727
Harvey	1,775	Finian's Rainbow	725
Born Yesterday	1,642	Claudia	722
The Voice of the Turtle	1,557	The Gold Diggers	720
Arsenic and Old Lace	1,444	I Remember Mama	714
Hellzapoppin	1,404	Junior Miss	710
Angel Street	1,295	Seventh Heaven	704
Lightnin'	1,291	Peg o' My Heart	692
Annie Get Your Gun	1,147	The Children's Hour	691
Pins and Needles	1,108	Dead End	687
*Mister Roberts	991	The Lion and the Mouse	686
Anna Lucasta	957	White Cargo	686
Kiss and Tell	956	Dear Ruth	683
Carousel	890	East Is West	680
Hats Off to Ice	889	*Where's Charley?	680
Follow the Girls	882	The Doughgirls	671
The Bat	867	Irene	670
My Sister Eileen	865	Boy Meets Girl	669
White Cargo	864	Blithe Spirit	657
Song of Norway	860	The Women	657
A Streetcar Named Desire	855	A Trip to Chinatown	657
You Can't Take It with You	837	Bloomer Girl	654
Three Men on a Horse	835	Rain	648
Stars on Ice	830	Janie	642
The Ladder	789	The Green Pastures	640
State of the Union	765	Is Zat So?	618
The First Year	760	Separate Rooms	613
		Star and Garter	609

388

Plays	Number Performances	Plays	Number Performances
Student Prince	608	Let's Face It	547
Broadway	603	Within the Law	541
Adonis	603	The Music Master	540
Street Scene	601	What a Life	538
Kiki	600	The Red Mill	531
A Society Circus	596	The Boomerang	522
*Kiss Me, Kate	596	Rosalinda	521
Blossom Time	592	Chauve Souris	520
The Two Mrs. Carrolls	585	Blackbirds	518
Brigadoon	581	Sunny	517
Brother Rat	577	Victoria Regina	517
Show Boat	572	The Vagabond King	511
The Show-Off	571	The New Moon	509
Sally	570	Shuffle Along	504
One Touch of Venus	567	Up in Central Park	504
Happy Birthday	564	Carmen Jones	503
The Glass Menagerie	561	Personal Appearance	501
Rose Marie	557	Panama Hattie	501
Strictly Dishonorable	557	*Detective Story	501
Ziegfeld Follies	553	Bird in Hand	500
Floradora	553	Sailor, Beware!	500
Good News	551	Room Service	500
*Death of a Salesman	550	Tomorrow the World	500

NEW YORK DRAMA CRITICS
CIRCLE AWARDS

When the drama critics met on April 5, 1950, to vote the "bests" for the period from April 1, 1949, to March 31, 1950, they were of pretty much the same mind. A hefty majority opined that Carson McCullers' "The Member of the Wedding" was the best play of the year, although there were scattered votes for William Inge's "Come Back, Little Sheba" and Gian-Carlo Menotti's libretto for "The Consul." T. S. Eliot's "The Cocktail Party" easily won the foreign play award, with the Maurice Valency-Jean Giraudoux "The Enchanted" slightly in the running. The Menotti opera, "The Consul," won decisively over Maxwell Anderson's and the late Kurt Weill's "Lost in the Stars."

In September, 1949, the Critics Circle debated a proposition that any play, no matter what its source, be eligible for the best play award. One faction argued that art knows no boundaries—and this faction lost. The critics voted to continue to confine their top prize to a play of American authorship. Many members of the "international set" believed that "The Cocktail Party" was the best drama of the year and should not have been given a secondary citation just because it was English.

Circle awards have been—

1935-36—Winterset, by Maxwell Anderson
1936-37—High Tor, by Maxwell Anderson
1937-38—Of Mice and Men, by John Steinbeck
1938-39—No award.
1939-40—The Time of Your Life, by William Saroyan
1940-41—Watch on the Rhine, by Lillian Hellman
1941-42—No award.
1942-43—The Patriots, by Sidney Kingsley
1943-44—No award.
1944-45—The Glass Menagerie, by Tennessee Williams
1945-46—No award.
1946-47—All My Sons, by Arthur Miller
1947-48—A Streetcar Named Desire, by Tennessee Williams
1948-49—Death of a Salesman, by Arthur Miller
1949-50—The Member of the Wedding, by Carson McCullers

PULITZER PRIZE WINNERS

The Pulitzer drama award committee confounded—not purposefully or impishly, however—the guessers who were speculating on various of the season's new plays. According to the committee's own calendar, "South Pacific" was eligible, even though it was a last-season show to the guessers. So the Pulitzer Prize went to Richard Rodgers, Oscar Hammerstein II and Joshua Logan for their fabulous musical. James A. Michener had previously won a Pulitzer fiction prize for the novel on which "South Pacific" was based. In the field of music, a Pulitzer citation went to Gian-Carlo Menotti's "The Consul."

Pulitzer awards have been—

1917-18—Why Marry?, by Jesse Lynch Williams
1918-19—No award.
1919-20—Beyond the Horizon, by Eugene O'Neill
1920-21—Miss Lulu Bett, by Zona Gale
1921-22—Anna Christie, by Eugene O'Neill
1922-23—Icebound, by Owen Davis
1923-24—Hell-bent fer Heaven, by Hatcher Hughes
1924-25—They Knew What They Wanted, by Sidney Howard
1925-26—Craig's Wife, by George Kelly
1926-27—In Abraham's Bosom, by Paul Green
1927-28—Strange Interlude, by Eugene O'Neill
1928-29—Street Scene, by Elmer Rice
1929-30—The Green Pastures, by Marc Connelly
1930-31—Alison's House, by Susan Glaspell
1931-32—Of Thee I Sing, by George S. Kaufman, Morrie Ryskind, Ira and George Gershwin
1932-33—Both Your Houses, by Maxwell Anderson
1933-34—Men in White, by Sidney Kingsley
1934-35—The Old Maid, by Zoe Akins
1935-36—Idiot's Delight, by Robert E. Sherwood
1936-37—You Can't Take It with You, by Moss Hart and George S. Kaufman
1937-38—Our Town, by Thornton Wilder
1938-39—Abe Lincoln in Illinois, by Robert E. Sherwood
1939-40—The Time of Your Life, by William Saroyan

1940-41—There Shall Be No Night, by Robert E. Sherwood
1941-42—No award.
1942-43—The Skin of Our Teeth, by Thornton Wilder
1943-44—No award.
1944-45—Harvey, by Mary Coyle Chase
1945-46—State of the Union, by Howard Lindsay and Russel
        Crouse
1946-47—No award.
1947-48—A Streetcar Named Desire, by Tennessee Williams
1948-49—Death of a Salesman, by Arthur Miller
1949-50—South Pacific, by Richard Rodgers, Oscar Hammerstein
        II and Joshua Logan

PREVIOUS VOLUMES OF BEST PLAYS

Plays chosen to represent the theatre seasons from 1899 to 1949 are as follows:

1899-1909

BARBARA FRIETCHIE, by Clyde Fitch. Life Publishing Co.
THE CLIMBERS, by Clyde Fitch. Macmillan.
IF I WERE KING, by Justin Huntly McCarthy. Samuel French.
THE DARLING OF THE GODS, by David Belasco. Little, Brown.
THE COUNTY CHAIRMAN, by George Ade. Samuel French.
LEAH KLESCHNA, by C. M. S. McLellan. Samuel French.
THE SQUAW MAN, by Edwin Milton Royle.
THE GREAT DIVIDE, by William Vaughn Moody. Samuel French.
THE WITCHING HOUR, by Augustus Thomas. Samuel French.
THE MAN FROM HOME, by Booth Tarkington and Harry Leon Wilson. Samuel French.

1909-1919

THE EASIEST WAY, by Eugene Walter. G. W. Dillingham and Houghton Mifflin.
MRS. BUMPSTEAD-LEIGH, by Harry James Smith. Samuel French.
DISRAELI, by Louis N. Parker. Dodd, Mead.
ROMANCE, by Edward Sheldon. Macmillan.
SEVEN KEYS TO BALDPATE, by George M. Cohan. Published by Bobbs-Merrill as a novel by Earl Derr Biggers; as a play by Samuel French.
ON TRIAL, by Elmer Reizenstein. Samuel French.
THE UNCHASTENED WOMAN, by Louis Kaufman Anspacher. Harcourt, Brace and Howe.
GOOD GRACIOUS ANNABELLE, by Clare Kummer. Samuel French.
WHY MARRY? by Jesse Lynch Williams. Scribner.
JOHN FERGUSON, by St. John Ervine. Macmillan.

1919-1920

ABRAHAM LINCOLN, by John Drinkwater. Houghton Mifflin.
CLARENCE, by Booth Tarkington. Samuel French.
BEYOND THE HORIZON, by Eugene G. O'Neill. Boni & Liveright.

DÉCLASSÉE, by Zoe Akins. Liveright, Inc.
THE FAMOUS MRS. FAIR, by James Forbes. Samuel French.
THE JEST, by Sem Benelli. (American adaptation by Edward Sheldon.)
JANE CLEGG, by St. John Ervine. Henry Holt.
MAMMA'S AFFAIR, by Rachel Barton Butler. Samuel French.
WEDDING BELLS, by Salisbury Field. Samuel French.
ADAM AND EVA, by George Middleton and Guy Bolton. Samuel French.

1920-1921

DEBURAU, adapted from the French of Sacha Guitry by H. Granville Barker. Putnam.
THE FIRST YEAR, by Frank Craven. Samuel French.
ENTER MADAME, by Gilda Varesi and Dolly Byrne. Putnam.
THE GREEN GODDESS, by William Archer. Knopf.
LILIOM, by Ferenc Molnar. Boni & Liveright.
MARY ROSE, by James M. Barrie. Scribner.
NICE PEOPLE, by Rachel Crothers. Scribner.
THE BAD MAN, by Porter Emerson Browne. Putnam.
THE EMPEROR JONES, by Eugene G. O'Neill. Boni & Liveright.
THE SKIN GAME, by John Galsworthy. Scribner.

1921-1922

ANNA CHRISTIE, by Eugene G. O'Neill. Boni & Liveright.
A BILL OF DIVORCEMENT, by Clemence Dane. Macmillan.
DULCY, by George S. Kaufman and Marc Connelly. Putnam.
HE WHO GETS SLAPPED, adapted from the Russian of Leonid Andreyev by Gregory Zilboorg. Brentano's.
SIX CYLINDER LOVE, by William Anthony McGuire.
THE HERO, by Gilbert Emery.
THE DOVER ROAD, by Alan Alexander Milne. Samuel French.
AMBUSH, by Arthur Richman.
THE CIRCLE, by William Somerset Maugham.
THE NEST, by Paul Geraldy and Grace George.

1922-1923

RAIN, by John Colton and Clemence Randolph. Liveright, Inc.
LOYALTIES, by John Galsworthy. Scribner.
ICEBOUND, by Owen Davis. Little, Brown.
YOU AND I, by Philip Barry. Brentano's.
THE FOOL, by Channing Pollock. Brentano's.

MERTON OF THE MOVIES, by George Kaufman and Marc Connelly, based on the novel of the same name by Harry Leon Wilson.

WHY NOT? by Jesse Lynch Williams. Walter H. Baker Co.

THE OLD SOAK, by Don Marquis. Doubleday, Page.

R.U.R., by Karel Capek. Translated by Paul Selver. Doubleday, Page.

MARY THE 3D, by Rachel Crothers. Brentano's.

1923–1924

THE SWAN, translated from the Hungarian of Ferenc Molnar by Melville Baker. Boni & Liveright.

OUTWARD BOUND, by Sutton Vane. Boni & Liveright.

THE SHOW-OFF, by George Kelly. Little, Brown.

THE CHANGELINGS, by Lee Wilson Dodd. Dutton.

CHICKEN FEED, by Guy Bolton. Samuel French.

SUN-UP, by Lula Vollmer. Brentano's.

BEGGAR ON HORSEBACK, by George Kaufman and Marc Connelly. Boni & Liveright.

TARNISH, by Gilbert Emery. Brentano's.

THE GOOSE HANGS HIGH, by Lewis Beach. Little, Brown.

HELL-BENT FER HEAVEN, by Hatcher Hughes. Harper.

1924–1925

WHAT PRICE GLORY? by Laurence Stallings and Maxwell Anderson. Harcourt, Brace.

THEY KNEW WHAT THEY WANTED, by Sidney Howard. Doubleday, Page.

DESIRE UNDER THE ELMS, by Eugene G. O'Neill. Boni & Liveright.

THE FIREBRAND, by Edwin Justus Mayer. Boni & Liveright.

DANCING MOTHERS, by Edgar Selwyn and Edmund Goulding.

MRS. PARTRIDGE PRESENTS, by Mary Kennedy and Ruth Warren. Samuel French.

THE FALL GUY, by James Gleason and George Abbott. Samuel French.

THE YOUNGEST, by Philip Barry. Samuel French.

MINICK, by Edna Ferber and George S. Kaufman. Doubleday, Page.

WILD BIRDS, by Dan Totheroh. Doubleday, Page.

1925–1926

CRAIG'S WIFE, by George Kelly. Little, Brown.

THE GREAT GOD BROWN, by Eugene G. O'Neill. Boni & Liveright.

THE GREEN HAT, by Michael Arlen.

THE DYBBUK, by S. Ansky, Henry G. Alsberg-Winifred Katzin translation. Boni & Liveright.

THE ENEMY, by Channing Pollock. Brentano's.

THE LAST OF MRS. CHEYNEY, by Frederick Lonsdale. Samuel French.

BRIDE OF THE LAMB, by William Hurlbut. Boni & Liveright.

THE WISDOM TOOTH, by Marc Connelly. George H. Doran.

THE BUTTER AND EGG MAN, by George Kaufman. Boni & Liveright.

YOUNG WOODLEY, by John Van Druten. Simon & Schuster.

1926-1927

BROADWAY, by Philip Dunning and George Abbott. George H. Doran.

SATURDAY'S CHILDREN, by Maxwell Anderson. Longmans, Green.

CHICAGO, by Maurine Watkins. Knopf.

THE CONSTANT WIFE, by William Somerset Maugham. George H. Doran.

THE PLAY'S THE THING, by Ferenc Molnar and P. G. Wodehouse. Brentano's.

THE ROAD TO ROME, by Robert Emmet Sherwood. Scribner.

THE SILVER CORD, by Sidney Howard. Scribner.

THE CRADLE SONG, translated from the Spanish of G. Martinez Sierra by John Garrett Underhill. Dutton.

DAISY MAYME, by George Kelly. Little, Brown.

IN ABRAHAM'S BOSOM, by Paul Green. McBride.

1927-1928

STRANGE INTERLUDE, by Eugene G. O'Neill. Boni & Liveright.

THE ROYAL FAMILY, by Edna Ferber and George Kaufman. Doubleday, Doran.

BURLESQUE, by George Manker Watters and Arthur Hopkins. Doubleday, Doran.

COQUETTE, by George Abbott and Ann Bridgers. Longmans, Green.

BEHOLD THE BRIDEGROOM, by George Kelly. Little, Brown.

PORGY, by DuBose Heyward. Doubleday, Doran.

PARIS BOUND, by Philip Barry. Samuel French.

ESCAPE, by John Galsworthy. Scribner.

THE RACKET, by Bartlett Cormack. Samuel French.

THE PLOUGH AND THE STARS, by Sean O'Casey. Macmillan.

1928-1929

STREET SCENE, by Elmer Rice. Samuel French.
JOURNEY'S END, by R. C. Sherriff. Brentano's.
WINGS OVER EUROPE, by Robert Nichols and Maurice Browne. Co-
vici-Friede.
HOLIDAY, by Philip Barry. Samuel French.
THE FRONT PAGE, by Ben Hecht and Charles MacArthur. Covici-
Friede.
LET US BE GAY, by Rachel Crothers. Samuel French.
MACHINAL, by Sophie Treadwell.
LITTLE ACCIDENT, by Floyd Dell and Thomas Mitchell.
GYPSY, by Maxwell Anderson.
THE KINGDOM OF GOD, by G. Martinez Sierra; English version by
Helen and Harley Granville-Barker. Dutton.

1929-1930

THE GREEN PASTURES, by Marc Connelly (adapted from "Ol' Man
Adam and His Chilllun," by Roark Bradford). Farrar & Rine-
hart.
THE CRIMINAL CODE, by Martin Flavin. Horace Liveright.
BERKELEY SQUARE, by John Balderston.
STRICTLY DISHONORABLE, by Preston Sturges. Horace Liveright.
THE FIRST MRS. FRASER, by St. John Ervine. Macmillan.
THE LAST MILE, by John Wexley. Samuel French.
JUNE MOON, by Ring W. Lardner and George S. Kaufman. Scribner.
MICHAEL AND MARY, by A. A. Milne. Chatto & Windus.
DEATH TAKES A HOLIDAY, by Walter Ferris (adapted from the Ital-
ian of Alberto Casella). Samuel French.
REBOUND, by Donald Ogden Stewart. Samuel French.

1930-1931

ELIZABETH THE QUEEN, by Maxwell Anderson. Longmans, Green.
TOMORROW AND TOMORROW, by Philip Barry. Samuel French.
ONCE IN A LIFETIME, by George S. Kaufman and Moss Hart. Far-
rar & Rinehart.
GREEN GROW THE LILACS, by Lynn Riggs. Samuel French.
AS HUSBANDS GO, by Rachel Crothers. Samuel French.
ALISON'S HOUSE, by Susan Glaspell. Samuel French.
FIVE-STAR FINAL, by Louis Weitzenkorn. Samuel French.
OVERTURE, by William Bolitho. Simon & Schuster.

THE BARRETTS OF WIMPOLE STREET, by Rudolf Besier. Little, Brown.

GRAND HOTEL, adapted from the German of Vicki Baum by W. A. Drake.

1931-1932

OF THEE I SING, by George S. Kaufman and Morrie Ryskind; music and lyrics by George and Ira Gershwin. Knopf.

MOURNING BECOMES ELECTRA, by Eugene G. O'Neill. Horace Liveright.

REUNION IN VIENNA, by Robert Emmet Sherwood. Scribner.

THE HOUSE OF CONNELLY, by Paul Green. Samuel French.

THE ANIMAL KINGDOM, by Philip Barry. Samuel French.

THE LEFT BANK, by Elmer Rice. Samuel French.

ANOTHER LANGUAGE, by Rose Franken. Samuel French.

BRIEF MOMENT, by S. N. Behrman. Farrar & Rinehart.

THE DEVIL PASSES, by Benn W. Levy. Martin Secker.

CYNARA, by H. M. Harwood and R. F. Gore-Browne. Samuel French.

1932-1933

BOTH YOUR HOUSES, by Maxwell Anderson. Samuel French.

DINNER AT EIGHT, by George S. Kaufman and Edna Ferber. Doubleday, Doran.

WHEN LADIES MEET, by Rachel Crothers. Samuel French.

DESIGN FOR LIVING, by Noel Coward. Doubleday, Doran.

BIOGRAPHY, by S. N. Behrman. Farrar & Rinehart.

ALIEN CORN, by Sidney Howard. Scribner.

THE LATE CHRISTOPHER BEAN, adapted from the French of René Fauchois by Sidney Howard. Samuel French.

WE, THE PEOPLE, by Elmer Rice. Coward-McCann.

PIGEONS AND PEOPLE, by George M. Cohan.

ONE SUNDAY AFTERNOON, by James Hagan. Samuel French.

1933-1934

MARY OF SCOTLAND, by Maxwell Anderson. Doubleday, Doran.

MEN IN WHITE, by Sidney Kingsley. Covici-Friede.

DODSWORTH, by Sinclair Lewis and Sidney Howard. Harcourt, Brace.

AH, WILDERNESS, by Eugene O'Neill. Random House.

THEY SHALL NOT DIE, by John Wexley. Knopf.

HER MASTER'S VOICE, by Clare Kummer. Samuel French.

NO MORE LADIES, by A. E. Thomas.

WEDNESDAY'S CHILD, by Leopold Atlas. Samuel French.

THE SHINING HOUR, by Keith Winter. Doubleday, Doran.

THE GREEN BAY TREE, by Mordaunt Shairp. Baker International Play Bureau.

1934-1935

THE CHILDREN'S HOUR, by Lillian Hellman. Knopf.

VALLEY FORGE, by Maxwell Anderson. Anderson House.

THE PETRIFIED FOREST, by Robert Sherwood. Scribner.

THE OLD MAID, by Zoe Akins. Appleton-Century.

ACCENT ON YOUTH, by Samson Raphaelson. Samuel French.

MERRILY WE ROLL ALONG, by George S. Kaufman and Moss Hart. Random House.

AWAKE AND SING, by Clifford Odets. Random House.

THE FARMER TAKES A WIFE, by Frank B. Elser and Marc Connelly.

LOST HORIZONS, by John Hayden.

THE DISTAFF SIDE, by John Van Druten. Knopf.

1935-1936

WINTERSET, by Maxwell Anderson. Anderson House.

IDIOT'S DELIGHT, by Robert Emmet Sherwood. Scribner.

END OF SUMMER, by S. N. Behrman. Random House.

FIRST LADY, by Katharine Dayton and George S. Kaufman. Random House.

VICTORIA REGINA, by Laurence Housman. Samuel French.

BOY MEETS GIRL, by Bella and Samuel Spewack. Random House.

DEAD END, by Sidney Kingsley. Random House.

CALL IT A DAY, by Dodie Smith. Samuel French.

ETHAN FROME, by Owen Davis and Donald Davis. Scribner.

PRIDE AND PREJUDICE, by Helen Jerome. Doubleday, Doran.

1936-1937

HIGH TOR, by Maxwell Anderson. Anderson House.

YOU CAN'T TAKE IT WITH YOU, by Moss Hart and George S. Kaufman. Farrar & Rinehart.

JOHNNY JOHNSON, by Paul Green. Samuel French.

DAUGHTERS OF ATREUS, by Robert Turney. Knopf.

STAGE DOOR, by Edna Ferber and George S. Kaufman. Doubleday, Doran.

THE WOMEN, by Clare Boothe. Random House.

ST. HELENA, by R. C. Sherriff and Jeanne de Casalis. Samuel French.

Yes, My Darling Daughter, by Mark Reed. Samuel French.
Excursion, by Victor Wolfson. Random House.
Tovarich, by Jacques Deval and Robert E. Sherwood. Random House.

1937-1938

Of Mice and Men, by John Steinbeck. Covici-Friede.
Our Town, by Thornton Wilder. Coward-McCann.
Shadow and Substance, by Paul Vincent Carroll. Random House.
On Borrowed Time, by Paul Osborn. Knopf.
The Star-Wagon, by Maxwell Anderson. Anderson House.
Susan and God, by Rachel Crothers. Random House.
Prologue to Glory, by E. P. Conkle. Random House.
Amphitryon 38, by S. N. Behrman. Random House.
Golden Boy, by Clifford Odets. Random House.
What a Life, by Clifford Goldsmith. Dramatists' Play Service.

1938-1939

Abe Lincoln in Illinois, by Robert E. Sherwood. Scribner.
The Little Foxes, by Lillian Hellman. Random House.
Rocket to the Moon, by Clifford Odets. Random House.
The American Way, by George S. Kaufman and Moss Hart. Random House.
No Time for Comedy, by S. N. Behrman. Random House.
The Philadelphia Story, by Philip Barry. Coward-McCann.
The White Steed, by Paul Vincent Carroll. Random House.
Here Come the Clowns, by Philip Barry. Coward-McCann.
Family Portrait, by Lenore Coffee and William Joyce Cowen. Random House.
Kiss the Boys Good-bye, by Clare Boothe. Random House.

1939-1940

There Shall Be No Night, by Robert E. Sherwood. Scribner.
Key Largo, by Maxwell Anderson. Anderson House.
The World We Make, by Sidney Kingsley.
Life with Father, by Howard Lindsay and Russel Crouse. Knopf.
The Man Who Came to Dinner, by George S. Kaufman and Moss Hart. Random House.
The Male Animal, by James Thurber and Elliott Nugent. Random House, New York, and MacMillan Co., Canada.
The Time of Your Life, by William Saroyan. Harcourt, Brace.
Skylark, by Samson Raphaelson. Random House.

MARGIN FOR ERROR, by Clare Boothe. Random House.
MORNING'S AT SEVEN, by Paul Osborn. Samuel French.

1940-1941

NATIVE SON, by Paul Green and Richard Wright. Harper.
WATCH ON THE RHINE, by Lillian Hellman. Random House.
THE CORN IS GREEN, by Emlyn Williams. Random House.
LADY IN THE DARK, by Moss Hart. Random House.
ARSENIC AND OLD LACE, by Joseph Kesselring. Random House.
MY SISTER EILEEN, by Joseph Fields and Jerome Chodorov. Random House.
FLIGHT TO THE WEST, by Elmer Rice. Coward-McCann.
CLAUDIA, by Rose Franken Meloney. Farrar & Rinehart.
MR. AND MRS. NORTH, by Owen Davis. Samuel French.
GEORGE WASHINGTON SLEPT HERE, by George S. Kaufman and Moss Hart. Random House.

1941-1942

IN TIME TO COME, by Howard Koch. Dramatists' Play Service.
THE MOON IS DOWN, by John Steinbeck. Viking.
BLITHE SPIRIT, by Noel Coward. Doubleday, Doran.
JUNIOR MISS, by Jerome Chodorov and Joseph Fields. Random House.
CANDLE IN THE WIND, by Maxwell Anderson. Anderson House.
LETTERS TO LUCERNE, by Fritz Rotter and Allen Vincent. Samuel French.
JASON, by Samson Raphaelson. Random House.
ANGEL STREET, by Patrick Hamilton. Constable & Co., under the title "Gaslight."
UNCLE HARRY, by Thomas Job. Samuel French.
HOPE FOR A HARVEST, by Sophie Treadwell. Samuel French.

1942-1943

THE PATRIOTS, by Sidney Kingsley. Random House.
THE EVE OF ST. MARK, by Maxwell Anderson. Anderson House.
THE SKIN OF OUR TEETH, by Thornton Wilder. Harper.
WINTER SOLDIERS, by Dan James.
TOMORROW THE WORLD, by James Gow and Arnaud d'Usseau. Scribner.
HARRIET, by Florence Ryerson and Colin Clements. Scribner.
THE DOUGHGIRLS, by Joseph Fields. Random House.

THE DAMASK CHEEK, by John Van Druten and Lloyd Morris. Random House.

KISS AND TELL, by F. Hugh Herbert. Coward-McCann.

OKLAHOMA!, by Oscar Hammerstein 2nd and Richard Rodgers. Random House.

1943-1944

WINGED VICTORY, by Moss Hart. Random House.

THE SEARCHING WIND, by Lillian Hellman. Viking.

THE VOICE OF THE TURTLE, by John Van Druten. Random House.

DECISION, by Edward Chodorov.

OVER 21, by Ruth Gordon. Random House.

OUTRAGEOUS FORTUNE, by Rose Franken. Samuel French.

JACOBOWSKY AND THE COLONEL, by S. N. Behrman. Random House.

STORM OPERATION, by Maxwell Anderson. Anderson House.

PICK-UP GIRL, by Elsa Shelley.

THE INNOCENT VOYAGE, by Paul Osborn.

1944-1945

A BELL FOR ADANO, by Paul Osborn. Knopf.

I REMEMBER MAMA, by John Van Druten. Harcourt, Brace.

THE HASTY HEART, by John Patrick. Random House.

THE GLASS MENAGERIE, by Tennessee Williams. Random House.

HARVEY, by Mary Chase.

THE LATE GEORGE APLEY, by John P. Marquand and George S. Kaufman.

SOLDIER'S WIFE, by Rose Franken. Samuel French.

ANNA LUCASTA, by Philip Yordan. Random House.

FOOLISH NOTION, by Philip Barry.

DEAR RUTH, by Norman Krasna. Random House.

1945-1946

STATE OF THE UNION, by Howard Lindsay and Russel Crouse. Random House.

HOME OF THE BRAVE, by Arthur Laurents. Random House.

DEEP ARE THE ROOTS, by Arnaud d'Usseau and James Gow. Scribner.

THE MAGNIFICENT YANKEE, by Emmet Lavery. Samuel French.

ANTIGONE, by Lewis Galantiere (from the French of Jean Anouilh). Random House.

O MISTRESS MINE, by Terence Rattigan. Published and revised by the author.

BORN YESTERDAY, by Garson Kanin. Viking.
DREAM GIRL, by Elmer Rice. Coward-McCann.
THE RUGGED PATH, by Robert E. Sherwood. Scribner.
LUTE SONG, by Will Irwin and Sidney Howard. Published version
    by Will Irwin and Leopoldine Howard.

1946-1947

ALL MY SONS, by Arthur Miller. Reynal & Hitchcock.
THE ICEMAN COMETH, by Eugene G. O'Neill. Random House.
JOAN OF LORRAINE, by Maxwell Anderson. Published by Maxwell
    Anderson.
ANOTHER PART OF THE FOREST, by Lillian Hellman. Viking.
YEARS AGO, by Ruth Gordon. Viking.
JOHN LOVES MARY, by Norman Krasna. Copyright by Norman
    Krasna.
THE FATAL WEAKNESS, by George Kelly. Samuel French.
THE STORY OF MARY SURRATT, by John Patrick. Dramatists' Play
    Service.
CHRISTOPHER BLAKE, by Moss Hart. Random House.
BRIGADOON, by Alan Jay Lerner and Frederick Loewe. Coward-
    McCann.

1947-1948

A STREETCAR NAMED DESIRE, by Tennessee Williams. New Direc-
    tions.
MISTER ROBERTS, by Thomas Heggen and Joshua Logan. Houghton
    Mifflin.
COMMAND DECISION, by William Wister Haines. Random House.
THE WINSLOW BOY, by Terence Rattigan.
THE HEIRESS, by Ruth and Augustus Goetz.
ALLEGRO, by Richard Rodgers and Oscar Hammerstein 2d. Knopf.
    Music published by Williamson Music, Inc.
EASTWARD IN EDEN, by Dorothy Gardner. Longmans, Green.
SKIPPER NEXT TO GOD, by Jan de Hartog.
AN INSPECTOR CALLS, by J. B. Priestley.
ME AND MOLLY, by Gertrude Berg.

1948-1949

DEATH OF A SALESMAN, by Arthur Miller. Viking.
ANNE OF THE THOUSAND DAYS, by Maxwell Anderson. Sloane.
THE MADWOMAN OF CHAILLOT, by Maurice Valency, adapted from
    the French of Jean Giraudoux. Random House.
DETECTIVE STORY, by Sidney Kingsley. Random House.

EDWARD, MY SON, by Robert Morley and Noel Langley.   Random House, New York, and Samuel French, London.

LIFE WITH MOTHER, by Howard Lindsay and Russel Crouse.   Knopf.

LIGHT UP THE SKY, by Moss Hart.   Random House.

THE SILVER WHISTLE, by Robert Edward McEnroe.   Dramatists' Play Service.

TWO BLIND MICE, by Samuel Spewack.   Dramatists' Play Service.

GOODBYE, MY FANCY, by Fay Kanin.   Samuel French.

WHERE AND WHEN THEY WERE BORN

(Compiled from the most authentic records available)

Abbott, George .... Forestville, N. Y. 1895
Abel, Walter .... St. Paul, Minn. 1898
Adams, Maude .... Salt Lake City, Utah 1872
Addy, Wesley .... Omaha, Neb. 1912
Aherne, Brian .... King's Norton, England 1902
Aldrich, Richard .... Boston 1902
Anders, Glenn .... Los Angeles, Cal. 1890
Anderson, Judith .... Australia 1898
Anderson, Maxwell .... Atlantic City, Pa. 1888
Andrews, A. G. .... Buffalo, N. Y. 1861
Arthur, Jean .... New York City 1905
Ashcroft, Peggy .... Croydon, Eng. 1907

Bainter, Fay .... Los Angeles, Cal. 1892
Bankhead, Tallulah .... Huntsville, Ala. 1902
Banks, Leslie .... West Derby, England 1890
Barrymore, Ethel .... Philadelphia, Pa. 1879
Barrymore, Lionel .... Philadelphia, Pa. 1878
Barton, James .... Gloucester, N. J. 1890
Behrman, S. N. .... Worcester, Mass. 1893
Bell, James .... Suffolk, Va. 1891
Bellamy, Ralph .... Chicago, Ill. 1905
Belmore, Bertha .... Manchester, England 1882
Bergman, Ingrid .... Stockholm 1917
Bergner, Elisabeth .... Vienna 1901
Berlin, Irving .... Russia 1888
Blackmer, Sidney .... Salisbury, N. C. 1898
Bolger, Ray .... Dorchester, Mass. 1906
Bondi, Beulah .... Chicago, Ill. 1892
Bourneuf, Philip .... Boston, Mass. 1912
Boyer, Charles .... Figeac, France 1899
Braham, Horace .... London, England 1896
Brent, Romney .... Saltillo, Mex. 1902
Brice, Fannie .... Brooklyn, N. Y. 1891
Bruce, Carol .... Great Neck, L. I. 1919
Bruce, Nigel .... San Diego, Cal. 1895

Burke, Billie .... Washington, D. C. 1885
Buckmaster, John .... Essex, Eng. 1915
Byington, Spring .... Colorado Springs, Colo. 1898

Cagney, James .... New York 1904
Cagney, Jeanne .... New York 1920
Calhern, Louis .... New York 1895
Cantor, Eddie .... New York 1894
Carlisle, Kitty .... New Orleans, La. 1912
Carnovsky, Morris .... St. Louis, Mo. 1898
Carradine, John .... New York City 1906
Carroll, Leo G. .... Weedon, England 1892
Carroll, Madeleine .... West Bromwich, England 1906
Catlett, Walter .... San Francisco, Cal. 1889
Caulfield, Joan .... New York City 1924
Chase, Ilka .... New York City 1905
Chatterton, Ruth .... New York 1893
Christians, Mady .... Vienna, Austria 1907
Claire, Ina .... Washington, D. C. 1892
Clark, Bobby .... Springfield, Ohio 1888
Clift, Montgomery .... Omaha, Neb. 1921
Clive, Colin .... St. Malo, France 1900
Coburn, Charles .... Macon, Ga. 1877
Collinge, Patricia .... Dublin 1894
Collins, Russell .... New Orleans, La. 1901
Colt, Ethel Barrymore ...... Mamaroneck, N. Y. 1911
Colt, John Drew .... New York 1914
Conroy, Frank .... London, England 1885
Cook, Donald .... Portland, Ore. 1902
Cook, Joe .... Evansville, Ind. 1890
Cooper, Melville .... Birmingham, England 1896
Corbett, Leonora .... London, England 1908
Cornell, Katharine .... Berlin, Germany 1898
Cossart, Ernest .... Cheltenham, England 1876
Coulouris, George .... Manchester, England 1906
Coward, Noel .... Teddington, England 1899
Cowl, Jane .... Boston, Mass 1887
Crothers, Rachel .... Bloomington, Ill. 1878
Cummings, Constance ...... Seattle, Wash. 1911

Dale, Margaret .... Philadelphia, Pa. 1880
Daniell, Henry .... London 1904
Davis, Owen .... Portland, Me. 1874
Derwent, Clarence .... London 1884

Kane, Whitford .... Larne, Ireland 1882
Kanin, Garson .... Rochester, N. Y. 1912
Karloff, Boris .... Dulwich, England 1887
Kaufman, George S. .... Pittsburgh, Pa. 1889
Kaye, Danny .... New York City 1914
Kazan, Elia .... Constantinople 1909
Keith, Robert .... Fowler, Ind. 1898
Kilbride, Percy .... San Francisco, Cal. 1880
King, Dennis .... Coventry, England 1897
Kingsford, Walter .... England 1881
Kingsley, Sidney .... New York City 1906
Kirkland, Patricia .... New York 1927
Knox, Alexander .... Ontario 1907
Kruger, Otto .... Toledo, Ohio 1885

Lackland, Ben .... Waco, Texas 1901
Landis, Jessie Royce .... Chicago, Ill. 1904
Laughton, Charles .... Scarborough, England 1899
Lawrence, Gertrude .... London 1898
LeGallienne, Eva .... London 1899
Leighton, Margaret .... Barnt Green, England 1922
Lillie, Beatrice .... Toronto, Canada 1898
Lindsay, Howard .... Waterford, N. Y. 1899
Linn, Bambi .... Brooklyn, N. Y. 1926
Loeb, Philip .... Philadelphia, Pa. 1892
Lockhart, Gene .... Ontario 1892
Lonergan, Lenore .... Toledo, Ohio 1928
Lord, Pauline .... Hanford, Cal. 1890
Lunt, Alfred .... Milwaukee, Wis. 1893
Lytell, Bert .... New York City 1885

MacMahon, Aline .... McKeesport, Pa. 1899
Mamoulian, Rouben .... Tiflis 1898
Mantle, Burns .... Watertown, N. Y. 1873
March, Fredric .... Racine, Wis. 1897
Margetson, Arthur .... London, England 1897
Martin, Mary .... Weatherford, Texas 1913
Mason, James .... Huddersfield, England 1909
Massey, Raymond .... Toronto, Canada 1896
Matteson, Ruth .... San Jose, Cal.... 1905
McClintic, Guthrie .... Seattle, Wash. 1893
McCormick, Myron .... Albany, Ind. 1907
McCracken, Joan .... Philadelphia, Pa. 1923

McGrath, Paul .... Chicago, Ill. 1900
McGuire, Dorothy .... Omaha, Neb. 1918
Menotti, Gian-Carlo .... Italy 1912
Meredith, Burgess .... Cleveland, Ohio 1908
Merman, Ethel .... Astoria, R. I. 1909
Middleton, Ray .... Chicago, Ill. 1907
Miller, Gilbert .... New York 1884
Mitchell, Thomas .... Elizabeth, N. J. 1892
Moore, Victor .... Hammondton, N. J. 1876
Morgan, Claudia .... New York 1912
Morley, Robert .... Semley, England 1908
Morris, McKay .... San Antonio, Texas 1890
Moss, Arnold .... Brooklyn, N. Y. 1910
Muni, Paul .... Lemberg, Austria 1895

Nagel, Conrad .... Keokuk, Iowa 1897
Natwick, Mildred .... Baltimore 1908
Nesbitt, Cathleen .... Cheshire, England 1889
Nugent, Elliott .... Dover, Ohio 1900

Odets, Clifford .... Philadelphia 1906
Oenslager, Donald .... Harrisburg, Pa. 1902
Olivier, Sir Laurence .... Dorking, Surrey, England 1907
Olsen, John Siguard (Ole) ... Peru, Ind. 1892
O'Malley, Rex .... London, England 1906
O'Neal, Frederick .... Brookville, Miss. 1905
O'Neill, Eugene Gladstone .... New York 1888

Palmer, Lilli .... Austria 1904
Petina, Irra .... Leningrad, Russia 1900
Picon, Molly .... New York City 1898
Pinza, Ezio .... Rome, Italy 1895
Porter, Cole .... Peru, Indiana 1892
Price, Vincent .... St. Louis, Mo. 1914

Raitt, John .... Santa Ana, Cal. 1917
Rathbone, Basil .... Johannesburg, ... 1892
Redman, Joyce .... Newcastle, Ireland 1918
Reed, Florence .... Philadelphia, Pa. 1883
Rennie, James .... Toronto, Canada 1890
Richardson, Sir Ralph ...... Cheltenham, England 1902
Rice, Elmer .... New York City 1892
Roberts, Joan .... New York City 1918

Rodgers, Richard ....New York City 1902
Ross, Anthony ....New York 1906
Royle, Selena ....New York 1905

Sarnoff, Dorothy ....Brooklyn, N. Y. 1919
Scheff, Fritzi ....Vienna, Austria 1879
Scott, Martha ....Jamesport, Mo. 1914
Segal, Vivienne ....Philadelphia, Pa. 1897
Shaw, Bernard ....Dublin 1856
Sherman, Hiram ....Boston, Mass. 1908
Sherwood, Robert Emmet ....New Rochelle, N. Y. 1896
Shubert, Lee ....Syracuse, N. Y. 1875
Simms, Hilda ....Minneapolis, Minn. 1920
Skinner, Cornelia Otis ....Chicago 1902
Smith, Kent ....Smithfield, Me. 1910
Stickney, Dorothy ....Dickinson, N. D. 1903
Stoddard, Haila ....Great Falls, Mont. 1914
Stone, Carol ....New York 1917
Stone, Dorothy ....New York 1905
Stone, Ezra ....New Bedford, Mass. 1918
Stone, Fred ....Denver, Colo. 1873
Sullavan, Margaret ....Norfolk, Va. 1910
Sullivan, Francis L. ....London 1903

Tandy, Jessica ....London, Eng. 1909
Tetzel, Joan ....New York 1923
Thomas, John Charles ......Baltimore, Md. 1887
Tozere, Frederick ....Brookline, Mass. 1901
Tracy, Lee ....Atlanta 1898
Truex, Ernest ....Red Hill, Mo. 1890

Van Druten, John ....London, Eng. 1902
Van Patten, Dick ....New York 1929
Van Patten, Joyce ....New York City 1934
Varden, Evelyn ....Venita, Okla. 1893

Walker, Nancy ....Philadelphia, Pa. 1922
Walker, June ....New York 1904
Wanamaker, Sam ....Chicago, Ill. 1919
Ward, Penelope ....London, England 1914
Warfield, David ....San Francisco, Cal. 1866
Waring, Richard ....Buckinghamshire, England ...1912
Waters, Ethel ....Chester, Pa. 1900

NECROLOGY

June 1, 1949—June 1, 1950

Allen, Lester, 58, actor. During 1920s was in many Ziegfeld and George White musicals. Began as circus acrobat. Born England; died Hollywood, November 6, 1949.

Andrews, Lyle D., 79, theatre manager and treasurer. Was box office man for Charles Frohman, general manager for Oscar Hammerstein of opera fame; built Vanderbilt Theatre, which housed such hits as "Irene." Born New York; died New York, January 17, 1950.

Arthur, Julia (Mrs. Benjamin P. Cheney), 81, actress. Began reciting Shakespeare at 12; early success in 1891 in "The Black Masque"; as a young actress attained critical acclaim in many Shakespeare roles; last appearance in 1925 in "Saint Joan." Born Hamilton, Ont.; died Boston, March 29, 1950.

Barry, Philip, 53, dramatist. Studied under Prof. George P. Baker at Harvard; his first play, "You and I," was a success; wrote "The Youngest," "White Wings," "Paris Bound," "The Animal Kingdom," "Here Come the Clowns," "The Philadelphia Story," and other plays. Born Rochester, N. Y.; died New York, December 2, 1949.

Batie, Frank, 69, actor. Was with Al Jolson in "Bombo," "Big Boy" and other Winter Garden shows; before that was with Dockstader, Primrose & West Minstrels. Born Norwich, N. Y.; died Norwich, December 31, 1949.

Benelli, Sem, 72, poet and playwright. Best known in this country for his play, "The Jest," and his opera libretto, "L'Amore dei Tre Re." Born Italy; died Zoagli, Italy, December 18, 1949.

Brady, William A., 86, producer and sports promoter. Began stage career as actor in "The White Slave" in San Francisco. Managed James J. Corbett and James J. Jeffries. Produced scores of plays, including many for his wife, Grace George. His greatest money-maker was "Way Down East." Born San Francisco; died New York, January 6, 1950.

Busley, Jessie, 80, actress. Made debut with Mantell in 1888; was with Charles Frohman fifteen years, starting with "Charley's Aunt"; hits included "The Girl I Left Behind Me," "The Admirable Crichton" and "Alien Corn." Born Albany, N. Y.; died New York, April 21, 1950.

Cavanaugh, Hobart, 63, actor. At age of 12 teamed with a schoolmate, Walter Catlett, in an act in San Francisco. Years later teamed with Catlett in vaudeville; acted in "Irene," "So Long Letty," "The Show Off," "As the Girls Go" and other musicals and plays, and was in many motion pictures. Born Virginia City, Nev.; died Hollywood, April 23, 1950.

Chesney, Arthur, 67, actor. Brother of Edmund Gwenn; acted mostly in England; played in New York in "A Little Bit of Fluff" and "Caroline"; was first husband of Estelle Winwood. Born London; died London, August 29, 1949.

Comstock, F. Ray, 69, producer. Began as assistant ticket seller at Criterion Theatre; first production was "The Runaways"; built the Princess Theatre for his productions, including "Leave It to Jane" and "Very Good, Eddie"; was associated in many productions with Morris Gest and William A. Brady; sponsored tours of the Russian ballet, Moscow Art Theatre and Eleanora Duse. Born Buffalo; died Boston, October 15, 1949.

Copeau, Jacques, 70, playwright. Founded the Vieux Colombier in Paris; staged French plays in New York during World War I; was art, drama and literary critic for *Figaro;* first success as dramatist was adaptation of "The Brothers Karamazov"; directed Lunt and Fontanne in this play in 1927. Born Paris; died Beaune, France, October 21, 1949.

Darnton, Charles, 80, drama critic. Began work as reporter in Adrian, Mich.; was reporter and drama critic on Detroit *Evening News;* became critic of New York *Evening World* in 1902 and held post for 21 years. Born, Adrian, Mich.; died, Hollywood, May 18, 1950.

Davenport, Harry, 83, actor. Youngest brother of Fanny Davenport; made debut with father in Philadelphia in "Damon and Pythias" in 1871; since 1934 was in movies; plays included "Three Wise Fools," "Lightnin'," "Trilby," "Coquette" and—with his sister—"La Tosca." Born New York; died Hollywood, August 9, 1949.

Desmond, William, 71, actor. Acted in New York and Los Angeles; appeared in "Quo Vadis?", "Ben Hur," and "Alias Jimmy Valentine," "Sign of the Cross"; became silent film star. Born California; died Hollywood, November 2, 1949.

Foote, John Taintor, 69, dramatist, novelist and screenwriter. For the stage wrote "Toby's Bow," "Flying Colors," "Tight Britches" and other plays. Born Leadville, Colo.; died Los Angeles, January 28, 1950.

Ford, Harriet, 86, playwright. Specialized in collaborations and in adapting novels. With Joseph Medill Patterson wrote "A Little Brother of the Rich" and "The Fourth Estate"; with Harvey O'Higgins wrote many plays, including "The Dummy." Born Seymour, Conn.; died New York, December 12, 1949.

Galloway, Louise, 70, actress. Was in original productions of "Way Down East," "The Music Master," "The Little Princess" and other hits; operated Summer theatres at Brookfield and Westboro, Mass. Born Michigan; died Brookfield, Mass., October 10, 1949.

Gardella, Tess, 52, actress. Known as Aunt Jemima, was in many Broadway musicals, including the 1932 revival of "Show Boat." Born Wilkes-Barre, Pa.; died New York, January 3, 1950.

Ginty, Elizabeth B., 86, playwright. For many years was secretary to David Belasco; in 1938 wrote play about Jesse James, "Missouri Legend." Died New York, November 15, 1949.

Gordon, G. Swayne, 69, actor. Started as property man; acted in "The Kick Back," "One Sunday Afternoon," "The Pursuit of Happiness," "Sailor, Beware" and many others. Born Baltimore; died New York, June 23, 1949.

Grey, Katherine, 77, actress. Joined Augustin Daly's company in San Francisco; had first personal success in "Shore Acres"; appeared with Richard Mansfield, Charles Coghlan, William Gillette, John Drew, Ada Rehan and others. Born San Francisco; died Orleans, Mass., March 21, 1950.

Hale, Alan, 57, actor. Best known for character roles on screen, beginning with "The Covered Wagon"; on New York stage played in "Friendly Enemies," "Baby Mine" and "The Rainbow Girl." Born Washington, D. C.; died Hollywood, January 22, 1950.

Hopkins, Arthur, 71, producer. Began as reporter in Cleveland; booked and produced vaudeville acts; first play was "The Poor Little Rich Girl" in 1912; produced and directed 76 plays, including "On Trial," "Anna Christie," "The Hairy Ape," "What Price Glory?" and "The Magnificent Yankee." Fostered and nurtured careers of John Barrymore, Robert Edmond Jones, Elmer Rice, Maxwell Anderson, Hal Skelly, Barbara Stanwyck, Philip Barry, Sidney Howard, Katharine Hepburn and many others. Set the style of naturalistic acting in this country. Born Cleveland; died New York, March 22, 1950.

Huston, Walter, 66, actor. Made stage debut in Toronto in 1902; in 1905 appeared on Broadway in "In Convict Stripes"; from 1909 to 1924 was in vaudeville; in 1924 played title role in "Mr. Pitt"; other plays included "Desire Under the Elms," "The Barker," "Dodsworth," "Othello" and "Knickerbocker

Holiday"; was in many films and won an "Oscar" for performance in "Treasure of the Sierra Madre." Born, Toronto; died Beverly Hills, April 7, 1950.

Kelly, Robert, 74, actor. Joined Augustin Daly's company in 1897; played Rev. Davidson in "Rain"; after retirement coached local plays in Lewiston, Me. Born Chicago; died Lewiston, June 19, 1949.

Kennedy, Charles Rann, 79, playwright. Was with Ben Greet's company as actor; his plays had religious or pacifist motives, and included "The Servant in the House" and "The Terrible Meek." Born England; died Los Angeles, February 16, 1950.

Lauder, Sir Harry, 79, actor. Began work in a Scottish flax mill at 11; from 12 to 22 worked in coal mines, and entertained local gatherings with song and comedy; made London debut in 1900; made 45 tours of United States, many of them "farewells"; was knighted for entertaining troops in World War I. Born Portobello, Scotland; died Strathaven, Scotland, February 26, 1950.

Leiber, Fritz, 67, actor. Played with Ben Greet, Mantell and Warfield; for many years managed his own Shakespearian touring company. Born Chicago; died Pacific Palisades, California, October 14, 1949.

Leverton, Garrett H., 52, editor. Taught drama at Northwestern and Columbia Universities; was editor-in-chief of Samuel French, Inc., play publishers and brokers; was credited with suggesting that Lynn Riggs' "Green Grow the Lilacs" be made into the musical, "Oklahoma!" Born Indiana; died New York, November 11, 1949.

MacArthur, Mary, 19, actress. Daughter of Helen Hayes and Charles MacArthur. Made debut in a single performance of her mother's "Victoria Regina" at age of 7; first professional appearance at New Hope, Pa., in "Alice Sit-by-the-Fire"; fell ill during Westport, Conn., tryout of "Good Housekeeping," which starred her mother. Before birth became famous as "act of God" baby when Miss Hayes withdrew from tour of "Coquette." Born New York; died New York, September 22, 1949.

McCabe, May North, 76, actress. Last appearance on Broadway in "Times Square," in 1931. Began in stock at 19; created role of Ann Berry in "Shore Acres"; was in "Arizona," "Oh, Boy," "Adam and Eva," "The Fool" and "If I Was Rich." Died New York, June 2, 1949.

McIntyre, Frank, 71, actor. Made debut in 1901; first success in lead of "The Traveling Salesman," 1908; was in "Sitting Pretty," "Becky Sharp," "Greenwich Village Follies of 1925" and many other plays and musicals. Born Michigan; died Ann Arbor, June 8, 1949.

McKenna, William J., 69, song writer. Wrote "Has Anybody Here Seen Kelly?" for Nora Bayes; wrote songs for Anna Held, George Primrose, Lew Dockstader, Nat Wills and others; collaborated on "The Mayor of Laughland," "The Mazuma Man" and other musicals. Born Jersey City, N. J.; died Jersey City, March 4, 1950.

Minsky, Abraham, 68, burlesque producer. Began in 1905 as nickelodeon movie exhibitor; joined brothers Herbert, Billy and Morton in producing vaudeville; began producing burlesque in 1915. Died New York, September 6, 1949.

Minzey, Frank, 70, actor. Began as juvenile with Boston's Castle Square Stock Company; was a pioneer in films, with Kalem, Biograph and Keystone; with his wife, the late Rose Melville, had phenomenal success in "Sis Hopkins," playing more than 5,000 performances. Born Massachusetts; died Lake George, N. Y., November 12, 1949.

Morgan, Frank, 59, actor. Was a star of stage, radio and screen. Made legitimate debut in 1914 in "Mr. Wu"; first success was "The Firebrand"; greatest stage success, "Topaz." Born New York; died Hollywood, September 18, 1949.

Moss, Paul, 70, producer. Was early associate of the Theatre Guild; last play production, "The Whole World Over"; as commissioner of licenses in New York, drove burlesque from the city; was director of the New York City Center of Drama and Music. Born New York; died New York, February 25, 1950.

Nash, Florence, 60, actress. First success as comedienne in "Within the Law"; hits included "Merton of the Movies"; was in film version of "The Women." Born Troy, N. Y., died Hollywood, April 2, 1950.

Nijinsky, Vaslav, 60, dancer. Made debut at age of 17 in Moscow; gave last performance in Montevideo in 1917, and two years later entered a private hospital for the insane in Switzerland. In latter years partially recovered from his ailment. Born of Polish parents in Kiev; died, London, April 8, 1950.

Odell, George Clinton Densmore, 83, historian. Joined teaching staff of Columbia University in 1895; succeeded Brander Matthews as professor of dramatic literature in 1924. Began compiling and writing his exhaustive *Annals of the New York Stage* in 1920, and before illness forced him to end his work had recorded in immense detail the history of the New York stage from 1700 to 1894. Born Newburgh, N. Y.; died New York City, October 17, 1949.

Ouspenskaya, Maria, 68, actress. Came to U. S. in 1924 with Moscow Art Theatre; remained for notable stage and screen career; made local debut with Provincetown Players, had great success in "Dodsworth." Born Russia; died Hollywood, December 3, 1949.

Patricola, Tom, 59, actor and dancer. Was in six of George White's "Scandals" and a popular vaudeville headliner. Born New Orleans; died Pasadena, Calif., January 1, 1950.

Pemberton, Brock, 64, producer. Was reporter on Emporia *Gazette*, drama editor on N. Y. *Evening Mail, World* and *Times;* became publicity man for Arthur Hopkins. His first play productions, "Enter Madame" and "Miss Lulu Bett," were successes; greatest success was "Harvey"; notable offerings included "Six Characters in Search of an Author," "Strictly Dishonorable," "Personal Appearance" and "Kiss the Boys Goodbye." Born Emporia, Kan.; died New York, March 11, 1950.

Robinson, Bill, 71, dancer. Most famous Negro tap dancer; began hoofing for "throw money" on sidewalks and in bars in Richmond, Va.; for many years a vaudeville headliner and music-show star. Born Richmond; died New York, November 25, 1949.

Shean, Al, 81, actor. Partner of the late Ed Gallagher; famed with him for song, "Absolutely, Mr. Gallagher? Positively, Mr. Shean." Was in vaudeville, burlesque, Ziegfeld "Follies" of 1923, "Princess Pat" and "Father Malachy's Miracle." Born Germany; died New York, September 12, 1949.

Shiels, George, 63, playwright. Dramatist of the Abbey Theatre, Dublin; wrote "The New Gossoon," "The Rugged Path" and "The Summit." Born Ireland; died Ballymoney, Ireland, September 19, 1949.

Short, Frank Lea, 75, actor, director. Played with Daniel Frohman's Lyceum Theatre Company and Murray Hill Stock Company; appeared with John Drew, Nazimova, Minnie Maddern Fiske; stage manager for Leslie Howard and Helen Hayes. Born Kansas City; died Yonkers, N. Y., June 14, 1949.

Silverman, Sid, 51, publisher. In 1931 succeeded his father, Sime Silverman, as publisher and editor of *Variety;* was inactive during his latter years because of ill health. Born New York; died Harrison, N. Y., March 10, 1950.

Starr, Muriel, 62, actress. Became star in Australia in "Within the Law," "Madame X" and other dramas; made New York debut in 1909 in "Going Some." Born Canada; died New York, April 19, 1950, in her dressing room during a performance of "The Velvet Glove."

Strauss, Richard, 85, composer. His most famous operas were "Der Rosenkavalier," "Elektra" and "Salomé." Born Munich; died Garmish-Partenkirken, Germany, September 8, 1949.

Vanbrugh, Dame Irene, 76, actress. Started in repertory in 1888; in 1941 was knighted Dame Commander of the British Empire; appeared in plays by Barrie, Wilde, Pinero, Milne and Coward; acted frequently in New York under Charles Frohman management, her first appearance here being in "The Chili Widow." Born Exeter, England; died London, November 30, 1949.

Vivian, Ruth, actress. Came to U. S. with Ben Greet Players; was in "The Man Who Came to Dinner," "Sweet Aloes," "The Damask Cheek" and other plays; was active in dramatic work for American Foundation for the Blind. Born England; died New York, October 24, 1949.

Weill, Kurt, 50, composer. Wrote operas in Germany, including "Three-Penny Opera"; in America wrote scores for "Johnny Johnson," "The Eternal Road," "Knickerbocker Holiday," "Lady in the Dark," "Street Scene," "Lost in the Stars" and other musicals. Born Dessau, Germany; died New York, April 3, 1950.

Yule, Joe, 55, actor. Vaudeville and burlesque comedian; motion picture actor; last stage assignment in road company of "Finian's Rainbow"; father of Mickey Rooney. Born Scotland; died Hollywood, March 30, 1950.

THE DECADES' TOLL

(Prominent Theatrical Figures Who Have Died
in Recent Years)

	Born	Died
Arliss, George	1869	1946
Baker, George Pierce	1866	1935
Barrymore, John	1882	1942
Bates, Blanche	1873	1941
Belasco, David	1856	1931
Bennett, Richard	1873	1944
Carroll, Earl	1893	1948
Carte, Rupert D'Oyly	1876	1948
Cohan, George M.	1878	1942
Collier, Willie	1866	1943
Craven, Frank	1890	1945
Crews, Laura Hope	1880	1942
Crosman, Henrietta	1865	1944
Digges, Dudley	1879	1947
Elliott, Maxine	1871	1940
Eltinge, Julian	1883	1941
Faversham, William	1868	1940
Fields, Lew	1867	1941
Fields, W. C.	1879	1946
Fiske, Harrison Grey	1861	1942
Frohman, Daniel	1851	1940
Gaige, Crosby	1883	1949
Gershwin, George	1898	1937
Gest, Morris	1881	1941
Hart, Lorenz	1895	1943
Hart, William S.	1870	1946
Hooker, Brian	1881	1947
Howard, Willie	1883	1949
Kern, Jerome D.	1885	1945
Lehar, Franz	1870	1948
Leonard, Eddie	1871	1941
Loftus, Cecilia	1876	1943
Mantle, Burns	1873	1948

	Born	*Died*
Merivale, Philip	1886	1946
Moore, Grace	1901	1947
Morgan, Helen	1900	1941
Nazimova, Alla	1879	1945
Patterson, Joseph Medill	1879	1946
Perry, Antoinette	1888	1946
Powers, James T.	1862	1943
Reinhardt, Max	1873	1943
Royle, Edwin Milton	1862	1941
Selwyn, Edgar	1875	1944
Sheldon, Edward	1886	1946
Skinner, Otis	1858	1942
Tarkington, Booth	1869	1946
Tauber, Richard	1890	1948
Tyler, George C.	1867	1946
Weber, Joe	1867	1942
Webster, Ben	1864	1947
Whitty, Dame May	1865	1948
Woollcott, Alexander	1887	1943
Youmans, Vincent	1899	1946

INDEX OF AUTHORS

INDEX OF PLAYS AND CASTS

Bold face page numbers refer to pages on which
Cast of Characters may be found.

427

INDEX OF PRODUCERS, DIRECTORS
AND DESIGNERS